C++ by Dissection

Ira Pohl

University of California
Santa Cruz

Addison
Wesley

Boston San Francisco New York
London Toronto Sydney Tokyo Singapore Madrid
Mexico City Munich Paris Cape Town Hong Kong Montreal

Senior Acquistions Editor	Maite Suarez-Rivas
Project Editor	Katherine Harutunian
Executive Marketing Manager	Michael Hirsch
Production Supervisor	Marilyn Lloyd
Project Management	Argosy Publishing
Copyeditor	Jeannie Smith
Proofreader	Janet Renard
Composition and Art	Debra Dolsberry and Argosy Publishing
Text and Cover Design	Leslie Haimes
Design Manager	Gina Hagen
Prepress and Manufacturing	Hugh Crawford

Access the latest information about Addison-Wesley titles from our World Wide Web site: http://www.aw.com/cs

Many of the designations used by manufacturers and sellers to distinguish their products are claimed as tradmarks. Where those designations appear in this book, and Addison-Wesley was aware of a trademark claim, the designations have been printed in initial caps or all caps.

Borland C/C++ is a registered trademark of Borland International, Inc.
GNU C/C++ is a registered trademark of Free Software Foundation, Inc.
Microsoft C/C++ is a registered trademark of Microsoft, Inc.
Turbo C/C++ is a registered trademark of Borland International, Inc.
MS-DOS is a registered trademark of Microsoft, Inc.
OS/2 is a registered trademark of International Business Machines, Inc.
UNIX is a registered trademark licensed through X/Open Company, Ltd.
Windows is a registered trademark of Microsoft, Inc.
FrameMaker is a registered trademark of Frame Technology, Inc.
PostScript is a registered trademark of Adobe Systems, Inc.

The programs and applications presented in this book have been included for their instructional value. They have been tested with care, but are not guaranteed for any particular purpose. The publisher does not offer any warranties or representations, nor does it accept any liabilities with respect to the programs or applications.

Library of Congress Cataloging-in-Publication Data

Pohl, Ira
  C++ by Dissection / Ira Pohl.
    p.   cm.
  ISBN 0-201-74396-5 (pbk.)
  1. C++ (Computer program language) I. Title.
  QA76.73.C153 P58 2002
  005.13'3--dc21   2001045829
                                        CIP

ISBN 0-201-74396-5
12345678910- RRD-04030201

About Ira Pohl

Ira Pohl, Ph.D., is a professor of Computer Science at the University of California, Santa Cruz. He has over 30 years of experience as a software methodologist. His teaching and research interests are in the areas of artificial intelligence, programming languages, practical complexity problems, heuristic search methods, deductive algorithms, and educational and social issues. He originated error analysis in heuristic search methods and deductive algorithms.

He is an ACM Fellow and has lectured at Berkeley, Stanford, the Vrije University in Amsterdam, the Courant Institute, Edinburgh University in Scotland, and Auckland University in New Zealand.

When not programming, he enjoys riding bicycles in Aptos, California, with his wife Debra and daughter Laura.

Other Publications by Ira Pohl

Ira is the sole author of the following Addison-Wesley or Benjamin Cummings publications:

C++ for C Programmers
C++ for Pascal Programmers
C++ for Fortran Programmers
Turbo C++
Object Oriented Programming Using C++
C++ Distilled

Ira is coauthor with Al Kelley for a series of books published by Addison-Wesley and Benjamin Cummings on the C programming language:

A Book on C: An Introduction to Programming in C
C by Dissection Turbo C: The Essentials of C Programming

Ira is also coauthor with Charlie McDowell of the following Addison-Wesley publication:

Java by Dissection: The Essentials of Java Programming

Ira's first book, coauthored with Alan Shaw, was a pioneering text on computer science (Computer Science Press, 1981):

The Nature of Computation: An Introduction to Computer Science

Dedicated to

Philip Pohl (1932–2001)

who gave me my first computer (a slide rule).

Preface

Today, the ANSI C++ programming language is widely used throughout the world in both academia and industry. In many educational institutions it is the language of choice for a first programming course and for a language to be used for computer science instruction. A key reason for this is that C++ has drifted down the curriculum from more advanced courses to more introductory courses. Further, C++ comes with many useful libraries, and is supported by sophisticated integrated environments. It is a language that efficiently supports object-oriented programming (OOP) the dominant contemporary programming methodology.

C++ by Dissection presents a thorough introduction to the programming process by carefully developing working programs to illuminate key features of the C++ programming language. Program code is explained in an easy-to-follow, careful manner throughout. The code has been tested on several platforms and is found on the bundled CD-rom accompanying this text. The code in *C++ By Dissection* can be used with most C++ systems, including those found in operating systems such as MacOS, MS-DOS, OS/2, UNIX, and Windows.

C++, invented at Bell Labs by Bjarne Stroustrup in the mid-1980s, is a powerful, modern, successor language to C. C++ adds to C the concept of class, a mechanism for providing user-defined types, also called abstract data types. C++ supports object-oriented programming by these means and by providing inheritance and runtime type binding.

Dissections

This book presents readers with a clear and thorough introduction to the programming process by carefully developing working C++ programs, using the method of dissection. Dissection is a unique pedagogical tool first developed by the author in 1984 to illuminate key features of working code. A dissection is similar to a structured walk-through of the code. Its intention is to explain to the reader newly encountered programming elements and idioms as found in working code. Programs and functions are explained in an easy-to-follow step-by-step manner. Key ideas are reinforced throughout by use in different contexts.

No Background Assumed

This book assumes no programming background and can be used by students and first time computer users. Experienced programmers not familiar with C++ will also benefit from the carefully structured presentation of the C++ language. For student use, the book is intended as a first course in computer science or programming.

It is suitable for a CS1 course or beginning programming course for other disciplines. Each chapter presents a number of carefully explained programs, which lead the student in a holistic manner to ever-improving programming skills. From the start, the student is introduced to complete programs, and at an early point in the text is introduced to writing functions as a major feature of structured programming. The function is to the program as the paragraph is to the essay. Competence in writing functions is the hallmark of the skilled programmer and hence is emphasized. Examples and exercises are plentiful in content and level of difficulty. They allow instructors to pick assignments appropriate to their audiences.

Special Features

C++ by Dissection: The Essentials of C++ Programming incorporates a number of special features:

- A CD-Rom with a working compiler

- A website with the full electronically searchable text of this book. Also included are active links to useful web-sites and complete working code for this text

- Software engineering practice is described throughout

- Dr. P's prescriptions are concise programming tips provided for the beginner for each chapter

- Early explanation of simple recursion to reflect its earlier introduction in beginning computer science courses

- Coverage of program correctness and type safety

- In-depth explanation of functions and pointers because these concepts are typically stumbling blocks for the beginner

- Object-oriented programming concepts are emphasized

- Generic programming and STL are carefully described

- UML diagrams are introduced as an aid to understanding object-oriented programming

- Comparison to Java, optional Java exercises and coordinating references to *Java by Dissection* (with Charlie McDowell)

Chapter Features

Each chapter contains the following pedagogical elements:

Dissections. Major elements of the important example programs are explained by the method of dissection. This step-by-step discussion of new programming ideas helps the reader encountering these ideas for the first time to understand them.

Object-oriented programming. The reader is led gradually to the object-oriented style. Chapter 4, *Classes and Abstract Data Types*, introduces classes, which are the basic mechanism for producing modular programs and implementing abstract data types. Class variables are the objects being manipulated. Chapter 8, *Inheritance and OOP*, develops inheritance and virtual functions, two key elements in this paradigm. Chapter 11, *OOP Using C++*, discusses OOP programming philosophy. This book develops in the programmer an appreciation of this point of view.

Programming Style and Software Engineering. Programming style and software methodology is stressed throughout. Important concepts such as structured branching statements, nested flow of control, top-down design, and object-oriented programming are presented early in the book. A consistent and proper coding style is adopted from the beginning with careful explanation as to its importance and rationale. The coding style used in the book is one commonly used by working programming professionals in the C++ community.

Working Code. Right from the start the student is introduced to full working programs. With the executable code, the student can better understand and appreciate the programming ideas under discussion. Many programs and functions are explained through dissections. Variations on programming ideas are often presented in the exercises.

Common Programming Errors. Many typical programming bugs, along with techniques for avoiding them, are described. Much of the frustration of learning a programming language is caused by encountering obscure errors. Many books discuss correct code but leave the reader to a trial-and-error process for finding out about bugs. This book explains how typical errors in C++ are made and what must be done to correct them.

Dr. P's Prescriptions. A series of programming tips is based on wide experience. A concise rationale is given for each tip.

Comparison to Java. An optional section describes the programming elements of Java that are comparable to the C++ examples. Exercises supporting these sections are included as well. For the most part, C++ and Java have equivalent elements. The text aids the student already conversant in Java to migrate to C++. Also the C++ student who later takes up Java will benefit from this section. Furthermore, as the book is a companion volume to *Java by Dissection* (with Charlie McDowell) the reader has access to complete explanations of the Java concepts fully utilizing this book's pedagogy.

Summary. A succinct list of points covered in the chapter serves as a review for the reader, reinforcing the new ideas that were presented in the chapter.

Exercises. The exercises test the student's knowledge of the language. Many exercises are intended to be done interactively while reading the text. This encourages self-paced instruction by the reader. In addition to exercising features of the language, some exercises look at a topic in more detail, and others extend the reader's knowledge to an advanced area of use.

Classroom Usage

This book can be used as a text in a one-semester course that teaches students how to program. Chapters 1 through 5 cover the C++ programming language through the use of arrays, pointers, and basic object programming. A second-semester course can be devoted to more advanced data types, OOP, generic programming and STL, file processing, and software engineering as covered in Chapters 6 through 11. In a course designed for students who already have some knowledge of programming, not necessarily in C++, the instructor can cover all the topics in the text. This book can also be used as a text in other computer science courses that require the student to use C++. In a comparative language course, it can be used with companion volumes for C, Java, and C# that follow the same dissection approach and share many of the same examples done uniquely in each language.

Interactive Environment

This book is written explicitly for an interactive environment. Experimentation via keyboard and screen is encouraged throughout. For PCs, there are many vendors that supply interactive C++ systems, including Borland, IBM, Metroworks, Microsoft, and Symantec.

Professional Use

While intended for the beginning programmer, *C++ by Dissection: The Essentials of C++ Programming* is a friendly introduction to the entire language for the experienced programmer as well. In conjunction with *A Book on C, Fourth Edition* by Al Kelley and Ira Pohl (Addison Wesley Longman, Inc., Reading, MA, 1998, ISBN 0-201183994), the computer professional will gain a comprehensive understanding of both languages. As a package, the two books offer an integrated treatment of the C/C++ programming language and its use that is unavailable elsewhere. Furthermore, in conjunction with *Java by Dissection* by Ira Pohl and Charlie McDowell (Addison Wesley Longman, Inc., Reading, MA, 1999, ISBN 0-201-61248-8), the student or professional is also given an integrated treatment of the object-oriented language Java.

This book is the basis of many on-site professional training courses given by the author, who has used its contents to train professionals and students in various forums since 1986. The text is the basis for Web-based training in C++ available from www.digitalthink.com.

Supplements

Support materials are available to instructors adopting this textbook for classroom use and include the following:

- Solutions to exercises
- Code for example programs
- Powerpoint slides of all the figures

Please check on-line information for this book at www.aw.com/cssupport for more information on obtaining these supplements.

Acknowledgments

Our special thanks go to Uwe F. Mayer, George Belotsky, and Bruce Montague, who were careful readers of the technical content of this work and suggested numerous improvements, without being responsible for my errors. Thanks to our reviewers, Charles Anderson, Colorado state University; Parris Egbert, Brigham Young University; Chris Eagle, Naval Postgraduate School; Nigel Gwee, Louisiana State University; Stephen P. Leach, Florida State University; and Steven C. Shaffer, Penn State University. Thanks also to John dePillis, Debra Dolsberry and Laura Pohl who developed and drew many of the cartoons. Most importantly further thanks to Debra Dolsberry, who acted as the chief technical editor for much of the material in this book and the CD-Rom. In addition, she was largely responsible for using FrameMaker to create files suitable for typesetting this book. Thanks also to Charlie McDowell and Al Kelley for writing companion volumes in C and Java.

We would also like to thank Maite Suarez-Rivas, Acquisitions Editor, Katherine Harutunian, Project Editor, and Patty Mahtani, Associate Managing Editor for their enthusiasm, support, and encouragement; and we would like to thank Caroline Roop and Sally Boylan at Argosy, for the careful attention to the production of this book.

Ira Pohl
University of California, Santa Cruz

Table of Contents

CHAPTER 1

Writing an ANSI C++ Program

T his chapter introduces the reader to the ANSI C++ programming world. Some general ideas on programming are discussed, and a number of elementary programs are thoroughly explained. The basic ideas presented here become the foundation for more complete explanations that occur in later chapters. An emphasis is placed on the basic input/output functions of C++. Getting information into and out of a machine is the first task to be mastered in any programming language.

C++ uses the operators << and >> for output and input, respectively. The use of both of these operators is explained. Other topics discussed in this chapter include the use of variables to store values and the use of expressions and assignments to change the value of a variable.

Throughout this chapter and throughout the text, many examples are given. Included are many complete programs, which often are dissected. This allows the reader to see in detail how each construct works. Topics that are introduced in this chapter are seen again in later chapters, with more detailed explanation where appropriate. This spiral approach to learning emphasizes ideas and techniques essential for the C++ programmer.

C++ is largely a superset of C. By learning C++, you are also learning the kernel language C. A companion book, *C by Dissection: Fourth*

Edition, by Al Kelley and Ira Pohl (Addison-Wesley, 2000), teaches the rest of C that is not found here.

Most chapters also have a comparison between C++ and Java programs. Java is partly based on C++. However, unlike C++, some C concepts do not work in Java or have a different meaning. Increasingly, people who begin to program in C++ have started from a Java background. An introduction to the Java programming process can be found in the companion volume *Java by Dissection,* by Ira Pohl and Charlie McDowell (Addison-Wesley, 1999). The modern programmer needs to be comfortable in all three C-based languages.

1.1 Getting Ready to Program

Programs are written to instruct machines to carry out specific tasks or to solve specific problems. A step-by-step procedure that accomplishes a desired task is called an algorithm. Thus, programming is the activity of communicating algorithms to computers. We have all given instructions to someone in English and then had that person carry out the instructions. The programming process is analogous, except that machines have no tolerance for ambiguity and must have all steps specified in a precise language and in tedious detail.

The Programming Process

1. Specify the task.

2. Discover an algorithm for its solution.

3. Code the algorithm in C++.

4. Test the code.

A computer is a digital electronic machine composed of three main components: processor, memory, and input/output devices. The processor is also called the central processing unit, or CPU. The processor carries out instructions that are stored in the memory. Along with the instructions, data also is stored in memory. The processor typically is instructed to manipulate the data in some desired fashion. Input/output devices take information from agents external to the machine and provide information to those agents. Input devices are typically terminal keyboards, disk drives, and tape drives. Output devices are typically terminal screens, printers, disk drives, and tape drives. The physical makeup of a machine can be quite complicated, but the user need not be concerned with the details.

The operating system consists of a collection of special programs and has two main purposes. First, the operating system oversees and coordinates the resources of the machine as a whole. For example, when a file is created on a disk, the operating system takes care of the details of locating it in an appropriate place and keeping track of its name, size, and date of creation. Second, the operating system provides tools to users, many of which are useful to the C++ programmer. Two of these tools are of paramount importance: the text editor and the C++ compiler.

We assume the reader can use a text editor to create and modify files containing C++ code. C++ code is also called source code, and a file containing source code is called a source file. After a file containing source code (a program) has been created, the C++ compiler is invoked. This process is system-dependent. (see Section 1.7, *Writing and Running a C++ Program*, on page 15.) For example, on many UNIX systems, we can invoke the C++ compiler with the command

   CC pgm.cpp

where *pgm.cpp* is the name of a file that contains a program. If there are no errors in *pgm.cpp*, this command produces an executable file—one that can be run, or executed. Although we think of this as compiling the program, what actually happens is more complicated.

When we compile a simple program, three separate actions occur: First the preprocessor is invoked, then the compiler, and finally the linker. The preprocessor modifies a copy of the source code by including other files and by making other changes. The compiler translates this into object code, which the linker then uses to produce the final executable file. A file that contains object code is called an object file. Object files, unlike source files, usually are not read by humans. When we speak of compiling a program, we really mean invoking the preprocessor, the compiler, and the linker. For a simple program, this is all done with a single command.

After the programmer writes a program, it has to be compiled and tested. If modifications are needed, the source code has to be edited again. Thus, part of the programming process consists of this cycle:

When the programmer is satisfied with the program performance, the cycle ends.

1.2   A First Program

A first task for anyone learning to program is to print on the screen. Let us begin by writing the traditional first C++ program, which prints the phrase *Hello, world!* on the screen. The complete program is

In file hello1.cpp

```
// Hello world in C++
// by Olivia Programmer

#include <iostream>        // I/O library
using namespace std;

int main()
{
    cout << "Hello, world!" << endl;
}
```

Using the text editor, the programmer types this code into a file ending in *.cpp*. The choice of a file name should be mnemonic. Let us suppose *hello.cpp* is the name of the file in which the program has been written. When this program is compiled and executed, it prints the following message:

```
Hello, world!
```

Hey, Heidi, Alpha Centauri says "Hello" and it's in C++!

Dissection of the *hello* Program

- ```
  // Hello world in C++
  // by Olivia Programmer
  ```

The `//` symbol is used as a rest-of-line comment symbol. Also, the program text can be placed in any position on the page, with white space between tokens being ignored. White space consists of characters such as blanks, tabs, and newlines. White space, comments, and indentation of text are all used to create a well-documented, readable program but do not affect program semantics.

- ```
  #include <iostream>        // I/O library
  ```

The C++ program is compiled after the preprocessor executes #-designated directives. The preprocessor precedes the compiler translation of the resulting program into machine code. The `#include` directive found in the example program *hello.cpp* imports any needed files, usually library definitions. In this case, the I/O library for a typical C++ compiler system is found in the file *iostream*. The compiler knows where to find this and other system files.

- ```
  using namespace std;
  ```

On C++ systems, standard C++ I/O header files are wrapped in `namespace std`. The `using` declaration allows names to be used without `std::` prepended to each name. The `include` files could have been coded without `namespace` and `using`, as follows:

```
#include <iostream.h>        // I/O library
```

Most systems provide older style *library_name.h* header files. These libraries do not require the `using namespace std;` statement.

- ```
  int main()
  {
  ```

A C++ program is a collection of declarations and functions that begins executing with the function `main()`.

- ```
  cout << "Hello, world!" << endl;
  ```

The identifier `cout` is defined in *iostream* as the standard output stream connected by most C++ systems to the screen. The identifier `endl` is a standard manipulator that flushes the output buffer, printing everything to that point and going to a new line. The operator `<<` is the put-to output operator, which writes out what comes after it to `cout`.
  ```

Note that without the `using std` statement, we could have written

■ `std::cout << "Hello, world!" << std::endl;`

The `::` operator is called the scope resolution operator. It tells the compiler what scope to examine to understand identifier `cout`. The scope of an identifier is the program text where the name may be used.

■ `}`

This ends the function `main()`. In C++, braces are paired; an open brace { can be understood as a begin construct and a closing brace } means end construct. A function in C++ has a return type that can be `void`, indicating that no value is to be returned. The special function `main()` returns an integer value to the runtime system. Implicitly the function `main()` returns 0, meaning that termination was normal. This could have been written explicitly, as

```
return 0;
```

just before the closing brace.

The expression `cout << `*some string* is used to print across the screen. It moves to a new line when a newline character is read or it sees the `endl`. The screen is a two-dimensional display that prints from left to right and top to bottom. To be readable, output must appear properly spaced on the screen.

Let us rewrite our program to make use of two `cout` statements. Although the program is different from our first one, its output is the same.

In file hello2.cpp

```
// Hello world in C++
// by Olivia Programmer
// Version 2

#include <iostream>        // I/O library
using namespace std;
int main()
{
    cout << "Hello, ";
    cout << "world!" << endl;
}
```

Notice that the string in the first statement ends with a blank character. If the blank were not there, the words `Hello, world!` would have no space between them in the output.

As a final variation to this program, let us add the phrase *Hello, universe!* and print the statements on two lines.

In file hello3.cpp

```cpp
// Hello universe in C++
// by Olivia Programmer

#include <iostream>        // I/O library
using namespace std;
int main()
{
    cout << "Hello, world!" << endl;
    cout << "Hello, universe!" << endl;
}
```

When we execute this program, the following appears on the screen:

```
Hello, world!
Hello, universe!
```

Notice that the two `cout` statements in the body of `main()` could be replaced by the single statement

```cpp
cout << "Hello, world!\nHello, universe!" << endl;
```

In this version, the special character \n is the newline character. This has the same effect as an `endl`.

1.3   Problem Solving: Recipes

Computer programs are detailed lists of instructions for performing a specific task or solving a particular type of problem. Instruction lists, called algorithms, are commonly found in everyday situations. Examples include instructions for cooking a meal, knitting a sweater, and registering for classes. Examining one of these examples is instructive. Consider this recipe for preparing a meat roast:

> Sprinkle the roast with salt and pepper. Insert a meat thermometer and place in oven preheated to 150°C. Cook until the thermometer registers between 80°C and 85°C. Serve roast with gravy prepared from either meat stock or from pan drippings, if there is a sufficient amount.

The recipe is typically imprecise—what does *sprinkle* mean, where *exactly* is the thermometer to be inserted, and what is a *sufficient amount* of pan drippings? However, the recipe can be formulated more precisely as a list of instructions by reading between the lines.

Cooking a Roast

1. Sprinkle roast with 1/8 teaspoon salt and pepper.
2. Turn oven on to 150°C.
3. Insert meat thermometer into center of roast.
4. Wait a few minutes.
5. If oven does not yet register 150°C, go back to step 4.
6. Place roast in oven.
7. Wait a few minutes.
8. Check meat thermometer. If temperature is less than 80°C, go back to step 7.
9. Remove roast from oven.
10. If there is at least 1/2 cup of pan drippings, go to step 12.
11. Prepare gravy from meat stock and go to step 13.
12. Prepare gravy from pan drippings.
13. Serve roast with gravy.

These steps comprise three categories of instructions and activities—those that involve manipulating or changing the ingredients or equipment, those that just examine or test the state of the system, and those that transfer to the next step. Steps 1 and 6 are examples of the first category; the temperature test in step 8 and the pan drippings test in step 10 are instances of the second category; and transfers in steps 5 and 8 (go to step *x*) are examples of the last category.

By using suitable graphical symbols for each of these categories, a simple two-dimensional representation of our cooking algorithm can be obtained, as shown in the following illustration:

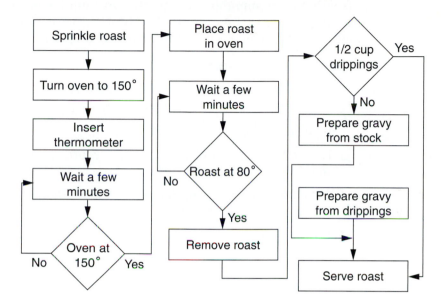

Such a figure is called a flowchart. To perform the program (prepare the roast), just follow the arrows and the instructions in each box. The manipulation activities are contained in rectangles, the tests are shown in diamonds, and the transfer or flow of control is determined by the arrows. Because of their visual appeal and clarity, flowcharts are often used instead of lists of instructions for informally describing programs. Some cookbook authors even employ flowcharts extensively.

1.3.1 Algorithms—Being Precise

Our recipe for preparing a roast can't be executed by a computer because the individual instructions are too loosely specified. Let's consider another example—one that manipulates numbers instead of food. You need to pay for some purchase with a dollar bill and get change in dimes and pennies. The problem is to determine the correct change with the fewest pennies. Most people do this simple, everyday transaction unthinkingly. But how do we precisely describe this algorithm?

In solving such a problem, trying a specific case can be useful. Let's say that you need to pay 77 cents and need change for a dollar. You can easily see that one dollar minus the 77 cents leaves you with

23 cents in change. The correct change having the fewest coins in dimes and pennies would be two dimes and three pennies. The number of dimes is the integer result of dividing 23 by 10 and discarding any fraction or remainder. The number of pennies is the remainder of dividing the 23 cents by 10. An algorithm for performing this change for a dollar is given by the following steps.

Change-Making Algorithm

1. Assume that the price is written in a box labeled `price`.

2. Subtract the value of `price` from 100 and place it in a box labeled `change`.

3. Divide the value in `change` by 10, discard the remainder, and place the result in a box labeled `dimes`.

4. Take the integer remainder of `change` divided by 10 and place it in a box labeled `pennies`.

5. Print out the values in the boxes `dimes` and `pennies` with appropriate labels.

6. Halt.

This algorithm has four boxes, namely, `price`, `change`, `dimes`, and `pennies`. Let's execute the algorithm with the values given. Suppose that the price is 77 cents. Always start with the first instruction. The contents of the four boxes at various stages of execution are shown in Table 1.1.

Table 1.1 Making Change					
Box	Step 1	Step 2	Step 3	Step 4	Step 5
price	77	77	77	77	77
change		23	23	23	23
dimes			2	2	2
pennies				3	3

To execute step 1, place the first number, 77, in the box `price`. At the end of instruction 2, the result of subtracting 77 from 100 is 23, which is placed in the box `change`. Each step of the algorithm performs a small part of the computation. By step 5, the correct values are in their respective boxes and are printed out. Study the example until you're convinced that this algorithm works correctly for any price under one dollar. A good way to do so is to act the part of a computer following the recipe. Following a set of instructions in this way, formulated as a computer program, is called hand simulation or bench testing. It is a good way to find errors in an algorithm or program. In computer parlance, these errors are called bugs, and finding and removing them is called debugging.

We executed the change-making algorithm by acting as an agent, mechanically following a list of instructions. The execution of a set of instructions by an agent is called a computation. Usually, the agent is a computer; in that case, the set of instructions is a computer program. In the remainder of this book, unless explicitly stated otherwise, we use *program* to mean *computer program*.

The algorithm for making change has several important features that are characteristic of all algorithms.

Algorithms

- The sequence of instructions will terminate.

- The instructions are precise. Each instruction is unambiguous and subject to only one interpretation.

- The instructions are simple to perform. Each instruction is within the capabilities of the executing agent and can be carried out exactly in a finite amount of time; such instructions are called effective.

- There are inputs and outputs. An algorithm has one or more outputs (answers) that depend on the particular input data.

Our description of the change-making algorithm, although relatively precise, is not written in any formal programming language. Such informal notations for algorithms are called pseudocode, whereas real code is something suitable for a computer. Where appropriate, we use pseudocode to explain an algorithm or computation to you without all the necessary detail needed by a computer.

The term *algorithm* has a long, involved history, originally stemming from the name of a well-known Arabic mathematician of the ninth century, Abu Jafar Muhammed Musa al-Khwarizmi. It later became associated with arithmetic processes and then, more particularly, with Euclid's algorithm for computing the greatest common divisor of two integers. Since the development of computers, the word has taken on a more precise meaning that defines a real or abstract computer as the ultimate executing agent—any terminating computation by a computer is an algorithm, and any algorithm can be programmed for a computer.

1.4 Implementing Our Algorithm in C++

In this section, we implement our change-making algorithm in the C++ programming language. You need not worry about following the C++ details at this point; we cover all of them fully in the next two chapters. For now, simply note the similarity between the following C++ program and the informal algorithm presented earlier. You not only have to be able to formulate a recipe and make it algorithmic, but you also have to express it in code.

In file change.cpp

```
// Change in dimes and pennies

#include <iostream>
using namespace std;

int main ()
{
    int  price, change, dimes, pennies;

    cout << "Enter price (0:100): ";
    cin >> price;
    change = 100 - price;      // how much change
    dimes = change / 10;       // number of dimes
    pennies = change % 10;     // number of pennies
    cout << "\n\nThe change is :"
         << dimes << " dimes   ";
    cout << pennies << " pennies." << endl;
}
```

Dissection of the *MakeChange* Program

■ `int price, change, dimes, pennies;`

This program declares four integer variables. These hold the values to be manipulated.

■ `cout << "Enter price (0:100): ";`

This line is used to prompt you to type the price. Whenever a program is expecting a user to do something, it should print out a prompt telling the user what to do. The part in quotes appears on the user's screen when the program is run.

■ `cin >> price;`

This statement obtains the input typed in from the keyboard. The value read is stored in the variable `price`. The symbol >> is called the insertion operator. At this point, you must type in an integer price. For example, you would type 77 and then hit Enter.

■ `change = 100 - price;`   `// how much change`

This computes the amount of change from one dollar.

■ `dimes = change / 10;`   `// number of dimes`
  `pennies = change % 10;`   `// number of pennies`

The number of dimes is the integer or whole part of the result of dividing `change` by 10. The symbol /, when used with two integers, computes the integer part of the division. The number of pennies is the integer remainder of `change` divided by 10. The symbol % is the integer remainder, or modulo operator. So if `change` is 23, the integer divide of 23/10 is 2 and the integer remainder, or modulo, of 23 % 10 is 3.

■ `cout << "\n\nThe change is :"`
        `<< dimes << " dimes   ";`
  `cout << pennies << " pennies." << endl;`

The quoted string prints out the characters between the quotation marks. This includes two newlines advancing the cursor down the screen. Then the value in `dimes` is printed, followed by the string " dimes ". Finally, the value of `pennies` is printed. For an input value of 77, the output would be

    `The change is : 2 dimes 3 pennies`

The `endl` in the last print statement indicates that a newline should be sent to the console, ending the line of output.

1.5 Software Engineering: Style

A good coding style is essential to the art of programming. It facilitates the reading, writing, and maintenance of programs. A good style uses white space and comments so that the code is easier to read and understand, and is visually attractive. Another important stylistic point is to choose names for variables that convey their use in the program to further aid understanding. A good style avoids error-prone coding habits.

Software needs to be maintained. Frequently, maintenance costs are higher than the cost of initially writing the code. Good programming style is part of good documentation, and programs need to be readable. This includes commenting the code, choice of identifiers, and associated documentation, such as a manual page or online help.

In this text, we are following the Bell Laboratories industrial programming style. We place all `#include`s, `int main()`s, and braces `{` and `}` that begin and end the body of `main()` in the leftmost position on the line:

```
#include <iostream>

int main()
{
   .....
}
```

The declarations and statements in the body of `main()` are indented three spaces. This visually highlights the beginning and ending of the function body. There is one blank line following the `#include`s, and one between the declarations and statements in the body of `main()`.

An indentation of two, three, four, five, or eight spaces is common. We use three spaces. Whatever is chosen as an indentation should be used consistently. To heighten readability, we put a blank space on each side of the binary operators. Some programmers do not bother with this, but it is part of the Bell Labs style.

There is no single agreed-upon good style. As we proceed through this text, we often point out alternate styles. Once you choose a style, use it consistently. Good habits reinforce good programming. *Caution:* Beginning programmers sometimes think they should dream up their own distinctive coding style. This should be avoided. The preferred strategy is to choose a style that is already in common use.

1.6   Common Programming Errors

When you first start programming, you make many frustrating, simple errors. One such error is to leave off a closing double quote character to mark the end of a string. When the compiler sees the first ", it starts collecting all the characters that follow as a string. If the closing " is not present, the string continues to the next line, causing the compiler to complain. Error messages vary from one compiler to another. Here is one possibility:

```
Unterminated string or character constant
```

Another common error is to misspell a variable name or forget to declare it. Compilers readily catch this kind of error and properly inform you of what is wrong. However, if you misspell the name of a function, such as `sqr()` instead of `sqrt()`, the compiler informs you that the function cannot be found. If you do not notice that the error message refers to `sqr` instead of `sqrt`, you may be quite mystified.

Even elementary errors, such as forgetting to place a semicolon at the end of a statement or leaving off a closing brace, can result in rather mystifying error messages from compilers. As you become more experienced, some of the error messages produced by your compiler will begin to make sense. Exercise 4 on page 24 suggests some programming errors you may want to introduce on purpose to experiment with the error message capability of your compiler.

1.7 **Writing and Running a C++ Program**

The precise steps you have to follow to create a file containing C++ code and to compile and execute it depend on three things: the operating system, the text editor, and the compiler. However, in all cases, the general procedure is the same. We first describe in some detail how it is done in a UNIX environment. Then we discuss how it is done in a Windows environment.

In the discussion that follows, we use the *CC* command to invoke the C++ compiler. In reality, however, the command depends on the compiler that is being used. For example, if we were using the command line version of the Borland C++ compiler, we would use the command *bcc or bcc32*.

Steps for Writing and Running a C++ Program

1. Using an editor, create a text file—say *pgm.cpp*—that contains a C++ program. The name of the file ends with *.cpp*, indicating that the file contains C++ source code. To use an editor, the programmer must know the appropriate commands for inserting and modifying text. For example, to use the *vi* editor on a UNIX system, we would give the command

   vi pgm.cpp

2. Compile the program. This can be done with the command

   CC pgm.cpp

   The *CC* command invokes the preprocessor, the compiler, and the linker in turn. The preprocessor modifies a copy of the source code according to the preprocessing directives and produces what is called a translation unit. The compiler translates the translation unit into object code. If there are errors, the programmer must start again at step 1, editing the source file. Errors that occur at this stage are called syntax errors or compile-time errors. If there are no errors, the linker uses the object code produced by the compiler, along with object code obtained from various libraries provided by the system, to create the executable file *a.out*. The program is now ready to be executed.

3. Execute the program. This is done with the command

> *a.out*

Typically, the program completes execution, and a system prompt reappears on the screen. Any errors that occur during execution are called runtime errors. If, for some reason, the program needs to be changed, the programmer must start again at step 1.

If we compile a different program, the file *a.out* is overwritten and its contents lost. If the executable file *a.out* is to be saved, the file must be moved or renamed. Suppose we give the command

> *CC hello.cpp*

This causes executable code to be written automatically into *a.out*. To save this file, we can give the command

> *mv a.out hello*

This moves *a.out* to *hello*. Now the program can be executed with the command

> *hello*

In UNIX, it is common practice to give the executable file the same name as the corresponding source file, except to drop the *.cpp* suffix. If we wish, we can use the *-o* option to direct the output of the *CC* command. For example, the command

> *CC –o hello hello.cpp*

causes the executable output from *CC* to be written directly into *hello*, leaving intact whatever is in *a.out*.

Different kinds of errors can occur in a program. Syntax errors are caught by the compiler, whereas runtime errors manifest themselves only during program execution. For example, if an attempt to divide by zero is encoded into a program, a runtime error may occur when the program is executed.

Let us now consider the Windows environment. Here, some other text editor would most likely be used. Some C++ systems, such as Borland C++, have both a command line environment and an integrated environment. The integrated environment includes both the text editor and the compiler. In Windows, the executable output produced by a C++ compiler is usually written to a file that has the same name as the source file, but with the extension *.exe* instead of *.cpp*. Suppose, for example, we are using the command line environment in Borland C++. If we give the command

> *bcc hello.cpp*

then the executable code is written to *hello.exe*. To execute the program, we give the command

> *hello.exe*

or, equivalently,

> *hello*

To invoke the program, we do not need to type the *.exe* extension. If we wish to rename this file, we can use the *rename* command.

No, mother, I didn't say "our secret pizza sauce code would make us rich," I said "our secret piece of source code would make us rich."

1.7.1   Interrupting a Program

The user may want to interrupt, or kill, a program that is running. For example, the program may be in an infinite loop. (In an interactive environment, it is not necessarily wrong to use an infinite loop in a program.) Throughout this text, we assume that the user knows how to interrupt a program. In Windows and in UNIX, a control-c is commonly used to effect an interrupt. On some systems a special key, such as *delete* or *rubout*, is used. Make sure you know how to interrupt a program on your system.

1.7.2 Typing an End-of-File Signal

When a program is taking its input from the keyboard, it may be necessary to type an end-of-file signal for the program to work properly. In UNIX, this is done by typing a control-d. In Windows, a control-z is typed instead.

1.8   Dr. P's Prescriptions

- Dr. P's first rule of style is *Have a style*.
- Be consistent in whatever style you choose.
- Check that your compiler supports full, modern C++.

In this book, we follow the traditional C and C++ style pioneered by Bell Laboratories programmers, such as Brian Kernighan, Dennis Ritchie, and Bjarne Stroustrup. Several elements of this style can be seen in our programs. Beginning and ending braces for function definitions line up under each other and under the first character of the function definition. Beginning braces after keywords, such as `do` and `while`, follow the keyword with the ending brace under the first character of that line. This style is in widespread use and makes it easy for others to read your code. The style allows us to distinguish key elements of the program visually, enhancing readability. Style should aim for clarity for both ourselves and others who need to read our code. Cleverness by its nature is usually obscure, and is the enemy of clarity. Hence, Kernighan and Plauger's maxim *Write clearly—don't be too clever*. Also, inconsistent style tends to obscure.

C++ compilers for ANSI C++, as described here, may still be incomplete. Make sure you know what the vendors support, especially when it comes to recent changes in the use of namespaces, exception handling, templates, and libraries.

1.9   C++ Compared with Java

Increasingly, beginning programmers start by studying Java. The roots of C++ and Java both are found in C. Most serious programmers will end up learning all three languages. This book is coordinated in its treatment with the book *Java by Dissection,* by Pohl and McDowell (Addison-Wesley, 1999), and with the book *C by Dissection, Fourth Edition* by Kelley and Pohl(Addison Wesley, 2000). These comparison sections are an enrichment for those readers who already know or wish to know Java. If they are a distraction to others, they can be skipped.

In this section, we implement our change-making algorithm from Section 1.3.1, *Algorithms—Being Precise*, on page 9, in the Java programming language. This is taken from *Java by Dissection*, pages 5–7.

In file MakeChange.java

```java
// Change in dimes and pennies

import tio.*; // use the package tio

class MakeChange {
    public static void main (String[] args) {
        int  price, change, dimes, pennies;

        System.out.println("type price (0:100):");
        price = Console.in.readInt();
        change = 100 - price;      // how much change
        dimes = change / 10;       // number of dimes
        pennies = change % 10;     // number of pennies
        System.out.print("The change is :");
        System.out.print(dimes);
        System.out.print(" dimes ");
        System.out.print(pennies);
        System.out.print(" pennies.\n");
    }
}
```

Dissection of the *MakeChange* Program

■ `import tio.*; // use the package tio`

A package is a library or collection of previously written program parts that you can use. This line tells the Java compiler that the program *MakeChange* uses information from the package `tio`. We developed this package especially for *Java by Dissection* to simplify keyboard input for you. It allows you to write `Console.in.readInt()`, which we explain shortly. The source code is presented in *Appendix D, The tio Library*, and is available for download on the Web at ftp://ftp.awl.com/cseng/authors/pohl-mcdowell/. You can also view it at http://www.cse.ucsc.edu/~charlie/java/tio/.

■ `int price, change, dimes, pennies;`

This program declares four integer variables. These hold the values to be manipulated.

■ `System.out.println("type price (0:100):");`

This line is used to prompt you to type the price. Whenever a program is expecting a user to do something, it should print out a prompt telling the user what to do. The part in quotes appears on the user's screen when the program is run.

■ `price = Console.in.readInt();`

The `Console.in.readInt()` is used to obtain the input from the keyboard. The value read is stored in the variable `price`. The symbol = is called the assignment operator. Read the first line as the variable `price` *is assigned the value obtained from* the input command `Console.in.readInt()`. At this point, you must type in an integer price. For example, you would type 77 and then hit Enter.

■ `change = 100 - price;`   `// how much change`

This line computes the amount of change.

■ `dimes = change / 10;`   `// number of dimes`
  `pennies = change % 10;`   `// number of pennies`

The number of dimes is the integer or whole part of the result of dividing `change` by 10. The symbol /, when used with two integers, computes the whole (nonfraction) part of the division. The number of pennies is the integer remainder of `change` divided by 10. The symbol % is the integer remainder, or modulo, operator in Java. So if `change` is 23, the integer divide of 23/10 is 2 and the integer remainder, or modulo, of 23 % 10 is 3.

■ `System.out.print("The change is :");`
  `System.out.print(dimes);`
  `System.out.print(" dimes ");`
  `System.out.print(pennies);`
  `System.out.print(" pennies.\n");`

In this example, the `System.out.print()` statements cause the values between the parentheses to be printed on the computer console. The first one just prints out the characters between the quotation marks. The second one converts the value in `dimes` to the sequence of digits and prints those digits. The other print statements are similar. For an input value of 77, the output would be

```
The change is : 2 dimes 3 pennies
```

The \n in the last print statement indicates that a newline should be sent to the console, ending the line of output.

Throughout this book we use the `tio` package in order to simplify the input and output required for Java. The source code is presented in Appendix D, *The tio Library*, and is available for download on the Web at ftp://ftp.awl.com/cseng/authors/pohl-mcdowell/. You can also view it at http://www.cse.ucsc.edu/~charlie/java/tio/.

Summary

- An algorithm is a computational procedure consisting of elementary steps. Programming is the art of communicating algorithms to computers.

- When we compile a simple program, three separate actions occur: First the preprocessor is invoked, then the compiler, and finally the linker.

- A simple program consists of optional preprocessing directives and the function `main()`. The body of the function is made up of declarations and statements written between the braces { and }. All variables must be declared. The declarations must occur before the statements that use the variables.

- The statement

  ```
  cout << "Hello, world!" << endl;
  ```

  prints output to the terminal. The `endl` places the cursor on a new line. It also flushes the output buffer, printing everything to that point.

- Following a set of instructions by writing out the results is called hand simulation or bench testing. It is a good way to find errors in an algorithm or program. Errors are called bugs, and finding and removing them is called debugging.

- An algorithm is a sequence of instructions that will terminate. The instructions are precise. Each instruction is unambiguous. The instructions are simple. Each instruction is within the capabilities of the executing agent and can be carried out

exactly in a finite amount of time. There are inputs and outputs. An algorithm has one or more outputs that depend on
the particular input data.

■ Informal notations for algorithms are called pseudocode,
whereas real code is something suitable for a computer.
Before coding in C++, it is useful to write pseudocode and
simulate its execution.

Review Questions

1. C++ uses the operators << and >> for _____ and _____,
respectively.

2. A step-by-step procedure that accomplishes a desired task is
called an _____.

3. The operating system has two main purposes. First, the operating
system oversees and coordinates _____ of the machine as a
whole. Second, the operating system provides _____.

4. The compiler takes _____ code and produces _____ code.

5. In the code std::cout, cout is _____, :: is the _____ operator,
and std is _____.

6. A _____ is a graphical means for displaying an algorithm.

7. `int price, change, dimes, pennies;`
This declares four _____. These hold the _____ to be manipulated.

8. The text uses _____ style. There is _____ following the
`#includes`, and between the declarations and statements in the
body of `main()`. An _____ of two, three, four, five, or eight spaces
is common.

9. In Windows and in UNIX, a _____ is commonly used to effect an
interrupt.

10. A common error is to _____ a variable name or to forget
to _____ it.

Exercises

1. Write on the screen the words

    she sells sea shells by the seashore

    (a) all on one line, (b) on seven lines, and (c) inside a box.

2. Here is part of a program that begins by having the user input three integers:

```
#include <iostream>
using namespace std;

int main()
{
    int   a, b, c, sum;

    cout << "Enter three integers:  ";
    .....
```

    Complete the program so that when the user executes it and types in 2, 3, and 7, this is what appears on the screen:

```
Enter three integers:  2  3  7
Twice the sum of your integers plus 7 is 31 - bye!
```

3. The following program is Laura Pohl's first program:

```
// Print L A U R A

#include <iostream.h>
int main()
{
cout << "L       A   U     U RRRRR     A"    << endl;
cout << "L      A A  U     U R    R   A A"   << endl;
cout << "L     A   A U     U R    R  A   A"  << endl;
cout << "LLL A       A  UUUUU R    R A     A "<<endl;
cout << endl;
```

```
// Print P O H L

cout << "PPPP 00000 H   H L "     << endl;
cout << "P  P O   O H   H L "     << endl;
cout << "P P  O   O HHHHH L "     << endl;
cout << "P    O   O H   H L "     << endl;
cout << "P      00000 H   H LLLLL" << endl;
cout << endl << endl;
cout << " By Laura Michelle Pohl " << endl << endl;
}
```

Rewrite this program so that it prints your name instead.

4. The purpose of this exercise is to help you become familiar with some of the error messages produced by your compiler. You can expect some error messages to be helpful and others to be less so. Correct each syntax error.

```
// Full of syntax mistakes.

#include <iostreem>
using namespace st;

int main()
{
    int   a = 1, b = 2, c = 3,

    cout << a + b * << " = a + b";
    cout <<"\nc = " << c;
}
```

5. Here is part of an interactive program that computes the sum of the value of some coins. The user is asked to input the number of half dollars, quarters, dimes, etc.

```
#include <iostream>
using namespace std;

int main()
{
    int   h,        // number of half dollars
          q,        // number of quarters
          d,        // number of dimes
          n,        // number of nickels
          p;        // number of pennies
    .....
```

```
cout << "Your change will be computed."<< endl;
cout << "Enter how many half dollars.";
cin >> h;
cout << "\nEnter how many quarters.";
cin >> q;
.....
```

Complete the program, causing it to print out relevant information. For example, you may want to create output that looks like this:

```
You entered:    0 half dollars
                3 quarters
                2 dimes
                17 nickels
                1 pennies
The value of your 23 coins is
equivalent to 181 pennies.
```

Notice that `pennies` is plural, not singular as it should be. After you learn about the `if-else` statement in Section 2.8.3, *The if and if-else Statements*, on page 59, you can modify your program so that its output is grammatically correct.

6. Modify the program that you wrote in the previous exercise so that the last line of the output looks like this:

```
The value of your 23 coins is $1.81
```

7. The purpose of this exercise is to find out what happens on your system when a runtime error occurs. Try the following code:

```
int   a = 1, b = 0;
cout << "int division by zero:" << a/b << endl;
```

On a UNIX system, you might get a core dump. That is, the system might create a file named core that contains information about the state of your program just before it ended abnormally. This file is not meant to be read by humans. A debugger can use the core dump to give you information about what your program was doing when it aborted. (Do not leave core dumps lying around. Because they are rather large, they eat up valuable disk space.

Also, George Belotsky points out that core dump files can be a security problem; someone could search in the core dump for potentially exploitable information.)

8. On some systems, dividing by a floating zero does not result in a runtime error. On other systems, it does. Try the following code:

```
double   x = 1.0, y = 0.0;
cout << "double division by zero:" << x/y << endl;
```

What happens on your system? If `Inf` or `NaN` gets printed, you can think of the value as *infinity* or *not a number*.

Native Types and Statements

This chapter, together with Chapter 3, *Functions, Pointers, and Arrays*, provides an introduction to programming in C++ using its native types and its nonOOP (object-oriented programming) features. C++ was designed to expand on the C language.

A native type is one provided by the language directly. In C++, this includes the simple types such as character, integer, and floating-point types; the boolean type; and derived types such as array, pointer, and structure types, which are aggregates of the simple types. This chapter focuses on the native simple data types and statements.

The intent of this and the next chapter is to enable programmers to use the kernel or core language, that subset of C++ that comes closest to forming a traditional imperative language such as C, Pascal, or FORTRAN. With the improvements to C in the kernel language of C++, it is now possible to use the C language without its more extensive additional object-oriented features. Three critical enhancements are type safety, an improved input/output library *iostream*, and the generic programming feature `template`. For example, in type safety, the compiler checks that a value of correct type is used within a statement or expression. Type safety enables the programmer to readily discover subtle errors.

An important object-oriented feature is type extensibility. This is the ability within the programming language to develop new types suitable to a problem domain. For this extensibility to work properly, the new type should work like the native types of the kernel language. Object-oriented design of user-defined types should mimic the look and feel of the native types. This is one reason why it is important to understand the design and use of the native types.

For the experienced C programmer, most of this chapter's material should be skimmed and read mainly with an eye for differences between C and C++. For a programmer coming from another language, such as Java or Pascal, or for rusty C programmers, this and the next chapter review the C++ core language.

I told you I had Cs at my core!

 ## 2.1   Program Elements

A program is composed of elements called tokens, which are collections of characters that form the basic vocabulary the compiler recognizes. Table 2.1 shows the C++ character set.

Table 2.1   C++ Character Set
a b c d e f g h i j k l m n o p q r s t u v w x y z
A B C D E F G H I J K L M N O P Q R S T U V W X Y Z
0 1 2 3 4 5 6 7 8 9
+ = _ - () * & % $ # ! | <> . , ; : " ' / ? {} ~ \ [ ] ^
white space and nonprinting characters, such as newline, tab, blank

In C++, tokens can be interspersed with white space and with comment text that is inserted for readability and documentation. There are five kinds of tokens: keywords, identifiers, literals, operators, and punctuators.

C++ distinguishes between uppercase and lowercase. As we shall see, C++ uses lowercase in its keyword list.

As a historical note, ALGOL60 was an ancestor language to C and C++, but it has not been used in any substantial way since the 1970s. It was the core language of Simula67, which was the first real object-oriented language.

2.1.1 Comments

C++ has a single-line comment, written as // *rest of line.*

```
// C++ by Dissection Chapter 2 - Example

#include <vector>     // vector is in STL
```

A multiline comment is written as /* *possibly multiline comment* */. Everything between /* and */ is a comment. Multiline comments do not nest.

```
/*  Multiline Comments Are Frequently Introductory
    Programmer:  Laura Pohl
    Date:        January 1, 1989
    Version:     DJD v4.2
*/
```

2.1.2 Keywords

Keywords in C++ are explicitly reserved words that have a strict meaning and may not be used in any other way. They include words used for type declarations, such as `int`, `char`, and `float`; words used for statement syntax, such as `do`, `for`, and `if`; and words used for access control, such as `public`, `protected`, and `private`. Table 2.2 shows the keywords in current C++ systems.

Table 2.2 Keywords			
asm	else	new	this
auto	enum	operator	throw
bool	explicit	private	true
break	export	protected	try
case	extern	public	typedef
catch	false	register	typeid
char	float	reinterpret_cast	typename
class	for	return	union
const	friend	short	unsigned
const_cast	goto	signed	using
continue	if	sizeof	virtual
default	inline	static	void
delete	int	static_cast	volatile
do	long	struct	wchar_t
double	mutable	switch	while
dynamic_cast	namespace	template	

2.1.3 Identifiers

An identifier in C++ is a sequence of letters, digits, and underscores. An identifier cannot begin with a digit. Uppercase and lowercase letters are treated as distinct. It is good practice to choose meaningful names as identifiers. One- or two-letter identifiers can be used when it is obvious what the name is being used for. Avoid using identifiers that are distinguished only by case differences. In principle, identifiers can be arbitrarily long, but many systems distinguish only up to the first 31 characters. Table 2.3 shows examples of identifiers.

Table 2.3 Valid Identifiers	
n	Typically an integer variable
count	Meaningful as documentation
buff_size	C++ style—underscore separates words
bufferSize	Java and Pascal style—capital separates words
q2345	Obscure
cout	Used in the standard library iostream
_Sysfoo	Underscore capital is for system use
too__bad	Double underscore is for system use

Table 2.4 has examples of illegal identifiers.

Table 2.4 Illegal as Identifiers	
for	Keyword
3q	Cannot start with digit
-count	Do not mistake – for _

No wonder she never gets asked out:
no one can remember her name or what she does!

2.1.4   Literals

Literals are constant values, such as 1 or 3.14159. There are literals for each C++ data type. String literals are also allowed, as illustrated in Table 2.5.

°Table 2.5 Literals	
5	An integer literal
5u	u or U specifies unsigned
5L	l or L specifies long
05	An integer literal written as octal
0x5	An integer literal written as hexadecimal
true	A `bool` literal
5.0	A floating-point literal treated as `double`
5.0F	f or F float—typically single precision
5.0L	l or L specifies long double

Character literals are written between single quotes. Special characters can be represented with the backslash character \. (See Appendix A, *ASCII Character Codes,* for the full character set.) Table 2.6 has examples of character literals.

Table 2.6 Character Literals	
'5'	Character literal—ASCII value 53
'A'	Letter capital A—ASCII value 65
'a'	Letter small a—ASCII value 97
'\0'	Null character—terminates strings
'\t'	Character printing a tab space
'\n'	Character printing a new line

String literals are stored as a series of characters terminated with the null character, whose value is 0. String literals are `static char[ ]` constants. The character '"' can be represented inside strings by escaping it with the backslash character \. Table 2.7 shows literals that contain characters requiring a backslash.

Table 2.7	Special Character Literals	
`"a"`	2 bytes	`'a' '\0'`
`"a\tb\n"`	5 bytes	`'a' '\t' 'b' '\n' '\0'`
`"1 \\"`	4 bytes	`'1' ' ' '\\' '\0'`
`"\""`	2 bytes	`'"' '\0'`

When printed, these strings would produce effects required by the special characters. Thus, the second string prints an a followed by a number of white-space characters as determined by the tab setting, and then a b followed by a newline character.

String literals that are separated only by white space are implicitly concatenated into a single string.

```
"This is a single string, "
"since it is separated only "
"by white space."
```

The character literals are usually represented as themselves. So the character `'A'` stands for the uppercase letter A. It also has an integer representation of 65. This can be written as the octal representation `'\101'` or the hexadecimal representation `'\x041'`.

Some nonprinting and special characters, such as blank or newline, require an escape sequence, as shown in Table 2.8.

Table 2.8	Character Constants
`'\a'`	Alert
`'\\'`	Backslash
`'\b'`	Backspace
`'\r'`	Carriage return
`'\"'`	Double quote
`'\f'`	Formfeed
`'\t'`	Tab
`'\n'`	Newline
`'\0'`	Null character
`'\''`	Single quote
`'\v'`	Vertical tab
`'\101'`	Octal 101 in ASCII 'A'
`'\x041'`	Hexadecimal ASCII 'A'
`L'00'`	`wchar_t` constant

Floating-point literals can be specified either with or without signed integer exponents, as illustrated by Table 2.9.

Table 2.9 Floating-Point Literals	
`0.1234567`	`double` is default floating-point literal
`1.234F`	`float` is smallest floating-point literal
`0.123456789L`	`long double` is longest floating-point literal
`3.  3.0  0.3E1`	All express `double 3.0`
`300e-2`	Also `3.0`

2.1.5   Operators and Punctuators

C++ allows operators, punctuators, and white space to separate language elements. C++ gives special meaning to many characters and character sequences, illustrated in Table 2.10.

Table 2.10 C++ Operators	
`+    -   *   /   %`	Arithmetic operators
`->      ->*`	Pointer and pointer-to-member operators
`&&    ||`	Logical operators
`=     +=    *=`	Assignment operators
`::`	Scope resolution operator
`new     delete`	Free-store operators

Operators are used in expressions and are meaningful when given appropriate arguments. C++ has many operators. Certain symbols stand for different operators, depending on context; for instance, − can be either unary or binary minus. A unary operator is an operator on one argument, and a binary operator is an operator on two arguments. The unary minus expression −(*expression*) is equivalent in value to the binary minus expression 0 − *expression*. C operators are all available in C++, but C++ has operators that are not found in C, such as the scope resolution operator ::.

Punctuators include parentheses, braces, commas, and colons and are used to structure elements of a program. For example, the following contain punctuators in C++:

```
foo(a, 7, b + 8)  // comma-separated argument list
{ a = b; c = d; } // { starts statement list or block
```

2.2   Input/Output

C++ input/output is not directly part of the language but rather is added as a set of types and routines found in a standard library. The C++ standard I/O library is *iostream* or *iostream.h*. The file name without the *.h* extension is the official ANSI standard name. Officially, the ANSI standard libraries that are taken from C libraries are *c* followed by their names without the *.h* extension. The ANSI C standard library *stdio.h* can be used as the ANSI C++ library *cstdio*. We use *iostream* because we are illustrating C++ practice. This section is introductory, intended to give the bare minimum of detail to get the reader up and running.

The *iostream* library overloads the two bit-shift operators:

```
<<    // "put to" output stream, normally left shift
>>    // "get from" input stream, normally right shift
```

This library also declares three standard streams:

```
cout      // standard out
cin       // standard in
cerr      // standard error
```

The use of the stream in conjunction with values and variables is analogous to assignment. C++ can use existing C library functions, such as `printf()` and `scanf()`, but the *iostream* library is type-safe and easier to use. For example, in the expression `cout << x,` the type of the variable x determines how it is to be printed. Therefore, there are fewer annoying formatting mismatch errors usually found in C, where with `printf("%`*format*`", x)`, the expression value x can be printed incorrectly when the format is mismatched.

The following example program *io.cpp* uses *iostream*. This ANSI C++ standard library is in `namespace std`. This means that all the identifiers defined in this scope are considered to have as their full name `std::`*identifier*. So the full name for the standard output stream is `std::cout`. We avoid having to use the `std::` prefix by inserting the `using namespace std` statement at the beginning of each program that uses files from the standard library. Some compilers provide a *.h* file where this is unnecessary.

In file io.cpp

```cpp
#include <iostream>
using namespace std;

int main()
{
   int  i;
   double x;

   cout << "\nEnter a double: ";
   cin >> x;
   cout << "Enter a positive integer: ";
   cin >> i;
   while (i < 1){
      cerr << "error i = " << i << endl;
      cout << "Enter a positive integer: ";
      cin >> i;
   };
   cout << "i * x = " << i * x << endl;
}
```

Here is some sample output:

```
Enter a double: 1.2
Enter a positive integer: 3
i * x = 3.6
```

In this example, the user entered the double 1.2 and the integer 3 with the result being outputted as the double value 3.6.

Dissection of the *io* Program

■ ```
int i;
double x;
```

The program uses two variables, one for integer input and the other for floating-point input. It is usual in short programs to place declarations at the head of the block. In longer programs, variables are often declared near to their first use.

■ ```
cout << "\nEnter a double: ";
cin >> x;
```

If we run this program, the first output statement in the preceding code places a string on the screen. This string, "\nEnter a double: ", first prints a newline character and then prompts the user for an input value of appropriate type. The second statement expects the double variable x to get a value converted from string input typed at the keyboard. The string represents a value that is either a double or assignment-convertible to a double. Other typed input fails. C++ I/O is type-safe.

■ ```
cout << "Enter a positive integer: ";
cin >> i;
while (i < 1){
    cerr << "error i = " << i << endl;
    cout << "Enter a positive integer: ";
    cin >> i;
};
```

Notice how the while statement insists on getting a positive integer value for input. When programs are to be heavily used, it is important to test that the input is correct. For example, if –1 was entered, the following would be printed:

```
error i = -1
Enter a positive integer:
```

The endl is a specially recognized identifier called a manipulator. It flushes the cerr output stream and adds a newline character to the output.

■ ```
cout << "i * x = " << i * x << endl;
```

The last statement prints the string i * x = , followed by the double value of the expression i * x.

2.3   Program Structure

A program in C++ is a collection of functions and declarations. The language is block-structured, and variables declared within blocks are allocated automatically on block entry and are freed on block exit. Unless otherwise specified, parameters are call-by-value. The following C++ program computes the greatest common divisor of two integers:

In file gcd.cpp

```
// GCD greatest common divisor program

#include <iostream>
using namespace std;

int gcd(int m, int n)      // function definition
{                          // block begin
   int  r;                 // declaration of remainder

   while (n != 0) {        // not equal
      r = m % n;           // modulus operator
      m = n;               // assignment
      n = r;
   }                       // end while loop
   return m;               // exit gcd with value m
}

int main()
{
   int  x, y, howMany;

   cout << "\nPROGRAM GCD C++";
   cout << "\nEnter how many GCD computations? ";
   cin >> howMany;
   for (int i = 0; i < howMany; ++i) {
      cout << "\nEnter two integers: ";
      cin >> x >> y;
      cout << "\nGCD(" << x << ", " << y << ") = "
           << gcd(x, y) << endl;
   }
}
```

As you can see, C++ is very terse. C++ compilers can compile multi-file programs. Large C++ programs are prepared as separate files. Each file is conceptually a module that contains related program declarations and definitions. On many systems, C++ source files have as their suffix either *.c, .cc,* or *.cpp.* One popular freely available compiler for UNIX systems is the GNU C++ translator. It is invoked with the command *g++.* So,

> *g++ module1.cpp module2.cpp my_main.cpp*

is the GNU C++ compile command *g++,* acting on three files: *module1.cpp, module2.cpp,* and *my_main.cpp.* If compilation shows no errors, an executable *a.out* is produced. It is important to rename the executable to something other than *a.out,* such as *program_name.* Otherwise, further compilation overwrites the previous *a.out.* It is convenient to be able to directly compile to an executable, such as *program_name.* As mentioned in Section 1.7, *Writing and Running a C++ Program,* on page 16, this can be done using *-o program_name* in the compile command. So,

> *g++ -o my_program module1.cpp module2.cpp my_main.cpp*

compiles directly to an executable named *my_program.*

Dissection of the *gcd* Program

■ `int gcd(int m, int n)`

The core language relies on functional encapsulation to produce well-designed modular programs. The function name should be chosen to be meaningful. In this case, gcd is a standard abbreviation for greatest common divisor. The function has two integer arguments passed by value. More on this in Section 3.2, *Function Invocation,* on page 88.

■
```
{                    // block begin
   int r;            // declaration of remainder
```

Function definitions are blocks. A block begins with an open (left) brace and includes declaration and executable statements. In C++, declaration statements can occur anywhere in a block. In small blocks, it is usual to place all declarations at the head of the block. In large blocks, it is often the case that declarations appear just before the first use of the associated variable.

```
■ while (n != 0) {          // not equal
      r = m % n;            // modulus operator
      m = n;                // assignment
      n = r;
  }                         // end while loop
```

The `while` statement is a basic looping construct controlled by a `bool` expression. In this case, as long as the expression "n is not equal to zero" is `true`, the compound statement after the `while` expression is executed. The compound statement is any number of contiguous statements between a matching set of braces. In this case, there are three assignment statements that constitute the heart of the greatest common divisor algorithm. The operator `%` is the integer modulo operator, meaning in this case that `r` is assigned `m` modulo `n`.

```
■     return m;             // exit gcd with value m
  }
```

The `return` statement terminates the function. Here, the `return` statement returns an integer value as the value of `gcd()` at the point the function was called in `main()`.

```
■ int main()
  {
      int  x, y, howMany;

      cout << "\nPROGRAM GCD C++";
```

The `main()` function initiates the running of a C++ program calling any subsidiary program, such as `gcd()`. Here, `main()` prints out to the user a message calling attention to its use. It is important to have input/output be clear and robust so that an untrained user of a program can readily use it without detailed knowledge of the program's components.

```
■ cout << "\nEnter how many GCD computations? ";
  cin >> howMany;
  for (int i = 0; i < howMany; ++i) {
```

The `for` statement is a loop that is executed `howMany` times. Here, just before the loop, the user is prompted for the value of `howMany`. Note that the `for` loop variable is declared inside the `for` statement; this is not possible in C.

```
    ■      cout << "\nEnter two integers: ";
           cin >> x >> y;
           cout << "\nGCD(" << x << ", " << y << ") = "
                << gcd(x, y) << endl;
    }
```

Inside the loop, the user is asked for two integer values. These are then used as arguments to gcd(). The final brace ends the loop.

2.3.1   Redirection

On most systems, input can be redirected from a file. Assume that the *gcd* program has been compiled into an executable file called *gcd*. The command

gcd < gcd.dat

takes its input from the file *gcd.dat* and writes the answers to the screen. Test this with a file containing

4   4   6   6   21   8   20   15   20

On most systems, output can also be redirected to a file. The command

gcd > gcd.ans

places its output in the file *gcd.ans,* taking its input from the keyboard. Note that the messages prompting the user for input also go to that file, and the user will have to know what to do without being prompted on the screen.

Enter the same data as before and check the file *gcd.ans* to see that it has the four correct answers. The two redirections can be combined as follows:

gcd < gcd.dat > gcd.ans

This takes its input from the file *gcd.dat* and places its output in the file *gcd.ans*. Test this on your system. Redirection is a very useful system feature.

2.4   Simple Types

The simple native types in C++ are `bool`, `int`, `double`, `char`, and `wchar_t`. These types have a set of values and representation that is tied to the underlying machine architecture on which the compiler is running. Both the `bool` and the `wchar_t` types are new to C++ and are not in C and early C++ systems. The `bool` type provides a native boolean type, and `wchar_t` provides a wide character type, used for representing character sets requiring more than the standard 255 characters.

C++ integral simple types can often be modified by the keywords `short`, `long`, `signed`, and `unsigned`, to yield further simple types. The floating-point types are `float`, `double`, and `long double`. Table 2.11 lists these types, shortest to longest. Length here refers to the number of bytes used to store the type.

Table 2.11	Fundamental Data Types	
Basic Type	Modifier	Modifier
bool		
char	signed char	unsigned char
wchar_t		
int	short int	long int
unsigned	unsigned short	unsigned long
double	float	long double

This basic type list runs from the conceptually shortest type, `bool`, to the conceptually longest type, `double`. Each longer type must be at least as long as its predecessor type. On most machines, a `bool` or a `char` is stored in a single byte. The basic types may have modifiers `short` or `long` that can change the range of values that they can represent. For example, on many machines a `short int` is 2 bytes and represents the range (-32,768, 32,767). The `unsigned` modifier also changes the range by making the values represented greater than or equal to zero. For example, on many machines an `unsigned short` is 2 bytes and represents the range (0, 65,535). On many current systems, `int` and `float` are each stored in 4 bytes. The longer types such as `long int` and `double` are often stored in 4 bytes also, but on some systems they might be stored in 8 bytes. The `wchar_t`, or wide character type, can represent distinct codes for any element of the largest extended character set in any language's alphabet, such as Japanese. A `wchar_t` type is often the same size as an `int` type.

C++ also has the `sizeof` operator, which is used to determine the number of bytes a particular object or type requires for storage.

```
// how many bytes it takes to store int and long

cout << "int size = " << sizeof(int) << endl;
cout << "long size = " << sizeof(long) << endl;
```

Using a Sun Microsystems compiler and system, this prints

```
int size = 4
long size = 4
```

This is not a mistake but an implementation decision for Sun Microsystems. The `long` type must be at least the size of the `int` type.

The range of integral values that can be represented on your system is defined in the standard header file *limits*. Some examples from our system are shown in Table 2.12.

Table 2.12 Range of Integral Values	
`#define CHAR_BIT 8`	Bits per `char`
`#define SCHAR_MIN (-128)`	`signed char` minimum
`#define SCHAR_MAX 127`	`signed char` maximum
`#define UCHAR_MAX 255`	`unsigned char` maximum
`#define INT_MAX 2147483647`	`int` maximum
`#define INT_MIN (-2147483648)`	`int` minimum
`#define UINT_MAX 4294967295U`	`unsigned int` maximum

The range of floating-point values that can be represented on your system is defined in the standard header file *cfloat*. Some examples from our system are illustrated in Table 2.13.

Table 2.13 Range of Floating-Point Values	
#define FLT_EPSILON ((float)1.19209290e-07)	Float
#define FLT_MIN ((float)1.17549435e-38)	Float min
#define FLT_MAX ((float)3.40282347e+38)	Float max
#define DBL_EPSILON 2.2204460492503131e-16	double
#define DBL_MIN 2.2250738585072014e-308	double min
#define DBL_MAX 1.7976931348623157e+308	double max

In Table 2.13, FLT_EPSILON is the smallest number that when added to 1 in that data type yields a result different from 1. The C++ standard library file *limits* contains the template numeric_limits, which allows the user to query the system about characteristics of different types. For example:

```
// determine the maximum value for int and float

cout << numeric_limits<int>::max()
     << " is the maximum int.\n";
cout << numeric_limits<float>::max()
     << " is the maximum float.\n";
```

Using a Borland compiler on a Windows system, this prints

```
2147483647 is the maximum int.
3.40282e+38 is the maximum float.
```

As a rule, use the int type for most integer arithmetic and double for most floating-point arithmetic. These types are the most efficient for their particular machines and compilers. Shorter types can be used if memory space is a priority. Longer types should be used when range of values or precision is needed.

2.4.1   Initialization

A variable declaration associates a type with the variable name. An important conceptual distinction is the following: A declaration of a variable constitutes a definition, if storage is allocated for it. In effect, the definition creates the object.

A definition can also initialize the value of the variable. Initialization is expressed by following the identifier name with an initializer. For simple variables, this is usually

type id = *expression*

Some examples of definitions are shown in the following code:

In file simple_variables.cpp

```cpp
#include <iostream>
using namespace std;

int main()
{
   int     i = 5;              // i is initialized to 5
   char    c1 = 'B', c2;      // c2 is uninitialized
   double  x = 0.777, y = x + i;

   cout << "i = " << i << endl;   // print i = 5
   cout << "x = " << x            // print x = 0.777
        << "\ty = " << y << endl; // print y = 5.777
   cout << "c1 = " << c1 << endl; // print c1 = B
   cout << "c2 = " << c2 << endl; // print c2 = ???
}
```

Initialization can involve an arbitrary expression, provided that all of the variables and functions used in the expression are defined. In the preceding example, y is initialized in terms of the just-defined x. The uninitialized variable c2 cannot be relied on to have any particular value associated with it. Using it in the computation before a well-defined value is assigned to it is a mistake. As a rule of thumb, when there is a choice, it is better to initialize a variable than to define it as uninitialized and later assign it a value. Initialization makes the code more readable, less error-prone, and more efficient.

Syntactically, C++ declarations are themselves statements and can occur intermixed with executable statements. This differs from C, in which declarations are not syntactically statements and must either be in global scope or at the head of a block. In the previous code, we could have placed the char declarations after the first cout statement without affecting the output.

```cpp
. . . . .
   cout << "x = " << x            // x = 0.777
        << "\ty = " << y << endl; // y = 5.777
   char    c1 = 'B', c2;          // c2 uninitialized
. . . . .
```

2.5   The Traditional Conversions

The expression x + y has both a value and a type. For example, if x and y are both variables of type int, x + y is also an int. However, if x and y are of different types, x + y is a mixed expression. Suppose that x is a short and y an int. The value of x is converted, or coerced, to an int, and the expression x + y has type int. The value of x as stored in memory is unchanged. It is only a temporary copy of x that is converted during the computation of the value of the expression. Now suppose that both x and y are of type short. Even though x + y is not a mixed expression, automatic conversion again takes place; both x and y are promoted to int, and the expression is of type int. The general rules are straightforward.

Automatic Arithmetic Expression Conversions

1. Any bool, char, short, or enum is promoted to int. Integral values that cannot be represented as int are promoted to unsigned.

2. If, after the first step, the expression is of mixed type, the following applies, according to the hierarchy of types:

   ```
   int <  unsigned <  long    <  unsigned long
        <  float    <  double <  long double
   ```

   The operand of the lower type is promoted to that of the higher type, and the value of the expression has that type.

To illustrate implicit conversion, we make some declarations and list a variety of mixed expressions along with their corresponding types in Table 2.14.

Table 2.14 Declarations			
char c; long lg; double d;			
short s; float f; unsigned u; int i;			
Expression	Type	Expression	Type
c - s / i	int	u * 3 - i	unsigned
u * 3.0 - i	double	f * 3 - i	float
c + 1	int	3 * s * lg	long
c + 1.0	double	d + s	double

An automatic conversion can occur with an assignment. For example, d = i causes the value of i, which is an `int`, to be converted to a `double` and then assigned to d; `double` is the type of the expression as a whole. A promotion, or widening, such as d = i, is usually reliable, but a demotion, or narrowing, such as i = d, can lose information. Here, the fractional part of d is discarded.

In addition to implicit conversions, which can occur across assignments and in mixed expressions, there are explicit conversions, called casts. If i is an `int`,

```
static_cast<double>(i)
```

casts the value of i so that the expression has type `double`. The variable i itself remains unchanged. The `static_cast` is available for a conversion that is well-defined, portable, and essentially invertible. This makes it a safe cast, namely, one with predictable and portable behavior. Some more examples are

```
y = static_cast<char>('A' + 1)
x = static_cast<double>(static_cast<int>(y) + 1)
```

Casts that are representation- or system-dependent use `reinterpret_cast`. For example:

```
i = reinterpret_cast<int>(&x)    // system-dependent
```

System-dependent casts are undesirable and should be avoided. They are considered unsafe.

Two other special casts exist in C++: `const_cast` and `dynamic_cast`. The `const` modifier means that a variable's value is nonmodifiable. Very occasionally, it is convenient to remove this restriction, by casting away constness. This is accomplished with the `const_cast`, as in

```
const int c_var = 5;
foo(const_cast<int&>(c_var));    // invoke foo(int&)
```

The type in `const_cast<type>` must be pointer, reference, or pointer-to-member type. Note that in the preceding example, c_var remains unchanged outside of `foo()`. The effect of the `const_cast<type>` (*arg*) is that a modifiable copy of its argument is created and passed as an argument to the called function.

To use `dynamic_cast`, we must have an inheritance hierarchy, which is studied in Section 8.7, *RTTI and Other Fine Points*, on page 403.

Older C++ systems allow an unrestricted form of cast with the following forms:

$$(type)\,expression \qquad or \qquad type(expression)$$

Some examples are

```
y = i / double(7);        // does division in double
ptr = (char*)(i + 88);    // C style int to pointer
```

The C cast notation (type) is considered obsolete and is not used in the text. The older casts do not differentiate among relatively safe casts, such as `static_cast`, and system-dependent unsafe casts, such as `reinterpret_cast`. The newer casts also are self-documenting; for example, a `const_cast` suggests its intent through its name.

The next program converts pounds to kilograms and then computes the body mass index.

In file body_fat.cpp

```cpp
// Pounds to Kilograms and Body Mass Index BMI

#include <iostream>
using namespace std;

// conversion constants

const double    lbs_to_kg = 2.2046,
                inches_to_meter = 39.370;
int main()
{
   int  weight, height;    // in pounds and inches
   double kilograms, meters;

   cout << "\nEnter weight in pounds: ";
   cin >> weight;
   kilograms = weight / lbs_to_kg;
   cout << "\nThis is approximately "
        << static_cast<int>(kilograms) << "kg."
        << endl;
   cout << "\nEnter height in inches: ";
   cin >> height;
   meters = height/inches_to_meter;
   cout << "\nYour BMI is approximately "
        << "body fat ratio is   "
        << kilograms/(meters * meters)
        << ". Under 25 is good."
        << endl;
}
```

Dissection of Casting in the *body_fat* Program

■ `// conversion constants`

```
const double  lbs_to_kg = 2.2046,
              inches_to_meter = 39.370;
```

The variables `lbs_to_kg` and `inches_to_meter` are global and are initialized to the values `2.2046` and `39.370`, respectively. The `const` modifier means these values are nonmodifiable. As a result, the identifiers are mnemonic and provide useful documentation. A `const` variable must be initialized on definition.

■ `int  weight, height;    // in pounds and inches`
  `double kilograms, meters;`

The variable names are chosen for the specific meanings they convey.

■ `cout << "\nThis is approximately "`
     `<< static_cast<int>(kilograms) << "kg."`
     `<< endl;`

The `double` value of the variable `kilograms` is narrowed to an `int`. The safe cast `static_cast<int>(kilograms)` truncates the `double` value to an `int` value. Without this explicit cast, the variable `kilometers` would have printed as a `double`.

2.6   Enumeration Types

The keyword `enum` is used to declare a distinct integer type with a set of named integer constants called enumerators. Consider the following declaration:

```
enum suit { clubs, diamonds, hearts, spades };
```

This declaration creates an integer type with the four suit names—`clubs`, `diamonds`, `hearts`, and `spades`—as integer constants, whose values are 0, 1, 2, and 3, respectively. These values are assigned by default, with the first enumerator being given the constant integer value 0. Each subsequent member of the list is one more than its left neighbor. The identifier `suit` is now its own unique type, distinct from other integer types. This identifier is called a tag name.

Enumerators can be defined and initialized to arbitrary integer constants.

```
enum ages { laura = 11, max, debra = 39,
              ira = debra + 7, robin };
```

The enumerators can be initialized to constant expressions. Note that the default rule applies when there is no explicit initializer; therefore, in the example, max is 12 and robin is 47.

The tag name and the enumerators must be distinct identifiers within scope. The values of enumerators need not be distinct. Enumerations can be implicitly converted to ordinary integer types, but not vice versa.

```
enum signal { off, on } a = on; // a initialized on
enum answer { no, yes, maybe = -1 } b;
enum neg { no, off} c; // illegal: no off redeclared
int  i, j = on;         // legal: on converted to 1

a = off;                // legal
i = a;                  // legal: i becomes 0
b = i;                  // illegal
b = static_cast<answer>(i); // legal: explicit cast
```

Enumerators can be declared anonymously, without a tag name. Some examples are

```
enum { LB = 0, UB = 99 };
enum { lazy, hazy, crazy } why;
```

The first declaration is a common means of declaring mnemonic integer constants. The second declares a variable why of enumerator type, with lazy, hazy, and crazy as its allowable values. Enumerators are useful to collect a small number of integral values and turn them into a type. This is good for program documentation, and for program safety as well. Type-checking allows the compiler to check that an appropriate type is used in a given context.

2.6.1   typedef Declarations

Synonyms for type declarations can be provided with typedef declarations.

```
typedef int   miles;      // miles synonym for int
typedef char* c_string;   // pointer to char
typedef void* gen_ptr;    // generic pointer type
typedef point* point_ptr; // pointer to point
```

Besides providing a form of documentation, typedef declarations reduce complicated declarations to simple identifiers.

2.7   Expressions

In C++, there are many special characters with particular meanings. Examples include the arithmetic operators

```
+       -       *       /       %
```

which stand for the usual arithmetic operations of addition, subtraction, multiplication, division, and modulus, respectively. In mathematics, the value of *a* modulus *b* is obtained by taking the remainder after dividing *a* by *b*. Thus, for example, 5 % 3 has the value 2, and 7 % 2 has the value 1. In a program, operators can be used to separate identifiers. Although not required, for style reasons we put white space around binary operators to heighten readability.

```
a + b  // a added to b
-a     // -a is unary minus equal to 0 - a
```

Some special characters are used in different ways in different contexts, and the context determines which way is intended. For example, parentheses are sometimes used to indicate a function name; at other times, they are punctuators. Another example is given by the expressions

```
a + b   // + binary operator add
++a     // ++ unary operator increment
a += b  // += add-assignment operator means a = a + b
```

All of these expressions use + as a character, but ++ is a single operator, as is +=. Having the meaning of a symbol depend on context makes for a small symbol set and a terse language.

2.7.1   Precedence and Associativity of Operators

Operators have rules of precedence and associativity that determine precisely how expressions are evaluated. Because expressions inside parentheses are evaluated first, parentheses can be used to clarify or change the order in which operations are performed. Consider the expression

```
1 + 2 * 3
```

The operator * has higher precedence than +, causing the multiplication to be performed first, followed by the addition. Hence, the value of the expression is 7. An equivalent expression is

```
1 + (2 * 3)
```

On the other hand, because expressions inside parentheses are evaluated first,

(1 + 2) * 3

is different; its value is 9. Now consider the equivalent expressions

1 + 2 – 3 + 4 – 5   and   (((1 + 2) – 3) + 4) – 5

Because the binary operators + and – have the same precedence, the associativity rule left to right is used to determine how an expression is evaluated. This means the operations are performed from left to right. Thus, they are equivalent expressions.

Table 2.15 gives the rules of precedence and associativity for the operators of C++ and is an important reference. We break out pieces of this table when dealing with subcategories of expressions, such as the logical expressions.

Table 2.15 Operator Precedence and Associativity	
Operators	**Associativity**
:: (*global scope*) :: (*class scope*)	Left to right
func() [] -> . (*postfix*) ++ (*postfix*) -- typeid(*e*) type(*e*) dynamic_cast<*type*>(*e*) static_cast<type>(*e*) reinterpret_cast<*type*>(*e*) const_cast<*type*>(*e*)	Left to right
++ (*prefix*) -- (*prefix*) ! ~ & (*address*) sizeof(*e*) + (*unary*) – (*unary*) *(*indirection*) delete new (*type*)*e*	Right to left
.* ->*	Left to right
* / %	Left to right
+ –	Left to right
<< >>	Left to right
< <= > >=	Left to right

Table 2.15 Operator Precedence and Associativity	
Operators	Associativity
== !=	Left to right
&	Left to right
∧	Left to right
|	Left to right
&&	Left to right
||	Left to right
?:	Right to left
= += -= *= /= %= >>= <<= &= ∧= |=	Right to left
throw(*e*)	Left to right
, (*comma operator*)	Left to right

All operators in a given table entry, such as ++, new, and &, have equal precedence with respect to one another but have higher precedence than all the operators in the entries below them. The associativity rule for all the operators in a given entry appears on the right side of the table. These rules are essential information for every C++ programmer, and this table is repeated in Appendix B, *Operator Precedence and Associativity*.

The operators include all the C operators but also have the following operators not found in C: the scope resolution operator ::; the memory management operators new and delete; the modern casting operators static_cast dynamic_cast reinterpret_cast const_cast; the member selection operators .* ->*; the throw expression for exception handling throw; and the runtime type identifier operator typeid.

From Table 2.15, we see that the unary operators have higher precedence than binary plus and minus. In the expression

```
- a * b - c
```

the first minus sign is unary, and the second, binary. Using the rules of precedence, we see that

```
((- a) * b) - c
```

is an equivalent expression.

C++ has many operators and expression forms. Arithmetic expressions in C++ are consistent with C practice. For example, in both C++

and C, the results of an operator, such as the division operator /, depend on its argument types.

```
a = 3 / 2;          // evaluates to integer value 1
a = 3 / 2.0;        // evaluates to double value 1.5
```

2.7.2 Relational, Equality, and Logical Operators

Just as with other operators, the relational, equality, and logical operators have rules of precedence and associativity that determine precisely how expressions involving them are evaluated. C++ systems use the `bool` values `true` and `false` to direct the flow of control in the various statement types. Table 2.16 contains the C++ operators that are most often used to affect flow of control.

The negation operator ! is unary. All of the other relational, equality, and logical operators are binary, operate on expressions, and yield the `bool` value, either `false` or `true`. Where a boolean value is expected, an arithmetic expression is automatically converted, in each case converting zero to `false` and nonzero to `true`.

Table 2.16 C++ Relational, Equality, and Logical Operators		
Relational operators	Less than	<
	Greater than	>
	Less than or equal to	<=
	Greater than or equal to	>=
Equality operators	Equal to	==
	Not equal to	!=
Logical operators	(Unary) negation	!
	Logical and	&&
	Logical or	||

One pitfall in C++ is that the equality operator and the assignment operator are easily confused because they are visually similar. The expression a == b is a test for equality, whereas a = b is an assignment expression. A common C++ programming mistake is to code something like

```
if (i = 1)
    // do something
```

intending

```
if (i == 1)
    // do something
```

The first `if` statement assigns 1 to `i` and evaluates to 1, so it is always `true`. This error can be very difficult to find. It is correct C++, and in certain very rare situations may be the code the programmer intends to write. Some compilers do provide a warning when they see a simple assignment expression as the controlling expression of a selection statement. To prevent this error, C++ programmers can adopt the style

```
if (1 == i)    // constant term on the left-hand side
    // do something
```

The logical operators `!`, `&&`, and `||`, when applied to expressions, yield the `bool` value `true` or `false`. Logical negation can be applied to an arbitrary expression. If an expression has value `false`, its negation yields `true`.

The precedence of `&&` is higher than `||`, but both operators are of lower precedence than all unary, arithmetic, and relational operators. Their associativity is left to right.

In the evaluation of expressions that are the operands of `&&` and `||`, the evaluation process stops as soon as the outcome `true` or `false` is known. This is called short-circuit evaluation. For example, suppose that *expr1* and *expr2* are expressions and that *expr1* has value `false`. In *expr1* `&&` *expr2*, the expression *expr2* is not evaluated, because the value of the logical expression is already determined to be `false`. Similarly, if *expr1* is `true`, then *expr2* in *expr1* `||` *expr2* is not evaluated, because the value of the logical expression is already determined as `true`. Table 2.17 shows some examples in C++.

Table 2.17 Declarations and Initialization		
`int a = 1, b = 2, c = 0;`		
C++	Parenthesized Equivalent	Value
`a + 5 && b`	`((a + 5) && b)`	`true`
`!(a < b) && c`	`((!(a < b)) && c)`	`false`
`(a == b) || c`	`((a == b)|| c)`	`false`

Short-circuit evaluation is an important feature. The following code illustrates its importance in a typical situation:

```
// Compute the roots of: a * x * x + b * x + c
.....
cin >> a >> b >> c;
assert(a != 0);
discr = b * b - 4 * a * c;
if (discr == 0)
    root1 = root2 = -b / (2 * a);
else if ((discr > 0) && (sqrt_discr = sqrt(discr))) {
    root1 = (-b + sqrt_discr) / (2 * a);
    root2 = (-b - sqrt_discr) / (2 * a);
}
else if (discr < 0) {          // complex roots
    .....
}
.....
```

The `sqrt()` function would fail on negative values, and short-circuit evaluation protects the program from this error.

Of all the operators in C++, the comma has the lowest precedence. It is a binary operator with expressions as operands. In a comma expression of the form

expr1 , *expr2*

expr1 is evaluated first and then *expr2*. The comma expression as a whole has the value and type of its right operand. For example, in

```
sum = 0, i = 1
```

if `i` has been declared an `int`, this comma expression has value 1 and type `int`.

The comma operator typically is used in the control expression part of an iterative statement, when more than one action is required. The comma operator associates from left to right.

The conditional operator `?:` is unusual in that it is a ternary operator. It takes three expressions as operands.

expr1 ? *expr2* : *expr3*

In this construct, *expr1* is evaluated first. If it is `true`, then *expr2* is evaluated, and that is the value of the conditional expression as a whole. If *expr1* is `false`, *expr3* is evaluated, and that is the value of the conditional expression as a whole. The following example uses a conditional operator to assign the smaller of two values to the variable `x`:

```
x = (y < z) ? y : z;
```

Because the conditional operator has precedence over the assignment operator, the parentheses are not necessary, but they help make clear the nature of the test.

The type of the conditional expression

expr1 ? *expr2* : *expr3*

is determined by *expr2* and *expr3*. If they are different types, the usual conversion rules apply. The conditional expression's type cannot depend on which of the two expressions *expr2* or *expr3* is evaluated. The conditional operator ?: associates right to left.

C++ provides bit-manipulation operators, shown in Table 2.18, which operate on the machine-dependent bit representation of integral operands. For example, the operand ~ changes an integral operand bit-representation into its one's complement. These operators can be ignored by programmers who don't manipulate underlying bit representations. In C++, we overload the shift operators to perform I/O.

Table 2.18 Bitwise Operators	
~	Unary one's complement
<<	Left shift
>>	Right shift
&	And
^	Exclusive or
|	Or

C++ considers function call ( ) and indexing or subscripting [ ] to be operators. C++ also has an address & operation and an indirection *, or dereferencing, operation. The unary address operator yields the address, or location, where an object is stored. The unary indirection operator is applied to a pointer that retrieves the value from the location it is pointed at. This operation is also known as dereferencing.

C++ also has a `sizeof` operator, which is used to determine the number of bytes a particular object or type requires for storage. This operator is important for obtaining an appropriate amount of storage for dynamically allocated objects.

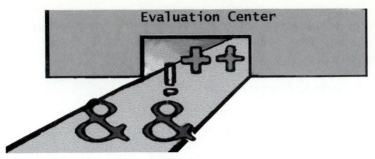

I know we were here first, but he has higher precedence!

2.8   Statements

C++ has a large variety of statement types, including an expression statement. For example, the assignment statement in C++ is syntactically an assignment expression followed by a semicolon. C++ and C both have assignment statements, procedure statements, transfer statements, conditional statements, selection statements, and iterative statements. A key difference is that, syntactically, C++ treats declarations as statements, allowing them to be most anywhere in blocks, but C allows declarations only at the head of blocks, before executable statements. In C++, declarations can also occur in the initializer part of the `for` loop.

2.8.1   Assignment and Expressions

In C++, assignment occurs as part of an assignment expression, which can occur in several forms.

```
a = b + 1;
```

This expression evaluates the right-hand side of the assignment and converts it to a value compatible with the variable on the left-hand side. This value is assigned to the left-hand side. The left-hand side must be an lvalue, a location in memory where a value can be stored or retrieved. Simple variables are lvalues.

C++ allows multiple assignments in a single statement.

```
a = b + (c = 3);
```

C++ provides assignment operators that combine an assignment operator and some other operator.

`a += b;`	*is equivalent to*	`a = a + b;`
`a *= a + b;`	*is equivalent to*	`a = a * (a + b);`

C++ also provides increment (++) and decrement (--) operators in both prefix and postfix form. In prefix form, the increment operator adds 1 to the value stored at the lvalue it acts on and returns the result. Similarly, the prefix form decrement operator subtracts 1 from the value stored at the lvalue it acts on and returns the result.

```
++i;          is equivalent to          i = i + 1;
--x;          is equivalent to          x = x - 1;
```

The postfix form behaves differently from the prefix form, changing the affected lvalue after the value has been returned.

```
j = ++i;      is equivalent to      i = i + 1; j = i;
j = i++;      is equivalent to      j = i; i = i + 1;
i = ++i + i++;      // awful practice, system-dependent
```

Note: These are not exact equivalencies. The compound assignment operators evaluate their left-hand side expression once. Therefore, for complicated expressions with side effects, results of the two forms can be different.

The null statement is written as a single semicolon and causes no action to take place. A null statement is usually used where a statement is required syntactically but no action is desired. This situation sometimes occurs in statements that affect the flow of control.

2.8.2   The Compound Statement

A compound statement in C++ is a series of statements surrounded by braces { and }. The chief use of the compound statement is to group statements into an executable unit. The body of a C++ function, for example, is always a compound statement. In C, when declarations come at the beginning of a compound statement, the statement is called a block. This rule is relaxed in C++, and declaration statements may occur throughout the statement list. Wherever it is possible to place a statement, it is also possible to place a compound statement.

2.8.3   The `if` and `if-else` Statements

The general form of an `if` statement is

```
if (condition)
    statement
```

If *condition* is `true`, then *statement* is executed; otherwise, *statement* is skipped. After the `if` statement has been executed, control passes to the next statement. A condition is an expression or a declaration with initialization that selects flow of control. Here is an example of an `if` statement:

```
if (temperature > 32)
    cout << "Above Freezing!\n";
cout << "Fahrenheit is " << temperature << endl;
```

`Above Freezing!` is printed only when `temperature` is greater than 32. The second statement is always executed.

The expression in an `if` statement is usually a relational, equality, or logical expression. Here is an example with a logical-and expression:

```
if (grade > 70 && grade < 80) {
    cout << " you passed ";
    letter_gr = 'C';
}
```

Notice how the statement that is executed is a compound statement. This allows one controlling `if` expression to execute a sequence of statements. In C++, *condition* evaluates as a `bool`. In C, there is no `bool` type, and the controlling expression depends on a nonzero value being considered *true*, and a zero value being considered *false*.

Closely related to the `if` statement is the `if-else` statement, which has the general form

```
if (condition)
    statement1
else
    statement2
```

If *condition* is `true`, then *statement1* is executed and *statement2* is skipped; if *condition* is `false`, then *statement1* is skipped and *statement2* is executed. After the `if-else` statement has been executed, control passes to the next statement. Consider the following code:

```
if (x < y)
    min = x;
else
    min = y;
cout << "min = " << min;
```

If `x < y` is `true`, then `min` is assigned the value of x; if `x < y` is `false`, `min` is assigned the value of y. After the `if-else` statement is executed, `min` is printed.

In the next program, we show how these statements can be used in a complete program. The program takes as input an integer grade and prints out a message and the equivalent letter grade. If the entered grade was outside the normal range, a grade of Z is printed. Notice how the `if-else` structure works to designate a series of logical cases. The last if is the error case. This is a frequent coding idiom, and the good programmer must master this form of decision making.

In file if_test.cpp

```cpp
// For printing out grade meanings

#include <iostream>
using namespace std;

int main()
{
    int  grade;              // from 0 to 100
    char letter_grade = 'Z';   // A, B, C, D, F, or Z

    cout << "Enter Your Number Score:" << endl;
    cin >> grade;

    if (grade == 100) {
        cout << " First in Class!\n";
        letter_grade = 'A';
    }
    else if (grade >= 90 && grade < 100) {
        cout << " Congratulations!\n";
        letter_grade = 'A';
    }
    else if (grade >= 80 && grade < 90) {
        cout << " Very Good\n";
        letter_grade = 'B';
    }
    else if (grade >= 70 && grade < 80) {
        cout << " Okay\n";
        letter_grade = 'C';
    }
    else if (grade >= 60 && grade < 70) {
        cout << " Work harder\n";
        letter_grade = 'D';
    }
    else if (grade >= 0 && grade < 60) {
        cout << " Sorry you failed\n";
        letter_grade = 'F';
    }
    else
        cout << " Not a recognizable grade" << endl;
    cout << " Your grade was  " << letter_grade
        << endl;
}
```

Dissection of the *if_test* Program

- ■
```
{
    int  grade;              // from 0 to 100
    char letter_grade = 'Z'; // A, B, C, D, F, or Z

    cout << "Enter Your Number Score:" << endl;
    cin >> grade;
```

The program converts an integer grade to a letter grade. The letter grade Z is reserved for an illegal integer grade. When asking a user for input, always prompt the user properly.

- ■
```
if (grade == 100) {
    cout << " First in Class!\n";
    letter_grade = 'A';
}
else if (grade >= 90 && grade < 100) {
```

In a nested `if-else` statement, we have an initial `if` expression followed by a series of `if-else` expressions. Here, each `if-else` expression brackets a particular grade range.

- ■
```
else if (grade >= 0 && grade < 60) {
    cout << " Sorry you failed\n";
    letter_grade = 'F';
}
else
    cout << " Not a recognizable grade" << endl;
```

The very last clause is an `else` part. This frequently takes care of irregular or illegal values. Here, it is an action for grades outside the range 0 to 100.

- ■
```
    cout << " Your grade was  " << letter_grade
         << endl;
}
```

The `if` selection picks a grade of A, B, C, D, or F and assigns it to the variable `letter_grade`. If no grade is selected, the default value Z prevails. The output statement prints the grade in an understandable phrase.

2.8.4   The `while` Statement

The general form of a `while` statement is

```
while (condition)
    statement
```

First, *condition* is evaluated. If it is `true`, *statement* is executed, and control passes back to the beginning of the `while` loop. The result: The body of the `while` loop, namely, *statement*, is executed repeatedly until *condition* is `false`. At that point, control passes to the next statement. In this way, *statement* can be executed zero or more times.

An example of a `while` statement follows.

In file while_test.cpp

```cpp
#include <iostream>
using namespace std;

int main()
{
   int  i = 1, sum = 0;

   while (i <= 10) {
      sum += i;
      ++i;
   }
   cout << "\nSum for i " << i << " is "
         << sum << endl;
}
```

The `while` loop increments the value of `sum` by the current value of `i` and then increments `i` by 1. After the body of the loop has been executed 10 times, the value of `i` is 11, and the value of the condition `i <= 10` is `false`. Thus, the body of the loop is not executed, and control passes to the next statement. When the `while` loop is exited, the value of `sum` is 55.

2.8.5   The for Statement

Consider the general form of a `for` statement:

> `for` (*for-init-statement*; *condition*; *expression*)
>   *statement*

First, the *for-init-statement* is evaluated and may be used to initialize variables used in the loop. Then *condition* is evaluated. If it is `true`, *statement* is executed, *expression* is evaluated, and control passes back to the beginning of the `for` loop again, except that evaluation of *for-init-statement* is skipped. This iteration continues until *condition* is `false`, at which point control passes to the next statement.

The *for-init-statement* can be an expression statement or a simple declaration. If it is a declaration, the declared variable has the scope of the for statement.

The for statement is an iterative statement, typically used with a variable that is incremented or decremented. As an example, the following code uses a for statement to sum the integers from 1 to 10:

In file for_test.cpp

```
// Use of typical for statement

#include <iostream>
using namespace std;

int main(){
   int  sum = 0;

   for (int i = 1; i <= 10; ++i)
      sum += i;
   cout << " sum of 1 to 10 is " << sum << endl;
}
```

Any or all of the parts inside the parentheses of a for statement can be missing, but the two semicolons must remain. If *for-init-statement* is missing, no initialization step is performed as part of the for loop. If *expression* is missing, no incrementation step is performed as part of the for loop. If *condition* is missing, no testing step is performed as part of the for loop. The special rule for when *condition* is missing is that the test is always true. Thus, the for loop in the code

```
for (int i = 1, sum = 0; ; ++i)
   sum += i;
```

is an infinite loop.

Sartre was right; there is no exit.

The `for` statement is one common case in which a local declaration is used to provide the loop control variable, as in

```
for (int i = 0; i < N; ++i)
    sum += a[i]; // sum array a[0] + · · · · · + a[N - 1]
```

Here, the `int` variable `i` is local to the given loop. This form of local declaration is not possible in C, but it can be simulated as follows:

```
{
    int  i;              /*local to block*/
    for (i = 0; i < N; ++i)
        sum += a[i];
}
```

2.8.6   The do Statement

The `do` statement can be considered a variant of the `while` statement. However, instead of making its test at the beginning of the loop, the `do` statement makes it at the end. The `do` statement always executes its body at least once. An example is

```
sum = i = 0;
do {                    // execute
    sum += i;
    cin >> i;
} while (i > 0);        // then test
```

Consider the general form of a do statement:

```
do
    statement
while (condition);
```

First, *statement* is executed, and then *condition* is evaluated. If it is
`true`, control passes back to the beginning of the do statement, and
the process repeats itself. When the value of *condition* is `false`, control passes to the next statement. As an example, suppose that we
want to add 10 positive numbers, such as the last 10 readings of your
blood pressure. We need to read in each integer and require that it be
positive. The following code accomplishes this:

In file do_test.cpp

```cpp
// Use of typical do statement

#include <iostream>
using namespace std;

int main() {
    int  sum = 0, n;

    cout << "\nYou must enter 10 positive integers";
    for (int i = 0; i < 10; ++i) {
        // loop until a positive integer is entered
        do {
            cout << "\nEnter a positive integer: ";
            cin >> n;
        } while (n <= 0);
        sum = sum + n;
    }
    cout << "Sum of 10 positive numbers is "
        << sum << endl;
}
```

The user is prompted for a positive integer. A negative or zero value
causes the loop to be executed again, asking for another value. Control exits the inner do loop only after a positive integer has been
entered.

2.8.7   ## The break **and** continue **Statements**

In C++, the break and continue statements are used to interrupt ordinary iterative flow of control in loops. In addition, the break statement is most importantly used within a switch statement, which can select among several cases. To interrupt the normal flow of control within a loop, the programmer can use the two special statements

break;   and   continue;

The following example illustrates the use of a break statement. A test for a negative value is made. If the test is true, the break statement causes the for loop to be exited. Program control jumps to the statement immediately following the loop.

```
for (i = 0; i < 10; ++i) {
    cin >> x;
    if (x < 0.0) {
        cout << "All done" << endl;
        break;         // exit loop if value is negative
    }
    cout << sqrt(x) << endl;
}
// break jumps to here
 .....
```

In this use of a break statement, a special condition is tested for inside the loop and, if met, the loop is exited.

The continue statement causes the current iteration of a loop to stop and causes the next iteration of the loop to begin immediately. The following code processes all characters except digits:

```
for (i = 0; i < MAX; ++i) {
    cin.get(c);
    if (isdigit(c)) {
        cout << c;         // echo digit
        .....              // do more stuff
        continue;          // terminate current iteration
    }
                           // process other characters
    count_non_digits++;
    .....                  // do more stuff
}
```

When the continue statement is executed, control jumps to just before the closing brace, causing the loop to begin execution at the top again. Notice that the `continue` statement ends the current iteration, whereas a `break` statement would end the loop.

A `break` statement can occur only inside the body of a `for`, `while`, `do`, or `switch` statement. The `continue` statement can occur only inside the body of a `for`, `while`, or `do` statement.

2.8.8   The `switch` Statement

The `switch` statement is a multiway conditional statement generalizing the `if-else` statement. The general form of the `switch` statement is given by

```
switch (condition)
    statement
```

where *statement* is typically a compound statement containing `case` labels, and optionally a `default` label. Typically, a `switch` is composed of many cases, and the *condition* in parentheses following the keyword `switch` determines which, if any, of the cases are executed.

A `case` label is of the form

```
case constant integral expression:
```

In a `switch` statement, each `case` label must be unique. Typically, the action taken after each `case` label ends with a `break` statement. If there is no `break` statement, execution falls through to the next statement in the succeeding `case` or `default`. If no `case` label is selected, control passes to the `default` label, if there is one. No `default` label is required, but including one is recommended. If no `case` label is selected, and if there is no `default` label, the `switch` statement is exited. The keywords `case` and `default` cannot occur outside a `switch`. To detect errors, include a `default`, even when all of the expected cases have been accounted for.

The Effect of a `switch` Statement

1. Evaluate the integral expression in the parentheses following `switch`.

2. Execute the `case` label having a constant value that matches the value of the expression found in step 1. If no match is found, execute the `default` label. If there is no `default` label, terminate the `switch`.

3. Terminate the `switch` when a `break` statement is encountered, or by falling off the end.

The following `switch` statement replaces the earlier `if-else` nested statement in the program *if_test.cpp*.

In file switch_test.cpp

```cpp
// Program for printing out grade meanings

#include <iostream>
using namespace std;

int main()
{
    int  grade;              // from 0 to 100
    char letter_grade = 'Z';    // A, B, C, D, F, or Z

    cout << "Enter Your Number Score:" << endl;
    cin >> grade;
    grade = (grade > 100) ? -1 : grade;

    switch (grade/10) {
    case 10: cout << " First in Class!\n";
        letter_grade = 'A';
        break;
    case 9: cout << " Congratulations!\n";
        letter_grade = 'A';
        break;
    case 8: cout << " Very Good\n";
        letter_grade = 'B';
        break;
    case 7: cout << " Okay\n";
        letter_grade = 'C';
        break;
    case 6: cout << " Work harder\n";
        letter_grade = 'D';
        break;
    case 5: case 4: case 3: case 2: case 1: case 0:
        cout << " Sorry you failed\n";
        letter_grade = 'F';
        break;
    default: cout << " Not a recognizable grade"
                  << endl;
    }
    cout << "Your grade was  " << letter_grade
                              << endl;
}
```

Dissection of the *switch_test* Program

■ `switch (grade/10) {`

The `switch` expression must be an integral expression. The various cases are a selection of the possible values computed here. In this case, the expression should evaluate to the integers from 0 to 10. Other values are considered illegal.

■ `case 8: cout << " Very Good\n";`
       `letter_grade = 'B';`
       `break;`

A typical case: The `case` label is followed normally by one or more actions and ended by the `break` statement. A `switch` case can be written without a `break`, but this is a dangerous practice. In that instance, there is a falling through to the next case. This logic can be confusing: It can result in error-prone, unmanageable code.

■ `case 5: case 4: case 3: case 2: case 1: case 0:`
       `cout << " Sorry you failed\n";`
       `letter_grade = 'F';`
       `break;`

It is permissible to have a series of `case` labels. Here, the program gives the same grade for scores less than 60.

■ `default: cout << " Not a recognizable grade"`
                 `<< endl;`
   `}`

The `default case` usually takes care of irregular or illegal values.

2.8.9   The `goto` Statement

The `goto` statement, the most primitive method of interrupting ordinary control flow, is an unconditional branch to an arbitrary labeled statement in the function. The `goto` statement is considered a harmful construct in most accounts of modern programming methodology. Thus, the statement can undermine all of the useful structure provided by other flow of control mechanisms (`for`, `while`, `do`, `if`, and `switch`).

A label is an identifier. By executing a `goto` statement of the form

   `goto` *label*;

control is unconditionally transferred to a labeled statement.

label:statement

Both the `goto` statement and its corresponding labeled statement must be in the body of the same function. In general, `goto` should be avoided.

2.9   Software Engineering: Debugging

Getting your code to work correctly is a crucial skill. Much of software engineering is about how to avoid or how to find errors. The general term for finding errors in programming is debugging.

Correct choice and use of type is one of the programmer's key techniques in avoiding errors. Languages that are strongly typed are usually safer to program in than languages that are weakly typed. C is considered a weakly typed, and therefore error-prone, language. C++ is a more strongly typed language than C but is less so than Java. C++ allows many different types to be mixed together in expressions with various conversions happening silently.

A classic C or C++ error is an expression of the form

```
double x, y = 2.5;
int i = 5;

x = y + i / 3;
cout << "x = " << x << endl;      // prints x = 3.5
```

when the programmer's intention was to have `i / 3.0`. With the denominator being a `double`, the division would be `double` and x would equal `4.13333`. All C++ expressions should be examined for suspicious conversions. Also, the programmer should test code on some simple data for which the results are already known.

C++ has greatly improved on C's primitive form of cast. In general, it is best to avoid explicit casting, also known as coercion or conversion. Type logic is a safety check that the compiler can perform statically to detect coding mistakes. However, if you must cast, try to stay with the most benign form of conversion, `static_cast<>`. A true, portable conversion is performed. At the other end of the spectrum is `reinterpret_cast<>`, with nonportable, system-dependent effects. This cast should be avoided.

C++ has changed C's rule on where declarations can occur. Use of local declarations is allowed in the `for` loop, for example. Because these rules have changed in C++ since its introduction in 1985, some legacy code is wrong and must be updated to conform to ANSI rules. In earlier compilers, variables that were declared in the initializer-statement part of the `for` statement had scope that extended beyond the `for` statement. This declaration would be in conflict with the same variable name declared at the head of the block.

It is perfectly acceptable to declare simple variables, including variables used for looping, at the head of a block, most likely the beginning of a function definition. Following this advice yields code that works in both C and C++. For example, here is an iterative version of the Fibonacci function:

In file fibonacci_1.c

```
// Fibonacci series compatible with C

unsigned fibonacci(unsigned n)
{
   unsigned i, sum = 0, f0 = 0, f1 = 1;

   for (i = 0; i < n - 1; ++i) {
      sum = f0 + f1;
      f0 = f1;
      f1 = sum;
   }
   if (n > 1)
       return sum;
   else
       return n;
}
```

Using the fact that declarations are allowed in the *for-init-statement* we recode this program as follows:

In file fibonacci_2.cpp

```
// Idiomatically correct C++
// Fibonacci series incompatible with C
// Code follows the rule of smallest enclosing scope
```

```
unsigned fibonacci(unsigned n)
{
    unsigned sum = 0;

    for (unsigned i = 0, f0 = 0, f1=1; i < n-1; ++i) {
        sum = f0 + f1;
        f0 = f1;
        f1 = sum;
    }
    if (n > 1)
        return sum;
    else
        return n;
}
```

Dissection of the *fibonacci* Program

■ `unsigned fibonacci(unsigned n)`

By using `unsigned`, we get a larger range of integer values that can be correctly calculated without causing overflow.

■ `{`
```
    unsigned sum = 0;

    for (unsigned i=0, f0=0, f1=1; i < n-1; ++i) {
```

In this version of `fibonacci()`, we have declarations both at the head of the block and inside the `for` statement. It is usual to declare and initialize the loop counter variable `i` as the first part of a `for` statement.

■ `if (n > 1)`
```
        return sum;
    else
        return n;
```

The variable sum was declared outside of the `for` loop because the `return` statement is outside of the `for` loop.

Notice what happens if we make the following coding error:

In file fibonacci_3.cpp

```cpp
// ERROR because of scopes

unsigned fibonacci(unsigned n)
{
   unsigned sum;

   for (unsigned i=0, f0=0, f1=1, sum=0; i<n-1; ++i){
      sum = f0 + f1;
      f0 = f1;
      f1 = sum;
   }
   if (n > 1)
      return sum;
   else
      return n;
}
```

In this last piece of code, an error was introduced by initializing `sum` in the `for` loop. This declares a second variable `sum` because it is interpreted by the compiler as part of the list of variables declared following the keyword `unsigned`. The program compiles and runs, but with system-dependent results, because there are two `sum` variables in `fibonacci()`. The variable `sum` declared at the head of the block is not initialized, and its value is the one that gets returned.

2.10   Dr. P's Prescriptions

- Use parentheses to make expressions readable.

- Use one statement to a line, except very short statements that are conceptually related, which can be on the same line.

- A compound statement brace comes on the same line as its controlling condition. Its matching terminating brace is lined up under the initial letter of the keyword starting the statement. A function body is a compound statement and starts on its own line.

- Everything after the opening (left) brace is indented a standard number of spaces—for example, as in this text, three spaces. The matching, closing (right) brace causes subsequent statements to be lined up under it.

- Global statements or declarations start in column 1.

- For readability, a space is added after each token, except for the semicolon and unary operators.

- Declarations at the head of a block are followed by a blank line.

- Parenthesize the `return` expression whenever it is not a simple expression.

- The return from `main()` of the integer constant `0` is considered implicit. The practice of explicitly returning `0`—or not—is discretionary.

- To detect errors, include a `default` in the `switch` statement, even when all the expected cases have been accounted for.

- Avoid side-effect operators, such as `++`, in complex expressions, unless they are used in a known idiomatic style.

- Use prefix increment and prefix decrement in preference to postfix when either can be used.

- Avoid casting expressions.

- When possible, use the `break` or `continue` statement, rather than a `goto`.

These spacing and layout guidelines conform to standard industry practice and are used to enhance readability. For example, a uniform indentation standard makes it easier to follow flow of control. One statement to a line gives adequate white space for easy readability.

Parentheses in expressions can be used to aid clarity by making grouping and precedence clear. For example, if the return expression statement is complicated, it should be parenthesized for readability. Within expressions, spaces around operators make them easier to read. Parentheses clarify associativity and precedence in expressions where these can be difficult to follow. They can also aid readability.

It is customary in C, and usual in C++, to place an opening brace on the same line as the starting keyword for a statement, such as an `if` or `for`. The closing brace lines up with the first character of this keyword. In the ALGOL and Pascal community, the practice was to put the equivalent to braces (begin - end tokens) on their own line, which is also acceptable. Whichever brace policy is adopted should be adhered to by the entire programmer team at a project or company.

Starting global statements and preprocessing directives in column 1 is consistent with historic practice, where in the earliest C systems, preprocessor directives had to be in column 1. Also, because of indentation and rest-of-line comments, this gives the most room to neatly lay out code.

The function `main()` is an integer function with the return value being passed to the system. Zero indicates correct termination and is implicitly assumed. Historically, it was required explicitly, so contemporary practice is to have a `return 0` inside `main()`. The ANSI committee endorses the new practice of not requiring it. Either practice is acceptable, but be consistent.

In most cases, you will write short function definitions. Keeping all declarations at the head of such blocks makes it easy to see what variables the function employs. These declarations should be separated for visual clarity from executable statements that follow them.

As previously mentioned, using both the prefix and postfix increment operators can be confusing. Stick to prefix most of the time. The same applies to the decrement operators. Avoid multiple use of these operators on the same variable within the same expression or statement, because the various increments, and when they occur, can be easily misunderstood. One reason for staying with prefix is that they can sometimes be more efficient than postfix on nonnative types.

In general, avoid casting. When using casts, try to use only the `static_cast<>`, as it is the safest of the casts. While casts can be convenient and efficient shortcuts in code, they are error-prone and often system-dependent.

The `goto` is unnecessary in C++. Other structured flow of control statements can better be used to maintain clear flow of control. In many instances, `break` and `continue` statements can be used. These also can be avoided by properly constructing `if-else` statements.

2.11   C++ Compared with Java

The primitive types in a Java program can be `boolean`, `char`, `byte`, `short`, `int`, `long`, `float`, and `double`. These types are always identically defined regardless of the machine or system they run on. For example, the `int` type is always a signed 32-bit integer, unlike in C++, where `int` can vary from system to system. The `boolean` type is not an arithmetic type and cannot be used in mixed arithmetical expressions. The `char` type uses 16-bit Unicode values. The `byte`, `short`, `int`, and `long` are all signed integer types, with length in bits of 8, 16, 32, and 64, respectively. Unlike in C++, unsigned types are not provided. The floating types comply with IEEE754 standards and are `float`, a 32-bit size, and `double`, a 64-bit size.

Java has the same basic set of operators as C++, with a few exceptions. For example, Java does not have the comma operator, scope resolution operator, or `delete` operator. Java added two operators: the `instanceof` and `>>>` operators.

The flow of control statements—`if`, `if-else`, `while`, `for`, and `switch`—available to C++ are also available in Java. Although `goto` is a reserved word in Java, the `goto` statement was not implemented. However, Java extended the `break` and `continue` statements so that they can use labels.

We write a program, *Moon*, to convert to kilometers the distance in miles from Earth to the Moon. In miles, this distance is, on average, 238,857 miles. This number is an integer. To convert miles to kilometers, we multiply by the conversion factor 1.609, a real number.

Our conversion program uses variables capable of storing integer values. The variables in the following program are declared in `main()`. Java cannot have variables declared as `extern` (in other words, as global or file scope variables).

In file Moon.java

```java
// Distance to the moon converted to kilometers

public class Moon {
    public static void main(String[] s) {
        int  moon = 238857;
        int  moon_kilo;

        System.out.println("Earth to moon = " + moon
                            + " mi.");
        moon_kilo = (int)(moon * 1.609);
        System.out.println("Kilometers = "
                            + moon_kilo +" km.");
    }
}
```

The output of the program is

```
Earth to moon = 238857 mi.
    Kilometers = 384320 km.
```

Dissection of the *Moon.java* Program

■ `int moon = 238857;`

Variables of type `int` are signed 32-bit integers. They can be initialized as in C.

■ `System.out.println("Earth to moon = " + moon`
`            + " mi.");`

The `println()` method prints a string. Either the string is a given literal string, or it is a string expression formed by concatenation. Here, the value of `moon` is printed as an integer. The symbol `+` represents string concatenation. By using the addition operator, `println()` can print a list of arguments. Each nonstring argument is converted from its specific type to an output string that is concatenated together and printed along with a newline character.

■ `moon_kilo = (int)(moon * 1.609);`

The mixed expression `moon * 1.609` is a `double` and must be explicitly converted to `int`. Java cast operators are notationally the same as in C, namely, (*type*).

Note that narrowing conversions that are implicit in C++ are not done in Java. Java, in this case, is more type-safe than C++. Also, in Java, all the primitive types are implementation-independent. So, numerically, a Java program gets the same answer regardless of the system it is running on. C++ continues C's tradition of having implementation-dependent choices of primitive types, so as to optimize performance on a given machine.

Summary

This summary emphasizes, in order of appearance, changes and differences from C in the C++ language.

- C++ comments include the `//` *rest of line comment* while retaining the multiline bracketed comments of C /* *comment here* */.

- C++ has many new tokens not found in C. In Table 2.2, *Keywords*, on page 30, there are 63 keywords, compared to 29 in C. New types include `bool` and `wchar_t`. New operators exist in C++, such as the free-store operators `new` and `delete`, and the scope resolution operator `::`. New constructs exist, such as exception handling, which uses `throw`, `catch`, and `try`. Object-building keywords include `class`, `private`, `public`, and `protected`.

- C++ has the new native types `bool` and `wchar_t`, and literals appropriate to each type.

- The new ANSI header file names, such as *iostream*, are embedded in the `namespace std`. In these cases, the construct `using namespace std;` allows access to the names in this library without the need for scope-resolved names, such as `std::cout`.

- At the conclusion of the execution of `main()`, there is an implicit `return 0`. Thus, it is proper C++ style to omit writing this explicitly, as is required by C.

- C++ relies on an external standard library to provide input/output. The information the program needs to use this library resides in the *iostream.h* or the *iostream* file. This library is type-safe and requires no formatting specifications, as found in C's use of `printf()` and `scanf()`. In C++, a typical output expression is

  `cout << expression1 << expression2 << endl;`

  Note that `cin` and `cout` are not keywords. They are identifiers used in a standard library. They should not be declared for other use.

- In addition to implicit conversions, which can occur across assignments and in mixed expressions, there are explicit conversions, called casts. New keywords introduced in C++, modern casts are `static_cast`, `reinterpret_cast`, `const_cast`, and `dynamic_cast`. Old-style C casts (*type*) should be avoided.

- The keyword `enum` is used to declare a distinct integer type with a set of named integer constants, called enumerators. In C++, the enumerator tag name is automatically a user-defined type.

- Both C++ and C have assignment, procedure, transfer, conditional, selection, and iterative statements. Two important differences are (1) C++ uses `bool` expressions to control flow of control statements; and (2) C++ allows declarations as statements instead of just being at the head of blocks or global.

- The general form of a `for` statement is different from that in C.

  `for` (*for-init-statement*; *condition*; *expression*)
     statement

  First, the *for-init-statement* is evaluated and may be used to initialize variables used in the loop. Then *condition* is evaluated. It is of type `bool`. If it is `true`, *statement* is executed, *expression* is evaluated, and control passes back to the beginning of the `for` loop again, except that evaluation of *for-init-statement* is skipped. This iteration continues until *condition* is `false`, whereupon control passes to the next statement. The *for-init-statement* can be an expression statement or a simple declaration. Where it is a declaration, the declared variable has the scope of the `for` statement.

  ```
  for (int i = 0; i < N; ++i)
     sum += a[i];    // sum a[0] + · · · · · + a[N - 1]
  ```

  The semantics are that the `int` variable `i` is local to the given loop. This form of local declaration is not possible in C.

Review Questions

1. A type in C++ that C and early C++ does not have is _____.

2. Three keywords in C++ that are not in C are _____, _____, and _____. Describe their use as far as you currently understand it.

3. What token does the new comment style in C++ involve? Why should it be used?

4. What two literal values does the `bool` type have? Can they be assigned to `int` variables? With what result?

5. What is the distinction between `static_cast<>` and `reinterpret_cast<>`? Which is the more dangerous? Why?

6. C++ uses the semicolon as a statement _____.

7. The general form of a `for` statement is

> `for` (*for-init-statement*; *condition*; *expression*)
>   *statement*

There are two important differences between the C++ `for` and the C `for`. What are they? Explain with an example.

8. The `goto` should _____ be used.

9. What happens when the condition part of the `for` statement is omitted?

10. It is customary in C++ to place an opening brace _____ line as the starting keyword for a statement, such as an `if` or `for`. The closing brace _____ of this keyword.

Exercises

1. Rewrite the `gcd()` function from Section 2.3, *Program Structure*, on page 38, with a `for` loop replacing the `while` loop.

2. Write a program that finds the maximum and minimum integer value of a sequence of inputted integers. The program should first prompt the user for how many values will be entered. The program should print this value out and ask the user to confirm this value. If the user fails to confirm the value, she must enter a new value.

3. Short-circuit evaluation is an important feature. The following code illustrates its importance in a typical situation:

```
// Compute the roots of: a * x * x + b * x + c
.....
cin >> a >> b >> c;
assert(a != 0);
discr = b * b - 4 * a * c;
if (discr == 0)
    root1 = root2 = -b / (2 * a);
else if ((discr > 0) && (sqrt_discr = sqrt(discr)))
{
    root1 = (-b + sqrt_discr) / (2 * a);
    root2 = (-b - sqrt_discr) / (2 * a);
}
else if (discr < 0) {        // complex roots
    .....
}
.....
```

The `sqrt()` function would fail on negative values, and short-circuit evaluation protects the program from this error. Complete this program by having it compute roots and print them out for the following values:

```
a = 1.0, b = 4.0, c = 3.0
a = 1.0, b = 2.0, c = 1.0
a = 1.0, b = 1.0, c = 1.0
```

4. Use the *complex* library to provide the C++ `complex` number type, and rewrite the preceding root-finding program to print out roots as complex numbers when appropriate. Compare this to a C implementation. In ANSI C++, use `#include <complex>`. In the main program, declare such variables as

```
complex<double> root1, root2;    // template type
```

5. What does the following program print? The last expression will cause an error on most machines.

```
// What is printed?

int main()
{
    char  c = 'A';
    int   i = 3, j = 1, m = 0;
    bool  p = false, q = true;
```

```
      cout << c << " is integer value " << int(c)
           << "  and !'A' is " << !c << endl;
      cout << "i = " << i << ", !i = " << !i << endl;
      cout << "!!i = " << !!i << ", !m = " << !m
           << endl;
      cout << "p = " << p << ", q = " << q << endl;
      cout << "!p = " << !p << ", !q = " << !q
           << endl;
      cout << "!(i + j) || m = " << (!(i + j) || m)
           << endl;
      cout << "q || (j / m) = " << (q || (j / m))
           << endl;
      cout << "(j / m) || q = " << ((j / m) || q)
           << endl;
   }
```

6. The C++ `switch` statement allows two or more cases to be executed for the same value by allowing the code to fall through.

```
   switch (i) {
   case 0: case 1:
      ++hopeless;                // fall through
   case 2: case 3:
      ++weak;
   case 4: case 5:
      ++fails; break;
   case 6: case 7:
      ++c_grades; break;
   case 8:
      ++b_grades; break;
   case 9:
      ++a_grades; break;
   default:
      cout << "incorrect grade " << i << endl;
   }
```

Hand simulate this statement for i equals 1. Write the equivalent `if-else` statements.

7. (George Belotsky) Rewrite the *if_test* program to avoid printing the Z grade. First, it is possible to print just the letter grade along with the descriptive message in every 'if' clause. This will prevent the Z grade from being printed. Another alternative is to wrap the final output in an 'if' statement that ensures the grade is not Z before printing. A common variant of the last alternative is to use a boolean variable as a flag to decide whether or not to print.

8. Use `sizeof` to determine the number of bytes each of the following requires on your local system: `bool`, `char`, `short`, `int`, `long`,
`float`, `double`, and `long double`. Also do this for the enumerated types

```
enum bounds { lb = -1, ub = 511 };
enum suit { clubs, diamonds, hearts, spades };
```

9. Write a program to convert from Celsius to Fahrenheit. The program should use integer values and print integer values that are
rounded. Recall that zero Celsius is 32 degrees Fahrenheit and
that each degree Celsius is 1.8 degrees Fahrenheit.

10. Write a program that prints whether water at a given Fahrenheit
temperature would be solid, liquid, or gas. In the computation,
use an enumerated type:

```
enum state { solid = STMP, liquid = LTMP,
             gas = GTMP };
```

11. Write a program that accepts either Celsius or Fahrenheit and
produces the other value as output. For example, input 0C, output 32F; input 212F, output 100C.

12. Simplify the following code:

```
for (sum =i = 0, j = 2, k = i+j; i < 10 || k < 15;
        ++i, ++j, ++k)
   sum += (i < j)? k : i;
```

Remember that comma expressions are sequences of left-to-right
evaluations, with each comma-separated subexpression evaluated
in strict order.

13. In the C world, more flexible file I/O is available by using the
`FILE` declaration and file operations found in *stdio*. The C++ community uses *fstream*, as discussed in Section 9.5, *Files*, on page
430. Familiarize yourself with this library. Convert the program in
the redirection exercise on page 41 to use *fstreams*. The program
should get its arguments from the command line, as in

gcd   gcd.dat   gcd.ans

14. The following code prints 100 random numbers:

```
int main()
{
    int  how_many = 100;

    cout << "Print " << how_many
         << " random integers." << endl;
    for (int i = 0; i < how_many; ++i)
        cout << rand() << '\t';
    cout << endl;
}
```

Add code that determines average, maximum, and minimum values generated. Note that the `rand()` function is found in the C *stdlib* library.

15. Alter the previous program to ask the user how many numbers should be generated. Have this be an outer loop. Exit this program when the user answers with zero or a negative number.

16. The constant `RAND_MAX` is the largest integer that `rand()` generates. Use `RAND_MAX/2` to decide whether a random number is to be heads or tails. Generate 1,000 randomly generated heads and tails. Print out the ratio of heads to tails. Is this a reasonable test to see whether `rand()` works correctly? Print out the size of the longest series of heads thrown in a row.

17. The conditions in selection and iterative statements can be declaration statements, such as `if (bool d = test()) ....`, where scope is restricted to the statement. Write a program that tests whether your compiler conforms to this latest ANSI rule change.

18. Rewrite `fibonacci()`, found in Section 2.9, *Software Engineering: Debugging*, on page 72, as a recursive function. Test it against the iterative form to see which is faster. Useful timing functions can be found in the *ctime* library.

19. *(Java)* Rewrite the convert from Celsius to Fahrenheit program in exercise 9 on page 84 in Java.

20. *(Java)* Rewrite the C++ Fibonacci program in Section 2.9, *Software Engineering: Debugging*, on page 72, in Java. Have it print out the first 40 Fibonacci numbers. Investigate the `for` loop scope rules in Java.

Functions, Pointers, and Arrays

This chapter focuses on functions, pointers, and arrays. It continues a discussion from Chapter 2, *Native Types and Statements*, on how to program classically in C++. In C++, a primary unit for structuring a program is the function. Aggregate data in C++ are either arrays or structures. In both cases, a pointer type is used as a mechanism for accessing such data.

C++ has C at its core.

3.1 Functions

A programmer can solve a simple problem in C++ with a single function. More difficult problems can be decomposed into subproblems, each of which can be either coded directly or further decomposed. Decomposing difficult problems until they are directly codable as single C++ functions is the software engineering method of stepwise refinement. The function construct in C++ is used to write code for these directly solvable subproblems. These functions are combined into other functions and are ultimately used in `main()` to solve the original problem.

The function mechanism is provided in C++ to perform distinct programming tasks. Some functions, such as `strcpy()` and `rand()`, are provided by libraries; others can be written by the programmer. C++ has default arguments, function overloading, and inlining of functions, features not available in C.

3.2 Function Invocation

A C++ program is made up of one or more functions, one of which is `main()`. Program execution always begins with `main()`. When program control encounters a function name, the function is called, or invoked. This means that program control passes to the function. The place at which a function is called is known as its calling environment. After the function does its work, program control is passed back to the calling environment, which continues execution from that point.

The pressure is getting to him. He doesn't want to get called.

As a simple example, consider the following program, *echo*, which uses the *string* library and echoes an input word:

In file echo1.cpp

```
#include <iostream>
using namespace std;

void echo(const string message)
{
    cout << message << endl;
}

int main()
{
    string word;

    cout << "Enter your word: ";
    cin >> word;                    // reads to white space
    echo(word);
}
```

If the word entered is *taxonomy,* the following appears on the screen:

```
Enter your word: taxonomy
taxonomy
```

Dissection of the *echo* Program

■ ```
void echo(const string message)
{
    cout << message << endl;
}
```

This very simple function performs the action of printing out a message and advancing to a new line on the screen. The keyword `void` as the function return type means no value is expected back from this function. A function without a return value is called a pure procedure. The `const` keyword indicates that the string `message` will not be modified by `echo()`. A discussion of this use of `const` is given in Section 3.15, *Reference Declarations*, on page 119.
```

```
■ string word;

  cout << "Enter your word: ";
  cin >> word;                     // reads to white space
```

The `string` type is found in the standard library but is not a native type. The user is prompted for the word that is to be echoed. The word is read in after the user hits the enter key.

```
■ echo(word);
```

At this point, the function `main()` calls, or invokes, the function `echo()`. Echo has as a parameter the variable `word`. The code defined by the `echo()` function is executed at this point using the variable `word`'s value.

3.3   Function Definition

The C++ code that describes what a function does is called the function definition. Its form is

function header
{
    statements
}

Everything before the first brace makes up the header of the function definition, and everything between the braces makes up the body of the function definition.

In its simplest form, the syntax of a function header is

type name(parameter-declaration-list)

The *type* specification that precedes the function name is the return type and determines the type of the value that the function returns, if any. We will see more involved functions headers in Section 10.7, *Exception Specification*, on page 467.

In the function definition for `echo()` in the *echo* program, the parameter list has one parameter. The body of the function consists of a block. Because the function does not return a value, the return type of the function is `void`.

Parameters are syntactically identifiers, and they can be used within the body of the function. The parameters in a function definition are called formal parameters to emphasize their role as place-holders for the values that are passed to the function when it is called. When the function is invoked, the value of the argument corresponding to a formal parameter is used within the body of the executing function. These parameters are call-by-value, meaning that only the values from the calling environment are passed, and not the variables themselves. This implies that if the called function changes the value of its formal parameters, the variables in the calling environment remain unchanged.

C++ functions can have declarations at the head of the block or elsewhere, as long as the variable is declared before its use. This differs from C, where variable declarations must be at the head of a block. So in the *echo* program, `main()` could have been written as

In file echo2.cpp

```
int main()
{
    cout << "Enter your word: ";
    string word;    // place declaration near its use
    cin >> word;
    echo(word);
}
```

In ANSI C++, the empty parameter list is always equivalent to using `void`. Thus, `main()` is equivalent to `main(void)`. The function `main()` implicitly returns the integer value 0 if no explicit `return` expression statement is executed.

Hey, I'm not a blockhead! I'm the head { } of a block.

3.4   The return Statement

The `return` statement is a flow of control statement. When a `return` statement is executed, the current function terminates, and program control is immediately passed back to the place where the function was invoked. In addition, if an expression follows the keyword `return`, the value of the expression is returned to the calling point as well. This value must be assignment-convertible to the return type of the function definition header.

A `return` statement has one of the following two forms:

```
return;
return expression;
```

Some examples are

```
return;
return (a + b);
```

Using parentheses in the `return` expression is optional, a stylistic device that some programmers use to enhance readability. Here is an example used to find the maximum of two values:

```
int maximum(int value1, int value2)
{
   if (value1 > value2)
      return value1;
   else
      return value2;
}
```

Notice how there are two `return` expressions. Some programming experts prefer that there be only one exit to a function. This is to simplify flow of control analysis of the program. We can rewrite the preceding code and avoid using two `returns`:

```
int maximum(int value1, int value2)
{
   int  answer;

   if (value1 > value2)
      answer = value1;
   else
      answer = value2;
   return answer;
}
```

This makes the program longer and less efficient by requiring an additional variable `answer` to be allocated and assigned. We can rewrite the preceding code and avoid this inefficiency by using the conditional operator:

```
int maximum(int value1, int value2)
{
   return (value1 > value2 ? value1 : value2);
}
```

Note that the return value from `int main()` is a special case. Modern C++ does not require a return statement from this `int` function but instead acts as if `return 0` is the last statement in `main()`.

3.5 Function Prototypes

The syntax of functions in C++ is type-safe, with the types of parameters listed inside the header parentheses. By explicitly listing the type and number of arguments, strong type-checking and assignment-compatible conversions are possible.

A function can be declared before it is defined. It can be defined later in the file or come from a library or user-specified file. Such a declaration is called a function prototype and has the general form

   type name(argument-declaration-list);

The *argument-declaration-list* is typically a comma-separated list of types. If a function has no parameters, the preferred style for such an empty parameter list is *function_name()*. The function's argument list can include the argument identifiers. This information allows the compiler to enforce type compatibility. Arguments are converted to these types as if they were following rules of assignment.

The use of the empty parameter list differs from that in traditional C, in which an empty parameter list can indicate an unknown number of arguments. Frequently, C programmers indicate an empty parameter list by using *function_name*(`void`). In C++, the empty parameter list is the same as the use of `void`. We used in the *echo* program the function `echo()`. Its prototype in `main()` would be

```
void echo(string);
```

Both the function return type and the argument-list types are explicitly mentioned. The definition of `echo()` that occurs in the file must match this declaration. The function prototype can also include the identifier names of the arguments. In the case of `echo()`, this is

```
void echo(const string message);
```

C++ uses the ellipsis symbol (. . .) for an unspecified argument list. The *stdio* function `printf()` is declared as the prototype:

```
int printf(const char* cntrl_str, ...);
```

Such a function can be invoked on an arbitrary list of parameters. This practice should be avoided because of loss of type safety. Type safety is when the compiler checks that appropriate values are used in an expression. The ellipsis deliberately avoids this check and places the onus on the programmer to provide correct arguments.

3.6   Call-By-Value

Functions are invoked by writing their name and an appropriate list of arguments within parentheses. These arguments match in number and type (or compatible type) the parameters in the parameter list in the function definition. The compiler enforces type compatibility. The basic argument-passing mechanism inherited from the C language is call-by-value. That is, each argument is evaluated and its value is used locally in place of the corresponding formal parameter. Thus, if a variable is passed to a function, the stored value of that variable in the calling environment will not be changed. Here is an example that clearly illustrates the concept of call-by-value:

In file compute_sum.cpp

```
#include <iostream>
using namespace std;

int compute_sum(int n)  // sum from 1 to n
{
   int   sum = 0;
   for ( ; n > 0; --n)  // value of n is changed
      sum += n;
   return sum;
}

int main()
{
   int   n = 3, sum;

   cout << n << endl;      // 3 is printed
   sum = compute_sum(n);
   cout << n << endl;      // 3 is printed
   cout << sum << endl;    // 6 is printed
}
```

Even though n is passed to `compute_sum()` and the value of n in the body of that function is changed, the value of n in the calling environment remains unchanged. It is the value of n that is being passed, not n itself.

This call-by-value mechanism is in contrast to that of call-by-reference. In Section 3.14.2, *Pointer-Based Call-By-Reference*, on page 115, we explain how to accomplish call-by-reference using pointers. In Section 3.15, *Reference Declarations*, on page 117, we show how to achieve call-by-reference using reference declarations. Call-by-reference is a way of passing addresses (references) of variables to a function that then allows the body of the function to make changes to the values of variables in the calling environment.

Function invocation with call-by-value means:

1. Each expression in the argument list is evaluated.

2. The value of the expression is converted, if necessary, to the type of the formal parameter, and that value is assigned to its corresponding formal parameter at the beginning of the body of the function. This means a local copy is made.

3. The body of the function is executed using the local copy of the parameter.

4. If a `return` statement is executed, then control is passed back to the calling environment.

5. If the `return` statement includes an expression, then the value of the expression is converted, if necessary, to the type given by the type specifier of the function, and that value is passed back to the calling environment, too.

6. If the `return` statement does not include an expression, then no useful value is returned to the calling environment.

7. If no `return` statement is present, then control is passed back to the calling environment when the end of the body of the function is reached. No useful value is returned.

8. All arguments are passed call-by-value. A change in the value of the local copy does not affect the passed in arguments value.

3.7   Recursion

A recursive function calls itself as part of its definition. A simple recursive function has two main parts: the base-case part, where it computes a value and terminates, and the recursive part, where it calls itself. Recursion is often used to define mathematical functions, such as the factorial function. Having recursive functions in C++ allows the programmer to use a simple code body to define these functions.

In file factorial.cpp

```
// Recursive factorial function

long factorial(int n)
{
    if (n <= 1)
        return 1;
    else
        return n * factorial(n - 1);
}
```

Notice how the recursive call is with the expression n - 1. This guarantees that the function `factorial()` terminates. Each recursion reduces the called expression by 1 until the termination condition n <= 1 is `true`. In running this computation, be aware that for even relatively small values of n (such as 13), the computation fails because of integer overflow.

Let us look at another simple example of recursion:

In file blast_off.cpp

```
// Recursive blast_off function

void count_down(unsigned int n)
{
    if (n <= 0)
        cout << "BLAST OFF" << endl;
    else {
        cout << "Count_down at time " << n << endl;
        count_down(n - 1);
    }
}
```

If `count_down(5)` were executed, the output would be:

```
Count_down at time 5
Count_down at time 4
Count_down at time 3
Count_down at time 2
Count_down at time 1
BLAST OFF
```

A pseudocode prescription for writing a simple recursion is

```
// base-case part
```

```
if (base-case condition)
    return base-case computed value;
```

```
// general case as a recursion
```

```
else
    return recursively computed expression;
```

The greatest common divisor of two integers is recursively defined in pseudocode as follows.

```
GCD(m,n) is:
    if m modulo n equals 0 then n;
    else GCD(n, m mod n);
```

Recall that the modulo operator in C++ is %. To test your understanding, do exercise 4 on page 152.

3.8   Default Arguments

A formal parameter can be given a default argument, usually a constant that occurs frequently when the function is called. Use of a default argument saves writing this default value at each invocation. The ability to provide default values to arguments does not exist in C or Java.

The default argument is placed in the function header by using initializing syntax within the argument list for one or more of its rightmost parameters. Here are some examples:

```
// Function headers with default arguments

void print_banner(string s = "PohlsBerry Inc.");
int add_increment(int i, int increment = 1);
int echo(const string s, int how_many = 2);
int compute_age(int year, month mth,
                int birth_year = 1989,
                month birth_month = january);
```

In the case of `print_banner()`, we expect to mostly print the default string `PohlsBerry Inc.` In the case of `add_increment()`, we expect to mostly add 1 to the argument substituted for `i`. In the case of `echo()`, we expect to repeat the argument string `s` twice. In the case of `compute_age()`, we expect to mostly use it for someone born in January 1989.

Where invoked, a function with a default argument can either substitute an actual argument for the default or omit the argument.

```
// Calls to the corresponding functions

void print_banner("Produced by ABC");  // not default
int add_increment(x);       // default and 1 is added
int echo("Boo Hoo", n);     // not default echo n times
int compute_age(2005, april);      // both args default
int compute_age(2005, april, 1954);  // 1 arg default
int compute_age(2005, may, 1954, july); // not default
```

The use of default values is a convenience. As a rule of thumb, use such a value when the majority of the calls to a function involve the default value. An example might be a printing function for printing authorship of the program. Because you are most likely the author, it can make sense to use your own name for the default.

```
void author_ship(string date,
                 string version,
                 string programmer = "Albie B. Coder")
{
    cout << programmer << endl;
    cout << "Version Number is " << version << endl;
    cout << date << endl;
}
```

Here are two calls with and without a `programmer` value:

```
author_ship("1/1/2005", "1.3");
            // Albie B. Coder is the programmer
author_ship("1/1/2003", "2.7", "L.M.P.");
            // L.M.P. is the programmer
```

Another example is the following recursive function:

In file powers.cpp

```
int sqr_or_power(int n, int k = 2)   // k = 2 is default
{
    assert(k > 1);                    // if false program aborts
    if (k == 2)
        return (n * n);
    else
        return (sqr_or_power(n, k - 1) * n);
}
```

We assume that most of the time the function is used to return the value of n squared. The `assert` is discussed in Section 3.25, *Software Engineering: Program Correctness*, on page 143.

```
sqr_or_power(i + 5)       // computes (i + 5) squared
sqr_or_power(i + 5, 3)    // computes (i + 5) cubed
```

Only trailing parameters of a function can have default values. This rule allows the compiler to know which arguments are defaulted when the function is called with fewer than its complete set of arguments. The rule substitutes the explicit arguments for the leftmost arguments and then uses defaults for any of the remaining contiguous unspecified arguments. Some examples are

```
void foo(int i, int j = 7);              // legal
void goo(int i = 3, int j);              // illegal
void hoo(int i, int j = 3, int k = 7);   // legal
void noo(int i, int j = 2, int k);       // illegal
```

3.9   Functions as Arguments

Functions in C++ can be thought of as the addresses of the compiled code residing in memory. Functions are therefore a form of pointer and can be passed as a pointer-value argument into another function. Using this idea, we write code that prints n values of a mathematical function *f(x)*, starting at an initial value using a specific increment. This plotting routine can be used to generate a function map that later is used to find properties of *f(x)*, such as a root of the function *f(x)*.

In file plot.cpp

```cpp
double f(double x) { return (x * x + 1.0 / x); }

void plot(double fcn(double), double x0,
          double incr, int n)
{
   for (int i = 0; i < n; ++i) {
      cout << " x :" << x0
              << "    f(x) : " << fcn(x0) << endl;
      x0 += incr;
   }
}

int main()
{
   cout << "mapping function x * x + 1.0 / x "
        << endl;
   plot(f, 0.01, 0.01, 100);
}
```

Dissection of the *plot* Program

■ `double f(double x) { return ( x * x + 1.0 / x); }`

This is a function that returns a `double`. The function has a single argument that is also a `double`. Functions are considered pointer values. They are the addresses in memory that store the function's code. A pointer has a type. In this case, this is a function of one argument that is `double` returning a `double`.

■ `void plot(double fcn(double), double x0,`
`            double incr, int n)`

Notice that the first argument to `plot()` is a function of a specific type. Functions as arguments are strongly typed. In this case, `plot()` takes a function with one argument that is `double` whose return type is `double`.

■ `for (int i = 0; i < n; ++i) {`
`      cout << " x :" << x0`
`              << "    f(x) : " << fcn(x0) << endl;`
`      x0 += incr;`
`   }`

The heart of `plot()` is a loop that prints out at intervals of size `incr` the value of the `fcn()` function.

```
■ int main()
  {
      cout << "mapping function x * x + 1.0 / x "
           << endl;
      plot(f, 0.01, 0.01, 100);
  }
```

The plot() function is called with f() inside main(), so there are three layers of function call. First, main() is called. Inside main(), the function plot() is called. Finally, inside the loop within plot(), the function f() is called repeatedly.

3.10 Overloading Functions

Function overloading is the ability to have multiple definitions for the same function name within the same scope. The usual reason for picking a function name is to indicate the function's chief purpose. Readable programs generally have a diverse and literate choice of identifiers. Sometimes different functions are used for the same purpose. For example, consider a function that averages a sequence of double values versus one that averages a sequence of int values. Both are conveniently named average(), as in the following code. An overloaded function can be written in which there are distinct argument lists. The list of arguments must differ in either type or number or both.

In file average.cpp

```
double average(const int size, int& sum)
{
    int  data;
    cout << "\nEnter " << size << " integers: "
                    << endl;

    for (int i = 0; i < size; ++i) {
       cin >> data;
       sum += data;
    }
    return static_cast<double>(sum) / size;
}
```

```
double average(const int size, double& sum)
{
    double data;
    cout << "\nEnter " << size << " doubles: "
        << endl;

    for (int i = 0; i < size; ++i) {
        cin >> data;
        sum += data;
    }
    return sum / size;
}
```

The following code shows how `average()` is invoked:

```
int main()
{
    int  isum = 0;
    double  dsum = 0.0;

    cout << average(10, isum) << " int average"
        << endl;
    cout << average(10, dsum) << " double average"
        << endl;
}
```

The compiler chooses the function with matching types and arguments. The signature-matching algorithm gives the rules for performing this. By *signature,* we mean the list of types that are used in the function declaration. The rules for this match are very detailed. We discuss them in more detail in Section 5.9, *Overloading and Signature Matching*, on page 238. Conceptually, the algorithm picks the best available match. Therefore, if the arguments are exactly matched to the signature, that is the match selected. In the preceding code, the arguments exactly matched the two versions of the overloaded function `average()`.

It is important not to abuse this feature. Multiple functions with the same name can often be confusing. It is not readily apparent to the programmer which version is being called. The use of function overloading is good design when each version of the overloaded function conceptually performs the same computation. In the previous example, the same computation of summing a sequence is done as discussed in Chapter 6, *Templates and Generic Programming*.

<table>
<tr><td>**3.11**</td><td># Inlining</td></tr>
</table>

The keyword `inline` can be placed at the beginning of a function declaration. It tells the compiler to attempt to replace the function call by the function body code. This avoids function call invocation. On most computers, this leads to a substantial speed-up when executing simple functions. This speed improvement can come at the expense of an increase in the size of the executable code.

In file inline.cpp

```
inline double cube(double x)
{
    return (x * x * x);
}
```

The compiler parses this function, providing semantics that are equivalent to a noninline version. Compiler limitations prevent complicated functions, such as recursive functions, from being inlined.

3.11.1 Software Engineering: Avoiding Macros

Macro expansion is a scheme for placing code inline that would normally use a function call. The `#define` preprocessor directive supports general macro substitution, as in the following:

```
#define  SQR(X)   ((X) * (X))
#define  CUBE(X)  (SQR(X)*(X))
#define  ABS(X)   (((X) < 0) ? -(X) : X)
    .....
    y = SQR(t + 8) - CUBE(t - 8);
    cout << sqrt(ABS(y));
```

The preprocessor expands the macros and passes on the resulting text to the compiler. So the preceding is equivalent to

```
    y = ((t+8) * (t+8)) - (((t-8) * (t-8)) * (t-8));
    cout << sqrt((((y) < 0)? -(y) : y));
```

One reason for all the parentheses is to avoid precedence mistakes, as would occur in the following:

```
#define  SQR(X)  X * X
    .....
    y = SQR(t + 8);        // expands to t + 8 * t + 8
```

Inlining makes you so much faster.

Macro expansion provides no type safety as is given by the C++ parameter-passing mechanism. Because the macro argument has no type, no assignment type conversions are applied to it, as they would be in a function. Although careful definition and use of macros can prevent such mistakes, C++ programmers avoid macro definitions by using inlining for purposes of code efficiency. Macros using `#define` are a holdover from C methodology.

3.12   Scope and Storage Class

The core language has two principal forms of scope: local scope and file scope. Local scope is scoped to a block. Compound statements that include declarations are blocks. Function bodies are examples of blocks. They contain a set of declarations that include their parameters. File scope has names that are external (global). There are also class scope rules, which are discussed in Section 4.6, *Class Scope*, on page 171. Every variable and function in C++ has two attributes: type and storage class. The four storage classes are automatic, external, register, and static, with corresponding keywords

`auto`   `extern`   `register`   `static`

The basic rule of scoping is that identifiers are accessible only within the block in which they are declared. Thus, they are unknown outside the boundaries of that block. A simple example follows:

In file scope_test.cpp

```
// Examples of scope rules

#include <iostream>
using namespace std;

int b = 15;                    // file scope

int main()
{
    int  a = 2;                // outer block a
    cout << a << endl;         // prints 2
    {                          // enter inner block
        int  a = b;            // inner block a
        cout << a << endl;     // prints 15
    }                          // exit inner block
    cout << ++a << endl;       // 3 is printed
}
```

Each block introduces its own nomenclature. An outer block name is valid unless an inner block redefines it. If redefined, the outer block name is hidden, or masked, from the inner block. Inner blocks may be nested to arbitrary depths that are determined by system limitations. In the preceding example, there is a global variable b, which is available throughout the code. Similarly, the output stream identifier cout is available as it is declared in the file *iostream*. The local variable a is declared in the outer block and redeclared in the inner block. In the inner block, the inner declaration of a masks the outer block variable a.

In C++, declarations can be almost anywhere in a block. An example shows this:

```
int max(int size)
{
    cout << "Enter " << size << " integers" << endl;

    int  comp, data;
    cin >> comp;
    for (int i = 1; i < size; ++i) {    // declare i
        cin >> data;
        if (data > comp)
            comp = data;
    }
    return comp;
}
```

In C++, the scope of an identifier begins at the end of its declaration and continues to the end of its innermost enclosing block.

Even though C++ does not require that declarations be placed at the head of blocks, it is frequently good practice to do so. Because blocks are often small, this practice provides a good documentation style for commenting on their associated use.

Sometimes it is appropriate to declare variables later on in a block. One circumstance is when placing declarations within blocks allows a computed or input value to initialize a variable. A second circumstance is when large objects need to be allocated for a short time toward the end of a block.

3.12.1   The Storage Class auto

Variables declared within function bodies are by default automatic, making automatic the most common of the four storage classes. An automatic variable is allocated within a block, and its lifetime is limited to the execution of that block. Once the block is exited, the value of such a variable is lost. If a compound statement contains variable declarations, these variables can be used within the scope of the enclosing compound statement. Recall that a compound statement with declarations is a block.

Declarations of variables within blocks are implicitly of storage class automatic. The keyword `auto` can be used to explicitly specify the storage class. An example is

```
auto int    a, b, c;
auto float  f = 7.78;
```

Because the storage class is automatic by default, the keyword `auto` is seldom used.

3.12.2   The Storage Class extern

One method of transmitting information across blocks and functions is to use external variables. When a variable is declared outside a function at the file level, storage is permanently assigned to it, and its storage class keyword is `extern`. A declaration for an external variable can look just like a declaration for a variable that occurs inside a function or a block. Such a variable is considered to be global to all functions declared after it. On block exit or function exit, the external variable remains in existence. Such variables cannot have automatic or register storage class.

The keyword `extern` is used to tell the compiler "Look for it elsewhere, either in this file or in some other file." Thus, two files can be compiled separately. The use of `extern` in the second file tells the compiler that the variable is to be defined elsewhere, either in this file or in another one. The ability to compile files separately is important for writing large programs.

Since external variables exist throughout the execution life of the program, they can be used to transmit values across functions. They may, however, be hidden if the identifier is redefined. Another way to conceive of external variables is as being declared in a block that encompasses the whole file.

Information can be passed into a function two ways: by external variables and by the parameter mechanism. The parameter mechanism is the preferred method, although there are exceptions. This tends to improve the modularity of the code and reduce the possibility of undesirable side effects.

Here is a simple example of using external declarations for a program that sits in two separate files:

In file circle.cpp

```
const double  pi = 3.14159;
double circle(double radius)
{
   return (pi * radius * radius);
}
```

In file circle_main.cpp

```
double circle(double);   // function of scope extern

int main()
{
   double  x;
   .....
   cout << circle(x)
        << " is area of circle of radius "
        << x << endl;
}
```

With the GNU system, this is compiled as *g++ circle.c circle_main.c*.

The `const` modifier causes `pi` to have local file scope, so `pi` cannot be directly imported into another file. When such a definition is required elsewhere, it must be modified explicitly with the keyword `extern`.

3.12.3   The Storage Class register

The storage class `register` tells the compiler that the associated variables should be stored in high-speed memory registers, provided it is physically and semantically possible to do so. Since resource limitations and semantic constraints sometimes make this impossible, the storage class `register` defaults to automatic whenever the compiler cannot allocate an appropriate physical register. Therefore, the `register` declaration can be used in place of an automatic declaration.

When speed is of concern, the programmer may choose a few variables that are most frequently accessed and declare them to be of storage class `register`. Common candidates for such treatment include loop variables and function parameters. Here is an example:

```
{
    for (register i = 0; i < LIMIT; ++i) {
        .....
    }
}
```

The declaration `register i;` is equivalent to `register int i;`. If a storage class is specified in a declaration and the type is absent, the type is `int` by default.

The storage class `register` is of limited usefulness. It is taken only as *advice* to the compiler. Furthermore, contemporary optimizing compilers are often more astute than the programmer.

3.12.4   The Storage Class static

Static declarations have two important and distinct uses. The more elementary use is to allow a local variable to retain its previous value when the block is reentered. By contrast, ordinary automatic variables lose their value on block exit and must be reinitialized. The second, more subtle use is in connection with external declarations and is discussed below.

As an example of the value-retention use of `static`, we write a function that maintains a count of the number of times it is called:

```
int f()
{
    static int  called = 0;

    ++called;
    .....
    return called;
}
```

The first time the function is invoked, the variable `called` is initialized to 0. On function exit, the value of `called` is preserved. When the function is invoked again, `called` is *not* reinitialized; instead, it uses its retained value from the previous time the function was called.

In its second, more subtle use, `static` provides a privacy mechanism that is very important for program modularity. By *privacy,* we mean *visibility* or *scope*—restrictions on otherwise accessible variables or functions.

This use restricts the scope of the function. Static functions are visible only within the file in which they are defined. Unlike ordinary functions, which can be accessed from other files, a static function is available throughout its own file but in no other. Again, this facility is useful in developing private modules of function definitions. Note that in C++ systems with namespaces, this mechanism should be replaced by anonymous namespaces (see Section 3.13, *Namespaces,* on page 113).

```
// C scheme of file privacy using static extern
// C++ should replace this with anonymous namespaces

static int goo(int a)
{
    .....
}
int foo(int a)
{
    .....
    b = goo(a);
    // goo() is available here but not in other files
    .....
}
```

In C++, the system initializes to 0 both external variables and static variables that are not explicitly initialized by the programmer. Such variables include arrays, strings, pointers, structures, and unions. For arrays and strings, this means that each element is initialized to 0; for structures and unions, it means that each member is initialized to 0. In contrast, automatic and register variables usually are not initialized by the system and can start with garbage values.

3.12.5   Header Files and Linkage Mysteries

Typically, a large program is written in a separate directory as a collection of *.h* and *.c* files, with each *.c* file containing one or more function definitions. Each *.c* file can be recompiled as needed, saving time for both the programmer and the machine. Let us suppose we are developing a large program called *pgm*. At the top of each of our *.c* files, we put the line

```
#include "pgm.h"
```

When the preprocessor encounters this directive, it looks first in the current directory for the file *pgm.h*. If there is such a file, it is included. If not, the preprocessor looks in other system-dependent places for the file. If the file *pgm.h* cannot be found, the preprocessor issues an error message and compilation stops.

Our header file *pgm.h* may contain `#includes`, `#defines`, declarations of enumeration types, declarations of class types, other programming constructs, and a list of function prototypes at the bottom. Thus *pgm.h* contains program elements that are appropriate for our program as a whole. Because the header file *pgm.h* occurs at the top of each *.c* file, it acts as the "glue" that binds our program together.

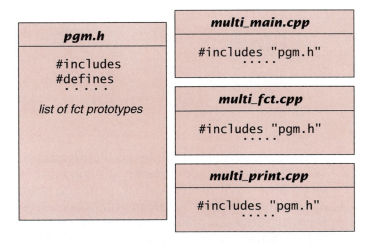

We show a very simple example of how this works. We write our program in a separate directory. It consists of a *.h* file and three *.cpp* files. Typically, the name of the directory and the name of the program are the same. Here is our *multi_main* program:

In file pgm.h:

```
#include <iostream>
#include <cstdlib>
using namespace std;

#define    N    3

void    fct1(int k);
void    fct2();
void    prn_info(const string& pgm_name);
```

In file multi_main.cpp:

```
#include "pgm.h"

int main()
{
    char    ans;
    int     k, n = N;

    cout << "This program does not do very much.\n";
    cout << "Do you want more information?   ";
    cout << "Enter either y or Y if yes. " << endl;
    cin >> ans;

    if (ans == 'y' || ans == 'Y')
        prn_info("multi_main");
    for (k = 0; k < n; ++k)
        fct1(k);
    cout << "Best Regards!" << endl;
}
```

In file multi_fct.cpp:

```
#include "pgm.h"

void fct1(int n)
{
    int    i;

    cout << "Hello from fct1()" << endl;
    for (i = 0; i < n; ++i)
        fct2();
}
```

```
void fct2()
{
    cout << "Hello from fct2()" << endl;
}
```

In file multi_prn.cpp:

```
#include "pgm.h"

void prn_info(const string& pgm_name)
{
    cout << "Usage:  " << pgm_name << endl;
    cout << "This program illustrates a " << endl;
    cout << "program in more than one file." << endl;
    cout << "In this example, a single" << endl;
    cout << ".h file is included at the" << endl;
    cout << "top of our three .cpp files." << endl;
    cout << "Thus pgm.h acts as the \"glue\"" << endl;
    cout << "that binds the program." << endl;
}
```

We compile the program with the command

cc -o multi_main multi_main.cpp multi_fct.cpp multi_prn.cpp

The compiler creates the executable file *multi_main,* along with three *.o* files that correspond to *.cpp* files. In Windows, they are *.obj* files.

Multifile programs require proper linkage. C++ requires some special rules to avoid hidden inconsistencies. As already indicated, a name declared at file scope as explicitly `static` is local and is hidden from other files. This form of linkage is called internal linkage. By default, `const` and `typedef` declarations have internal linkage. A `const` variable that is at file scope but is not static can be given external linkage by declaring it `extern`. Finally, linkage to C code is possible using the form

```
extern "C" { code or included file }
```

Linkage to languages other than C is system-dependent. For example, some systems might allow `"Java"`.

It is the coder's responsibility to make sure that all names referring to the identical construct are consistent. It is beyond the scope of this text to discuss all the nuances of linkage.

Tips for Avoiding Linkage Problems

- Use header files for function prototypes, class definitions, constants, typedefs, templates, inline functions, and named namespaces.

- Use these header files with an `#ifdef __`*filename* as a guard against multiple inclusion.

- Think in terms of the one-definition rule (ODR), which states that classes, enumerations, templates, and so forth must be defined exactly once in the program.

- As a heuristic, envision writing the code into one monolithic file and seeing whether this causes conflicts.

 3.13

Namespaces

C++ inherited C's single global namespace. Programs written by two or more parties can have inadvertent name clashes when combined. C++ encourages multivendor library use. This motivates the addition of a namespace scope to ANSI C++.

```
namespace LMPinc {
    class puzzles { ····· };
    class toys { ····· };
    ·····
}
```

The namespace identifier can be used as part of a scope-resolved identifier, which has the form

namespace_id::id

A `using` declaration lets a client have access to all names from that namespace.

```
using namespace LMPinc;
toys  top;                              // LMPinc::toys
```

Namespaces can also nest.

```
namespace LMPinc{
   int  n;
   namespace dolls {                // inner namespace
      int  sq(){ return n * n; }// LMPinc::n
      void  pr_my_logo();
   }
   void  LMPdolls::pr_my_logo()
      { cout << "Dolls by Laura" << endl; }
}
```

As mentioned in Section 3.12.4, *The Storage Class* `static`, on page 108, namespaces can be used to provide a unique scope that replaces static global declarations. This is done by an anonymous namespace definition, as in

```
namespace { int count = 0; }    // count is unique here

// count is available in the rest of the file
void  chg_cnt(int i) { count = i; }
```

Library headers conforming to the ANSI C++ standard no longer use the *.h* suffix. Files such as *iostream* and *complex* are declared within the `namespace std`. Vendors no doubt will continue shipping old-style headers, such as *iostream.h* or *complex.h*, as well, so that old code can run without change.

3.14   Pointer Types

C++ pointers, used to reference variables and machine addresses, are intimately tied to array and string processing. C++ arrays can be considered a special form of pointer associated with a contiguous piece of memory for storing a series of indexable values.

Pointers are used in programs to access memory and to manipulate addresses. If v is a variable, &v is the address, or location in memory, of its stored value. The address operator & is unary and has the same precedence and right-to-left associativity as the other unary operators. Pointer variables can be declared in programs and then used to take addresses as values. The following declares p to be of type "pointer to `int`":

```
int*  p;
```

The legal range of values for any pointer always includes the special address 0, as well as a set of positive integers that are interpreted as machine addresses on a particular system. Some examples of assignment to the pointer p are

```
p = &i;                      // address of object i
p = 0;                       // special sentinel value
p = static_cast<int*>(1507);// absolute address
```

In the first example, we think of p as "referring to i," "pointing to i," or "containing the address of i." The compiler decides what address to assign the variable i. This varies from machine to machine and most likely differs for various executions on the same machine. The second example is the assignment of the special value 0 to the pointer p. This value is typically used to indicate a special condition. For example, a pointer value of 0 is returned by a call to the operator new when free storage is exhausted. By convention, a pointer value of 0 is also used to indicate the end of a dynamic data structure, such as a tree or a list. In the third example, the cast is necessary to avoid a type error, and an actual memory address is used.

3.14.1   Addressing and Dereferencing

As in C, the dereferencing, or indirection, operator * is unary and has the same precedence and right-to-left associativity as the other unary operators. If p is a pointer, *p is the value of the variable that p points to. The direct value of p is a memory location, whereas *p is the indirect value of p—namely, the value at the memory location stored in p. In a certain sense, * is the inverse operator to &. Here is code showing some of these relationships:

```
int   i = 5, j;
int*  p = &i;    // pointer p is init to address of i

cout << *p << " = i stored at " << p << endl;
j = p;           // illegal pointer not convert to int
j = *p + 1;      // legal
p = &j;          // p points to j
```

3.14.2   Pointer-Based Call-By-Reference

The addresses of variables can be used as arguments to functions so that the stored values of the variables can be modified. Experienced C programmers should skip this discussion and go to Section 3.15, *Reference Declarations*, on page 117. In pointer-based call-by-reference, pointers must be used in the parameter list in the function definition. Then, when the function is called, addresses of variables must be passed as arguments. For example, let us code a function order() that exchanges two values if the first value is greater than the second value:

In file order1.cpp

```
// Pointer-based call-by-reference

void  order(int*, int*);

int main()
{
    int  i = 7, j = 3;

    cout << i << '\t' << j << endl;     // 7  3 printed
    order(&i, &j);
    cout << i << '\t' << j << endl;     // 3  7 printed
}
void order(int* p, int* q)
{
    int  temp;

    if (*p > *q) {
        temp = *p;
        *p = *q;
        *q = temp;
    }
}
```

Most of the work of this program is carried out by the function call to
order(). Notice that the addresses of i and j are passed as arguments. As we shall see, this allows the function call to change the values of i and j in the calling environment.

Dissection of the order() Function

■ void order(int* p, int* q)
  {
      int temp;

The parameters p and q are both of type pointer to int. The variable
temp is local to this function and is of type int.

```
■ if (*p > *q) {
      temp = *p;
      *p = *q;
      *q = temp;
  }
```

If the value of what is pointed to by p is greater than the value of what is pointed to by q, the following is done: First, `temp` is assigned the value of what is pointed to by p; second, what is pointed to by p is assigned the value of what is pointed to by q; and third, what is pointed to by q is assigned the value of `temp`. This interchanges in the calling environment the stored values of whatever p and q are pointing to.

The rules for using pointer arguments to achieve call-by-reference can be summarized as follows.

Call-By-Reference Using Pointers

1. Declare a pointer parameter in the function header.

2. Use the dereferenced pointer in the function body.

3. Pass an address as an argument when the function is called.

3.15   Reference Declarations

Reference declarations, a C++ feature not available in C, declare the identifier to be an alternative name, or alias, for an object specified in an initialization of the reference. Reference declarations allow a simpler form of call-by-reference parameters. Some examples are

```
int      n;
int&     nn = n;      // nn is an alternative name for n
double   a[10];
double&  last = a[9];// last is an alias for a[9]
```

Declarations of references that are definitions must be initialized and are usually initialized to simple variables. The initializer is an lvalue expression, which gives the variable's location in memory. In these examples, the names n and nn are aliases for each other; that is, they refer to the same object. Modifying nn is equivalent to modifying n, and vice versa. The name `last` is an alternative to the single array element a[9]. These names, once initialized, cannot be changed.

When a variable i is declared, it has an address and memory associated with it. When a pointer variable p is declared and initialized to

&i, it has an identity separate from i. The pointer p has memory associated with it that is initialized to the address of i. When a reference variable r is declared and initialized to i, it is identical to i. It does not have an identity separate from the other names for the same object. In effect, r is just another name for i, that is, an alias.

The following definitions are used to demonstrate the use of dereferencing and aliasing. The definitions assume that memory at location 1004 is used for integer variable a and that memory at 1008 is used for pointer variable p.

```
int    a = 5;          // declare and define a
int*   p = &a;         // p points to a
int&   ref_a = a;      // alias for a
*p = 7;        // *p is lvalue of a, so a is assigned 7
a = *p + 1;    // rvalue 7 added to 1 and a assigned 8
```

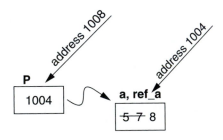

Pointer Declarations

Notice in the preceding figure of pointer declarations that any change to the value of a is equivalent to changing ref_a. Such a change affects the dereferenced value of p. The pointer p can be assigned another address and lose its association with a. However, a and ref_a are aliases and within scope must refer to the same object. These declarations can be used for call-by-reference arguments, which allows C++ to have call-by-reference arguments directly. The function order(), using this mechanism, is recoded as follows:

In file order2.cpp

```
void order(int& p, int& q)
{
    int  temp;

    if (p > q) {
        temp = p;
        p = q;
        q = temp;
    }
}
```

The function would be prototyped and invoked in main() as follows:

```
void  order(int& p, int& q);

int main()
{
    int  i, j;
    .....
    order(i, j);
    .....
}
```

If i and j are int variables, then order(i, j) uses the reference to i and the reference to j to exchange, if necessary, their two values. In traditional C, this operation must be accomplished by using pointers and dereferencing.

When function arguments are to remain unmodified, it can be efficient and correct to pass them const call-by-reference. This is the case for types that are structures. The const is not strictly necessary, but it indicates the programmer's intent not to modify these values and allows the compiler to check this.

```
struct large_size {
    int  mem[N];
    .....
};
```

```
void print(const large_size& s)      // efficient
{
    // when invoked only a pointer value is passed
.....
}

int add(large_size s) // inefficient
{
    // when invoked a local copy of s is made
.....
}
```

3.16   The Uses of void

The keyword void is used to declare the generic pointer type—
pointer to void. The keyword void is also used as the return type of
a function not returning a value. In programming, such a function is
sometimes called a pure procedure. In addition, void can be used in
a cast to indicate that a value is unneeded.

Most interesting is the use of void* as a generic pointer type. A
pointer declared as type pointer to void, as in void* gp, may be
assigned a pointer value of any type but may not be dereferenced.
Dereferencing is the operation * acting on a pointer value to obtain
what is pointed at. It would not make sense to dereference a pointer
to a void value.

```
void*  gp;                        // generic pointer
int*   ip;                        // int pointer
char*  cp;                        // char pointer

gp = ip;                          // legal conversion
ip = reinterpret_cast<int*>(gp);// legal conversion
cp = ip;                          // illegal conversion
*ip = 15;      // legal dereference of pointer to int
*ip = *gp;     // illegal generic pointer dereference
```

A key use for this type is as a formal parameter. For example, the
library function memcpy() is declared in *cstring*:

```
void* memcpy(void* s1, const void* s2, size_t n);
```

On older C++ systems or on C systems, this is declared in *string.h*.
This function copies n characters from the object based at s2 into the
object based at s1. The function works with any two pointer types as

arguments. The type `size_t` is defined in *cstddef* and is often a synonym for `unsigned int`.

A further use of `void` given as the parameter list in a function declaration means that the function takes no arguments. Thus, `int foo()` is equivalent in C++ to `int foo(void)`.

3.17 Arrays

An array is a data type used to represent a large number of values of the same type. An array might be used to represent all the salaries in a company or all the weights of participants in a fitness program. Each element in an array has a position, with the initial element having position zero. An array element's position can be used as an index or subscript to access that element. The elements of an array are randomly accessible through the use of subscripts. Arrays of all types are possible, including arrays of arrays. A typical array declaration allocates memory starting from a base address. An array name is, in effect, a pointer constant to this base address. In C++, only one-dimensional arrays are provided, with the first element always indexed as element zero.

To illustrate some of these ideas, let us write a small program that fills an array, prints out values, and sums the elements of the array.

In file sum_array1.cpp

```cpp
// Simple array processing

const int  SIZE = 5;

int main()
{
    int  a[SIZE];      // get space for a[0],······,a[4]
    int sum = 0;

    for (int i = 0; i < SIZE; ++i) {
        a[i] = i * i;
        cout << "a[" << i << "] = " << a[i] << "  ";
        sum += a[i];
    }
    cout << "\nsum = " << sum << endl;
}
```

The output of this program is

```
a[0] = 0  a[1] = 1  a[2] = 4  a[3] = 9  a[4] = 16
   sum = 30
```

The preceding array requires enough memory to store five integer values. Thus, if `a[0]` is stored at location 1000, the remaining array elements on a system needing 4 bytes for an `int` are successively stored at locations 1004, 1008, 1012, and 1016. It is considered good programming practice to define the size of an array as a constant. Since much of the code may depend on this value, it is convenient to be able to change a single `const int SIZE` declaration to process various size arrays. Notice how the various parts of the `for` statement are neatly tailored to provide a terse notation for dealing with array computations.

3.17.1   Subscripting

Assume that a declaration has the form

```
int  i, a[size];
```

We can write `a[i]` to access an element of the array. More generally, we may write `a[expr]`, where *expr* is an integral expression, to access an element of the array. We call *expr* a subscript, or index, of `a`. The value of a C++ subscript should lie in the range 0 to *size* – 1. An array subscript value outside this range often causes a runtime error. When this happens, the condition is called "overrunning the bounds of the array," or "subscript out of bounds." It is a common programming error. The effect of the error in a C++ program is system-dependent and can be quite confusing. One frequent result is that the value of an unrelated variable is returned or modified. Thus, the programmer must ensure that all subscripts stay within bounds.

3.17.2   Initialization

Arrays can be initialized by a comma-separated list of expressions enclosed in braces:

```
int array[4] = { 9, 8, 7 }; // a[0]=9, a[1]=8, a[2]=7
```

When the list of initializers is shorter than the size of the array, the remaining elements are initialized to 0. If uninitialized, external and static arrays are automatically initialized to 0. This is not so for automatic arrays, which start with undefined values.

An array declared with an explicit initializer list and no size expression is given the size of the number of initializers. The following two arrays are equivalent:

```
char laura[] = { 'l', 'm', 'p' };
char laura[3] = { 'l', 'm', 'p' };
```

3.18   Arrays and Pointers

An array name by itself is an address, or pointer value, and pointers and arrays are almost identical in terms of how they are used to access memory. However, there are subtle and important differences. A pointer is a variable that takes addresses as values. An array name is a particular fixed address that can be thought of as a constant pointer. When an array is declared, the compiler must allocate a base address and a sufficient amount of storage to contain all of the elements of the array. The base address of the array is the initial location in memory where the array is stored; it is the address of the first element (index 0) of the array. Suppose that we write the declaration

```
const int  N = 100;

int  a[N], *p;
```

and the system causes memory bytes 300, 304, 308, . . . , 696 to be the addresses of a[0], a[1], a[2], . . . , a[99], respectively, with location 300 being the base address of a. We are assuming that each byte is addressable and that 4 bytes are used to store an int. The two statements p = a; and p = &a[0]; are equivalent and would assign 300 to p. Note that [] has higher precedence than &, so &a[0] is equivalent to &(a[0]).

Pointer arithmetic provides an alternative to array indexing. The two statements p = a + 1; and p = &a[1]; are equivalent and would assign 304 to p. Assuming that the elements of a have been assigned values, we can use the following code to sum the array:

In file sum_array2.cpp

```
sum = 0;
for (p = a; p < &a[N]; ++p)
   sum += *p;
```

is equivalent to

```
sum = 0;
for (i = 0; i < N; ++i)
   sum += a[i];
```

In this loop, the pointer variable p is initialized to the base address of the array a. Then the successive values of p are equivalent to &a[0], &a[1], . . . , &a[N-1]. In general, if i is a variable of type int, p + i is the ith offset from the address p. In a similar manner, a + i is the ith offset from the base address of the array a. Here is another way to sum the array:

```
sum = 0;
for (i = 0; i < N; ++i)
   sum += *(a + i);
```

Just as the expression *(a + i) is equivalent to a[i], the expression *(p + i) is equivalent to p[i]. In many ways, arrays and pointers can be treated alike, but there is one essential difference. Because the array a is a constant pointer and not a variable, and we thus cannot change the address of a, expressions such as the following are illegal:

```
a = p          ++a          a += 2
```

3.19 Passing Arrays to Functions

In a function definition, a formal parameter that is declared as an array is a pointer. When an array is being passed, its base address is passed call-by-value. The array elements themselves are not copied. As a notational convenience, the compiler allows array bracket notation to be used in declaring pointers as parameters. This notation reminds the programmer and other readers of the code that the function should be called with an array. To illustrate this, we write a function that sums the elements of an array of type int:

In file sum_array3.cpp

```
int sum(int a[], int n)        // n is the size of a[]
{
   int  s = 0;

   for (int i = 0; i < n; ++i)
      s += a[i];
   return s;
}
```

As part of the header of a function definition, the declaration int a[] is equivalent to int *a. In other contexts, the two are not equivalent.

Suppose that v has been declared to be an array with 100 elements of type `int`. After the elements have been assigned values, we can use the function `sum()` to add various elements of v. Table 3.1 illustrates some of the possibilities.

Table 3.1 Summing Elements of an Array	
Invocation	What Gets Computed and Returned
sum(v, 100)	v[0] + v[1] + . . . + v[99]
sum(v, 88)	v[0] + v[1] + . . . + v[87]
sum(v + 7, k)	v[7] + v[8] + . . . + v[k+6]

The first call sums all 100 elements of the array v[]. The second call sums the first 88 elements. The third function call again illustrates the use of pointer arithmetic. The base address of v is offset by 7, and `sum()` initializes the local pointer variable a to this address. This causes all address calculations inside the function call to be similarly offset. The number of elements summed is the value of the variable k. If the value of k is 10, then we sum elements from v[7] up to and including v[16].

In C++, a function with a formal array parameter can be called with an array argument of any size, provided the array has the right base type.

3.20 Problem Solving: Random Numbers

Random numbers have many uses in computers. One use is to serve as data to test code; another use is to simulate a real-world event that involves a probability. The method of simulation is an important problem-solving technique. Programs that use random number functions to generate probabilities are called Monte Carlo simulations. The Monte Carlo technique can be applied to many problems that otherwise would have no possibility of solution.

A random number generator is a function that returns integers that appear to be randomly distributed in some interval 0 to *n*, where *n* is system-dependent. The function `rand()` in the standard library *cstdlib* is provided to do this. This function generates a pseudorandom sequence. It is called pseudorandom because the numbers are generated by a deterministic algorithm but appear to be random. In order to start the pseudorandom sequence at different points, you should use the *cstdlib* function `srand(n)` to start the sequence with the number seed n.

Let us write a program that displays some random numbers generated by `rand()`. Here is the first part of the program:

In file random.cpp

```
#include <iostream>
#include <cstdlib>
using namespace std;

void    prn_random_numbers(int k);

int main(void)
{
    int   n, seed;

    cout << "\nSome random numbers will be printed.";
    cout << "\nEnter how many you want?   " << endl;
    cin >> n;
    cout << "Enter seed number:   ";
    cin >> seed;
    srand(seed);
    prn_random_numbers(n);
}
```

Because the function prototype for `rand()` is in the standard header file *cstdlib*, we have included it at the top of the file.

The user is asked to enter how many random numbers are wanted. In order not to repeat the same sequence each time the program is run, the user is asked for a seed. The seed is used to start `rand()` at different points in the pseudorandom sequence. The value entered for n is passed as an argument to the function `prn_random_numbers()`.

In the remainder of the file, we write the function definition for `prn_random_numbers()`. Here is the function:

```
void prn_random_numbers(int k)
{
    int   r, biggest, smallest;

    r = biggest = smallest = rand();
    cout << endl << r;
```

```
for (int i = 1; i < k; ++i) {
    if (i % 5 == 0)
        cout << endl;
    else
        cout << '\t';
    r = rand();
    biggest = r > biggest ? r : biggest;
    smallest = r < smallest ? r : smallest;
    cout << r;
}
cout << endl << "\n\nCount: " << k
     << "\nMaximum: " << biggest
     << "\nMinimum: " << smallest << endl;
}
```

We want to dissect this function definition, but before we do so, let us see what the output of the program looks like. Suppose we run this program and input 23 when prompted. Here is what appears on the screen:

```
Some random numbers will be printed.
Enter how many you want?
15

Enter seed number:
6

31820    32473    17167    31717    17190
4449     16050    7311     6478     29467
9562     14170    21117    29323    14006


Count: 15
Maximum: 32473
Minimum: 4449
```

3.21 Software Engineering: Structured Programming

Let us write a program that will find the maximum, minimum, and average value of an array of doubles. This could be part of package of routines that does data analysis. The key to simplifying this project is to use a single function for each part of the problem. This is the heart of structured programming. A large problem is decomposed or refined into a series of small problems.

Another key problem-solving technique is to reuse already tested code. We already programmed the routine for summing an array of int, as we saw in Section 3.19, *Passing Arrays to Functions*, on page 124.

In file sum_array3.cpp

```
// n is the size of a[]
int sum(const int a[], const int n)
{
   int s = 0;

   for (int i = 0; i < n; ++i)
      s += a[i];
   return s;
}
```

This can be readily modified to produce an average of an array of double:

In file average_array1.cpp

```
double average(const double a[], const int n)
{
   double s = 0.0;

   for (int i = 0; i < n; ++i)
      s += a[i];
   return s / n;
}
```

Notice how little was changed. Problem solving is greatly aided by mastering key programming idioms. Here, the key idiom is the use of the for loop to process the elements of a one-dimensional array.

Writing minimum() also follows this idiom.

```
double minimum(const double a[], const int n)
{
   double min = a[0];

   for (int i = 1; i < n; ++i)
       if (min > a[i])
           min = a[i];
   return min;
}
```

We leave as an exercise the writing of `maximum()`. (See exercise 11 on page 155.)

Another important part of software engineering is to have a testing strategy. When testing array routines, it is appropriate to first test the program with a small data set that the programmer can easily bench-check. This allows the programmer to readily find logical errors.

```
// Simple test of our program

const int size = 6;

int main()
{
   double a[size] = {0.5, 1.5, 6.0, 7.5, 2.3, 4.6 };

   cout << "Test array data processing" << endl;
   cout << "average = " << average(a, size) << endl;
   cout << "minimum = " << minimum(a, size) << endl;
   cout << "maximum = " << maximum(a, size) << endl;
}
```

Obviously we expect as output:

```
Test array data processing
average = 3.7333
minimum = 0.5
maximum = 7.5
```

Now, to test this on a large amount of data, we can call on our random number generator to fill up a large array.

In file average_array2.cpp

```
void fill(double a[], const int n)
{
   for (int i = 0; i < n; ++i)
      a[i] = (2.0 * rand()) / RAND_MAX;
}
```

The constant RAND_MAX is the largest integer random number that rand() generates. Therefore, the double expression used to fill the array will range between 0.0 and 2.0.

```
// Generate data using fill()

const int size = 20000;

int main()
{
   double a[size];

   fill(a, size);
   cout << "Test array data processing" << endl;
   cout << "average = " << average(a, size) << endl;
   cout << "minimum = " << minimum(a, size) << endl;
   cout << "maximum = " << maximum(a, size) << endl;
}
```

We expect as output something like:

```
Test array data processing
average = 0.998711
minimum = 0.000244148
maximum = 1.8990750
```

Note that the minimum is very nearly 0 and the maximum approaches 2, and that the output will vary from run to run. Random number generators are very useful for producing large data sets that have predictable properties when used for testing.

3.22   Core Language ADT: char* String

The C++ community has agreed to treat the type `char*` as a form of string type. The understanding is that such strings are terminated by the `char` value `'\0'`, and that the *cstring* (or *string.h* on older systems) package of functions is called using this representation. In ANSI C++, the library *string* provides as a template class a standardized string type that is preferred to this use of `char*`. The language partly supports this abstraction by defining string literals as being null-terminated. A `char*` or `char[]` can be initialized with a literal string. Note that the terminating `'\0'` is part of the initializer list. Also, a `char[]` cannot be assigned to and is a constant, while a `char*` can be assigned to.

```
char*  s = "c++";      // s[0] = 'c', s[1] = '+',
                       // s[2] = '+', s[3] = '\0';
```

How smart can humans be if strings give them trouble?

The *cstring* package contains more than 20 functions.

Some Functions in the *cstring* Library

- `size_t strlen(const char* s);`
  Computes the string length. The number of characters terminated by `'\0'` is returned.

- `char* strcpy(char* s1, const char* s2);`
  Copies the string s2 into s1. The value of s1 is returned.

- `int strcmp(const char* s1, const char* s2);`
  Returns an integer that reflects the lexicographic comparison of s1 and s2. When the strings are the same, 0 is returned. When s1 is less than s2, a negative integer is returned. When s1 is greater than s2, a positive integer is returned.

By adhering to these conventions, the programmer can reuse a lot of string code. The library routines ensure that portable, readily understood code is available.

In file string_func.cpp

```
// String function implementations

size_t strlen(const char* s)
{
   int  i;
   for (i = 0; s[i] != '\0'; ++i)
      continue;
   return i;
}
int strcmp(const char* s1, const char* s2)
{
   int  i;
   for (i=0; s1[i] && s2[i] && (s1[i]==s2[i]); ++i)
      continue;
   return (s1[i] - s2[i]);
}
char* strcpy(char* s1, const char* s2)
{
   for (int i = 0; s1[i] = s2[i]; ++i)
      continue;
   return s1;
}
```

Dissection of the *cstring* Library Functions

■ `size_t strlen(const char* s)`

This function does not modify its argument, so it is declared as `const`. The return type `size_t` is defined as an `unsigned int` in our library *cstddef* and is convertible to `size_t` in any case.

■ `for (i=0; s[i] != '\0'; ++i)`
   `continue;`

Notice how these functions use the convention that a string is null-terminated to end their major loops. The function `strlen()` terminates this loop when `s[i] != '\0'`. Pointers to `char` strings are by convention terminated with the value `'\0'`. The `continue` statement could have been omitted. It is the equivalent here to an empty statement. However, an empty statement is less readable and more enigmatic.

■ `return i;`

The value is 0 if the empty string is the argument. Note that this can be readily hand-simulated as a check on the code. The variable `i` could not have been declared inside the loop because it needs to be in scope in this `return` statement.

■
```
int strcmp(const char* s1, const char* s2)
{
    int  i;
    for(i=0; s1[i] && s2[i] && (s1[i]==s2[i]); ++i)
        continue;
```

Again, `const` declarations are good practice to indicate that the pointer arguments are not used to change underlying contents of the memory they point at. The major loop relies on short-circuit evaluation of the logical and expression. The test on equality of the two string characters relies on both strings not yet being terminated.

■ `return (s1[i] - s2[i]);`

The difference in the final tested characters is returned, with 0 indicating string equality.

■
```
char* strcpy(char* s1, const char* s2)
{
    for (int i = 0; s1[i] = s2[i]; ++i)
        continue;
```

Here, we have a signature where `s1` is not declared as `const`. This is the pointer to which the copying occurs, so it cannot point at nonmodifiable memory. Notice that loop termination occurs when `s2[i]` is value `'\0'`. Here, the expression is an assignment and is a highly unusual coding practice. No checking is done as to whether `s1` points to allocation big enough to contain `s2`.

The following function implements a string-equality test. Note its use of pointer arithmetic. The construct `*s1++` means "dereference the pointer `s1`, and after using this value in the expression, add `sizeof(char)` to its pointer value." Because of operator precedence, `*s1++` is equivalent to `*(s1++)`. This pointer calculation gets us the next element address.

```
bool streq(const char* s1, const char* s2)
{
    while (*s1 != 0 && *s2 != 0)
        if (*s1++ != *s2++)
            return false;
    return (*s1 == *s2);
}
```

To better understand the relationship between arrays and pointers, we reimplement the preceding function using array notation:

```
bool streq2(const char s1[], const char s2[])
{
    int  i;

    for (i = 0; (s1[i] != 0) && (s2[i] != 0); ++i)
        if (s1[i] != s2[i])
            return false;
    return (s1[i] == s2[i]);
}
```

Finally, it is also natural to implement these functions as recursions. Here is the recursive form of `strlen()`:

```
// Recursive string function implementations

size_t strlen(const char* s)
{
    if (*s == '\0')
        return 0;         // the end
    else                  // add 1 and recur on the rest
        return (1 + strlen(s + 1));
}
```

While recursion is an elegant coding technique, it is not usual, for efficiency reasons, to find heavily used functions coded this way. (See exercise 3 on page 152.)

3.23 Multidimensional Arrays

C++ allows arrays of any type, including arrays of arrays. With two bracket pairs, we obtain a two-dimensional array. This idea can be iterated to obtain arrays of higher dimension, as shown in Table 3.2. With each bracket pair, we add another array dimension.

Table 3.2 Declarations of Arrays	
`int a[100];`	One-dimensional array
`int b[3][5];`	Two-dimensional array
`int c[7][9][2];`	Three-dimensional array

A k-dimensional array has a size for each of its k dimensions. If we let s_i represent the size of its ith dimension, the declaration of the array allocates space for s_1 3 s_2 3 . . . 3 s_k elements. In Table 3.2, b has 3 3 5 elements, and c has 7 3 9 3 2 elements. Starting at the base address of the array, all the array elements are stored contiguously in memory, row by row.

Initialization of multidimensional arrays can be done using a brace-enclosed list of initializers, where each row is initialized from a brace-enclosed list. There are a number of ways to initialize a two-dimensional array. The following three initializations are equivalent:

```
int   a[2][3] = {1, 2, 3, 4, 5, 6};
int   a[2][3] = { {1, 2, 3}, {4, 5, 6} };
int   a[ ][3] = { {1, 2, 3}, {4, 5, 6} };
```

If there are no inner braces, then each of the array elements a[0][0], a[0][1], . . ., a[1][2] is initialized in turn. Note that the indexing is by rows. If there are fewer initializers than elements in the array, then the remaining elements are initialized to zero. If the first bracket pair is empty, then the compiler takes the size from the number of inner brace pairs. All sizes except the first must be given explicitly. This data structure is an important scientific abstract data type and is central to all of linear algebra.

Even though array elements are stored contiguously one after the other, it is often convenient to think of a two-dimensional array as a rectangular collection of elements with rows and columns. For example, if we declare

```
int   a[3][5];
```

then we can think of the array elements arranged as in Table 3.3.

Table 3.3 Array Elements					
	col 1	col 2	col 3	col 4	col 5
row 1	`a[0][0]`	`a[0][1]`	`a[0][2]`	`a[0][3]`	`a[0][4]`
row 2	`a[1][0]`	`a[1][1]`	`a[1][2]`	`a[1][3]`	`a[1][4]`
row 3	`a[2][0]`	`a[2][1]`	`a[2][2]`	`a[2][3]`	`a[2][4]`

To illustrate these ideas, let us write a program that fills a two-dimensional array, prints out values, and sums the elements of the array:

In file sum_2d_array1.cpp

```cpp
#include <iostream>
using namespace std;

const int M = 3;    // number of rows
const int N = 4;    // number of column

int main()
{
   int   a[M][N], i, j, sum = 0;

   for (i = 0; i < M; ++i)          // fill the array
      for (j = 0; j < N; ++j)
         a[i][j] = i + j;
   for (i = 0; i < M; ++i) {        // print array
      for (j = 0; j < N; ++j)
         cout << "a[" << i << "][" << j
              << "] = " << a[i][j] << '\t';
      cout << endl;
   }
   for (i = 0; i < M; ++i)          // sum the array
      for (j = 0; j < N; ++j)
         sum += a[i][j];
   cout << "\nsum =  " << sum << endl;
}
```

The output of this program is

```
a[0][0] = 0    a[0][1] = 1    a[0][2] = 2    a[0][3] = 3
a[1][0] = 1    a[1][1] = 2    a[1][2] = 3    a[1][3] = 4
a[2][0] = 2    a[2][1] = 3    a[2][2] = 4    a[2][3] = 5

sum = 30
```

In processing every element of a multidimensional array, each dimension requires a single for loop.

Because of the relationship between arrays and pointers, there are numerous ways to access elements of a two-dimensional array, as shown in Table 3.4.

Table 3.4   Expressions Equivalent to a[i][j]

`*(a[i] + j)`
`(*(a + i))[j]`
`*((*(a + i)) + j)`
`*(&a[0][0] + 5*i + j)`

The parentheses are necessary because the brackets [ ] have higher precedence than the indirection operator *. We can think of `a[i]` as the *i*th row of a (counting from 0), and we can think of `a[i][j]` as the element in the *i*th row, *j*th column of the array (counting from 0). The array name a by itself is equivalent to `&a[0]`; it is a pointer to an array of five `int`s. The base address of the array is `&a[0][0]`, not a. Starting at the base address of the array, the compiler allocates contiguous space for 15 `int`s. For any array, the mapping between pointer values and array indices is called the storage mapping function. For the array a, the storage mapping function is specified by noting that

  `a[i][j]`   *is equivalent to*   `*(&a[0][0] + 5*i + j)`

When a multidimensional array is a formal parameter in a function definition, all sizes except the first must be specified, so that the compiler can determine the correct storage mapping function. After the elements of the array a just given have been assigned values, the following function can be used to sum the elements of the array. Note carefully that the column size must be specified.

In file sum_2d_array2.cpp

```
int sum(int a[][5])
{
   int   i, j, sum = 0;

   for (i = 0; i < 3; ++i)
      for (j = 0; j < 5; ++j)
         sum += a[i][j];
   return sum;
}
```

In the header of the function definition, the following parameter declarations are equivalent:

```
int a[][5]      int (*a)[5]      int a[3][5]
```

Because of operator precedence, the parentheses are necessary. The constant 3 acts as a reminder to human readers of the code, but the compiler disregards it.

The `for` loop and the output statement in `main()` can be replaced by an output statement:

```
cout << "\nsum = " << sum(a) << endl;
```

3.24   Operators `new` and `delete`

The unary operators `new` and `delete` are available to manipulate free store. They are more convenient than, and replace, the C standard library functions `malloc()`, `calloc()`, and `free()` in most applications. Free store is a memory pool for objects whose lifetime is directly managed by the programmer. The programmer creates an object using `new` and destroys the object using `delete`. This is important for dynamic data structures, such as lists and trees.

In C++, the operator `new` is typically used in the following forms:

> `new` *type-name*
> `new` *type-name initializer*
> `new` *type-name*[*expression*]

In each case, there are at least two effects. First, an appropriate amount of store is allocated from free store to contain an object of the named type. Second, the base address of the object is returned as the value of the `new` expression.

The operator `new` can either throw a `bad_alloc` exception or return the value 0, when memory is unavailable.

The following example uses `new`:

```
int*  p, *q, *r;
p = new int(5);   // allocation and initialization
q = new int[10];  // gets q[0] to q[9] with q = &q[0]
r = new int;      // allocate int but uninitialized
```

In this code, the pointer to `int` variable p is assigned the address of the store obtained in allocating an object of type `int`. The location pointed at by p is initialized to the value 5. This use is not usual for a simple type, such as `int`, in that it is far more convenient and natural to automatically allocate an integer variable on the stack or globally.

Usually, an array of elements is allocated, as is done in the example with the pointer q. The array values are uninitialized. Some compilers may choose as an implementation decision to initialize elements to 0, but this is not a language specification and should not be relied on.

The operator `delete` destroys an object created by `new`, in effect returning its allocated storage to free store for reuse. The operator `delete` is used in the following forms:

```
delete expression
delete [ ] expression
```

The first form is used when the corresponding `new` expression has not allocated an array. The second form has empty brackets, indicating that the original allocation was an array of objects. The operator `delete` does not return a value. Equivalently, one can say that its return type is `void`. The following example uses these constructs to dynamically allocate an array:

In file dynamic_array.cpp

```cpp
// Use of new to dynamically allocate an array
// assumes older-style return of 0 for
// allocation error

int main()
{
   int*  data;
   int   size;

   cout << "\nEnter array size: ";
   cin >> size;
   assert(size > 0);

   data = new int[size];   // allocate array of ints
   assert(data != 0);      // data != 0 allocation OK
   for (int j = 0; j < size; ++j)
      cout << (data[j] = j) << '\t';
   cout << "\n\n";
   delete[] data;          // deallocate an array
}
```

Dissection of the *dynamic_array* Program

- ```
  int*  data;
  int   size;

  cout << "\nEnter array size: ";
  cin >> size;
  assert(size > 0);

  data = new int[size];    // allocate array of ints
  assert(data != 0);       // data != 0 allocation OK
  ```

  The pointer variable `data` is used as the base address of a dynamically allocated array whose number of elements is the value of `size`. The user is prompted for the integer valued `size`. The `new` operator is used to allocate storage from free store capable of storing an object of type `int[size]`. On a system on which integers take 4 bytes, this would allocate 4 3 `size` bytes. At this point, `data` is assigned the base address of this store. The second `assert` guarantees that allocation succeeded. In newer C++ systems, if the `new` operator fails, it can throw an exception of type `bad_alloc`, automatically aborting the program.

- ```
  for (int j = 0; j < size; ++j)
      cout << (data[j] = j) << '\t';
  ```

  This statement initializes the values of the `data` array and prints them.

- ```
  delete[] data;              // deallocate an array
  ```

  The operator `delete` returns the storage associated with the pointer variable `data` to free store. This can be done only with objects allocated by `new`. The bracket form is used because the corresponding allocation was of an array.

This introductory discussion of the free-store operators treats the basic cases. The free-store operators are addressed in greater detail in Section 5.19, *Overloading new and delete*, on page 256.

It is becoming a standard practice to use C++ libraries for accessing both `char*` arrays and general arrays instead of coding the array functions directly. Here, we discuss two such libraries: one for vectors and one for string processing.
  ```

3.24.1   Vector Instead of Array

The standard C++ library contains the template for the vector data structure. In almost all cases, the vector is an improvement over the simple C++ array but can be used essentially as an array. Many writers, including myself, recommend that the vector be used in place of arrays for most programming. For example, the function in Section 3.19, *Passing Arrays to Functions*, on page 124, for summing an array uses `int sum(int a[], int n)`. We can trivially change this to use vector as follows:

In file sum_array4.cpp

```
int sum(vector<int> a, int n)
{
   int  s = 0;

   for (int i = 0; i < n; ++i)
      s += a[i];
   return s;
}
```

Notice that the only change was to transform the array declaration to a vector declaration. Without investigating the details of template syntax, we can use a simple rule:

  Type id[ ]   *is replaced by*   `vector<`*Type*`>` *id*

If the declaration requires an array size, we can extend the rule as follows:

  Type id[*size*]   *is replaced by*   `vector<`*Type*`>` *id*(*size*)

One improvement of `vector` is that it knows the number of elements associated with it. The expression *id*.`size()` gives the current number of elements contained in the vector. Using this information improves the `sum()` function by making it simpler and by avoiding errors that come about in C and C++ when the wrong size is passed as a parameter. This prevents out-of-range errors that are the bane of C array programmers.

In file sum_array5.cpp

```
// Sum written to use a.size() in place of N

int sum(vector<int> a)
{
    int  i, s = 0;

    for (i = 0; i < a.size(); ++i)
        s += a[i];
    return s;
}
```

3.24.2   String Instead of char*

In C++, the standard library provides both *cstring* and *string*. Both libraries can be used for string processing, and they can be used jointly. However, C++ style is to prefer the use of the `string` type, which is more robust and has a more extensive interface. In certain cases, it is both more efficient and more elegant.

The following simple program uses `string`. The program is easy to understand and easy to use, because the operator + provides concatenation.

In file pr_statements.cpp

```
// Print a string with a line number

void pr_numbered_statement(const string& statement)
{
    static int ln = 0;

    ln++;              // start the line numbers at 1
    cout << "line " << ln << ":" + statement + "\n";
}
```

```
// Test pr_numbered_statement() using two strings

int main()
{
   string s1, s2;

   cout << "Enter two words: " << endl;
   cin >> s1 >> s2;
   pr_numbered_statement(s1);
   pr_numbered_statement(s2);
   cout << endl;
}
```

3.25 Software Engineering: Program Correctness

An assertion is a program check for correctness that, if violated, forces an error exit. One point of view is that an assertion is a contractual guarantee among the provider of a piece of code, the code's manufacturer, and the code's client or user. In this model, the client needs to guarantee that the conditions for applying the code exist, and the manufacturer needs to guarantee that the code works correctly under these provisions. In this methodology, assertions provide various guarantees.

Program correctness can be viewed in part as a proof that the computation terminated with correct output dependent on correct input. The user of the computation has the responsibility of providing correct input. This is a precondition. The computation, if successful, satisfies a postcondition. Such assertions can be monitored at runtime to provide very useful diagnostics. Indeed, the discipline of thinking out appropriate assertions frequently allows the programmer to avoid bugs and pitfalls.

In the C++ community, there is an increasing emphasis on the use of assertions. The standard library *assert* provides the macro `assert` and is invoked as though its function signature were

```
void assert(expression);
```

If the *expression* evaluates as `false`, execution is aborted with diagnostic output. The assertions are discarded if the macro NDEBUG is defined. The following program provides assertions to demonstrate this. The program examines a slice of an array for its minimum element and places that element in the first examined array position.

In file order3.cpp

```cpp
// Find minimum element in array slice

void order(int& p, int& q)
{
   int  temp = p;

   if (p > q) {
      p = q;
      q = temp;
   }
}

int place_min(int a[], int size, int lowbnd = 0)
{
   assert(size >= 0);                    // precondition
   assert(lowbnd >= 0);                  // precondition
   for (int i = lowbnd; i < lowbnd + size - 1; ++i)
      order(a[lowbnd], a[i + 1]);
   return a[lowbnd];
}

int main()
{
   int   a[9] = { 6, -9, 99, 3, -14, 9, -33, 8, 11 };

   cout << "Minimum = " << place_min(a, 3, 2)
        << endl;
   assert(a[2]<=a[3] && a[2]<=a[4]); // postcondition
}
```

Dissection of the `place_min()` Function

- `int place_min(int a[], int size, int lowbnd = 0)`
  `{`

The function finds the minimum element from a number of adjacent array elements and by swapping the minimum element into the first examined array position `lowbnd`. Normally, `lowbnd` is 0, making it a default parameter candidate.

```
■ assert(size >= 0);                          // precondition
  assert(lowbnd >= 0);                        // precondition

  for (int i = lowbnd; i < lowbnd + size - 1; ++i)
      order(a[lowbnd], a[i + 1]);
```

The precondition assertions in place_min() guarantee that a nonnegative number of elements at a nonnegative index is searched.

```
■ int main()
  {
      int a[9] = { 6, -9, 99, 3, -14, 9, -33, 8, 11};

      cout << "Minimum = " << place_min(a, 3, 2)
           << endl;
      assert(a[2]<=a[3] && a[2]<=a[4]);// postcondition
  }
```

The place_min(a, 3, 2) call is supposed to place the minimum of three elements, starting at position 2, into position 2. The postcondition in main() checks that the minimum element was found and placed in the correct position. The assert states that a[2] is the smallest of the three elements. Therefore, the value of a[2] should be -14.

Assertions and general exception handling are discussed at length in Chapter 10, *Exceptions and Program Correctness*.

3.26   Dr. P's Prescriptions

- Functions should be short.

- Functions should do one job.

- Avoid subtle type conversions in overloading.

- Use explicit conversions to provide an exact match.

- Avoid the use of ellipsis notation.

- Overload only conceptually coherent function definitions.

- In C++, use explicit call-by-reference.

- Use const in your declarations.

- Use string in preference to char*.

- Use vector<> in preference to array.

A large part of the art of writing code is properly writing functions. Think of functions as the paragraph elements in an essay and statements as sentences. Structured programming is a methodology that decomposes parts of a program into elements that are readily coded as functions. Keeping functions short makes them easier to test for correctness, maintain, and document. Like a paragraph in writing, they are meant to be a basic coherent unit that is easily grasped.

A function should have a readily grasped purpose as indicated by the function name; for example, `print()`, which is clear as to intent. Do not obscure what a function does by giving it unrelated tasks. For example, if you want to print an array and find its maximum element, write two different functions.

In C++, there is little need for untyped functions with the ellipsis signature. Functions of appropriate type can be overloaded or generated from templates. This leads to type safety, which the compiler can statically test for.

Overloading is frequently overused, making code difficult to follow and debug. In the extreme, by using function `foo()` with different signatures, one can produce any computation—clearly a poor programming practice.

In C++, we usually have two choices for a call-by-reference parameter declaration. It can be either a pointer declaration or a reference declaration. Our advice is to stay primarily with reference declarations. These require less notation, such as the use of the address-of operator in the actual argument and the dereferencing operator inside the code body. Less notation leads to fewer mistakes.

The keyword `const` is an important type constraint. It allows the compiler to check your code automatically for critical errors. It also allows a smart compiler to further optimize your code.

The `string` type found in the standard template library is much safer and more flexible than the `char*` type. It should be used in preference to the traditional C use of `char*` for strings.

The `vector` container type found in the standard template library is much safer and more flexible than the native array type. It should be used in preference to traditional C arrays.

3.27 C++ Compared with Java

Java does not have pointers but instead has nonprimitive variables that are references. Java avoids much of the direct programmer management of memory that causes so many bugs in C and C++. Java does have arrays, which are reference types. Java does not have functions that are outside the scope of a class. Java's term for functions is *methods,* which indicates that all functions are members of a class. The closest construct to an ordinary C or C++ function is a static method. Java can overload methods but does not allow default arguments or inlining.

The following program initializes an array, prints its values, and computes its sum and average value:

In file SumArray.java

```java
class SumArray {
   public static void main(String[] args)
   {
      int[]  data = {1, 2, 3, 4, 5, 6, 7};
      int  sum = 0;
      double average;

      for (int i = 0; i < 7; ++i) {
         sum = sum + data[i];
         System.out.print(data[i] + ", ");
      }
      average = sum / 7.0;
      System.out.println("\n\n sum = " + sum
         + " average = " + average);
   }
}
```

Dissection of the *SumArray.java* **Program**

■ `int[] data = {1, 2, 3, 4, 5, 6, 7};`

The variable data is declared to refer to an array of integers. It is allocated seven integer elements, which are initialized to the values 1 through 7.

■ `for (int i = 0; i < 7; ++i) {`

The `for` statement declares the local variable i to be used as an index or a subscript variable. This `for` statement is the most common array code idiom. The initial subscript for array objects in Java is 0, so the subscript variable is usually initialized to 0. The array length is 7, so the terminating condition is usually `i < 7` so that the array index stops at 7 - 1. The last part of the `for` statement header is the autoincrement of the index variable, so that each array element gets processed in turn.

■ `sum = sum + data[i];`
   `System.out.print(data[i] + ", ");`

The element `data[i]` is selected by computing the index value. A common error that results in an exception is for this to be out of range. These subscripted or indexed elements can be used as simple variables of type `int`. In this code, each element's integer value is added to the variable `sum`. Then, in turn, each element's value is printed.

Note: In this example, `main()` is `static`. In Java, a `static` method more or less corresponds to an ordinary C function. This example is nearly identical to one found on pages 145 to 146 of *Java by Dissection*, by Pohl and McDowell (Addison-Wesley, 1999). A complete explanation of Java arrays that is consistent with our treatment here can be found in that text. It is also available as an e-book through MightyWords at http://www.mightywords.com/.

Summary

■ In ANSI C++, the empty parameter list is always equivalent to using `void`, so `main()` is equivalent to `main(void)`. The function `main()` implicitly returns the integer value 0 if no explicit `return` expression statement is executed.

■ A formal parameter can be given a default argument, usually a constant that occurs frequently when the function is called. Use of a default argument saves writing this default value at each invocation. The following function header shows the syntax:

```
int sqr_or_power(int n, int k = 2);   // k=2 default
```

■ Overloading refers to using the same name for multiple meanings of an operator or a function. The meaning selected depends on the types of the arguments used by the operator or function. In the following code, we overload `average()`:

```
// Average the values in an input sequence

double average(int size, int sum);
double average(int size, double sum);
```

- Reference declarations allow an object to be given an alias, or alternative name. These declarations can be used for call-by-reference arguments. For example, the function `order()`, using this mechanism, is declared as

```
void order(int &p, int &q);
```

- C++ provides the keyword `inline` to preface a function declaration when the programmer intends the code replacing the function call to be inline. In most cases, this should be used in place of `#define` macros.

- C++ inherited C's single global namespace. Programs written by various parties can inadvertently have name clashes when combined. C++ adds namespace scope, as in

```
namespace StellarSoft {
    class S_widget { ..... };
    class update{ ..... };
    .....
}
```

- The namespace identifier can be used as part of a scope-resolved identifier. This has the form

namespace_id`::`*id*

There is also a `using` declaration, which lets a client have access to all names from that namespace.

```
using namespace StellarSoft;
S_widget  w;            // StellarSoft::S_widget
```

Namespaces can be used to provide a unique scope that replaces static global declarations.

- The declaration `void*` is a generic pointer type. A pointer declared as type pointer to `void`, as in `void* gp`, can be assigned a pointer value of any underlying base type, but it may not be dereferenced. Unlike in C, a generic pointer may not be assigned to a nonvoid pointer type without an explicit cast. In this regard, C++ is again more type-safe than C.

- The C and C++ communities have agreed to treat the type char* as a form of string type. The understanding is that these strings are terminated by the char value '\0', and that the *cstring* (or *string.h* on older systems) package of functions is called on this abstraction. In ANSI C++, the library *string* provides as a template class a standardized string type that is preferred over the use of char*.

- The unary operators new and delete are available to manipulate free store. Free store is a memory pool for objects whose lifetime is directly managed by the programmer. The programmer creates an object by using new and destroys the object by using delete. This is important for dynamic data structures, such as lists and trees.

- The standard library contains the template for the vector data structure. In almost all cases, the vector is an improvement over the simple C++ array but can be used essentially as an array. Many experts recommend that it be used in place of arrays for most programming.

Review Questions

1. If not explicitly returned, the value _____ is returned by main().

2. Replace #define ABS(X)   ((X <0) ? -X: X) with inline code.

3. Discuss the difference between using the macro ABS(f(y)) and the equivalent inline call. Assume that f(y) calls a nontrivial function.

4. What is wrong with overloading int foo(); and void foo(); in the same scope? Note that the only difference in their declarations is the return types.

5. The C++ STL vector can be used to replace _____ in C and C++ programs.

6. In C, control of an if statement depends on whether an if statement expression is zero or nonzero. In C++, this condition is type _____.

7. In C, the function `strlen()` is found in _____; in C++, it is found in _____. Can you think of a reason for this difference?

8. The _____ exception is thrown when _____ fails to properly allocate memory.

9. The operator _____ is used in place of the *cstdlib* function `free()` to return memory to free store.

10. In C, call-by-reference requires the use of pointers, but in C++, _____ may be used as well.

Exercises

1. Pointers to `char` strings are by convention terminated with the value 0. The following function implements a string-equality test. Note its use of pointer arithmetic. The construct `*s1++` means "dereference the pointer `s1`, and after using this value in the expression, add `sizeof(char)` to its pointer value." Here is `streq()` from Section 3.22, *Core Language ADT: char* String*, on page 134:

```
bool streq(const char* s1, const char* s2)
{
    while ( *s1 != 0 && *s2 != 0)
        if ( *s1++ != *s2++)
            return false;
    return (*s1 == *s2);
}
```

Write and test a function

```
bool streq_n(const char* s1, const char* s2, int n);
```

that returns `true` if the first *n* characters of the two strings are the same and that otherwise returns `false`. It should also return true if the strings are shorter than n characters and equal.

When testing this code, use a technique called boundary condition testing. For each control structure in the code, such as an `if` statement or a `while` loop, test right at these boundaries that the code works properly. For example, on a small piece of data the loop should execute the correct number of times. It easiest to check on an empty or length 1 string in this example. It is observed in practice that most mistakes are made at these boundaries.

2. Reimplement the preceding functions using array notation, both in the header and the body of the code. So the header for `streq()` is

   ```
   bool streq(char s1[], char s2[]);
   ```

3. Write a recursive version of

   ```
   bool streq(const char* s1, const char* s2);
   ```

   Discuss and, if necessary, run tests to see which version is more efficient. Will your system allow these functions to be inlined?

4. The greatest common divisor of two integers is recursively defined in pseudocode as follows, as seen in Section 3.7, *Recursion*, on page 97:

   ```
   GCD(m,n) is:
       if m mod n equals 0 then n;
       else GCD(n, m mod n);
   ```

   Recall that the modulo operator in C++ is %. Code this routine using recursion in C++. We have already done this iteratively.

5. We wish to count the number of recursive function calls by `gcd()`. It is generally bad practice to use globals inside functions. In C++, we can use a local `static` variable instead of a global. Complete and test the following C++ `gcd()` function:

   ```
   int gcd(int m, int n)
   {
       static int  fcn_calls = 1;      // happens once
       int         r;                  // remainder

       fcn_calls++;
       .....
   }
   ```

6. The following C program uses traditional C function syntax:

   ```
   /* Compute a table of cubes. */

   #include <stdio.h>
   #define  N    15
   #define  MAX  3.5
   ```

```
int main()
{
    int  i;
    double  x, cube();

    printf("\n\nINTEGERS\n");
        for (i = 1; i <= N; ++i)
            printf("cube(%d) = %f\n", i, cube(i));
    printf("\n\nREALS\n");
    for (x = 1; x <= MAX; x += 0.3)
        printf("cube(%f) = %f\n", x, cube(x));
    return 0;
}

double  cube(x)
double  x;
{
    return (x * x * x);
}
```

The program gives the wrong answers for the integer arguments because integer arguments are passed as if their bit representation were double. It is unacceptable as C++ code. Recode, as a proper function prototype, and run, using a C++ compiler. C++ compilers enforce type compatibility on function argument values. Therefore, the integer values are properly promoted to double values.

7. Predict what the following program prints:

```
int foo(int n)
{
    static int  count = 0;

    ++count;
    if ( n <= 1) {
        cout << " count = " << count << endl;
        return n;
    }
    else
        foo(n / 3);
}

int main()
{
    foo(21);
    foo(27);
    foo(243);
}
```

8. The `static` storage class is useful in multifile compilation. Predict what the following program prints:

```
// file A.c

static int  foo(int i)
{
    return (i * 3);
}

int  goo(int i)
{
    return (i * foo(i));
}
```

```
// file B.c

int foo(int i)
{
    return (i * 5);
}

int  goo(int i);          // imported from file A.c

int main()
{
    cout << "foo(5) = " << foo(5) << endl;
    cout << "goo(5) = " << goo(5) << endl;
}
```

The program is compiled as follows: *g++ A.c B.c.* File-scope functions are by default `extern`. The `foo()` in file *A.c* is private to that file, but `goo()` is not. Thus, redefining `foo()` in file *B.c* does not cause an error. Try this again, this time dropping `static`, to see what error message your compiler gives. Then try a third time, making `goo()` `inline` in *A.c*, to see what error message your compiler gives. Recode these files, using anonymous namespaces to replace the `static` declarations.

9. C++ provides a method to pass command line arguments into the function `main()`. The following code prints its command line arguments:

```
// Print command line arguments rightmost first

int main(int argc, char **argv)
{
    for (--argc; argc >= 0; --argc)
        cout << argv[argc] << endl;
}
```

Compile this into an executable called *echo*. Run it with the following command line arguments:

echo a man a plan a canal panama

The argument `argc` is passed the number of command line arguments. Each argument is a string placed in the two-dimensional array `argv`.

10. Modify the previous program to print the command line arguments from left to right and to number each of them.

11. Write the function `double maximum(double a[], int n)`. This is a function that finds the maximum of the elements of an array of `double` of size n. (See Section 3.21, *Software Engineering: Structured Programming*, on page 128.)

12. The problem with using `void*` is that it cannot be dereferenced. Thus, to perform useful work on a generic pointer, one must cast it to a standard working type, such as a `char*`. Write and test

```
void* memcpy(void* s1, const void* s2, unsigned n)
{
    char*  from = s2, *to = s1;    // uses char type
    .....
}
```

13. Write a program that performs string reversal. Assume that `s1` ends up with the reverse of the string `s2` and that `s1` points at enough store that is adequate for reversal. (See Section 3.22, *Core Language ADT: char* String*, on page 132, for some examples of string-handling functions.)

```
char* strrev(char* s1, const char* s2);
```

14. Write a program that performs string reversal, using storage allocated with new. Assume that s1 ends up with the reverse of the string s2, and use new to allocate s1 of length strlen(s2) + 1, which is adequate store for s1.

```
char* strrev(char*& s1, const char* s2);
```

15. (Uwe F. Mayer) Rewrite

```
void order(int& p, int& q)
{
    int  temp = p;

    if (p > q) {
        p = q;
        q = temp;
    }
}
```

to make it more efficient. This can be done by reordering some of the operations. This can be important in an application that calls this simple routine repeatedly.

16. Write a function

```
double findmin(double fcn(double),
               double x0,        // initial point
               double x1,        // terminal point
               double incr,      // increment
               double& xmin)
```

that returns the value fcn(xmin), where f(xmin) is the minimum value of fcn(x) in the interval (x0, x1), evaluated at increments of incr, and xmin is an argument producing that minimum. Rewrite the function findmin() so that the range (0, 1.0) and the increment 0.00001 are used by default, unless explicitly passed in. Note that to do this, the preceding function arguments should be used but in a different order. Why?

17. Write a function

```
double plot(double y[],
            double fcn(double),
            double x0 = 0.0,
            double x1 = 1.0,
            double incr = 0.001)
```

that computes $y[i] = fcn(x_i)$, where x_i is in the interval (x0, x1), evaluated at increments of incr. Use the defaults (0, 1.0) and an increment of 0.001, with y expected to have 1,000 elements.

18. Redo the previous exercise to use `vector<double> y`.

19. Write a function `findzero()` that finds `xzero`, the value of `x` for which the function `fcn(x)` is closest to zero in a specified interval. The function `findzero()` should have the same arguments as `findmin()`. Again write it to have standard default values for its parameters.

20. Modify the dynamic array program in Section 3.24, *Operators new and delete*, on page 139, so that it is initialized by pseudorandom numbers in the range `(0, RAND_MAX)`. For 5,000 such random numbers, find their average value. See whether, while using the operator `new`, you can do this problem for 50,000, 500,000, 5,000,000, . . ., until you find a value on your system that causes `new` to fail. If you rewrote this code to use ordinary stack-allocated arrays, at what size on your system did it fail to allocate the array? Also try the same problem using `vector<int>`, and see how large a problem can be run.

21. Write a program that simulates a roulette wheel with the numbers 0 to 35. This is where the wheel has the numbers 0–35. You should use a random number generator that gets you one of these values with equal probability. Test your simulation by spinning the wheel 36, 360, 3,600, and 36,000 times. Store the results in an array of 36 integer values, one for each wheel location. Print the results. Were your results in agreement with what you expected? In order to start the pseudorandom sequence at different points, you should use the *cstdlib* function `srand(n)` to start the sequence with the number seed n.

22. Using the functions written in the previous exercise, simulate a gambler making 1,000 bets of one dollar at odds of 35 to 1. Notice that the real odds should be 36 to 1. This favors the casino running the roulette wheel and is why casinos are so profitable. The gambler starts with 1,000 dollars. Print out how much the gambler has at the end of her 1,000 bets. Consider this one trial. Now do this 1,000 times and see what the average bankroll is after each 1,000 bets. Does this conform with what you expected?

23. When a gambler persists at a game that favors the casino, it is likely that the gambler will lose his shirt—this is called gambler's ruin. Give your gambler 100 dollars. Let him keep betting until he runs out of money. Count how many bets this took. Notice that if you are very unlucky, this might take only 100 bets. Store this number in an array, call it `ruinLength[]`. Do this for 1,000 trials and see what the minimum, maximum, and average length to ruin was. Notice that by using a structured programming approach,

you should be able to easily design your program and complete this exercise.

24. Write a function `index` (BMI) to compute body mass as follows:

    BMI = (*weight in kilograms*) / (*height in meters*)^2

    If the BMI is over 25, you are considered overweight; if it is over 40, you are considered obese. Test the program on data taken from at least five individuals, printing out for each name a weight, height, BMI, and BMI category of normal, overweight, or obese. Store the data in arrays or in vectors.

25. *(Java)* Recode the BMI program in Java. Use Java arrays to store values for each individual.

Classes and Abstract Data Types

This chapter introduces the reader to classes. The original name given by Bjarne Stroustrup to his language was "C with classes." The name C++ was coined by Rick Mascitti in 1983, being a pun on the ++ increment operator. Stroustrup had extensive experience with Simula67, the first object-oriented language. It was developed in 1967 to be a simulation language and added the construct class to its base language, ALGOL60.

A class in C++ is an extension of the idea of `struct` found in C. A class packages a data type with its associated functions and operators. This in turn can be used to implement abstract data types (ADTs). An abstract data type, such as a stack, is a set of values and operations that define the type. The type is abstract in that it is described without its implementation. It is the job of the C++ programmer to provide a concrete representation of the ADT. This is usually done with the class.

C++ classes bundle data declarations with function declarations, thereby coupling data with behavior. The class description also has access modifiers `public` and `private` that allow data hiding. Allowing private and public visibility for members gives the programmer control over what parts of the data structure are modifiable. The private parts are hidden from client code, and the public parts are available. It is possible to change the hidden representation, but not to change the public access or functionality. If this is done properly, client code need not change when the hidden representation is modified. A large part of the object-oriented programming (OOP) design process involves thinking up the appropriate ADTs for a problem. Good ADTs not only model key features of the problem but also are frequently reusable in other code.

4.1   The Aggregate Type `class` and `struct`

The `class` or `struct` type allows the programmer to aggregate components into a single named variable. A class has components, called members, that are individually named. Since the members of a structure can be of various types, the programmer can create aggregates that are suitable for describing complicated data.

Student   **Cards**   **Stack**

As a simple example, let us define a structure that describes a point. We can declare the structure type as follows:

```
struct point {
    double x, y;
};
```

In C++, the structure name, or tag name, is a type. In the preceding declaration, `struct` is a keyword, `point` is the structure tag name, and the variables x and y are members of the structure. The declaration `point` can be thought of as a blueprint; it creates the type `point`, but no instances are allocated. The declaration

```
point  pt;
```

allocates storage for the variable `pt`. To access the members of `pt`, we use the member access operator, represented by a period, or dot. It is a construct of the form

structure_variable . member_name

The construct is used as a variable in the same way that a simple variable or an element of an array is used. Suppose that we want to assign to `pt` the value (–1, +0.5). To do this, we can write

```
pt.x = -1;
pt.y = 0.5;
```

The member name must be unique within the specified structure. Since the member must always be prefaced or accessed through a unique structure variable identifier, there is no confusion between two members that have the same name in different structures, as in

```
struct fruit {
   char   name[15];
   int    calories;
};
struct vegetable {
   char   name[15];
   int    calories;
};

fruit      a;         // struct fruit    a; in C
vegetable  b;         // struct vegetable b; in C
```

Having made these declarations, we can access `a.calories` and `b.calories` without ambiguity.

In general, a structure is declared with the keyword `struct`, followed by an identifier (tag name), followed by a brace-enclosed list of member declarations, followed by a semicolon. The tag name is optional but should be expressive of the ADT concept being modeled. When there is no tag name, the structure declaration is anonymous and can be used only to declare variables of that type immediately:

```
struct {
   int  a, b, c;
} triples [2] = { {3, 3, 6}, {4, 5, 5} };
```

Note: Omitting the semicolon at the end of a declaration is a typical syntax error.

We use the two-dimensional point example in much of this chapter. You should see at different places in the text whether you can extend these ideas to a three-dimensional point. To test your understanding, do exercise 2 on page 203.

4.2 Member Selection Operator

Now we introduce the member selection operator ->, which provides access to the members of a structure via a pointer. This operator is typed on the keyboard as a minus sign followed by a greater-than sign. If a pointer variable is assigned the address of a structure, a member of the structure can be accessed by a construct of the form

pointer_to_structure -> member_name

An equivalent construct is given by

(**pointer_to_structure*).*member_name*

The operators -> and ., along with () and [ ], have the highest precedence, and they associate left to right. In complicated situations, the two accessing modes can be combined. Here is the `point` structure:

```
struct point {
    double  x, y;
};
```

Table 4.1 illustrates its use.

Table 4.1 Declarations and Initialization		
point w, *p = &w; point v[5]; w.x = 1; w.y = 4; v[0] = w;		
Expression	Equivalent Expression	Value
w.x	p -> x	1
w.y	p -> y	4
v[0].x	v -> x	1
(*p).y	p -> y	4

The member `w.x` was assigned 1. Therefore, the equivalent expression "pointer `p` accessing member x" is 1. The assignment `v[0] = w` assigns values member by member. Therefore, `v[0].x` is 1. A more complete example using `point` is the following:

In file struct_point1.cpp

```cpp
// Compute an average point

struct point { double x, y; };

point average(const point* d, int size)
{
    point sum = {0, 0};

    for (int i = 0; i < size; i++) {
        sum.x += d->x;
        sum.y += d->y;
        d++;        // d is iterator accessing each point
    }
    sum.x = sum.x / size;
    sum.y = sum.y / size;
    return sum;
}

int main()
{
    point data[5] = { {1.0, 2.0}, {1.0, 3.3},
                      {5.1, 0.5}, {2.0, 2.0}, {0, 0} };
    point average_point;

    average_point = average(data, 5);
    cout << "average point = (" << average_point.x
         << ", " << average_point.y << ") " << endl;
}
```

4.3   Member Functions

C++ allows functions to be members. C allows only data members. The function declaration is included in the structure declaration. The idea is that the functionality required by the structure or class should often be directly included in the `class` or `struct` declaration. Such functions are called class methods. This term *method,* meaning member function, comes from object-oriented programming methodology. This construct improves the encapsulation of the ADT `point` operations by packaging it directly with its data representation. An informal idea for designing an object is to think of the object as a noun, such as `point`, and to think of methods as verbs that apply to the noun, such as `print()`. Let us add a printing operation and an initializing operation to the ADT `point`.

In file point1.cpp

```
struct point {
    double x, y;
    void  print() const { cout << "(" << x << ","
                                << y << ")"; }
    void  set(double u, double v) { x = u; y = v; }
};
```

The member functions, or methods, are written in much the same way that other functions are. One difference is that they can use the data member names directly. Thus, the member functions in `point` use x and y in an unqualified manner. When invoked on a particular object of type `point`, they act on the specified member in that object.

Let us use these member functions in an example.

```
int main()
{
    point w1, w2;
    w1.set(0, 0.5);
    w2.set(-0.5, 1.5);
    cout << "\npoint w1 = ";
    w1.print();
    cout << "\npoint w2 = ";
    w2.print();
    cout << endl;
}
```

This prints

```
point w1 = (0,0.5)
point w2 = (-0.5,1.5)
```

Dissection of the point Structure

■ `struct point {`
    `double x, y;`

In classical programming, structures are user-defined data types that bundle previously defined data types into a new type. In this case, the new type is `point`. Its constituents are two `double`s, the coordinates represented by variables x and y.

```
■ void  print() const { cout << "(" << x << ","
                           << y << ")"; }
  void  set(double u, double v) { x = u; y = v;}
```

Object-oriented programming requires that functions be bundled with data and become the actions available to the type. These member functions are also called methods. Here is a simple `print()` method that prints out a value for a `point`. The `set()` method is used to change the values of the point's coordinates. As we shall see in further examples, it is part of the object-oriented programming style to use member functions to access the data representation of an object type. It is considered poor programming practice to directly manipulate these values in an unrestrained fashion. The `const` modifier after the function declaration indicates that the function will not modify any class members. (See Section 4.10, *const Members*, on page 183.)

```
■ int main()
  {
      point w1, w2;
```

The newly defined type looks like any of the native types. Here, two points are declared in `main()`.

```
■ w1.set(0, 0.5);
  w2.set(-0.5, 1.5);
  cout << "\npoint w1 = ";
  w1.print();
```

Notationally, to call methods of type `point` requires a `point` variable dotted to the method name. In the first line, the `point w1` is set to the coordinates (0, 0.5). In the last line, these coordinates would be printed out by the method `print()`.

Member functions that are defined within the `struct` are implicitly inline. As a rule, only short, heavily used member functions should be defined within the `struct`, as in the example just given. To define a member function outside the `struct`, the scope resolution operator is used (see Section 4.6, *Class Scope*, on page 171). Let us illustrate this by adding a member function, `point::plus()`. We write it out fully, using the scope resolution operator. In this case, the function is not implicitly inline.

In file point1.cpp

```
struct point {
   .....
   void plus(point c);        // function prototype
   .....
};

// offset the existing point by point c

void  point::plus(point c)    // definition not inline
{
   x += c.x;
   y += c.y;
}
```

Member functions within the same `struct` can be overloaded. Consider adding to the data type `point` a print operation that has a string parameter printed as the name of the point. The print operation could be added as the following function prototype within the struct.

In file point1.cpp

```
struct point {
   .....
   void  print(const string& name) const;
   .....
};

void point::print(const string& name) const
{
   cout << name << " (" << x << "," << y << ")";
}
```

The definition that is invoked depends on the arguments to `print()`:

```
w1.print();                        // standard print
w1.print("\npoint w1 = ");         // print with name
```

A member function is conceptually part of the type. The `inline` specification can be used explicitly, with member functions defined at file scope, which avoids having to clutter the class definition with function bodies. The grouping of operations with data emphasizes their objectness. Objects have a description and a behavior. Thinking of an object as a noun and its behavior as the verbs that are most often associated with that noun is key to good object design. OOP is a data-centered design approach.

4.4   Access: Private and Public

In C++, structures have `public` and `private` members. The keyword `private` followed by a colon is used to declare subsequent members to have private access. The private members can be used by only a few categories of functions. Class member functions can use `private` members, and friend functions of the class can use `private` members. Friend functions are discussed in Section 5.10, *Friend Functions*, on page 241.

The keyword `public` followed by a colon is used to declare subsequent members to have public access. The public members can be used by any code.

We modify our example of `point` to hide its data representation, as follows:

In file point2.cpp

```
struct point {
public:
   void  print() const { cout << "(" << x << ","
                                     << y << ")"; }
   void  print(const string& name) const;
   void  set(double u, double v) { x = u; y = v; }
   void  plus(point c);
private:
   double x, y;
};
```

In the following code, an attempt by a nonmember function, `foo()`, to access the now private members x and y results in a syntax error:

```
void foo(point w)
{
   .....
   cout << " x coordinate = " << w.x; // syntax error
   .....
}
```

The keyword `protected` followed by a colon is used to declare subsequent members to have protected access. The protected members can be thought of as private members but with special rules when they are used by a derived class. This is not used here but is explained in Section 8.1, *A Derived Class*, on page 378.

Hiding data is an important component of OOP. It allows for more easily debugged and maintained code because errors and modifications are localized. Client programs need be aware only of the type's interface specification. This is also known as the black box principle. A good design hides unnecessary implementation detail and presents the simplest possible useful user interface to the client.

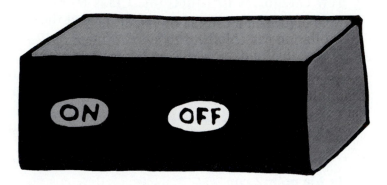

The interface is great, but what does it do?

4.5   Classes

Classes in C++ are introduced by the keyword `class`. A form of `struct`, classes have a default privacy specification of `private`, in contrast to structures defined with `struct`, which have a default privacy specification of `public`. Thus, `struct` and `class` can be used interchangeably with the appropriate access specifications. In the following example, we modify `point` to use `class`:

In file point3.cpp

```
class point {
   double x, y;          // implicitly private
public:
   void   print() const { cout << "(" << x << ","
                                << y << ")"; }
   void   print(const string& name) const;
   void   set(double u, double v) { x = u; y = v; }
   void   plus(point c);
};
```

Contemporary C++ style is to use access specifiers explicitly rather than rely on defaults. The use of implicit features is labor-saving but error-prone. Therefore, it is better style to declare `point` as follows:

In file point4.cpp

```
class point {
public:                    // place public members first
   void  print() const { cout << "(" << x << ","
                                << y << ")"; }
   void  print(const string& name) const;
   void  set(double u, double v) { x = u; y = v; }
   void  plus(point c);
private:
   double x, y;
};
```

When access keywords are used, `struct` and `class` are interchange-able. Stylistically, professional C++ programmers use `class` in pref-erence to `struct` unless the `struct` has only public data members. This text uses access keywords explicitly and places public members first and private members last. In this need to know style, everyone needs to know the public interface, but only the class provider needs to know the private implementation details.

At this point, you should be able to write a `class pair`. The `class pair`, like `point`, has two fundamental values; for example, the first value might be a name and the second value a telephone number. Such a `pair` could provide you an online way of keeping your per-sonal phone list.

I'm sorry, sir, but I really cannot let you have access unless you are a member.

As a second example, let us write an ADT for `customer`, which many business applications require. As part of this representation, we will use the Standard Template Library (STL) `string` type. This type over-loads the binary operator + to produce string concatenation.

In file customer.cpp

```
enum c_kind { general, wholesale, retail };

class customer {
public:
   void  set_name(const string& l, const string& f)
            { last_name = l; first_name = f; }
   c_kind  get_kind() const { return t; }
   void  set_kind(c_kind k) { t = k; }
   void  print() const { cout << (first_name + "   "
                          + last_name) << endl; }
   double price_discount() const;
private:
   string  last_name, first_name;
   int  id_number;
   c_kind  t;
};

double customer::price_discount() const
{
   if (t == wholesale)
      return 0.20;
   else
      return 0.1;
}
```

The class `customer` is an ADT in which the `enum` type c_kind distinguishes among three categories of customer so that a different pricing structure can be applied for each category.

Let us write a `main()` that tests the use of this new type:

```
int main()
{
   customer c, d;

   c.set_name("Pohl", "Ira");
   c.set_kind(wholesale);
   c.print();
   cout << "\nYour PC costs "
        << 900 * (1 - c.price_discount())
        << " dollars." << endl;
}
```

Here is the output from this test program:

```
Ira Pohl
Your PC costs 720 dollars.
```

Dissection of the customer Class

■ `enum c_kind { general, wholesale, retail };`

Simple ADTs are expressible as an **enum** type. The enumeration can be declared inside or outside the class.

■ `c_kind  get_kind() const { return t; }`
  `void  set_kind(c_kind k) { t = k; }`

These are typical member functions. There is usually a `set()` and a `get()` method for each data member of the internal representation. This is part of the public interface for the ADT. It allows, in a controlled fashion, access to key values for the `customer` type.

■ `private:`
  `    string last_name, first_name;`
  `    int  id_number;`
  `    c_kind  t;`
  `};`

Implementation is almost always hidden in accord with the black box principle.

4.6   Class Scope

Classes add new scope rules to those of the kernel language. Classes provide an encapsulation technique. Conceptually, it makes sense that all names declared within a class be treated within their own scope, as distinct from external names, namespace names, function names, and other class names, creating a need for a scope resolution operator.

4.6.1   Scope Resolution Operator

The scope resolution operator, the highest-precedence operator in the language, comes in two forms. The unary form is used to uncover or to access a name that has external scope and has been hidden by local or class scope. The binary form places the class or namespace identifier before the operator and the identifier after the operator.

```
::i               // unary  - refers to external scope
point::x          // binary - refers to class scope
std::cout         // binary - refers to namespace scope
```

In file how_many1.cpp

```
int  count = 0;                        // global count

void how_many(double w[], double x, int& count)
{
    for (int i = 0; i < N; ++i)
        count += (w[i] == x);          // local count
    ++::count;               // global count tracks calls
}
```

To understand this program fragment, change the parameter `int& count` to `int& cnt`. Now there is no need for the scope resolution operator, as the two identifiers are distinct.

In file how_many2.cpp

```
int  count = 0;                        // global count

void how_many(double w[], double x, int& cnt)
{
    for (int i = 0; i < N; ++i)
        cnt += (w[i] == x);
    ++count;                 // global count tracks calls
}
```

Binary scope resolution is used to clarify names that are reused within classes.

```
class widgets { public: void  f(); };
class gizmos  { public: void  f(); };

void  f() { ····· }              // ordinary external f
void  widgets::f() { ····· }    // f scoped to widgets
void  gizmos::f() { ····· }     // f scoped to gizmos
```

One way to think about the scope resolution operator is to view it as providing a path to the identifier. If there is no scope modifier, normal scope rules apply. Continuing with the previous example:

```
widgets  w;
gizmos   g;

g.f();
w.f();
g.gizmos::f();  // legal but redundant
g.widgets::f(); // illegal—widgets can't act on gizmo
```

4.6.2   Nested Classes

Like blocks and namespaces, classes are scopes and can nest. Nesting allows local hiding of names and local allocation of resources. This is often desirable when a class is needed as part of the implementation of a larger construct. The following nested classes illustrate current C++ rules:

In file nested.cpp

```
char   c;            // external scope  ::c

class X {            // outer class declaration  X::
public:
   char   c;         // X::c
   class Y {         // inner class declaration  X::Y::
   public:
      void foo(char e) { X t; ::c = t.c = c = e; }
   private:
      char   c;      // X::Y::c
   };
};
```

In class Y, the member function foo(), when using ::c, references the global variable c; when using X::c, it references the outer class variable; when using c, it references the inner class variable X::Y::c. All three variables named c are accessible using the scope resolution operator. Furthermore, purely locally scoped classes can be created within blocks. Their definitions are unavailable outside their local block context.

```
void foo()
{
   class local { ..... } x;
}

local y;      // illegal—local is scoped within foo()
```

Notice that C++ allows you to nest function definitions by using class nesting, which is a restricted form of function nesting. The member functions must be defined inside the local class and cannot be referred to outside this scope.

So which nest is mine?

Avoid unnecessary nesting as it creates hard-to-follow, complex designs. Good choice of distinct names is preferable to distinguishing identifiers by scope.

4.7 An Example: Flushing

We want to estimate the probability of being dealt a flush in poker. A flush occurs when at least five cards are of the same suit. We simulate shuffling cards by using a random number generator. This is a form of Monte Carlo calculation, named after the famous gambling resort. As was already mentioned in Section 3.20, *Problem Solving: Random Numbers*, on page 125, a Monte Carlo calculation is a computer simulation program requiring a probability calculation. The program uses classes to represent the necessary data types and functionality. The key data type is `card`, which consists of a `suit` value and a `pips` value. A `pips` value is between 1 and 13. On an actual card, these 13 `pips` values are ace, 2, 3, · · · · ·, 10, jack, queen, and king.

In file poker.cpp

```
enum suit { clubs, diamonds, hearts, spades };
```

```cpp
class pips {
public:
   void  set_pips(int n) { p = n % 13 + 1; }
   int   get_pips() const { return p; }
   void  pr_pips() const { cout << p; }
private:
   int  p;            // meant to hold values [1,13]
};
class card {
public:
   void  set_card(int n)
      { s = static_cast<suit>(n/13); p.set_pips(n); }
   void  pr_card() const;
   suit  get_suit() const { return s; }
   pips  get_pips() const { return p; }
private:
   suit  s;
   pips  p;
};
class deck {
public:
   void  set_deck();
   void  shuffle();
   void  deal(int, int, card*);
   void  pr_deck() const;
private:
   card  d[52];
};
void deck::set_deck()
{
   for (int i = 0; i < 52; ++i)
      d[i].set_card(i);
}

void  deck::shuffle()
{
   for (int i = 0; i < 52; ++i) {
      int   k = i + (rand() % (52 - i));
      card  t = d[i];               // swap cards
      d[i] = d[k];
      d[k] = t;
   }
}
```

```
void deck::deal(int n, int pos, card* hand)
{
    for (int i = pos; i < pos + n; ++i)
        hand[i - pos] = d[i];
}
```

Dissection of the deck Class

- ```
  enum suit { clubs, diamonds, hearts, spades };
  ```

```
class pips {
public:
    void  set_pips(int n) { p = n % 13 + 1; }
    .....
private:
    int  p;            // meant to hold values [1,13]
};
```

The class pips and the enum suit are used to build the card type. The set_pips() method uses integers 0 to 51 to set an appropriate pips value for a card. The clustering of member functions and the data members they act on improves modularity. Behavior and description are logically grouped together.

- ```
  class card {
  public:
      void  set_card(int n)
          {s=static_cast<suit>(n/13); p.set_pips(n);}
      .....
  private:
      suit  s;
      pips  p;
  };
  ```

Each level of declaration hides the complexity of the previous level. The class card uses suit and pips in its representation. The set_card() method uses integer division to generate an enumerator value. To recode suit as a class type, you could have a set_suit() method do the same computation.

```
■ class deck {
  public:
     void  set_deck();
     void  shuffle();
     void  deal(int, int, card*);
     void  pr_deck() const;
  private:
     card  d[52];
  };
```

The class deck declares only the class member functions; definitions come later.

```
■ void deck::set_deck()
  {
     for (int i = 0; i < 52; ++i)
        d[i].set_card(i);
  }
```

The set_deck() function calls card::set_card() to map the integers into card values. Again we notice how each part of the design enables us to segregate function and description into appropriate object types.

```
■ void  deck::shuffle()
  {
     for (int i = 0; i < 52; ++i) {
        int  k = i + (rand() % (52 - i));
        card  t = d[i];               // swap cards
        d[i] = d[k];
        d[k] = t;
     }
  }
```

The shuffle() function uses the library-supplied pseudorandom number generator rand() in *stdlib* to exchange two cards for every deck position.

We now write main() to test these classes by computing the odds of getting a dealt-out flush in a poker game. We allow the user to decide how many cards to play, as there are many poker variants that require between five and nine cards per hand.

```cpp
#include <iostream>
#include <ctime>        // needed for time()
#include <cstdlib>      // needed for rand() and srand()
using namespace std;

int main()
{
    card one_hand[9]; // max hand is 9 cards
    deck dk;
    int  i, j, k, flush_count = 0, sval[4];
    int  ndeal, nc, nhand;

    do {
        cout << "\nEnter no. cards in a hand (5-9): ";
        cin  >> nc;
    } while (nc < 5 || nc > 9);

    nhand = 52 / nc;
    cout << "Enter no. of hands to deal: ";
    cin  >> ndeal;
    srand(time(NULL)) // seed rand() from time()
    dk.set_deck();
    for (k = 0; k < ndeal; k += nhand) {
        if ((nhand + k) > ndeal)
            nhand = ndeal - k;
        dk.shuffle();
        for (i = 0; i < nc * nhand; i += nc) {
            for (j = 0; j < 4; ++j)// zero suit counts
                sval[j] = 0;
        dk.deal(nc, i, one_hand); // deal next hand

        for (j = 0; j < nc; ++j)
            sval[one_hand[j].get_suit()]++; // +1 to suit
        for (j = 0; j < 4; ++j)
            if (sval[j] >= 5)        // 5 or more is flush
                flush_count++;
        }
    }
    cout << "\nIn " << ndeal << " ";
    cout << nc << "-card hands there were ";
    cout << flush_count << " flushes\n";
}
```

Dissection of the *poker* Program

-
```
do {
   cout << "\nEnter no. cards in a hand (5-9): ";
   cin  >> nc;
} while (nc < 5 || nc > 9);
nhand = 52 / nc;
cout << "Enter no. of hands to deal: ";
cin  >> ndeal;
```

We first ask the user to enter a number of cards per hand. We insist with a do loop that we get an integer between 5 and 9. We then input the number of hands to run the computation on. For a relatively rare hand, such as a flush, we need a high number of hands to get a reasonable estimate of the probability of flushing. Notice we did not insist on checking that the number of hands dealt was between some integer values. A more robust program might also use a do loop for this input as well.

-
```
srand(time(NULL));        // seed rand() from time()
dk.set_deck();
for (k = 0; k < ndeal; k += nhand) {
   if ((nhand + k) > ndeal)
      nhand = ndeal - k;
   dk.shuffle();
```

The deck is initialized and then shuffled using the random number generator. Each time the deck is dealt, the number nhand represents how many poker hands per shuffle can be arranged. If we were dealing six-card hands, this would be 8, as 6*8 is 48, but 7*8 is 56 (too many cards for a 52-card deck). Also note that the library *ctime* needs to be included for the call to time().

-
```
for (j = 0; j < nc; ++j)
   sval[one_hand[j].get_suit()]++; // +1 to suit
```

For each card, we get its suit value. The suit value is an enumerator that can be used as an index into the sval array. Each of the four elements of sval stores how many of each suit is found in a given hand. If one of these values is at least 5, the hand is a flush.

You can test your understanding of the poker program by modifying it to compute the probability of other poker hands. It is straightforward to compute whether a hand has a straight. A straight is a hand that has five cards whose pips value are in sequence, such as having a (3, 4, 5, 6, 7).

A Bold Bluff

One of a series of
Dogs Playing Poker
by C. M. Coolidge

4.8   The this Pointer

The keyword this denotes an implicitly declared self-referential pointer that can be used in a nonstatic member function. Later, we discuss static member functions, where the this pointer is not available. A simple illustration of the pointer's use follows.

In file point5.cpp

```
// Class illustrating the use of the this pointer

class point {
public:                      // place public members first
   void   print() const { cout << "(" << x << ","
                                << y << ")"; }
   void   print(const string& name) const;
   void   set(double u, double v) { x = u; y = v; }
   void   plus(point c);
   point  inverse() {x = -x; y = -y; return (*this);}
   point* where_am_I() { return this; }
private:
   double x, y;
};

// Offset the existing point by point c

void point::plus(point c)
{
   x += c.x;
   y += c.y;
}
```

```
int main()
{
    point   a, b;

    a.set(1.5, -2.5);
    a.print();
    cout << "\na is at " << a.where_am_I() << endl;
    b = a.inverse();
    b.print();
    cout << "\nb is at " << b.where_am_I() << endl;
}
```

The output on our system is

```
(1.5,-2.5)
a is at 0x0064fdd4
(-1.5,2.5)
b is at 0x0064fdc4
```

Note that machine addresses are displayed in hexadecimal and are system-dependent. In this case, the two addresses differ by hexadecimal 0x10, or decimal 16 bytes, the size of the two `double`s required to represent a point.

Dissection of the `this` Pointer

■ `point inverse() { x = -x; y = -y; return (*this);}`

The member function `inverse()` inverts the value of the `point` it acts on. It then uses the built-in self-referential `this` pointer to return the value of that point.

■ `point* where_am_I() const { return this; }`

The member function `where_am_I()` returns the address in memory of the given object. In the output from `main()`, we see how it can be used for tracing the program execution by showing the address of the `point` object that it is applied to.

4.9   **static Members**

C++ allows static members. Using the modifier `static` when declaring a data member means that the data member is independent of any given class variable. The data member is part of the class but separate from any single class object. Nonstatic data members are created for each instance of the class. A static data member is commonly accessible by all instances of its class; it is a global member within class scope. Another difference between static and nonstatic members is that `static` members cannot use the `this` pointer.

Since a static member is independent of a particular instance, it can be accessed in the form

>   *class-name* `::` *identifier*

Note the use of the scope resolution operator. A static member of a global class must be explicitly declared and defined in file scope. For example, if we want a counter to keep track of how many points are declared at any time, we can add to class `point` as follows:

```
class point {
public:
    static int how_many;        // declaration
    .....
};
int point::how_many = 0;        // initialization
    .....
++point::how_many; // use independent of any instance
```

The static member `point::how_many` needs a definition separate from an ordinary `point` variable, since it exists independently from these variables. The static member can be used with scope resolution, since it exists independent of `point` objects. Syntactically, a `static` member function has the modifier `static` precede the return type inside the class declaration. The preferred style for accessing static members is to use scope resolution. Pointer and dot operator access are misleading and give no indication that the member is `static`. The definition outside the class must not have this modifier.

```
class point {
    .....
    static print_how_many();     // static goes first
    .....
};

int point::print_how_many()     // no static keyword here
{ cout << "How many points " << how_many << endl; }
```

The next section discusses the `const` modifier applied to member functions and shows a further example using `static` members.

4.10   const Members

A data member declared with the `const` modifier cannot be modified after initialization. A nonstatic member function can also have the `const` modifier. Syntactically, a `const` member function has the modifier `const` follow the argument list inside the class declaration, and its definition outside the class must also have this modifier. A `const` member function is not allowed to modify any of its implicit arguments.

```
class person {
    .....
    int  print_age() const;
private:
    int  age;
};

int person::print_age() const     // age unmodifiable
{ cout << "age is " << age << endl; }
```

An ordinary member function invoked as

```
x.method(i, j, k);
```

has an explicit argument list i, j, k and an implicit argument list that includes the members of x. The implicit arguments can be thought of as a list of arguments accessible through the `this` pointer. A `const` member function cannot modify its implicit arguments. Writing out `const` member functions and parameter declarations is called const-correctness and is an important aid in writing code. In effect, it is an assertion that the compiler should check that an object does not have its values modified. Const-correctness can also allow the compiler to apply some special optimizations, such as placing a `const` object in read-only memory. The following example illustrates these ideas:

In file salary.cpp

```cpp
// Calculate salary using static members

class salary {
public:
   void  set(int b) { b_sal = b; your_bonus = 0; }
   void  calc_bonus(double perc)
      { your_bonus = b_sal * perc; }
   static void  set_all_bonus(int p)
      { all_bonus = p; }
   int  comp_tot() const
      { return (b_sal + your_bonus + all_bonus); }
private:
   int         b_sal;
   int         your_bonus;
   static int  all_bonus;      // declaration
};

// declaration and definition
int salary::all_bonus = 100;

int main()
{
   salary  w1, w2;

   w1.set(1000);
   w2.set(2000);
   w1.calc_bonus(0.2);
   w2.calc_bonus(0.15);
   salary::set_all_bonus(400);
   cout << " w1 " << w1.comp_tot() << "    w2 "
        << w2.comp_tot() << endl;
}
```

Dissection of the *salary* Program

■
```
class salary {
   .....
private:
   int        b_sal;
   int        your_bonus;
   static int all_bonus;        // declaration
};
```

There are three private data members. The `static` member `all_bonus` requires a file-scope declaration and can exist independently of any specific variables of type `salary` being declared.

■
```
void  set(int b) { b_sal = b; your_bonus = 0; }
```

This assigns the value of `b` to the member `b_sal`. This member function initializes the base salary. The variable `your_bonus` is also initialized. Although our small example did not require this, it is a good habit to initialize all member variables. As we see in Section 5.1, *Classes with Constructors*, on page 211, special functions called constructors are used when initialization and object creation are needed.

■
```
void  calc_bonus(double perc)
   { your_bonus = b_sal * perc; }
```

The right-hand side of the assignment is a calculation of an `int` times a `double`. This results in a `double`. The assignment to an `int` causes a narrowing conversion resulting in the value for `your_bonus`.

■
```
static void  set_all_bonus(int p)
   { all_bonus = p; }
```

The modifier `static` must come before the function return type.

■
```
int  comp_tot() const
   { return (b_sal + your_bonus + all_bonus); }
```

The `const` modifier comes between the end of the argument list and the beginning of the code body. This modifier indicates that no data member has its value changed. Thus, it makes the code more robust. In effect, the self-referential pointer is passed as `const salary* const this`.

■
```
salary::set_all_bonus(400);
```

A `static` member function can be invoked by using the scope resolution operator. The member function could also have been invoked as `w1.set_all_bonus(400)`, but this is misleading since there is nothing special about the class variable `w1`.

Also allowed in C++ is `static const` initialization within a class declaration.

```
class salary {
    .....
private:
    const static int  all_bonus = 1000; // initializer
    .....
};

const int salary::all_bonus;  // declaration required
```

Note: This is ANSI C++, but the GNU compiler g++ allows a user to avoid the further declaration outside the class. If `all_bonus` is initialized in this way, then `set_all_bonus()` no longer works, because `all_bonus` is now a constant.

4.10.1   Mutable Members

The keyword `mutable` allows data members of class variables that have been declared `const` to remain modifiable. It also allows `const` member functions to modify that data member. This reduces the need to cast away constness using `const_cast<>`. The keyword is used as follows:

In file person.cpp

```
class person {                  // Class with mutable members
public:
    person(const string namep, int agep,
            unsigned long ssn)
        : name(namep), age(agep), soc_sec(ssn) { }
    void  bday() const { ++age; }
    void  print() const { cout << name << " is " << age
            << " years old. SSN = " << soc_sec << endl; }
private:
    mutable int    age;    // always modifiable
    const unsigned long   soc_sec;
    const string   name;
};
```

```
int main()
{
    const person ira("ira pohl", 38, 1110111);

    ira.print();
    ira.bday();          // okay, ira.age is mutable
    ira.print();
}
```

The key point is that without the `mutable` modifier on the declaration of `age`, `bday()` could not modify `ira`'s `age` normally because `ira` was declared `const`. To fully understand this example, you will need to read about constructors and initializer syntax in Chapter 5, *Ctors, Dtors, Conversions, and Operator Overloading.*

4.11   A Container Class Example: `ch_stack`

A container is a data structure whose main purpose is to store and retrieve a large number of objects. In the kernel language, an array acts as such a structure. In this section, we develop code that is used to store character values in a stack, which is a last-in-first-out (LIFO) container. We code the stack class `ch_stack` that stores characters.

In file ch_stack1.h

```
class ch_stack {
public:
    void   reset() { top = EMPTY; }
    void   push(char c) { +s[++top] = c; }
    char   pop() { return s[top--]; }
    char   top_of() const { return s[top]; }
    bool   empty() const { return (top == EMPTY); }
    bool   full() const { return (top == FULL); }
private:
    enum { max_len = 100, EMPTY = -1,
           FULL = max_len - 1 };
    char   s[max_len];
    int    top;
};
```

The basic operations on a stack are push and pop. The push operation places a value on the top of the stack, and the pop operation removes the value at the top of the stack. We use a fixed-length `char` array to implement the stack. Later, we talk about other, more flexible implementations.

We now write `main()` to test the same operations.

In file ch_stack1.cpp

```
// Reverse a string with a ch_stack

int main()
{
   ch_stack  s;
   char    str[40] = { "My name is Don Knuth!" };
   int     i = 0;

   cout << str << endl;
   s.reset();                // s.top = EMPTY; is illegal
   while (str[i] && !s.full())
      s.push(str[i++]);
   while (!s.empty())     // print the reverse
      cout << s.pop();
   cout << endl;
}
```

The output from this version of the test program is

```
My name is Don Knuth!
!htunK noD si eman yM
```

Dissection of the ch_stack Class

- `private:`
  ```
  enum { max_len = 100, EMPTY = -1,
         FULL = max_len - 1 };
  char   s[max_len];
  int    top;
  ```

As usual, we hide the implementation details. In this case, we represent the stack of characters with a fixed-length array.

- ```
  bool  empty() const { return (top == EMPTY); }
  bool  full() const { return (top == FULL); }
  ```

These functions do not modify the stack, hence we declare them `const`. They are known as accessor functions. They access information describing the stack.
  ```

- ```
  void  push(char c) { s[++top] = c; }
  char  pop() { return s[top--]; }
  ```

These functions manipulate and change the stack. They are known as mutator functions and cannot be declared `const`.

- ```
  s.reset();          // s.top = EMPTY; is illegal
  while (str[i] && !s.full())
     s.push(str[i++]);
  ```

As the comment in `main()` states, access to the hidden variable `top` is controlled. The variable can be changed by the member function `reset()` but cannot be accessed directly. Also, notice how the variable `s` is passed to each member function, using the member access operator form, as in `s`.*function*.

4.12   Software Engineering: Class Design

The access order for classes has traditionally been `private` first:

```
class ch_stack {
  // private by default
  int   top;
  enum { max_len = 100, EMPTY = -1,
         FULL = max_len - 1 };
  char  s[max_len];
public:
  void  reset() { top = EMPTY; }
  void  push(char c) { s[++top] = c; }
  char  pop() { return s[top--]; }
  char  top_of() const { return s[top]; }
  bool  empty() const { return (top == EMPTY); }
  bool  full() const { return (top == FULL); }
};
```

The reason is that in the original form of C++, only the access keyword `public` was present. The access keywords `private` and `protected` did not exist. By default, member access for `class` was `private`; therefore, the private members had to come first.

The style of `public` first is becoming the norm. It follows the rule that the widest audience needs to see the public members. More specialized information is placed later in the class declaration. This can be thought of as a need-to-know principle or newspaper principle. In a newspaper, the first sentence gives the most important and most widely disseminated information. Details are left for later.

Data members should in general be private. This is an important coding heuristic. Generally, data are part of an implementation choice and should be accessed through public member functions. Such member functions are called accessor functions when they do not change, or mutate, the data. This is not necessarily inefficient because simple accessor member functions can be inline. In the class `ch_stack`, the member functions `top_of()`, `empty()`, and `full()` are all inline accessor functions. Accessor functions should be declared `const`. The member function `reset()` is a mutator. It allows a constrained action on the hidden variable `top`. Notice how much safer such a design is. If `top` were directly accessible, it would be easy for it to be inappropriately changed.

In OOP design, the public members are usually functions and are thought of as the type's interface. These are the actions, or behaviors, publicly expected of an object. If we think of the object type as a noun, the behaviors are verbs. In the implementation, data members are generally placed in private access. This is a key data-hiding principle; namely, that implementation is kept inside a black box that cannot be directly exploited by the object's user.

There is a way through indirection to provide additional data hiding. This is through the use of a separate class for the underlying data representation. This technique is called the Cheshire Cat technique, in honor of Lewis Carroll's cat that disappeared leaving only a smile. Let us recode `class ch_stack` to use this technique:

```
class ch_stack {
public:
   void   reset() { ptr -> reset(); }
   void   push(char c)
     { ptr->push(c); }
   char   pop() { return ptr->pop(); }
   char   top_of() const { return ptr->top_of(); }
   bool   empty() const
     { return ptr -> empty(); }
   bool   full() const
     { return ptr -> full(); }
private:
   ch_stk_rep* ptr;              // opaque pointer
};
```

All the data and underlying operations are handled through the `ch_stk` pointer. The class `ch_stack` is therefore known as a wrapper class. The relationship between the wrapper class and the underlying representation class is called the handle design pattern. We will illustrate this relationship when we introduce Unified Modeling Language

(UML) diagrams in Section 4.12.2, *Unified Modeling Language (UML) and Design*, on page 192.

```
class ch_stk_rep {
public:
   void   reset() { top = EMPTY; }
   void   push(char c)
     { s[top++] = c; }
   char   pop() { return s[top--]; }
   char   top_of() const { return s[top]; }
   bool   empty() const
     { return (top == EMPTY); }
   bool   full() const
     { return (top == FULL); }
private:
   enum { max_len = 100, EMPTY = -1,
          FULL = max_len - 1 };
   int    top;
   char   s[max_len];
}
```

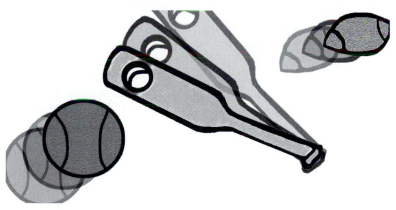

Noun: Ball   **Verbs: Bounce   Hit   Throw**

4.12.1   Trade-Offs in Design

Design is all about trade-offs. Recall our poker example and our use of an enum type to describe suit. What if this were recoded as a class?

Change the suit declaration from an enumerated type to a class as follows:

```
class suit {
public:
   void  set(int n) { s = n / 13; }
   int   get_suit() const { return s; }
   void  print() const;
private:
   enum  suit_val
         { clubs, diamonds, hearts, spades } s;
};
```

We add the member function `get_suit()` to access the hidden integer value of a `suit` variable. The advantage is that `suit` and `pips` are now treated symmetrically, with both being given class definitions. The disadvantage is that we have added more code and a layer of methods to access what is basically a simple type having four unique values. There is no clear answer as to which choice for `suit` is better. In one sense, the curse of C++ is that there are too many opportunities, but this is also its great benefit over simpler languages such as Java.

4.12.2   Unified Modeling Language (UML) and Design

The Unified Modeling Language (UML) is a graphical depiction of class relationships that helps the coder design, document, and maintain object-oriented code. The simplest diagram is a rectangle that represents a class. Generally, the class has three things depicted: its name, placed at the top; its data members, placed in the middle; and its methods, placed at the bottom. The following UML diagram corresponds to the `person` class in Section 4.10.1, *Mutable Members*, on page 186.

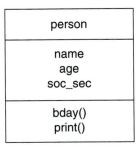

UML Diagram for Class person

A class diagram describes the types and relationships in the system. It is very useful documentation, and a number of systems, such as

Rational Rose, now provide automated tools to develop such documentation along with coding. A relationship that can be depicted by UML includes the part-whole, or aggregation, relationship (*HASA*). For example, a handle type such as `ch_stack` has a representation class `class ch_stk_rep` pointer.

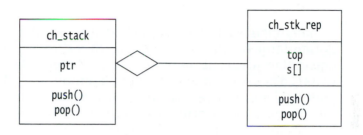

Handle Class in UML

The representation class is used to concretely implement the handle class. This relationship recurs in many object-oriented coding schemes. It is called the bridge or handle design pattern. A design pattern is a recurring software solution to a problem, usually involving several classes collaborating to solve the problem. The book *Design Patterns: Elements of Reusable Object-Oriented Software,* by Erich Gamma et al. (Addison-Wesley, 1995) popularized this approach by listing over 20 such patterns with catchy names, such as the bridge pattern.

4.13   Dr. P's Prescriptions

- Indentation is as follows: `class`, access keywords, and closing brace all line up and are placed on separate lines. Member declarations are indented and line up vertically.

- Access privileges are in order: `public`, `protected`, and `private`.

- Data members should be `private`.

- `const` your member functions where possible.

- Provide a uniform set of methods, such as `set()`, `get()`, and `print()`.

- Use inlining only when vital to performance.

The indentation rules are consistent with industry practice. The idea behind placing more visible members first is based on the same logic used in newspaper articles—namely, what everyone needs to know comes first. What everyone needs to know are the public members. This is the interface available to all users of the class.

In most designs, it is appropriate to make data members `private`. As we explained, this is the black box principle. The builder (read: programmer) hides the details of the implementation. The client benefits by having to see and understand fewer details and being protected from obvious misapplications.

Many member functions, such as print methods, are accessor but not mutator functions. This means they do not change values of the object they are using. In these cases, the methods should be declared `const`. This is good programming methodology. It allows the compiler to check for key correctness attributes of the code. It also allows the compiler to perform certain optimizations that come from knowing the object's value is not changed by the method. *Note:* `const` does not have an effect on what the function computes, so many lazy programmers choose to not use it.

A client expects to print information about a data type, so almost all data types need print methods in their interface. A client expects to retrieve and change key values of the object. A proper choice of set and get methods allows the class programmer to provide these services. Providing these functions with like names and uses makes it easier to code new types and have clients easily use them.

Inlining comes at a cost. The inline function is expanded to a body of code rather than just a function call. This can cause code bloat. More important, inlining forces developers to recompile their entire code base when these functions are rewritten. Changing a non-inline function requires only a relink as long as the interface remains the same. (George Belotsky mentioned this in a private note.)

4.14   C++ Compared with Java

Java classes are based on the C++ aggregate type `class`. A `class` provides the means for implementing a user-defined data type and associated functions. Therefore, a `class` can be used to implement an ADT. Unlike in C++, however, functions, or methods, as they are called in Java, cannot exist outside a class construct. Also, Java `class` types are always reference types. The Java primitive types, such as `int` or `char` are value types. Let us write a `class` called `Person` that is used to store information about people:

In file Person.java

```java
// An elementary Java implementation of type Person

class Person {
   public void  setName(String nm) { name = nm; }
   public void  setAge(int a) { age = a; }
   public void  setGender(char b) { gender = b; }
   public String toString()
      { return (name + " age is " + age
                      + " gender is " + gender); }
   private String name;
   private int age;
   private char gender;   // male 'M', female 'F'
};
```

As with C++ classes, Java has two important additions to the structure concept of traditional C. First, Java has members called class methods that are functions, such as setAge(). Second, Java has both public and private members. The keyword public indicates the visibility of the members that follow it. Without this keyword, the members are private to the class. Private members are available for use only by other member functions of the class. Public members are available anywhere the class is available. Privacy allows part of the implementation of a class type to be hidden and prevents unanticipated modifications to the data structure. Restricted access, or data hiding, is a feature of object-oriented programming.

The declaration of methods inside a class allows the ADT to have actions, or behaviors, that can act on its private representation. For example, the member function toString() has access to private members and gives Person a string representation used in output. This method is common to many class types.

We can now use this data type Person as if it were a basic type of the language. Other code that uses this type is a client. The client can use only the public members to act on variables of type Person.

```java
// PersonTest.java uses Person

public class PersonTest {
    public static void main (String[] args)
    {
        System.out.println("Person test:");
        Person p1 = new Person();    // create Person
        p1.setAge(20);
        p1.setName("Alan Turing");
        p1.setGender('M');
        System.out.println(p1.toString());
    }
}
```

The output of this example program is

```
Person test:
Alan Turing age is 20 sex is M
```

Notice the use of `new Person()` to create an instance of `Person`. The `new` operator goes off to the heap, as it does in C++, and obtains memory for creating an instance of object `Person`. The value of `p1` is a reference to this object. In effect, this is the address of the object. For a more detailed look of a similar example, and explanation of the nuances of Java classes, read *Java by Dissection,* by Ira Pohl and Charlie McDowell (Addison-Wesley, 1999), pages 234 to 242.

4.15   Advanced Topics

This section can be omitted on a first reading, as it is about less used and arcane facilities.

4.15.1   Pointer to Class Member

A pointer to class member is distinct from a pointer to class. A pointer to class member's type is $T::*$, where T is the class name. C++ has two operators that act to dereference a pointer to class member. The two pointer-to-member operators are `.*` and `->*`. Think of *obj.*ptr_mem* and *pointer->*ptr_mem* as first accessing the object and then accessing and dereferencing the member that is specified. The following code shows how to use these operators:

In file show_hide.cpp

```cpp
//Pointer to class member

class X {
public:
   int  visible;
   void print() const
      { cout << "\nhide = " << hide
             << " visible = " << visible; }
   void reset() { visible = hide; }
   void set(int i) { hide = i; }
private:
   int  hide;
};

typedef void (X::*pfcn)();

int main()
{
   X   a, b, *pb = &b;
   int X::*pXint = &X::visible;
   pfcn pF = &X::print;

   a.set(8); a.reset();
   b.set(4); b.reset();
   a.print();
   a.*pXint += 1;
   a.print();
   cout << "\nb.visible = " << pb ->*pXint;
   (b.*pF)();
   pF = &X::reset;
   (a.*pF)();
   a.print();
   cout << endl;
}
```

The output is as follows:

```
hide = 8 visible = 8
hide = 8 visible = 9
b.visible = 4
hide = 4 visible = 4
hide = 8 visible = 8
```

The `typedef void (X::*pfcn)();` statement says that `pfcn` is a pointer to class X member whose base type is a function with no arguments that returns `void`. Member functions `X::print` and `X::reset` match this type.

The declaration

```
int X::*pXint = &X::visible;
```

declares `pXint` to be a pointer to class X member whose base type is `int`. It is initialized by `pfcn pF = &X::print` to point at the member `X::visible`. The pointer `pF` is initialized to point at the member function `X::print`. Given the pointer assignments in the program, the following equivalencies hold:

a.*pXint += 1	*is equivalent to*	++a.visible
pb ->*pXint	*is equivalent to*	pb -> visible
b.*pF()	*is equivalent to*	b.print()
(a.*pF)()	*is equivalent to*	a.reset().

Consider the memory layout for representing an object. The object has a base address, and the various nonstatic members are offset relative to this base address. In effect, a pointer to class member is used as an offset and is not a true pointer; a true pointer has general memory addresses as values. A static member is not offset and, as such, a pointer to a static member is a true address.

4.15.2 Unions

This section is about a dangerous type-construction facility, the union. A union is a derived type whose syntax is the same as for structures except that the keyword `union` replaces `struct`. The member declarations share storage, and their values are overlaid. Therefore, a union allows its value to be interpreted as a set of types that correspond to the member declarations.

A union initializer is a brace-enclosed value for its first member. Consider the following declaration:

In file union.cpp

```
union int_dbl {
    int    i;
    double x;
} n = { 0 };            // i member is set to zero
```

Now we write `main()` to show how the variable `n` can be used as either an integer type or a double type.

```
int main()
{
   n.i = 7;              // int value 7 is stored in n
   cout << n.i << " is integer. ";
   cout << n.x << " is double-machine dependent.\n";
   n.x = 7.0;            // double value 7.0 in n
   cout << n.i << " is integer - machine dependent.";
   cout << n.x << " is double." << endl;
}
```

This example also illustrates why unions can be dangerous and are often system-dependent. On some systems, it is possible that not all bit patterns are legal values for the overlaid types. In that case, a legal value with one type might, when accessed as the other type, lead to an exception.

A union can be anonymous, as in the following code:

In file weekend.cpp

```
enum week { sun, mon, tues, weds, thurs, fri, sat };

static union {
   int    i;
   week   w;
};

int main()
{
   i = 5;

   if (w == sat || w == sun)
      cout << " It's the weekend! ";
}
```

The anonymous union allows the individual member identifiers to be used as variables. The member names must be unique within scope, and no variables of the anonymous type can be declared. Note that an anonymous union declared in file scope must be static.

4.15.3   Bit Fields

This next topic is also arcane and system-dependent, and it may be omitted by readers who do not use bit manipulation in their programs.

A member that is an integral type can consist of a specified number of bits. Such a member is called a bit field, and the number of associated bits is called its width. The width is specified by a nonnegative constant integral expression following a colon.

```
struct pcard {          // packed representation of card
    unsigned  s : 2;
    unsigned  p : 4;
};
```

The compiler attempts to pack the bit fields sequentially within memory, but it is at liberty to skip to a next byte or word for purposes of alignment. Arrays of bit fields are not allowed. Also, the address operator & cannot be applied to bit fields.

Bit fields are used to address information conveniently in packed form. On many machines, words are 32 bits, and bit operations can be performed in parallel. In this case, bit manipulation is an implementation technique for sets that contain up to 32 elements, as shown next.

In file set.cpp

```
struct word {
unsigned w0:1, w1:1, w2:1, w3:1, w4:1, w5:1, w6:1,
    w7:1,  w8:1,  w9:1,  w10:1, w11:1, w12:1, w13:1,
    w14:1, w15:1, w16:1, w17:1, w18:1, w19:1, w20:1,
    w21:1, w22:1, w23:1, w24:1, w25:1, w26:1, w27:1,
    w28:1, w29:1, w30:1, w31:1;
};
```

We can overlay word and unsigned within a union to create a data structure for manipulating bits.

```
union set {
    word      m;
    unsigned  u;
};
int main()
{
    set  x, y;

    x.u = 0x0f100f10;
    y.u = 0x01a1a0a1;
    x.u = x.u | y.u;              // set union
    cout << "element 9 = "
         << ((x.m.w9)? "true" : "false") << endl;
}
```

The set operation union is performed as a word-parallel operation on most systems. A word-parallel operation means an operation that executes simultaneously on all the distinct bits contained in the machine word. This is far more efficient than processing each bit sequentially.

C++ provides bit-manipulation operators (see Table 4.2). They operate on the machine-dependent bit representation of integral operands. It is customary that the shift operators be overloaded to perform I/O.

Table 4.2 Bitwise Operators	
~	Unary one's complement
<<	Left shift
>>	Right shift
&	And
^	Exclusive or
|	Or

Summary

- The original name Stroustrup gave to his language was "C with classes." A class is an extension of the idea of structure in traditional C. A class is a way of implementing a data type and associated functions and operators. It is the mechanism in C++ for implementing ADTs, such as complex numbers and stacks.

- The structure type allows the programmer to aggregate components into a single named variable. A structure has components, called members, that are individually named. Critical to processing structures is the accessing of their members. This is done with either the member access operator . or the member selection operator -> . These operators, along with () and [], have the second-highest precedence. Highest precedence belongs to scope resolution, ::.

- The concepts of structure and class are augmented in C++ to allow functions to be members. The function declaration is included in the structure declaration and is invoked using access methods for structure members. The functionality required by the `struct` data type should often be directly included in the `struct` declaration.

- Member functions defined within the structure or class are implicitly inline. As a rule, only short, heavily used member functions should be defined within the structure. When defined outside the structure, the scope resolution operator is used.

- The scope resolution operator allows member functions of various structure types to have the same names; which member function is invoked depends on the type of object it acts on. Member functions within the same `struct` can be over-loaded.

- Structures have public and private members that provide data hiding. Inside a structure or class, the keyword `private` followed by a colon restricts the access of the members that follow it. The private members are used by only a few categories of functions, whose privileges include access to these members. These functions include the member functions of the class.

- Classes in C++ are a form of `struct`, whose default access specification is private. Thus, `struct` and `class` can be used interchangeably with the appropriate access specification.

- Data members can be declared with the storage class modifier `static`. A data member that is declared `static` is shared by all variables of that class and is stored in one place only. Therefore, the data member can be accessed using the form

  class-name `::` *identifier*

- Classes can be nested. The inner class is inside the scope of the outer class. This is not in accordance with C semantics.

Review Questions

1. In C++, the structure name, or _____, is a type.

2. Member functions that are defined within `class` are implicitly _____.

3. A function invocation `w1.print();` means that print is a _____ function.

4. A private member (can or cannot) _____ be used by a member function of that class.

5. The `static` modifier used in declaring a data member means that the data member is _____.

6. The preferred style is to have members of _____ given first and members of _____ access declared last in a class declaration.

7. A stack is a LIFO container. A container is a data structure whose main purpose is _____.

8. LIFO means _____.

Exercises

1. Design a C++ structure to store a dairy product name, portion weight, calories, protein, fat, and carbohydrates. Twenty-five grams of American cheese have 375 calories, 5 grams of protein, 8 grams of fat, and 0 carbohydrates. Show how to assign these values to the member variables of your structure. Write a function that, given a variable of type `struct dairy` and a weight in grams (portion size), returns the number of calories for that weight.

2. Write a structure `point` that has three coordinates x, y, and z. How can you access the individual members?

3. Use the structure `card` defined in the *poker* program in Section 4.7, *An Example: Flushing*, on page 175, to write a hand-sorting routine. In card games, most players keep their cards sorted by pip value. The routine places aces first, kings next, and so forth, down to twos. A hand is five cards.

4. The following declarations do not compile correctly. Explain what is wrong.

```
struct brother {
    char          name[20];
    int           age;
    struct sister sib;
} a;

struct sister {
    char           name[20];
    int            age;
    struct brother sib;
} a;
```

5. In this exercise, use the class `ch_stack`, defined in Section 4.11, *A Container Class Example: ch_stack*, on page 187. Write the function

```
void  reverse(char s1[], char s2[]);
```

The strings `s1` and `s2` must be the same size. String `s2` should become a reversed copy of string `s1`. Internal to `reverse`, use a `ch_stack` to perform the reversal.

6. Rewrite the functions `push()` and `pop()` discussed in Section 4.11, *A Container Class Example: ch_stack*, on page 188, to test that `push()` is not acting on a full `ch_stack` and that `pop()` is not acting on an empty `ch_stack`. If either condition is detected, print an error message, using `cerr`, and use `exit(1)` (in *cstdlib*) to abort the program. Contrast this to an approach using asserts.

7. Write `reverse()` as a member function for type `ch_stack`, discussed in Section 4.11, *A Container Class Example: ch_stack*, on page 187. Test it by printing normally and reversing the string

Gottfried Leibniz wrote Toward a Universal Characteristic

8. For the `ch_stack` type in Section 4.4, *Access: Private and Public*, on page 167, write as member functions

```
// Push n chars from s1 onto the ch_stack

void  pushm(int n, const char s1[]);

// Pop n chars from ch_stack into char string

void  popm(int n, char s1[]);
```

Hint: Be sure to put a terminator character into the string before outputting it.

9. Explain the difference in meaning between the structure

```
struct a {
    int  i, j, k;
};
```

and the class

```
class a {
    int  i, j, k;
};
```

Explain why the class declaration is not useful. How can you use the keyword `public` to change the class declaration into a declaration equivalent to `struct a`?

10. Recode as a class the data type `deque`, which is a double-ended queue that allows pushing and popping at both ends.

```
class deque {
public:
    void reset() {top=bottom = max_len / 2; top--; }
    .....
private:
    char   s[max_len];
    int    bottom, top;
};
```

Declare and implement `push_t()`, `pop_t()`, `push_b()`, `pop_b()`, `print_stack()`, `top_of()`, `bottom_of()`, `empty()`, and `full()`. The function `push_t()` stands for push on top and `pop_t()` for pop on top; `push_b()` stands for push on bottom and `pop_b()` for pop on bottom. The `print_stack()` function should output the stack from bottom to top. An empty stack is denoted by having the top fall below the bottom. Test each function. Draw the UML diagram for this class.

11. Extend the data type `deque` by adding a member function `relocate()`. If the `deque` is full, `relocate()` is called, and the contents of the `deque` are moved to balance empty storage around the center `max_len/2` of array `s`. Its function declaration header is

```
// Returns true if it succeeds, false if it fails
bool deque::relocate()
```

12. Recode `deque` to hide the representation in a `class deque_rep`. Draw an appropriate UML diagram for this handle class design.

13. Write a function that swaps the contents of two strings. If you pushed a string of characters onto a `ch_stack` and popped them into a second string, they would come out reversed. In a swap of two strings, we want the original ordering. Use a `deque` to do the swap. The strings are stored in character arrays of the same length, but the strings themselves may be of differing lengths. The function prototype is

```
void   swap(char s1[], char s2[]);
```

14. Write the following member functions and add them to the *poker* program found in Section 4.7, *An Example: Flushing*, on page 174. Let `pr_deck()` use `pr_card()` and `pr_card()` use `print()`. Print the deck after it is initialized.

    ```
    void  pips::print() const;
    void  card::pr_card() const;
    void  deck::pr_deck() const;
    ```

15. Write a function `pr_hand()` that prints out card hands. Add it to the *poker* program and use it to print out each flush.

16. In Section 4.7, *An Example: Flushing*, on page 174, `main()` detects flushes. Write a function

    ```
    bool  isflush(const card hand[], int nc) const;
    ```

    that returns `true` if a `hand` is a flush.

17. Write a function

    ```
    bool  isstraight(const card hand[], nc) const;
    ```

    that returns `true` if a `hand` is a straight. A straight is five cards that have sequential pip values. The lowest straight is ace, 2, 3, 4, 5, and the highest straight is 10, jack, queen, king, ace. Run experiments to estimate the probability that dealt cards result in a straight, and compare the results of five-card hands with results of seven-card hands. *Hint:* You may want to set up an array of 15 integers to correspond to counters for each pip value. Be sure that a pip value of 1 (corresponding to ace) is also counted as the high card corresponding to a pip value of 14.

18. Use the previous exercises to determine the probability that a poker hand results in a straight flush. This is the rarest poker hand and has the highest value. Note that, in a hand of more than five cards, it is not sufficient to merely check for the presence of both a straight and a flush to determine that the hand is a straight flush.

19. Change the `suit` declaration from an enumerated type to a class:.

    ```
    enum  suit_val { clubs, diamonds, hearts, spades };

    class suit {
    public:
        void  assign(int n) { s = n / 13; }
        int   getsuit() const { return s; }
        void  print() const;
    private:
        suit_val  s;
    };
    ```

    We add the member function `getsuit()` to access the hidden integer value of a `suit` variable. Now recode all references to `suit` throughout the program.

20. Change class `ch_stack` to `int_stack` by substituting type `int` for type `char` in the class definition as appropriate. In Section 6.1, *Template Class stack*, on page 283, we see how to use templates to automate this process.

21. Redesign the roulette simulation problem of Chapter 3, *Functions, Pointers, and Arrays*, exercise 21, through exercise 23 on page 158, to be a class-based program. You might have a roulette class and a gambler class. Recompute an estimate of the gambler's ruin length for a gambler whose initial capital is 2,000 dollars. Draw the UML for this program.

22. *(Java)* Recode `point` in Section 4.5, *Classes*, on page 169, as a Java class.

23. *(Java)* Recode and test `ch_stack` in Section 4.11, *A Container Class Example: ch_stack*, on page 187, as a Java class. Add a method `reverse()` that does the same basic operation as the code in `main()` on page 188 and test it.

24. *(Java to C++)* Recode the Java program *PersonTest.java* in Section 4.14, *C++ Compared with Java*, on page 195, to run as C++.

CHAPTER 5

Ctors, Dtors, Conversions, and Operator Overloading

Objects are class instances. An object requires memory and an initial value, which C++ provides through declarations that are definitions. Variables of any type require memory and an initial value. For example, in

```
void foo()
{
    int     n = 5;
    double  z[10] = { 0.0 };
    struct  gizmo { int i, j; } w = { 3, 4 };
    .....
}
```

all of the variables are created at block entry when `foo()` is invoked. A typical implementation uses a runtime system stack. Thus, the `int` variable n on a system with 4-byte integers gets its space allocated off the stack and initialized to the value 5. The `gizmo` variable w requires 8 bytes to represent its two-integer members. The array of `double` variable z requires 10 times `sizeof(double)` to store its elements. In each case, the system provides for the construction and initialization of these variables. On exit from `foo()`, deallocation occurs automatically.

In creating complicated aggregates, the user expects similar management of a class-defined object. The class needs a mechanism to specify object creation and destruction so that a client can use objects like native types.

A constructor (ctor) is a member function whose name is the same as the class name; it creates objects of the class type. This process involves initializing data members and, frequently, allocating storage from the heap by using `new`. A destructor (dtor) is a member function whose name is the class name preceded by the tilde character, ~. A destructor's usual purpose is finalizing or destroying objects of the class type. Finalizing objects involves retrieving resources allocated to the object. Frequently this requires using `delete` to deallocate store assigned to the object.

Whereas constructors can be overloaded and take arguments, destructors can do neither. A constructor is invoked when its associated type is used in a definition, when call-by-value is used to pass a value to a function, or when the return value of a function must create a value of associated type. Destructors are invoked implicitly when an object goes out of scope. Constructors and destructors do not have return types and cannot use `return` *expression* statements.

Hey, you must have the wrong address for demolition. We don't need a destructor yet! We are still constructing this thing!

5.1   Classes with Constructors

The simplest use of a constructor is for initialization. In this and later sections, we develop some examples that use constructors to initialize the values of the data members of the class. Our first example is an implementation of a data type `counter` to store numbers that are computed with a modulus of 100. A car's trip odometer is a counter.

In file counter.cpp

```
// Counter and constructor initialization

class counter {
public:
    counter(int i);          // ctor declaration
    void  reset() { value = 0; }
    int   get() const { return value; }
    void  print() const { cout << value << '\t'; }
    void  click() { value = (value + 1) % 100; }
private:
    int  value;              // 0 to 99
};

// Constructor definition

inline counter::counter(int i) { value = i % 100; }
```

Dissection of the counter Class

■ ```
class counter {
public:
    counter(int i);   // ctor declaration
```

The `class counter` is to be used as a simple data type that counts from 0 to 99. It has a constructor that initializes variables to a value between these limits. Here, we have the constructor declared but not defined.

■ ```
void  reset() { value = 0; }
int   get() const { return value;}
void  print() const { cout << value << '\t'; }
void  click() { value = (value + 1) % 100; }
```

Here, we have a typical group of methods. The counter's click operation is implemented by adding 1 and using the modulus operator to guarantee that the value of the counter stays inside its limits.

- ```
  private:
      int  value;              // 0 to 99
  };
  ```

The integer `value` is restricted in value to 0, 1, 2, . . . , 99. It is the class implementer's responsibility to enforce this restriction by having all member functions guarantee this behavior.

- ```
  // Constructor definition

  inline counter::counter(int i){ value = i % 100; }
  ```

The member function `counter::counter(int)` is a constructor. It does not have a return type. This constructor is invoked when objects of type `counter` are declared. It is a function of one argument. When invoked, the constructor requires an expression that is assignment-compatible with its `int` parameter. It then creates and initializes the declared variable. Notice we have placed the definition of the constructor outside the class braces. We can then define it by using the scope resolution operator `::`. Methods defined inside the class brackets are automatically inlined. When defining a method outside the class braces, we can indicate that is to be inlined by using the keyword `inline` explicitly in the definition. When providing an inline function definition outside of the class brackets, you must include it in any file with code that uses it.

Some examples of this are

```
counter   a(0);      // a.value = 0;
counter   b(1);      // b.value = 1;
```

but not

```
counter   a;         // illegal: no parameter list
```

Since this class has only the one constructor of argument list `int`, a `counter` declaration must have an integral expression passed as an initializing value. Not allowing a `counter` variable to be declared without an initializing expression prevents runtime errors due to uninitialized variables. In the next section, we provide a constructor that remedies the preceding illegal declaration. This is a constructor, termed the default constructor, that does not require an initializing value. Such a constructor should perform initialization of a class variable to a default value.

Man, oh, man, I wish I could automate this counting!

5.1.1   The Default Constructor

A constructor requiring no arguments is called the default constructor. It can be a constructor with an empty argument list or one whose arguments all have default values. It has the special purpose of initializing arrays of objects of its class.

It is often convenient to overload the constructor with several function declarations. In the preceding example, it could be desirable to have the default value be 0. If the default constructor

```
counter() { value = 0; }
```

is added as a member function of `counter`, the following declarations are possible:

```
counter   s;          // initializes s.value to 0
counter   d[5];       // arrays properly initialized
```

In both of these declarations, the empty parameter-list constructor is invoked.

If a class has no constructor, the system provides a default constructor. If a class has constructors but not a default constructor, array allocation causes a syntactic error.

In our `counter` example, the following constructor could serve as both a general initializer and a default constructor:

```
inline counter::counter(int i = 0) { value = i % 100 }
```

This initializes `counter` variable's `value` to 0 by default, unless the user provides in an argument list an explicit initial value.

5.1.2   Constructor Initializer

A special syntax is used for initializing subelements of objects with constructors. Constructor initializers for structure and class members are specified by a colon and a comma-separated list that follows the constructor parameter list and that precedes the code body. A constructor initializer is a data member identifier followed by a parenthesized expression. Using this syntax, the `counter` constructor can be recoded as

```
// Default constructor for counter

inline counter::counter(int i = 0) :
      value(i % 100) { }
```

The member variable `value` is initialized by the expression `i % 100`. The constructor definition has a compound statement that is empty. Notice that initialization replaces assignment. The individual members must be initializable as

member-name (*expression list*)

It is not always possible to assign values to members in the body of the constructor. An initializer list is required when a nonstatic member is either a `const` or a reference type.

5.1.3   Constructors as Conversions

Constructors of a single parameter are used automatically for conversion unless declared with the keyword `explicit`. For example, `Metal::Metal(Ore)` provides code that can be used to convert an `Ore` object to a `Metal` object. Consider the following class, whose purpose is to print invisible characters with their ASCII designation; for example, the code 07 (octal) is `alarm` or `bel`. (See Appendix A, *ASCII Character Codes,* for the full character set.)

In file printable.cpp

```
// ASCII printable characters

class pr_char {
public:
   pr_char(int i = 0) : c(i % 128) { }
   void  print() const { cout << rep[c]; }
private:
   int  c;
   static const char*  rep[128];
};
```

```
const char*  pr_char::rep[128] = { "nul", "soh", "stx",
    ·····// filled in with table of ASCII characters
    "w", "x", "y", "z","{", "|", "}", "~", "del" };

int main()
{
    pr_char  c;
    for (int i = 0; i < 128; ++i) {
        c = i;        // or: c = static_cast<pr_char>(i);
        c.print();
        cout << endl;
    }
}
```

Dissection of the *printable* Program

■
```
class pr_char {
public:
    pr_char(int i = 0) : c(i % 128) { }
```

The constructor creates an automatic conversion from integers to pr_char. Its signature is of type int.

■
```
    static const char*  rep[128];
};
const char*  pr_char::rep[128] = { "nul", "soh",
"stx",
    ·····// filled in with table of ASCII characters
    "w", "x", "y", "z","{", "|", "}", "~", "del" };
```

The table of characters is declared static. This is important here. We want the representation not to be attached to a given object. Being declared static means that there is only one such array rep[] and it is independent of any given class variable.

■ pr_char c;

The declaration invokes the default constructor and is equivalent to pr_char c(0).

■
```
for (int i = 0; i < 128; ++i) {
    c = i;        // or: c = static_cast<pr_char>(i);
    c.print();
```

The integer value of i is converted implicitly by calling the constructor of signature int, namely, pr_char::pr_char(int), to produce the equivalent pr_char value and assign it to c. You need to be careful with such conversions and assignments. In cases where the objects that are converted use significant resources, there can be considerable overhead in this technique.

%$#\n\b !!!

Gee, we'd better use printable characters in a family publication.

5.1.4   Improving the point Class

The class `point` from Section 4.5, *Classes*, on page 169, is readily improved by adding constructors. It is also the case that usually there are several constructors per class. Each constructor signature represents a useful way to declare and initialize an object of that type. Notice that the class contains the ordinary member function `point::set()`, which can be used to change the value of a `point` object but cannot be used to create a `point` object.

In file parabola.cpp

```
class point {
public:
    point() : x(0), y(0) { }          // default
    point(double u) : x(u), y(0) { }  // double to point
    point(double u, double v) : x(u), y(v) { }
    void print() const { cout << "(" << x << ","
                              << y << ")"; }
    void set(double u, double v) { x = u; y = v; }
    void plus(point c);
private:
    double x, y;
};

// Offset existing point by point c

void point::plus(point c)
{
    x += c.x;
    y += c.y;
}
```

This class has three individually coded constructors. They could be combined using default arguments as follows:

```
inline point::point(double u = 0, double v = 0) :
                    x(u), y(v) { }
```

Many scientific problems require producing a table of points or a graph by using a function. For example, a parabola can be coded as

```
double parabola(double x, double p)
        { return(x * x) / p; }
```

We produce a table of points graphing the parabola from 0 to 2 in increments of 0.1.

In file parabola.cpp

```
void graph(double a, double b, double incr,
    double f(double, double), double p, point gr[])
{
     double x = a;
     for (int i = 0; x <= b; ++i, x += incr)
         gr[i].set(x, f(x, p));
}

const int no_of_pts = 20;

int main()
{
   point g[no_of_pts];  // uses default ctor

   graph(0, 2, 0.1, parabola, 5, g);
   cout << "First 20 samples:" << endl;
   for (int i = 0; i < no_of_pts; ++i) {
      g[i].print();
      if (i % 5 == 4)
         cout << endl;
      else
         cout << "  ";
   }
}
```

5.1.5   Constructing a Stack

A constructor can also be used to allocate space from the heap also known as free store. We shall modify the ch_stack type from Section 4.11, *A Container Class Example: ch_stack*, on page 187, so that its maximum length is initialized by a constructor. The length of the stack is a parameter to a constructor. This parameter is used to call the operator new, which can allocate storage dynamically.

The design of the object ch_stack includes hidden implementation detail. Data members are placed in the private access region of class ch_stack. The public interface provides clients with the expected stack abstraction. These are all public member functions, such as push() and pop(). Some of these functions are accessor functions that do not change the stack object, such as top_of() and empty(). It is usual to make these const member functions. Some of these functions are mutator functions that do change the ch_stack object, such as push() and pop(). The constructor member functions have the job of creating and initializing ch_stack objects.

In file ch_stack2.h

```
class ch_stack {
public:
// public interface for ch_stack
    explicit ch_stack(int size) :
            max_len(size), top(EMPTY)
            { assert(size > 0); s = new char[size];
            assert(s != 0); }
    void   reset() { top = EMPTY; }
    void   push(char c) { s[++top]= c; }
    char   pop() { return s[top--]; }
    char   top_of() const { return s[top]; }
    bool   empty() const { return (top == EMPTY); }
    bool   full() const { return (top == max_len-1); }
private:
    enum   { EMPTY = -1 };
    char*  s;                    // changed from s[max_len]
    int    max_len;
    int    top;
};
```

Dissection of `ch_stack` Class

- ```
  explicit ch_stack(int size) :
      max_len(size), top(EMPTY)
      { assert(size > 0); s = new char[size];
        assert(s != 0); }
  ```

The keyword `explicit` is used with a constructor of one argument. Normally, this would be a conversion constructor, but the keyword `explicit` disables this feature. It is clear that we do not want an `int` type to be inadvertently turned into a stack.

For example, if this constructor did not have the keyword `explicit`, then

```
ch_stack s(200); // s is size 200
int n = 5;
. . . . .
s = n;              // s assigned a stack of size 5;
. . . . .
```

This would be an unwanted behavior, which is prevented by using the keyword `explicit`.

In the preceding code and in the rest of this chapter, we use assertions to test whether a pointer value is 0. This is done after calling `new` and indicates that `new` has failed. The `assert` technique requires that a debug option be turned on for the compiler. Also, we are assuming that memory allocation exception handling is turned off. An alternative scheme is to have the `bad_alloc` exception thrown. This is discussed in detail in Section 10.9, *Standard Exceptions and Their Uses*, on page 469. This code has no destructor and leads to memory leaks. We show an appropriate destructor in Section 5.2, *Classes with Destructors*, on page 223. It should also have a copy construction nd overload assignment operator.

- ```
  enum   { EMPTY = -1 };
  char*  s;         // changed from s[max_len]
  int    max_len;
  int    top;
  ```

Here is the `ch_stack` implementation for a dynamically sized array. We use a base pointer `s` rather than a fixed-length array.

Constructors are important because they create possibilities for conveniently initializing the abstract data type. For example, we can code two additional constructors for `ch_stack`. One would be a default constructor to allocate a specific-length `ch_stack`, and a second would be a two-parameter constructor whose second parameter would be a `char*` to initialize the `ch_stack`. The two constructors are as follows:

```
// Default constructor for ch_stack

ch_stack::ch_stack() : max_len(100), top(EMPTY)
{
   s = new char[100];
   assert(s != 0);
}

// Copy a char* string into the ch_stack

ch_stack::
ch_stack(int size, const char str[]) : max_len(size)
{
   int  i;
   assert(size > 0);
   s = new char[size];
   assert(s != 0);
   for (i = 0; i < max_len && str[i] != 0; ++i)
      s[i] = str[i];
   top = --i;
}
```

The corresponding function prototypes would be included as members of the class `ch_stack`. We show the use of these constructors:

```
ch_stack  data;       // creates data.s[100]
ch_stack  d[N];       // creates N 100 element ch_stacks
ch_stack  w(4, "ABCD"); // w.s[0]='A'·····w.s[3]='D'
```

5.1.6   The Copy Constructor

The semantics of call-by-value for functions require that a local copy of the argument type be created and initialized from the value of the expression passed as the actual argument. For example,

```
int cube_plus(int i)
{
   i = i + 1;
   return i * i * i;
}
```

when called as in

```
int j = 2;
cout << cube_plus(j + 2) << endl;
```

is equivalent to placing a block of code

```
{ int i_local = j + 2;      // call by value copy
      i_local = i_local + 1;
      return i_local * i_local * i_local;
}
```

In this example, the local variable `i_local` is initialized to 4. One is then added to the local variable, and a value of 125, or 5 cubed, is returned.

For a native type, a local copy is made and the value inside the block of the local copy is not passed back after function execution.

For class types, call-by-value requires a copy constructor. The compiler provides a copy constructor whose signature is

```
class_name::class_name(const class_name&);
```

The compiler copies by memberwise initialization. This is usually correct for simple classes that have nonpointer data members, such as `class point`. This is incorrect in other circumstances, such as for classes with members that are pointers. In many cases, the pointer is the address of an object. The act of duplicating the pointer value but not the object pointed at can lead to buggy code. This form of copying is called shallow copying. Shallow copying is wrong for classes such as `ch_stack`. In these cases, deleting the original object may cause the copied object to incorrectly disappear.

The `class ch_stack` explicitly defines its own copy constructor, as is appropriate.

In file ch_stack2.h

```
// Copy ctor for ch_stack of characters

ch_stack::ch_stack(const ch_stack& stk) :
                    max_len(stk.max_len), top(stk.top)
{
    s = new char[stk.max_len];
    assert(s != 0);
    memcpy(s, stk.s, max_len);
}
```

The *stdlib* routine `memcpy()` copies `max_len` characters from the base address `stk.s` into memory, starting at base address `s`. This is called a deep copy. The character arrays are distinct because they refer to different memory locations. If instead the body of this routine were `s = stk.s;` this would be a shallow copy, with `ch_stack` variables sharing the same representation. Any change to one variable would change the other.

Suppose that we wish to examine our stack and count the number of occurrences of a given character. We can repeatedly pop the stack, testing each element in turn, until the stack is empty. But what if we want to preserve the contents of the stack? Call-by-value parameters accomplish this.

In file ch_stack2.cpp

```
// Count the number of c's found in s

int cnt_char(char c, ch_stack s)
{
   int   count = 0;

   while (!s.empty())            // done when empty
      count += (c == s.pop());   // found a c
   return count;
}
```

In this case, the explicitly written copy constructor does a deep copy. If we had allowed the compiler to provide a default copy constructor, we would have potentially buggy code. A copy constructor is invoked when there is call-by-value of the object, return-by-value for the object, or initialization of one object by another of the same type.

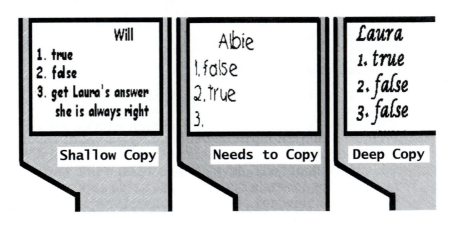

5.2 Classes with Destructors

A destructor is a member function whose name is the class name preceded by a tilde, ~. Destructors are almost always called implicitly, usually at the exit of the block in which the object was declared. They are also invoked when a `delete` operator is called on a pointer to an object having a destructor or where needed to destroy a subobject of an object being deleted.

Let us augment our `ch_stack` example with a destructor:

In file ch_stack2.h

```
// Implementation with ctors and dtor

class ch_stack {
public:
   ch_stack();                        // default ctor
   explicit ch_stack(int size) :
      max_len(size), top(EMPTY)
      { assert(size > 0); s = new char[size];
        assert(s != 0); }
   ch_stack(const stack& stk);        // copy ctor
   ch_stack(int size, const char str[]);
   ~ch_stack() { delete []s; }        // dtor
   // rest of the methods ·····
private:
   enum    { EMPTY = -1 };
   char*   s;
   int     max_len;
   int     top;
};
```

The addition of the destructor allows the class to return unneeded heap-allocated memory during program execution. All of the public member functions perform in exactly the same manner as before. However, the destructor is implicitly invoked on block and function exit to clean up storage no longer accessible.

5.3   Members That Are Class Types

In object-oriented programming (OOP) methodology, complicated objects are built from simpler objects. For example, a house is built with a foundation, rooms, and a roof. The house has a roof as a subobject. This part-whole relationship is called in OOP the HASA relationship. Complicated objects can be designed from simpler ones by incorporating them with the HASA relationship. In this section, the type `address` is used as a member of the class `person`.

In file address.cpp

```
class address {
public:
    address(string street, string city)
             :street_name(street),city_name(city) { }
    void   print() const;
    string get_street() const { return street_name; }
    string get_city() const { return city_name; }
private:
    string city_name;
    string street_name;
};

class person {
public:
    person(string n, address h);
    void print() const;
    void set_address();
private:
    address home;
    const string name;
};

person::person(string n, address h) :
                name(n), home(h) { }
```

Notice that the `person` constructor is a series of initializers. The initializers of the `address` member invoke the `address` copy constructor. Also, the methods `get_street()` and `get_city()` could be written to return a `const` reference as follows:

```
const string& get_street() const
                { return street_name; }
```

For large objects, this is more efficient, as it does not require making a copy. Making the return type `const` also keeps the user of the class from altering the data member without an access function.

5.4   Example: A Singly Linked List

The singly linked list data type is the prototype of many useful dynamic abstract data types (ADTs) called self-referential structures. These data types have pointer members that refer to objects of their own type and are the basis of many useful container classes. The following declaration implements such a type:

In file slist.cpp

```
struct slistelem {
   char       data;
   slistelem*  next;
};

class slist {                    // singly linked list
public:
   slist() : h(0) { }         // 0 denotes empty slist
   ~slist() { release(); }
   void   prepend(char c);   // adds to front of slist
   void   del();
   slistelem*  first() const { return h; }
   void   print() const;
   void   release();
private:
   slistelem*  h;             // head of slist
};
```

Singly Linked List

Note that slist is really only an interface for `slistelem*`.

Selected List Operations

1. `prepend`: Adds to front of list

2. `first`: Returns first element

3. `print`: Prints list contents

4. `del`: Deletes first element

5. `release`: Destroys list

The link member `next` points to the next `slistelem` in the list. In this example, `data` is a simple variable, but it could be replaced by a complicated type capable of storing a range of information. The constructor initializes the head of `slist` pointer h to the value 0, which is called the null-pointer constant and can be assigned to any pointer type. In linked lists, this constant typically denotes the empty list or end-of-list value. The member function `prepend()` builds the list structure as follows:

```
void slist::prepend(char c)
{
    slistelem*  temp = new slistelem;// create element

    assert(temp != 0);
    temp -> next = h;                       // link to slist
    temp -> data = c;
    h = temp;                       // update head of slist
}
```

A list element is allocated from the heap, and its data member is initialized from the single argument c. Its link member `next` is set to the old list head. The head pointer h is updated to point at this element as the new first element of the list.

The member function `del()` has the inverse role.

```
void slist::del()
{
    slistelem*  temp = h;

    h = h -> next;              // presumes nonempty slist
    delete temp;
}
```

This function returns the first element of the list to the heap by using the `delete` operator on the head of `slist` pointer h. The new head-of-list is the value of the `next` member. This function can be modified to work on the empty list without aborting.

Much of list processing consists of repetitively chaining down the list until the null-pointer value is found. The following two functions use this technique:

In file slist.cpp

```cpp
void slist::print() const        // object is unchanged
{
    slistelem*  temp = h;

    while (temp != 0) {              // detect end of slist
        cout << temp -> data << " -> ";
        temp = temp -> next;
    }
    cout << "\n###" << endl;
}

// Elements returned to the heap

void slist::release()
{
    while (h != 0)
        del();
}
```

Dissection of the `print()` and `release()` Functions

- ```cpp
  void  slist::print() const   // object is unchanged
  {
      slistelem*  temp = h;
  ```

An auxiliary pointer `temp` chains down the list. The pointer is initialized to the address of the `slist` head h. The pointer h cannot be used because its value would be lost, in effect destroying access to the list.

- ```cpp
  while (temp != 0) {              // detect end of slist
      cout << temp -> data << " -> ";
      temp = temp -> next;
  }
  ```

The value 0 is guaranteed to represent the end-of-list value because the constructor `slist::slist()` initialized it as such and the `slist::prepend()` function maintains it as the end-of-list pointer value. Notice that the internals of this loop could be changed to process the entire list in another manner.

- ```cpp
  void slist::release()
  ```

The `release` function is used to return all list elements to the heap. It does this by continually removing the head of the list until there are no more elements.
  ```

```
■ while (h != 0)
     del();
```

Each element of the list must be returned to the heap in sequence by `slist::del()`, which manipulates the hidden pointer h. Since we are destroying the list, it is unnecessary to preserve the original value of pointer h. This function is the body of the destructor `slist::~slist()`. The following incorrect destructor deletes only the first element in the list:

```
slist::~slist()
{
    delete h;
}
```

The following code demonstrates the use of this type. The destructor has been modified to print a message.

In file slist.cpp

```
slist::~slist()
{
    cout << "destructor invoked" << endl;
    release();
}

int main()
{
    slist*  p;
    {
        slist  w;
        w.prepend('A');
        w.prepend('B');
        w.print();
        w.del();
        w.print();
        p = &w;
        p -> print();
        cout << "exiting inner block" << endl;
    }
    // p -> print();  gives system-dependent behavior
    cout << "exiting outer block" << endl;
}
```

Notice that `main()` contains an inner block, which is included to test that the destructor is invoked on block exit, returning storage associated with w to the heap. The output of this program is

```
B -> A ->
###
A ->
###
A ->
###
exiting inner block
destructor invoked
exiting outer block
```

The first `print()` call prints the two-element `slist`, which stores A and B. After a `del` operation is performed, the list contains one element, which stores A. The outer block pointer to `slist` p is assigned the address of the `slist` variable w. When the list is accessed through p in the inner block, it prints A. This output shows that the destructor works at block exit on the variable w.

The behavior of the commented-out invocation of `slist::print()` is system-dependent. It is a runtime error to dereference p here because the address it refers to may have been overwritten at block exit by the deletion routine.

5.5   Strings Using Reference Semantics

Allocation at runtime of large aggregates can readily exhaust memory resources. The list example in Section 5.4, *Example: A Singly Linked List*, on page 226, shows one scheme for handling this: The system reclaims memory by traversing each list and disposing of each element. This model of reclamation is a form of garbage collection. In Java, LISP, and SmallTalk, the system itself is responsible for this reclamation. Such systems periodically invoke a garbage collector to identify all memory locations currently accessible by the executing program and reclaim those that are inaccessible. Most such schemes require traversal and marking of memory locations accessible from pointers with a computationally expensive procedure.

A disposal scheme that avoids this is reference counting, in which each dynamically allocated object tracks its active references. When an object is created, its reference count is set to 1. Every time the object is newly referenced, the reference count is incremented; every time it loses a reference, the count is decremented. When the reference count becomes 0, the object's memory is disposed of.

The following example creates a `my_string` class that has reference semantics for copying. The class uses both the *cstring* and the *assert* libraries. This class has shallow copy semantics because pointer assignment replaces copying. The techniques illustrated are common for this type of aggregate. We use the class `str_obj` to create object values. The type `str_obj` is a required implementation detail for `my_string`. It could not be directly placed in `my_string` without destroying the potential many-to-one relationship between objects of type `my_string` and referenced values of type `str_obj`. The values of `my_string` are in the class `str_obj`, which is an auxiliary class for `my_string`'s use only. The publicly used class `my_string` handles the `str_obj` instances and is called a handler class.

In file my_string.cpp

```
// Reference counted my_strings

class str_obj {
public:
   int     ref_cnt;
   char*   s;
   str_obj() : ref_cnt(1), len(0)
         { s = new char[1];
            assert(s != 0); s[0] = 0; }
   str_obj(const char* p) : ref_cnt(1)
         { len = strlen(p); s = new char[len + 1];
            assert(s != 0); strcpy(s, p); }
   ~str_obj() { delete []s; }
private:
   int  len;
};
```

The `str_obj` declares objects that are used by `my_string`. For now, we leave the data members `ref_cnt` and `s` public. They are needed in some of the methods of `class my_string`. We explain later how data members can be made private and accessed using the `friend` mechanism. Notice how the `str_obj` class is used for construction and destruction of objects using the heap. On construction of a `str_obj`, the `ref_cnt` variable is initialized to 1.

```
class my_string {
public:
   my_string() { st = new str_obj; assert(st != 0); }
   my_string(const char* p)
      { st = new str_obj(p); assert(st != 0); }
   my_string(const my_string& str)
       { st = str.st; st -> ref_cnt++; }
   ~my_string();
   void  assign(const my_string& str);
   void  print() const { cout << st -> s; }
private:
   str_obj*  st;
};

my_string::~my_string()
{
   if (--st -> ref_cnt == 0)
      delete st;
}

void my_string::assign(const my_string& str)
{
   if (str.st != st) {
      if (--st -> ref_cnt == 0)
         delete st;
      st = str.st;
      st -> ref_cnt++;
   }
}
```

Dissection of the `my_string` Class

■ `str_obj(const char* p) : ref_cnt(1)`
   `{ len = strlen(p); s = new char[len + 1];`
   `assert(s != 0); strcpy(s, p); }`

This constructor initialized the `ref_cnt` variable to 1. It used the *cstring* library function `strcpy()` to copy the characters in the string. It needs an internal array s of length `len + 1`, because the last character stored is the null character \0.

■ `my_string() { st = new str_obj; assert(st != 0); }`

The default constructor creates a `str_obj` and asserts that `new` worked. Recall that this is tested by checking that the assigned pointer value is not 0.

■ `my_string(const char* p)`
```
     { st = new str_obj(p); assert(st != 0); }
```

This C-style string constructor relies on the conversion constructor in `str_obj`.

■ `my_string(const my_string& str)`
```
     { st = str.st; st -> ref_cnt++; }
```

The copy constructor is particularly efficient. It is here that you see shallow copying. Only the pointer value, an address, is copied, and the reference count is incremented. In a deep copy, the entire string, character by character, needs to be copied. This requires space and time proportional to the length of the string.

■ `my_string::~my_string()`
```
{
    if (--st -> ref_cnt == 0)
    delete st;
}
```

The destructor acts when `ref_cnt` of the associated `str_obj` goes to 0. Otherwise, `my_string` variables still reference the underlying `str_obj` representation.

■ `void my_string::assign(const my_string& str)`
```
{
    if (str.st != st) {
        if (--st -> ref_cnt == 0)
            delete st;
        st = str.st;
        st -> ref_cnt++;
    }
}
```

The semantics of `assign()` show some of the subtleties of using reference counting. The assignment occurs if the `my_string` is not being assigned its same value. The assignment causes the assigned variable to lose its previous value. This is equivalent to decrementing the reference count of the pointed-at `str_obj` value. Whenever an object's reference count is decremented, it gets tested for deletion. The advantage of this over normal copying is clear. A very large aggregate is copied by reference, using a few operations and a small amount of storage for the reference counter. Also, each possible change to a pointer adds a reference-count operation. The destructor must also test the reference count before deletion.

Don't shut me off, fool. There are still 3 users attached!

5.6   Constructor Issues and Mysteries

Object creation for native types is usually the task of the compiler. The writer of a class wishes to achieve the same ease of use for the class. Let us reexamine some issues in simple terms. Does every class need an explicitly defined constructor? Of course not. If no constructor is written by the programmer, the compiler provides a default constructor, if needed.

In file tracking.cpp

```cpp
// Personal data tracking

struct pers_data {
   int   age;         // in years
   int   weight;      // in kilograms
   int   height;      // in centimeters
   char  name[20];    // last name
};

void print(pers_data d)
{
   cout << d.name << " is " << d.age
        << " years old\n";
   cout << "weight : " << d.weight
        << "kg,  height : " << d.height << "cm."
        << endl;
}
```

```
int main()
{
    pers_data  laura = { 3, 14, 88, "POHL" };
                        // construction off the stack

    print(laura);       // calls copy ctor
}
```

What if we use constructors and allow the copy constructor to be provided by the compiler? Recall that this means that the copy constructor does member-by-member copy, which can result in the wrong semantics—namely, shallow copy semantics—in which no new value is created; instead, a pointer variable is assigned the address of the existing value.

Take the case of reference semantics, whereby a copy implies that the reference counter is incremented. This does not happen with the compiler-provided copy constructor. Thus, objects copied in this manner are undercounted and prematurely returned to the heap. As a rule of thumb, the class provider should explicitly write out the copy constructor unless it is self-evident that memberwise copy is safe. Be cautious if the aggregate has any pointer-based members.

The union data type is little used in C++ and need not be studied at first. Recall, it is a `struct`-like type in which the members share the same memory. This means that the same storage can be interpreted as different types without using a cast. There are special rules for unions. This should not be surprising, since unions are a technique for having various objects share space. Unions cannot have members that have constructors or destructors, nor can they have `static` data members. Anonymous unions can have only `public` data members, and a global anonymous union must be declared `static`.

5.6.1 Destructor Details

A destructor is implicitly invoked when an object goes out of scope. Common cases include block exit and function exit.

```
my_string sub_str(char c, my_string b)
{
    my_string  temp;
    .....
    return temp;
}
```

In `sub_str()`, we have `b`, a call-by-value argument of type `my_string`. Therefore, the copy constructor is invoked to create a local copy when the function is invoked. Correspondingly, a destructor is called on function exit. A local `my_string` variable, `temp`, is constructed on block entry to this function and therefore must have its destructor invoked on block exit. Finally, the `return` argument must be constructed and passed back into the calling environment. The corresponding destructor is invoked, depending on the scope of the object to which it is assigned.

5.6.2 Constructor Pragmatics

In constructors, initialization is preferred to assignment:

```
ch_stack::ch_stack(int size)
    { s = new char[size]; assert(s != 0);
      max_len = size; top = EMPTY; }
```

is better written as

```
ch_stack::ch_stack(int size) : max_len(size),
top(EMPTY)
    { s = new char[size]; assert(s != 0); }
```

The compiler is often more efficient about initialization. Initialization order follows declaration order inside the class and not the ordering of the initializer list.

In classes that use `new` to construct objects, a copy constructor should be explicitly provided. The default compiler-provided copy constructor usually has the wrong semantics for such an object. Usual practice is to provide a default and a copy constructor with any class that uses pointers in its implementation. As we shall see in Section 5.14, *Overloading the Assignment Operator*, on page 250, such classes should have their own explicit definition of `operator=()`. This ensures that copying and assignment are done safely.

5.7   Polymorphism Using Function Overloading

Polymorphism is a means of giving different meanings to the same function name or operator, dependent on context. The appropriate meaning is selected on the basis of the type of data being processed. We have encountered one form of polymorphism when writing expressions of mixed type. Depending on the type of the operands, the division operator on native types might be either an integer division or a floating-point division.

Object orientation takes advantage of polymorphism by linking behavior to the object's type. Operators, such as + and <<, have distinct meanings overloaded by operand type. For example, the expression `cout << x` is by convention expected to display an appropriate representation of `x`, depending on the type of object `x`.

Overloading of functions gives the same function name different meanings. The name has several interpretations that depend on function selection. This is called ad hoc polymorphism. The remainder of this chapter discusses overloading, especially operator overloading, and conversions of data types.

Operators are overloaded and selected based on the signature-matching algorithm. Overloading operators gives them new meanings. For example, the meaning of the expression `a + b` differs depending on the types of the variables `a` and `b`. Overloading the operator + for user-defined types allows them to be used in addition expressions in much the same way native types are used. The expression `a + b` could mean string concatenation, complex-number addition, or integer addition, depending on whether the variables were the user-defined ADT `my_string`, the standard library class `complex`, or the native type `int`. Mixed-type expressions are also made possible by defining conversion functions.

One principle of OOP is that user-defined types must enjoy the same privileges as native types. Where the C++ standard library adds the complex number type, the programmer expects the convenience of using it without regard to a native/nonnative distinction. Operator overloading and user-defined conversions let us use complex numbers in much the same way as we can use `int` or `double`.

Later, we will discuss two other powerful forms of polymorphism, namely, parametric polymorphism using templates and pure polymorphism using virtual functions.

5.8   ADT Conversions

Explicit type conversion of an expression is necessary when either the implicit conversions are not desired or the expression is not otherwise legal. One aim of OOP using C++ is the integration of user-defined ADTs and built-in types. To achieve this, C++ makes a constructor of one argument a type conversion from the argument's type to the constructor's class type. For example,

```
point::point(double u);
```

is automatically a type conversion from `double` to `point`, unless it is disabled by declaring such a conversion constructor with the modifier `explicit`. The conversion is available both explicitly and implicitly. Explicitly, it is used as a conversion operation in either cast or functional form. Thus,

```
point    s;
double   d = 3.5;

s = static_cast<point>(d);
```

and

```
s = d;              // implicit invocation of conversion
```

both work.

These are conversions from an already defined type to a user-defined type. However, it is not possible for the user to add a constructor to a built-in type such as `int` or `double`. A conversion function for a user-defined type can be created by defining a special conversion function inside the class. The general form of such a member function is

```
operator type() { ····· }
```

Such a member function must be nonstatic, cannot have parameters, and does not have a declared return type. It must return an expression of the designated type.

In the `point` example, one may want a conversion from `point` to `double`. This can be done for the `point` class, as follows:

```
point::operator double()   // use distance from origin
{
    return sqrt(x * x + y * y);
}
```

Notice that we used a specific conversion that is by no means unique or universally understood. Another possibility is to return the x value only. A class having a particular meaning for a conversion should be fully documented and intended for custom use. When such a class is intended for general use, it is best to omit such conversions, as they can readily lead to unintended results.

5.9   Overloading and Signature Matching

Overloaded functions are an important polymorphic mechanism in C++. The overloaded meaning is selected by matching the argument list of the function call to the argument list of the function declaration. When an overloaded function is invoked, the compiler must have a selection algorithm with which to pick the appropriate function. The algorithm that accomplishes this depends on what type conversions are available and is called the signature matching algorithm. A best match must be unique, must be best on at least one argument, and must be as good as any other match on all other arguments. The following list shows the signature matching algorithm for each argument.

Basic Signature Matching Algorithm

1. Use an exact match if found.

2. Try standard type promotions.

3. Try standard type conversions.

4. Try user-defined conversions.

5. Use a match to ellipsis if found.

Standard promotions—conversions from `float` to `double` and from `bool`, `char`, `short`, or `enum` to `int`—are better than other standard conversions. Standard conversions also include pointer conversions.

An exact match is clearly best. Casts can be used to force such a match. The compiler complains about ambiguous situations. Thus, it is poor programming practice to rely on subtle type distinctions and implicit conversions that obscure the overloaded function. When in doubt, use explicit conversions to provide an exact match.

Let us write an overloaded function `greater()` and follow our algorithm for various invocations. In this example, the user type `rational` is available.

In file rational.cpp

```
// Overloading functions

class rational {
public:
   rational(int n = 0) : a(n), q(1) { }
   rational(int i, int j) : a(i), q(j) { }
   rational(double r) : a(static_cast<long>(r * BIG)),
                        q(BIG) { }
   void  print() const { cout << a << " / " << q; }
   operator double()
             { return static_cast<double>(a) / q; }
private:
   long  a, q;
   enum { BIG = 100 };
};
```

```
inline int     greater(int i, int j)
      { return (i > j ? i : j); }
inline double  greater(double x, double y)
      { return (x > y ? x : y); }
inline rational greater(rational w, rational z)
      { return (w > z ? w : z); }

int main()
{
   int     i = 10, j = 5;
   float   x = 7.0;
   double  y = 14.5;
   rational w(10), z(3.5), zmax;

   cout << "\ngreater(" << i << ", " << j << ") = "
        << greater(i, j);
   cout << "\ngreater(" << x << ", " << y << ") = "
        << greater(x, y);
   cout << "\ngreater(" << i << ", ";
   z.print();
   cout << ") = "
        << greater(static_cast<rational>(i), z);
   zmax = greater(w, z);
   cout << "\ngreater(";
   w.print();
   cout << ", ";
   z.print();
   cout << ") = ";
   zmax.print();
   cout << endl;
}
```

The output from this program is

```
greater(10, 5) = 10
greater(7, 14.5) = 14.5
greater(10, 350 / 100) = 10
greater(10 / 1, 350 / 100) = 10 / 1
```

A variety of conversion rules, both implicit and explicit, are being applied.

Dissection of the *rational* Program

■ `rational(double r) : a(static_cast<long>(r * BIG)),`
                        `q(BIG) { }`

This constructor converts from `double` to `rational`.

■ `operator double()`
        `{ return static_cast<double>(a) / q; }`

This member function converts from `rational` to `double`. This is only approximately an arithmetically correct conversion.

■ `inline int      greater(int i, int j)`
    `{ return (i > j ? i : j); }`
`inline double  greater(double x, double y)`
    `{ return (x > y ? x : y); }`
`inline rational greater(rational w, rational z)`
    `{ return w > z ? w : z); }`

Three distinct functions are overloaded. The most interesting has `rational` type for its argument list variables and its return type. The conversion member function `operator double()` is required to evaluate `w > z`. Later, we shall show how to overload `operator>()` to take `rational` types directly.

■ `cout << "\ngreater(" << i << ", " << j << ") = "`
    `<< greater(i, j);`
`cout << "\ngreater(" << x << ", " << y << ") = "`
    `<< greater(x, y);`

The first statement selects the first definition of `greater()` because of the exact-match rule. The second statement selects the second definition because of a standard widening promotion `float` to `double` where variable x is widened to `double`.

■ `<< greater(static_cast<rational>(i), z);`

The third definition of `greater()` is selected because of the best-match rule. The explicit conversion of i to a `rational` is necessary to avoid ambiguity. Then the `rational` is implicitly converted to `double`.

■ `zmax = greater(w, z);`

This is an exact match for the third definition.

5.10 Friend Functions

The keyword `friend` is a function specifier that gives a nonmember function access to the hidden members of the class and provides a method of escaping the data-hiding restrictions of C++. However, we must have a good reason for escaping these restrictions, as they are important to reliable programming.

One reason for using friend functions is that some functions need privileged access to more than one class. A second reason is that friend functions pass all of their arguments through the argument list, and each argument value is subject to assignment-compatible conversions. Conversions apply to a class variable passed explicitly and are especially useful in cases of operator overloading, as seen in the next section.

A friend function must be declared inside the class declaration to which it is a friend. The function is prefaced by the keyword `friend` and can appear in any part of the class without affecting its meaning. The preferred style is to place the `friend` declaration in the public part of the class. Since access has no effect on `friend` declarations, they are conceptually public. A `friend` function to one class could be a private member of another class, and hence not be public. Member functions of one class can be friend functions of another class. In this case, they are written in the `friend`'s class, using the scope resolution operator to qualify its function name. In order to specify that all member functions of one class are friend functions of a second class, write `friend class` *class-name*.

The following declarations illustrate the syntax:

```
void alice()
{
   // use some private stuff from tweedledee
   .....
      cout << "Have some more tea.\n";
}
class tweedledee {
   .....
      friend void  alice();        // friend function
      int  cheshire();             // member function
   .....
};
```

```
class tweedledum {
   .....
   // friend member function
   friend int  tweedledee::cheshire();
   .....
};
class tweedledumber {
   .....
   // all member functions of tweedledee have access
   friend class tweedledee;
   .....
};
```

The global function `alice()` has access to all members of `tweedledee`. The member function `tweedledee::cheshire()` is given access to all the members of `tweedledum`. All member functions of `tweedledee` are given access to all the members of `tweedledumber`.

Tweedledee
and
Tweedledum

by
Sir John
Tenniel
(1820-1914)

Let us revisit our implementation of `my_string` and make the data variables private. This is appropriate, as objects should hide their implementation.

In file my_string.cpp

```
class str_obj {
public:
    friend class my_string;// my_string access members
    str_obj() : len(0), ref_cnt(1)
        { s = new char[1]; assert(s != 0); s[0] = 0; }
    str_obj(const char* p) : ref_cnt(1)
        { len = strlen(p); s = new char[len + 1];
            assert(s != 0); strcpy(s, p); }
    ~str_obj() { delete []s; }
private:
    int    len, ref_cnt;
    char*  s;
};
```

The `friend` declaration gives `my_string` privileged access to the private members of `str_obj`. Its member functions would not otherwise be able to use the variables `ref_cnt` and `s`.

The OOP paradigm is that objects (in C++, class variables) should be accessed through their public members. Only member functions should have access to the hidden implementation of the ADT. This is a neat, orderly design principle. The friend function, however, straddles this boundary. The friend function has access to private members but is not itself a member function. The friend function can be used to provide quick fixes to code that needs access to the implementation details of a class. But the mechanism is easily abused.

5.11   Overloading Operators

The keyword `operator` is used to define a type-conversion member function, as well as to overload the built-in C++ operators. Just as a function name such as `print()` can be given a variety of meanings depending on its arguments, so can an operator such as + be given additional meanings. Overloading operators allows infix expressions of both ADTs and built-in types to be written. In many instances, this important notational convenience leads to shorter, more readable programs.

Unary and binary operators can be overloaded as nonstatic member functions. Implicitly, they are acting on a class value. Most unary operators can be overloaded as ordinary functions, taking a single argument of class or reference-to-class type. Most binary operators can be overloaded as ordinary functions, taking one or both arguments of class or reference-to-class type. The operators =, ( ),

[ ], and -> must be overloaded with a nonstatic member function. Here, we expand our `rational` class from Section 5.9, *Overloading and Signature Matching*, on page 239.

In file rational.cpp

```
// Overloading operators

class rational {
public:
    friend bool operator>(rational w, rational z);
};

bool operator>(rational w, rational z)
{
    return (static_cast<double>(w.a) / w.q >
            static_cast<double>(z.a) / z.q);
}
```

Although meanings can be added to operators, their associativity and precedence remain the same. For example, the multiplication operator remains of higher precedence than the addition operator. Almost all operators can be overloaded. The exceptions are the member operator `.`, the member object selector `.*`, the ternary conditional expression operator `? :`, the `sizeof` operator, and the scope resolution operator `::`.

Available operators include all of the arithmetic, logical, comparison, equality, assignment, and bit operators. Furthermore, the increment and decrement operators, ++ and --, can have distinct prefix and postfix meanings. The subscript or index operator [] and the function call () can also be overloaded. The structure pointer operator -> and the member pointer selector operator ->* can be overloaded. It is also possible to overload `new` and `delete`. The assignment, function call, subscripting, and class pointer operators can be overloaded only by nonstatic member functions.

5.12 Unary Operator Overloading

To continue the discussion of operator overloading, we demonstrate how to overload unary operators, such as !, ++, ~ and []. For this purpose, we develop the class `my_clock`, which can be used to store time as days, hours, minutes, and seconds. We shall develop familiar operations on `my_clock`.

In file my_clock.cpp

```cpp
class my_clock {
public:
   my_clock(unsigned long i = 0);// ctor & conversion
   my_clock set(unsigned long i = 0);
   void   print() const;          // formatted printout
   void   tick();                 // add one second
   my_clock operator++() { tick(); return *this; }
private:
   unsigned long   tot_secs, secs, mins, hours, days;
};

inline my_clock::my_clock(unsigned long i) :
         tot_secs(i), secs(i % 60),
         mins ((i / 60) % 60),
         hours((i / 3600) % 24),
         days(i / 86400) { }

my_clock my_clock::set(unsigned long i)
{
   tot_secs = i;
   secs = i % 60;
   mins = (i / 60) % 60;
   hours = (i / 3600) % 24;
   days = i / 86400;
   return *this;
}

void my_clock::tick()
{
   *this = static_cast<my_clock>(++tot_secs);
}

void my_clock::print() const
{
   cout << days << " d :" << hours << " h :"
        << mins << " m :" << secs << " s" << endl;
}
```

Dissection of the `my_clock` Class

- ```
  inline my_clock::my_clock(unsigned long i) :
        tot_secs(i), secs(i % 60),
        mins ((i / 60) % 60),
        hours((i / 3600) % 24),
        days(i / 86400) { }
  ```

This is both the default constructor and the conversion constructor from `unsigned long` to `my_clock`. It is the default constructor because inside the class it is declared as

```
my_clock(unsigned long i = 0);
```

Therefore, if no argument is passed into the constructor, everything is set to 0. Notice also that there are conversion opportunities for any type convertible to `unsigned long`. So an ordinary `int` or a `double` would also convert where necessary to a `my_clock` time.

- ```
  my_clock my_clock::set(unsigned long i)
  {
      tot_secs = i;
      secs = i % 60;
      mins = (i / 60) % 60;
      hours = (i / 3600) % 24;
      days = i / 86400;
      return *this;
  }
  ```

This `set()` function mimics the constructor logic. It cannot use the special initializing syntax allowed of constructors.

- ```
  void my_clock::tick()
  { *this = static_cast<my_clock>(++tot_secs); }
  ```

The member function advances the `my_clock` time by 1 second. We could have, after adding 1 to `tot_secs`, used the `set()` method to recompute time. But here we use some of the sophistication found in C++. The cast expression causes the conversion constructor to properly compute `my_clock` time. The use of assignment to the dereferenced self-referential pointer `this` is a common idiom when the code needs to affect the entire object. This is a subtle concept and one you should study carefully.

- ```
  my_clock operator++() { tick(); return *this; }
  ```

The overloaded `operator++()` also updates the implicit `my_clock` variable and returns the updated value as well. The return of the dereferenced `this` pointer is needed to return the proper `my_clock` value. Note that `operator ++()` always denotes the prefix version.

Let us test this class to check that everything works.

In file my_clock.cpp

```
// my_clock and overloaded operators

int main()
{
    my_clock  t1(59), t2(172799); // t2=2 days-1 sec

    cout << "initial times are" << endl;
    t1.print();
    t2.print();
    ++t1; // invokes the overloaded member function
    ++t2;
    cout << "after one second times are" << endl;
    t1.print();
    t2.print();
}
```

The output is

```
initial times are
0 d :0 h :0 m :59 s
1 d :23 h :59 m :59 s
after one second times are
0 d :0 h :1 m :0 s
2 d :0 h :0 m :0 s
```

It is also possible to overload prefix ++ using an ordinary function.

```
my_clock operator++(my_clock& cl)
{
    cl.tick();
    return cl;
}
```

Notice that the `my_clock` variable must advance by 1 second, so we can use call-by-reference to accommodate this change.

The decision to choose between a member function representation and a nonmember function typically depends on whether implicit conversion operations are available and desirable. Explicit argument passing allows the argument to be automatically coerced, if necessary and possible. When overloaded as a member function, `++c` is equivalent to `c.operator++()`, and implicit conversions to `c` do not happen. When overloaded as a nonmember function, `++c` is equivalent to `operator++(c)`. This allows implicit conversions to `c`. See exercise 21 on page 276 on how to overload the postfix versions of the increment and decrement operators.

5.13   Binary Operator Overloading

We continue with our `my_clock` example and show how to overload binary operators. The same principles hold: When a binary operator is overloaded using a member function, it has as its first argument the implicitly passed class variable and as its second argument the lone argument-list parameter. Friend functions and ordinary functions have both arguments specified in the parameter list. Of course, ordinary functions cannot access private members.

Let us create an addition operation for type `my_clock` that adds two values:

In file my_clock.cpp

```
class my_clock {
    .....
    friend my_clock operator+(my_clock c1,
                              my_clock c2);
};
my_clock operator+(my_clock c1, my_clock c2)
{
    return (c1.tot_secs + c2.tot_secs);
}
```

The `int` return expression is implicitly converted to a `my_clock` by the conversion constructor `my_clock::my_clock(unsigned long)`. Both `my_clock` values are passed as function arguments, and both are candidates for assignment conversions. Because `operator+()` is a symmetric binary operator, the arguments should be treated identically. Thus, it is normal for symmetric binary operators to be over-loaded by friend functions.

In contrast, let us overload binary minus with a member function:

```
class my_clock {
    .....
    my_clock  operator-(my_clock c);
};
my_clock my_clock::operator-(my_clock c)
{
    return (tot_secs - c.tot_secs);
}
```

Remember that there is an implicit first argument. This takes some getting used to. It is better to use a friend function for binary minus because of the symmetric treatment of the arguments.

We define a multiplication operation as a binary operation, with one argument an `unsigned long` and the second a `my_clock` variable. The operation requires the use of a friend function. It cannot be done with a member function because, as was already stated, member functions have as their implicit first argument the `this` pointer.

```
my_clock operator*(unsigned long m, my_clock c)
{
    return (m * c.tot_secs);
}
```

This requirement forces the multiplication to have a fixed ordering that is type-dependent. In order to avoid this, it is common practice to write a second overloaded function. The second function is defined in terms of the first, as follows:

```
my_clock operator*(my_clock c, unsigned long m)
{
    return (m * c);
}
```

Defining the second implementation in terms of the first implementation reduces code redundancy and maintains consistency.

5.14 Overloading the Assignment Operator

The assignment operator for a class type is by default generated by the compiler to have member-by-member assignment. This is fine for many user-defined types such as `rational` or `point`. For types such as `my_string` and `slist`, which need deep copying, this is incorrect. As a rule of thumb, anytime a class needs an explicit copy constructor defined, it also needs an assignment operator defined. As we have seen with copy constructors, this is usually the case when the object allocates its own memory.

We augment `my_string` with an assignment operator. This is in accord with the OOP design principle that user-defined types should have the look and feel of native objects. The class programmer can specify the behavior of assignment by overloading it. It is good style to be consistent with standard usage. The following member function overloads assignment for class `my_string`:

In file my_string.cpp

```cpp
my_string& my_string::operator=(const my_string& str)
{
    if (str.st != st) {
        if (--st -> ref_cnt == 0)
            delete st;
        st = str.st;
        st -> ref_cnt++;
    }
    return *this;
}
```

Dissection of the `my_string::operator=()` Function

■ `my_string& my_string::operator=`
        `(const my_string& str)`

The `operator=()` function returns reference to `my_string` and has one explicit argument of type reference to `my_string`. The first argument of the assignment operator is the implicit argument. If the function had been written to return `void`, it would not have allowed multiple assignment.

```
■ if (str.st != st) {
```

This tests for the case a = a, in other words, self-assignment. Don't do anything if assignment is to the current variable.

```
■ if (--st -> ref_cnt == 0)
      delete st;
```

This implements reference-counting semantics. The old value of the left-hand variable is reduced in reference count by 1, which can cause its underlying string representation to be deleted.

```
■ st = str.st;
  st -> ref_cnt++;
```

The right-hand side of the assignment str.st is the new left-hand side string representation.

```
■ return *this;
```

The self-referential pointer is dereferenced and passed back as the value of the expression. This allows multiple assignment with right-to-left associativity to be defined.

The preceding definition of assignment allows ordinary and multiple assignment of my_string objects. Here are some examples:

```
// Code fragment using overloaded assignment

my_string  a, b("do "), c("do not "), d;

a = b;             // a is now "do "
d = b = c;         // these are "do not "
c = "do not but";  // invoke conversion ctor
d = c.assign(b);   // illegal-assign() returns void
d += c;            // illegal even if + exists
```

Notice that overloading both the assignment and plus operators does not imply that operator+= is overloaded. Indeed, it is the class designer's responsibility to make sure that the various operators have consistent semantics. It is customary to overload related sets of operators consistently.

Note, when the assignment operator and the copy constructor are not needed, they can be diabled by declaring them without definitions in the private section of a class. If necessary, they can be coded later, if required.

5.15 Overloading the Subscript Operator

The subscripting operator is usually overloaded where a class type represents an aggregate for which indexing is appropriate. The index operation is expected to return a reference to an element contained within the aggregate. Overloading assignment and subscripting share several characteristics. Both must be done as nonstatic member functions, and both usually involve a reference return type.

An overloaded subscript operator can have any return type and any argument list type. However, it is good style to maintain the consistency between a user-defined meaning and standard usage. Thus, the most common function prototype is

element-type& `operator[]`(*integral type*);

Such functions can be used on either side of an assignment. Let us continue with our `my_string` example. We overload `operator[]` to return the reference to the ith character in the `my_string`. If there is no such character, the reference to the null string character is returned.

In file my_string.cpp

```
char& my_string::operator[](int position)
{
   char* s = st -> s;
   for (int i = 0; i != position; ++i) {
      if (*s == 0)
         break;
      s++;
   }
   return *s;
}
```

5.16 Overloading Operator () for Indexing

The function call operator () can be overloaded as a nonstatic member function with respect to various signatures. It is frequently used to provide an operation requiring multiple indices. For example, we can code a substring operation for `my_string` by overloading as a member function `my_string::operator()`. It has two arguments so that `my_string(from, to)` returns a substring, with `from` being the beginning of the substring and `to` the end.

```
my_string my_string::operator()(int from, int to)
{
    my_string temp(to - from + 1);

    for (int i = from; i < to + 1; ++i)
        temp.st -> s[i - from] = st -> s[i];
    temp.st[to - from + 1] = 0;
    return temp;
}
```

It is also possible to use the function call operator to develop other methods requiring multiple arguments. For example:

```
// Search substring for the character c
// and return true if it is found and false if not

bool my_string::operator()(int from, int to, char c)
```

5.17   Overloading << and >>

In keeping with the spirit of OOP, it is important to overload << to output user-defined types. The operator << has two arguments—an ostream& and the ADT—and must produce an **ostream&**. Whenever overloading << or >>, you want to use a reference to a stream and return a reference to a stream, because you do not want to copy a stream object. Let us write these functions for the type `rational`:

In file rational.cpp

```
class rational {
public:
    friend ostream&
        operator<<(ostream& out, const rational& x);
    friend istream& operator>>(istream& in,rational& x);
    .....
private:
    long  a, q;
};

ostream& operator<<(ostream& out, const rational& x)
{
    return (out << x.a << " / " << x.q << '\t');
}
```

When the operator >> is overloaded to produce input to a user-defined type, its typical form is

```
istream& operator>>(istream& p, user-defined type& x)
```

I wanted to make "rational" be a more complete ADT, so I overloaded "<<" to operate on my "rational" data type. Now I just use a regular "cout" statement and voila! The output is just what I wanted.

If the function needs access to private members of x, it must be made a friend of its class. A key point is to make x a reference parameter so that its value can be modified. To do this for `rational` requires placing a `friend` declaration for this operator in the class `rational` and providing its function definition.

```
istream& operator>>(istream& in, rational& x)
{
    return (in >> x.a >> x.q);
}
```

You can improve on this input function by allowing it to read the input a/q where the "/" acts a separator for the two integer values.

5.18   Overloading ->

The structure pointer operator -> is overloaded as a nonstatic class member function. The overloaded structure pointer operator is a unary operator on its left operand. The argument must be either a class object or a reference of this type. The function should return a pointer to a class object, an object of a class for which `operator ->` is defined, or a reference to a class for which `operator ->` is defined. The idea is to provide additional functionality to a pointer type. This type of object is a smart pointer. This technique is used for implementing the proxy design pattern.

One smart pointer

We overload the structure pointer operator inside class t_ptr in the following example. Objects of type t_ptr act as controlled-access pointers to objects of type triple. The template class auto_ptr is an example of a smart pointer that is defined in the standard library.

In file triple.cpp

```
// Overloading the structure pointer operator

class triple {
public:
   triple(int a, int b, int c) : i(a), j(b), k(c) { }
   void print() const { cout << "i = " << i
                          << ", j = " << j << ", k = "
                          << k << endl; }
private:
   int  i, j, k;
};

triple   unauthor(0, 0, 0);
class t_ptr {
public:
   t_ptr(bool f, triple* p) : access(f), ptr(p) { }
   triple*  operator ->();
private:
   bool  access;
   triple*  ptr;
};
```

```
triple* t_ptr::operator->()
{
    if (access)
        return ptr;
    else {
        cout << "unauthorized access" << endl;
        return &unauthor;
    }
}
```

The overloaded operator -> tests the variable `t_ptr::access`. If it is `true`, access is granted. The following code illustrates this:

```
int main()
{
    triple  a(1, 2, 3), b(4, 5, 6);
    t_ptr ta(false, &a), tb(true, &b);

    ta -> print();          // access denied
    tb -> print();          // access granted
}
```

The output of this program is

```
unauthorized access
i = 0, j = 0, k = 0
i = 4, j = 5, k = 6
```

5.19 Overloading new and delete

Most classes involve free-store memory allocation and deallocation. Sometimes, more sophisticated use of memory than is provided by simple calls to operators new and `delete` is needed for efficiency or robustness.

Operator new has the general form

$::_{opt}$ new $placement_{opt}$ *type* $initializer_{opt}$

Some examples are

```
::new char[10];         // insist on global new
new(buff) X(a);         // call with buff using X::X(a)
```

Up to now, we have been using the global operator new() to allocate free store. The system provides a sizeof(*type*) argument to this function implicitly. Its function prototype is

```
void* operator new(size_t size);
```

The operators new and delete can be overloaded. This feature provides a simple mechanism for user-defined manipulation of the heap. For example, traditional C programming uses malloc() to access the heap and to return a void* pointer to the allocated memory. In this scheme, memory is deallocated by the *stdlib* function free(). We use operator overloading of new and delete to allow an X object to use C's traditional free-store management.

```
class X {
public:
    void* operator new(size_t size)
        { return (malloc(size)); }
    void  operator delete(void* ptr) { free(ptr); }
    X(size_t size);
    ~X() { delete(p); }
    .....
private:
    char* p;
};

X::X(size_t size)
{
    p = reinterpret_cast<char*>(operator new(size));
    assert(p!= 0);
}
```

In this example, the class X has provided overloaded forms of new() and delete(). When a class overloads operator new(), the global operator is still accessible using the scope resolution operator ::.

One reason to overload these operators is to give them additional semantics, such as providing diagnostic information or being more fault-tolerant. Also, the class can have a more efficient memory-allocation scheme than that provided by the system.

The placement syntax provides a comma-separated argument list used to select an overloaded operator new() with a matching signature. These additional arguments are often used to place the constructed object at a particular address. This form of operator new uses the *new* library.

```
// Placement syntax and new overloaded

char*  buf1 = new char[1000];    // in place of heap
char*  buf2 = new char[1000];
```

```
class object {
public:
   .....
private:
   .....
};

int main()
{
   object *p = new(buf1) object;   // allocate at buf1
   object *q = new(buf2) object;   // allocate at buf2
   .....
}
```

This placement syntax allows an arbitrary signature for the overloaded `new` operator. This signature—which is distinct from the initializer argument—calls `new` to select an appropriate constructor.

The `delete` operator comes in two flavors. There are two possible signatures:

```
void operator delete(void* p);
void operator delete(void* p, size_t);
```

The first signature makes no provision for the number of bytes to be returned by `delete`; in this case, the programmer provides code that supplies this value. The second signature includes a `size_t` argument passed to the `delete` invocation. This argument is provided by the compiler as the size of the object pointed at by `p`. Only one form of `delete` can be provided as a static member function in each class. These class `new()` and `delete()` member functions are always implicitly static. The `new()` is invoked before the object exists and therefore cannot have a `this` yet. The `delete()` is called by the destructor, so the object is already destroyed.

It is possible to explicitly call a destructor:

```
p = new my_string("I don't need you long");
    // invokes my_string::my_string(const char*);
.....
p -> ~my_string(); // or p -> my_string::~my_string()
.....              // but delete p strongly preferred
```

This is most often done when `new` is used with placement.

5.20   More Signature Matching

Rules for signature matching are given in simplified form in Section 5.9, *Overloading and Signature Matching*, on page 238. A further clarification of these rules with examples is given here.

For a given argument, a best match is always an exact match. An exact match also includes trivial conversions. These are shown in Table 5.1 for type T.

Table 5.1 Trivial Conversions	
From	**To**
T*	const T*
T*	volatile T*

The use of `volatile` is specialized. It means that a variable can be modified external to the program code. So a variable representation of an address that gets data from an external device, such as a real-time clock, would be `volatile`. Also, `volatile` is used to suppress compiler optimizations that involve such variables.

It is important to remember that user-defined conversions include constructors of a single argument that can be implicitly called to perform conversions from the argument type to their class type. This can happen for assignment conversions, as in the argument-matching algorithm. The following example is modified from the one in Section 5.12, *Unary Operator Overloading*, on page 245:

In file my_clock.cpp

```
// Modify my_clock program

class my_clock {
public:
    my_clock(unsigned long i);// ctor & conversion
    void   print() const;      // formatted printout
    void   tick();             // add one second
    my_clock  operator++()
        { tick(); return *this; }
    void   reset(const my_clock& c);
private:
    unsigned long  tot_secs, secs, mins, hours, days;
};
```

```
void my_clock::reset(const my_clock& c)
{
    tot_secs = c.tot_secs;
    secs = c.secs;
    mins = c.mins;
    hours = c.hours;
    days = c.days;
}

int main()
{
    my_clock  c1(900), c2(400);
    .....
    c1.reset(c2);
    c2.reset(100);
    .....
}
```

The call to `reset(100)` involves an argument match between `int` and `my_clock` that is a user-defined conversion invoking the constructor `my_clock(unsigned)`. Where these conversions are unintended, `explicit` can be used in declaring the constructor to disable its use as an implicit conversion.

5.21 Software Engineering: When to Use Overloading

Explicitly casting arguments can be both an aid to documentation and a useful way to avoid poorly understood conversion sequences. It is not an admission of ignorance to cast or to parenthesize arguments or expressions that otherwise could be converted or evaluated properly.

Operator overloading is easily misused. Do not overload operators when doing so can lead to misinterpretation. Typically, operator overloading is appropriate when there is a widely used notation that conforms to your overloading, such as complex arithmetic. Also, overload related operators in a manner consistent with C++ community expectations. For example, the relational operators <, >, <=, and >= should all be meaningful and provide expected inverse behaviors.

Generally speaking, overload symmetric binary operators, such as +, *, ==, !=, and &&, with friend functions. Both arguments are then passed as ordinary parameters, which subjects them to the same rules of parameter passing. Recall that using a member function to provide overloading for symmetric binary operators causes the first argument to be passed via the `this` pointer.

Anytime a class uses `new` to construct objects, it should provide an explicitly overloaded `operator=()`. This advice is analogous to our rule that such a class provide an explicit copy constructor. The compiler-provided default assignment operator semantics in most cases result in spurious behavior. This leads to a suggested normal form for classes with heap-managed memory. Normal form means that the class provides explicit constructors, including the default and copy constructor and the overloaded assignment operator, as well as an appropriate destructor. Class behaviors should be consistent with other C++ types.

In file my_string.cpp

```
// Normal form for heap-managed classes

class my_string {
public:
   my_string() { st = new str_obj; assert(st != 0); }
   my_string(const char* p)
      { st = new str_obj(p); assert(st != 0); }
   my_string(const my_string& str)
      { st = str.st; st -> ref_cnt++; }
   ~my_string();
   my_string& operator=(const my_string& str);
   // other methods  .....
private:
   str_obj*  st;
};
```

5.22   Dr. P's Prescriptions

- Constructors should be public methods.

- Constructors come first, then a destructor, and then other member functions.

- All friend functions are placed in the `public` section.

- Classes with dynamically allocated memory should have both a copy constructor and an assignment operator explicitly defined.

- Initialization is preferable to assignment in constructors.

- Constructors have three uses: allocation, initialization, and conversion. Avoid other purposes.

- Destructors have two uses: deallocation and finalization. Avoid other purposes.

- Use friends for binary operator overloading.

- Use friends when a special relationship exists between two classes.

- A set of overloaded operators should be developed for scientific types and not for nonstandard purposes. The standard library provides one such type: complex number.

- Overload the `operator=()` whenever the constructor uses `new`.

- Overloaded `operator=()` should check for assignment to itself. It should assign a value to each data member and return `*this`.

The idea behind placing more visible members first is the newspaper principle—namely, what everyone needs to know comes first. What everyone needs to know are the public members. This is the interface available to all users of the class. The friend functions are to be considered part of that interface and therefore in the public access section as well. Constructors and destructors are needed by anyone using the class, so they go first. Construction or object initialization is needed to use an ordinary type, so it is usual to have a constructor be public.

Classes that use pointers as part of their implementation should provide explicit default and copy constructors. This avoids problems from inadvertent shallow copies in which the pointer value is copied, but no new implementation is created. Usually, such classes require a related overloaded definition of `operator=`.

Constructors are for initialization. In the debugging and prototyping phase of code development, it is also useful to add code that outputs or tests behavior. Other work should not be carried out by a constructor, for this would be unexpected. For example, if in initializing an integer variable the system printed out its square root and whether it was prime, we would be properly upset.

Similarly, destructors are for finalization. They should retrieve resources connected with variables going out of scope. They are conceptually the inverse operation to a corresponding constructor.

For `const` and reference members, an initializer list is required because they cannot be given values through assignment. Even when member values can be assigned, initializers are preferable, because they can be more efficient and are notationally clear in purpose.

The `friend` declaration should be used for special situations and not merely as a way of circumventing access restrictions. Friends are commonly used for overloading operators. When a member function overloads a binary operator, the first argument is passed through the `this` pointer and the second argument is passed through the function's argument list. The second argument is subjected to assignment conversions. For example, `a + b` is equivalent to `a.operator+(b)` when overloaded with a member function, and to `operator+(a, b)` when overloaded with an ordinary function. In the second case, both arguments are symmetrically subjected to assignment conversion. This symmetry is expected for most operators. Usually, writing these overloaded operators as nonmember functions requires that the function be given access to private implementation and therefore needs the `friend` designation.

The `friend` designation is also appropriate between tightly coupled classes. These classes are designed to work together intimately. An example is a container class, such as a list, and an iterator class for navigating the list.

Idiosyncratic algebras and personal notations are a bad idea. They lead to writing dense and obscure code that is hard for others to follow and test. Where community-understood algebras exist, as in the mathematical and scientific disciplines, operator overloading should follow normal definitions and contain no surprises. One guideline is to be complete. For example, if the `operator==()` is defined, then define the corresponding `operator!=()`. The type complex number is provided by the C++ library and is an example of a scientific type using overloaded operators. Other such types might include polynomials, vectors, matrices, and rational numbers.

The assignment operator is especially important and is frequently a candidate for overloading. Anytime the copy constructor of a class is explicitly defined, an analogous definition of `operator=()` should be coded. The default semantics of assignment are member-by-member, which is often incorrect when pointers are involved in a class implementation. When overloading assignment, test that `x = x` works correctly.

5.23   C++ Compared with Java

Like a C++ constructor, a Java constructor is a function whose job is to initialize an object of its class. Constructors are invoked after the instance variables of a newly created class object have been assigned default initial values and any explicit initializers are called. Constructors are frequently overloaded. A constructor is a member function whose name is the same as the class name. The constructor does not have a return type.

Let us write a program for making change. We can encapsulate the logic of that program in a class. We can look at change as an object returned when we have a purchase. We have to decide which data members are needed for making change. Generally, objects mimic the real world. In this case, we need members that track the number of coins of each denomination. We also need actions that are useful with these types. For example, what would be the value of a set of coins containing three quarters and two dimes?

In file Change.java

```java
class Change {
    private int dollars, quarters, dimes, pennies;
    private double total;

    Change(int dlrs, int qtr, int dm, int pen) {
        dollars = dlrs;
        quarters = qtr;
        dimes = dm;
        pennies = pen;
        total = dlrs + 0.25 * qtr + 0.1 * dm + 0.01
                    * pen;
    }
    static Change makeChange(double paid, double owed)
    {
        double  diff = paid - owed;
        int  dollars, quarters, dimes, pennies;
        dollars = (int)diff;
        pennies = (int)((diff - dollars) * 100);
        quarters = pennies / 25;
        pennies -= 25 * quarters;
        dimes = pennies / 10;
        pennies -= 10 * dimes;
        return new Change(dollars, quarters, dimes,
                          pennies);
    }
```

```
        public String toString() {
            return ("$" + total + "\n"
                    + dollars + " dollars\n"
                    + quarters + " quarters\n"
                    + dimes + " dimes\n"
                    + pennies + " pennies\n");
        }
    }
```

Dissection of the *Change.java* Program

■ `private int dollars, quarters, dimes, pennies;`
`private double total;`

Here, we declare the various data members bundled inside a Change object. We gave them private access to protect them from arbitrary manipulations by nonmember methods.

■ `Change(int dlrs, int qtr, int dm, int pen) {`
`    dollars = dlrs;`
`    quarters = qtr;`
`    dimes = dm;`
`    pennies = pen;`
`    total = dlrs + 0.25 * qtr + 0.1 * dm + 0.01`
`            * pen;`
`}`

As defined, the only way to construct a Change object is by specifying the number of each type of coin. We chose not to use nickels or half-dollars, just to keep the code shorter. Because there is not a no-argument constructor (in C++ terminology, the default constructor) in this class, we can't create a Change object by using the expression new Change(). We intentionally left the no-argument constructor out because, as currently implemented, there is no use for it. Java does not have initializing syntax for its constructors.

■
```java
static Change makeChange(double paid, double owed) {

    double  diff = paid - owed;
    int  dollars, quarters, dimes, pennies;
    dollars = (int)diff;
    pennies =(int)((diff-dollars) * 100);
    quarters = pennies / 25;
    pennies -= 25 * quarters;
    dimes = pennies / 10;
    pennies -= 10 * dimes;
    return new Change(dollars, quarters, dimes,
                      pennies);
}
```

This method is a static method because it isn't operating on a `Change` object. Instead, it is a helper function, used to compute change for an amount paid and an amount owed. Once we've computed the numbers of each of the coin types, we then create a new `Change` object using the values. This new `Change` object is then returned as the result of the method. Note that we are using an object to encapsulate many related values—the counts of the various coins. The return type, rather than being a single primitive value, is an object. This type allows a complex calculation to bundle and return many related values as an object.

■
```java
public String toString() {
    return ("$" + total + "\n"
            + dollars + " dollars\n"
            + quarters + " quarters\n"
            + dimes + " dimes\n"
            + pennies + " pennies\n");
}
```

In Java, all classes include a method `toString()`, which returns a `string` representation of the class.

If we don't provide the method, the Java system provides one by default—but it isn't useful for most purposes. It simply returns the name of the class of which the object is an instance and the address of the object in the computer's memory. One version of the method `println()` takes as an argument any reference. The method then prints whatever the `toString()` method for the referenced object returns. Here, we use string concatenation to build the result string. This `toString()` method gives slightly nonstandard output for values when no pennies are involved. For example, the total for $1.50 prints out as $1.5, with no trailing 0. The `toString()` method is a polymorphic conversion method.

The following simple program, taken from *Java by Dissection*, by Ira Pohl and Charlie McDowell (Addison-Wesley, 1999), pages 210 to 212, uses the class Change.

In file ChangeTest.java

```
public class ChangeTest {
    public static void main(String[] args) {
        double owed = 12.37;
        double paid = 15.0;
        System.out.println("You owe $" + owed);
        System.out.println("You gave me $" + paid);
        System.out.println("Your change is " +
                    Change.makeChange(paid, owed));
    }
}
```

The output of this program is

```
You owe $12.37
You gave me $15.0
Your change is $2.63
2 dollars
2 quarters
1 dimes
3 pennies
```

As with C++, methods and constructors are typically overloaded.

```
// Constructor to be placed in Java class Person

public Person() { name = "Unknown"; }
public Person(String nm) { name =nm; }
public Person(String nm, int a, char b)
    { name = nm; age =a; gender = b; }
```

These constructors would be invoked when new is used to associate a created instance with the appropriate type reference variable. For example:

```
p1 = new Person();
// make Unknown 0 M
p1 = new Person("Laura Pohl");
// make Laura Pohl 0 M
p1 = new Person("Laura Pohl", 12, 'F');
// make Laura Pohl 12 F
```

The overloaded constructor is selected by the set of arguments that match the constructor's parameter list.

Destruction is done automatically by the system, using automatic garbage collection. This differs from C++, in which the programmer must provide the destructor. When the object can no longer be referenced—for example, when the existing reference is given a new object—the now inaccessible object is called garbage. Periodically, the system sweeps through memory and retrieves these dead objects. The programmer need not be concerned with such apparent memory leaks.

Unlike C++, Java does not have operator overloading. Java's use of new is similar to that in C++ but does not allow for overloading of the new operator. In general, this simplifies and restricts what the Java programmer can do and needs to worry about. Java allows ordinary casts but does not allow nonportable casts.

Java performs an automatic conversion only if the conversion does not result in any information loss. The exception is that some numeric conversions from integer types to floating-point types can result in loss of precision, but the most significant digits of the result are unchanged. For example, the following results in an automatic conversion when n is assigned to f:

```
int n = 2;
float f;

f = n;
```

Trying to assign f to n requires a cast.

```
n = (int)f;
```

In this case, the floating-point value stored in f is rounded *toward zero* and the resulting value is stored in n. String conversion is used in println():

```
System.out.println("x = " + x);
```

in which x is a numeric primitive type variable. String conversion occurs when exactly one operand of the operator + is a string. In this case, the nonstring operand is converted to a string. For the primitive types, the result of string conversion is a value of type String that represents the primitive value. For example, the result of doing a string conversion on the int value 123 is the String "123".

Summary

- A constructor, a member function whose name is the class name, constructs objects of its class type. This can involve initializing data members and allocating the heap, using the operator `new`. A constructor is invoked when its associated type is used in a definition.

```
TYPE_foo y(3);      // invoke TYPE_foo::TYPE_foo(int)
extern TYPE_foo x;// declaration but not definition
```

Again, not all declarations are definitions. In those cases, no constructor is invoked.

- A destructor is a member function whose name is the class name preceded by the tilde character, ~. Its usual purpose is to destroy values of the class type, typically by using `delete`.

- A constructor requiring no arguments is called the default constructor. It can be a constructor with an empty argument list or one whose arguments all have default values. It has the special purpose of initializing arrays of objects of its class.

- A copy constructor of the form

  type::*type*(`const` *type*& *x*)

  is used to copy one type value into another when a variable is initialized by a value, a value is passed as an argument in a function or a value is returned from a function. If the copy constructor is not present, the compiler provides one that does member-by-member initialization of values.

- A class having members whose type requires a constructor uses initializers, a comma-separated list of constructor calls following a colon. The constructor is invoked by using the member name followed by an argument list in parentheses. The initialization is in the order of the declaration of the members.

- Constructors of a single parameter are automatically conversion functions. They convert from the parameter type to the class type. `my_type::my_type(int);` is a conversion from `int` to `my_type`. This property can be disallowed by declaring the constructor `explicit`.

- Overloading operators gives them new meanings. For example, the meaning of the expression `a + b` depends on the types of the variables `a` and `b`. The expression could mean string concatenation, complex number addition, or integer addition, depending on whether the variables were the ADT `my_string`, the ADT `complex`, or the built-in type `int`, respectively.

■ The keyword `friend` is a function specifier that allows a nonmember function access to the nonpublic members of the class of which it is a friend.

■ It is common to overload >> and << to provide input and output for class types.

■ The structure pointer operator -> , or smart pointer, is overloaded as a nonstatic class member function. The argument must be a class object or a reference of this type. The function should return a pointer to a class object, an object of a class or reference to a class for which `operator` -> is defined.

■ Overloading functions are selected using the signature matching algorithm.

Basic Signature Matching Algorithm

1. Use an exact match if found.

2. Try standard type promotions.

3. Try standard type conversions.

4. Try user-defined conversions.

5. Use a match to ellipsis if found.

Review Questions

1. What is the signature in the following declaration: `void f(int x, double y);`?

2. How can you disable a conversion constructor?

3. How many arguments can a user-defined conversion have?

4. Outline the signature matching algorithm.

5. Explain how `cout << x` uses operator overloading and why this is important.

6. The keyword `friend` is a function specifier. It gives a nonmember function _____.

7. One reason for using friend functions is _____.

8. Binary operators, such as +, should be overloaded by _____ non-member functions because _____.

9. When a pointer operator is overloaded, it must be a _____ function.

10. Some operators can be overloaded only as nonstatic member functions. Name three such operators.

Exercises

1. Table 5.2 contains a variety of mixed-type expressions. Fill in both the type the expression is converted to and its value when well defined.

Table 5.2 Declarations and Initializations		

`int    i = 3, *p = &i;`
`char c = 'b';`
`float x = 2.14, *q = &x;`		

Expression	Type	Value
`i + c`		
`x + i`		
`p + i`		
`p == & i`		
`* p - * q`		
`static_cast<int>(x + i)`		

2. To test your understanding, use the `slist` type to code the following member functions:

```
// slist ctor with initializer char* string
slist::slist(const char* c);
```

```
// length returns the length of the slist
int slist::length() const ;
```

```
// return number of elements whose data value is c
int slist::count_c(char c) const ;
```

3. For the type `rational` in Section 5.9, *Overloading and Signature Matching*, on page 238, explain why the conversions of integer 7 and double 7.0 lead to different internal representations.

4. The following line of code is from the *rational.cpp* program in Section 5.9, *Overloading and Signature Matching*, on page 238.

```
cout << ") = "
                << greater(static_cast<rational>(i),
z);
```

If the preceding statement is replaced by

```
cout << ") = " << greater(i, z);
```

what goes wrong?

To test your understanding, write a `rational` constructor that, given two integers as dividend and quotient, uses a greatest common divisor algorithm to reduce the internal representation to its smallest a and q value.

5. Overload the equality and comparison operators for `rational`. Notice that two `rational`s are equal in the form given by the previous exercise if and only if their dividends and quotients are equal. (See Section 5.9, *Overloading and Signature Matching*, on page 238.)

6. Define class `complex` as

```
class complex {
public:
    complex(double r) : real(r), imag(0) { }
    void  assign(double r, double i)
        { real = r; imag = i; }
    void  print()
        { cout << real << " + " << imag << "i "; }
    operator double()
        { return (sqrt(real * real + imag * imag));}
private:
    double real, imag;
};
```

We wish to augment the class by overloading a variety of operators. For example, the member function `print()` could be replaced by creating the friend function `operator<<()`:

```
ostream& operator<<(ostream& out, complex x)
{
    out << x.real << " + " << x.imag << "i ";
    return out;
}
```

Also, code and test a unary minus operator. It should return a `complex` whose value in each part is negated.

7. For the type `complex`, write the binary operator functions add, multiply, and subtract. Each should return `complex`. Write each as a friend function. Why not write them as member functions?

8. Write two friend functions:

```
friend complex  operator+(complex, double);
friend complex  operator+(double, complex);
```

In the absence of a conversion from type `double` to type `complex`, both types are needed to allow completely mixed expressions of `complex` and `double`. Explain why writing one with an `int` parameter is unnecessary when these friend functions are available.

9. Overload assignment for `complex`:

```
complex& complex::operator=(complex c) {return c;}
```

If this definition were omitted, would this be equivalent to the default assignment that the compiler generates? In the presence of the conversion operator for converting `complex` to `double`, what is the effect of assigning a `complex` to a `double`? Try to overload assignment with a friend function in class `complex`.

```
friend double  operator=(double d, complex c);
// assign d = real_part(c)
```

Why won't this work?

10. Program a class `vec_complex` that is a safe array type whose element values are `complex`. Overload operators + and * to mean, respectively, element-by-element `complex` addition and dot-product of two `complex` vectors. For added efficiency, you can make the class `vec_complex` a friend of class `complex`.

11. Redo the `my_string` ADT by using operator overloading. (See Section 5.5, *Strings Using Reference Semantics*, on page 230.) The member function `assign()` should be changed to become `operator=`. Also, overload `operator[]` to return the `i`th character in the `my_string`. If there is no such character, the value –1 is to be returned.

12. Test your understanding of `my_string` by implementing additional members of `my_string`.

```
// strcmp is negative if s < s1,
//          is 0 if s == s1,
//          and is positive if s > s1
//          where s is the implicit argument

int my_string::strcmp(const my_string& s1);

// strrev  reverses the my_string
void my_string::strrev();

// print overloaded to print the first n characters
void my_string::print(int n) const;
```

13. Explain why friendship to `str_obj` was required when overloading `<<` to act on objects of type `my_string`. (See Section 5.5, *Strings Using Reference Semantics*, on page 230.) Rewrite `my_string` by adding a conversion member function `operator char*()`. This now allows `<<` to output objects of type `my_string`. Discuss this solution.

14. What goes wrong with the following client code when the overloaded definition of `operator=()` is omitted from `my_string`? (See Section 5.5, *Strings Using Reference Semantics*, on page 230.)

```
// Swapping my_strings that are reference counted
class my_string {
    .....
};

void swap(my_string x, my_string y)
{
    my_string temp;
    temp = x;
    x = y;
    y = temp;
}

int main()
{
    my_string  b("do not try me "), c(" try me");

    cout << b << c << endl;
    swap(b, c);
    cout << b << c << endl;
}
```

15. We can further develop our `my_string` class with a substring operation by overloading the function call operator (). The notation is `my_string(from, to)`, where `from` is the beginning of

the substring and to is the end. Use this to search a string for a character sequence and return true if the subsequence is found.

```
my_string my_string::operator()(int from, int to)
{
    my_string temp(to - from + 1);   //code this

    for (int i = from; i < to + 1; ++i)
        temp.st -> s[i - from] = st -> s[i];
    temp.st[to - from + 1] = 0;
    return temp;
}
```

16. Given this code for overloaded [] for my_string from Section 5.1.6, *The Copy Constructor*, on page 222, why would the following be buggy?

```
char& my_string::operator[](int position)
{
    return st -> s[position];
}
```

17. Rewrite the substring function, using a char* constructor. Is this better or worse? If you have a profiler, run this example with both forms of substring creation on the following client code:

```
int main()
{
    my_string large("A verbose phrase to search");

    for (i = 0; i < MANY; ++i)
        count += (large(i, i + 3) == "ver");
}
```

For this exercise, code operator==() to work on my_strings.

18. To test your understanding, use the preceding substring operation to search a string for a given character sequence and to return true if the subsequence is found. To further test your understanding, recode this function to test that the positions are within the actual string. This means that they cannot have negative values and they cannot go outside the null character terminator of the string.

19. Code a class int_stack. Use this to write out integer subsequences in increasing order by value. In the sequence (7, 9, 3, 2, 6, 8, 9, 2), the subsequences are (7, 9), (3), (2, 6, 8, 9), (2). Use a stack to store increasing values. Pop the stack when a next sequence value is no longer increasing. Keep in mind that the stack pops

values in reverse order. Redo this exercise using a queue, thus avoiding this reversal problem.

20. Redo the list ADT by using operator overloading. (See Section 5.4, *Example: A Singly Linked List*, on page 225.) The member function `prepend()` should change to `operator+()`, and `del()` should change to `operator--()`. Also, overload `operator[]()` to return the `i`th element in the list.

21. The postfix operators `++` and `--` can be overloaded distinct from their prefix meanings. Postfix can be distinguished by defining the postfix overloaded function as having a single unused integer argument, as in

```
class T {
public:
    // postfix invoked as t.operator++(0);
    T   operator++(int);
    T   operator--(int);
};
```

There is no implied semantic relationship between the postfix and prefix forms. Add postfix decrement and increment to class `my_clock` in Section 5.12, *Unary Operator Overloading*, on page 245. Have them subtract a second and add a second, respectively. Write these operators to use an integer argument `n` that is subtracted or added as an additional argument.

```
my_clock c(60);
```

```
c++;                   // adds a second
c--;                   // subtracts a second
c.operator++(5);       // adds 1 + 5 seconds
c.operator--(5);       // subtracts 6 seconds
```

22. (Uwe F. Mayer) Rewrite `istream& operator>>(istream& in, rational& x)`. You can improve on this input function by allowing it to read the input `a/q` where the "/" acts a separator for the two integer values.

23. *(Project)* You should start by writing code to implement a polynomial class with overloaded operators + and * for polynomial addition and multiplication. You can base the polynomial on a linked list representation. Then write a full-blown polynomial package that is consistent with community expectations. You could include differentiation and integration of polynomials as well.

24. *(Project)* Write code that fleshes out the `rational` type of Section 5.17, *Overloading << and >>*, on page 253. Have the code work appropriately for all major operators. Allow it to properly mix with other number types, including integers, floats, and complex numbers. There are several ways to improve the `rational` implementation. You can try to improve the precision of going from `double` to `rational`. Also, many algorithms are more convenient when the `rational` is in a canonical form in which the quotient and divisor are relatively prime. This can be accomplished by adding a greatest common division algorithm to reduce the representation to the canonical form. (See exercise 4 on page 272.)

25. *(Java)* Rewrite in Java the class `rational` in Section 5.9, *Overloading and Signature Matching*, on page 238. You must substitute ordinary methods for any operator overloading.

Templates and Generic Programming

A key problem in programming is programmer productivity. An important technique is code reuse. Generic programming is a critical methodology for enhancing code reuse. Generic programming is about code that can be used over a wide category of types. In C++, there are three different ways to employ generic coding techniques: void* pointers, templates, and inheritance. We show a simple use of each of these methods. This lets us concentrate on C++ templates and how they are used effectively.

We start with a small piece of code that can benefit from genericity: assigning the contents of one array to a second array.

In file transferArray.cpp

```
// Simple array assignment function

int transfer(int from[], int to[], int size)
{
    for (int i = 0; i < size; i++)
        to[i] = from[i];
    return size;
}
```

This code works for the int array type and depends on an appropriate size array being allocated. This piece of code can be readily replicated for different types, but replication has a cost and can introduce errors.

For the following declarations,

```
int a[10], b[10];
double c[20], d[20];

transfer(b, a, 10);          // works fine
transfer(d, c, 20);          // syntax error
```

C++ has a void pointer type that can be used to create generic code. Generic code is code that can work with different types.

In file voidTransferArray.cpp

```
// void* generic assignment function

int transfer(void* from, void* to,
             int elementSize, int size)
{
    int  nBytes = size * elementSize;

    for (int i = 0; i < nBytes; i++)
        static_cast<char*>(to)[i] =
        static_cast<char*>(from)[i];
    return size;
}
```

Dissection of the transfer() Function Using void*

■ int transfer(void* from, void* to,
              int elementSize, int size)

This code works for any array type. Since void* is a universal pointer type, any array type can be passed as a parameter. However, the compiler does not catch type errors. Here are some declarations and function calls:

```
int a[10], b[10];
double c[20], d[20];

transfer(a, b, sizeof(int), 10);      // works fine
transfer(c, d, sizeof(double), 20);   // works fine
transfer(a, c, sizeof(int), 10);   // sys dependent
```

In this last call, a is an `int*` type but c is a `double*`. On many machines, an `int` fits in 4 bytes and a `double` fits in 8 bytes. The effect of these transfers can be very different where the underlying size limits differ.

- `int nBytes = size * elementSize;`

The number of bytes to be transferred is computed as the `element-Size` times the `size` for an individual element. For a 10-element array of 4-byte `int`s, this would be 40 bytes.

- ```
  for (int i = 0; i < nBytes; i++)
      static_cast<char*>(to)[i] =
      static_cast<char*>(from)[i];
  ```

This `for` loop performs the actual transfer. It does it byte by byte, with each byte being treated as a character.

C++ has template functions that can be used to create generic code. Template functions are written using the keyword `template` followed by angle brackets. The angle brackets contain an identifier that is used as a placeholder for an arbitrary type. Here, we write the `transfer()` function using templates.

In file templateTransferArray.cpp

```
// Template generic assignment function

template<class T>
int transfer(T* from, T* to, int size)
{
  for (int i = 0; i < size; i++)
    to[i] = from[i];
   return size;
}
```
```

Dissection of the `transfer()` Function Using `template`

- ```
  template<class T>
    int transfer(T* from, T* to, int size)
  ```

This code works for any array type. T can be any type. Here are some declarations and function calls:

```
int a[10], b[10];
double c[20], d[20];

transfer(a, b, 10);      // works fine
transfer(c, d, 20);      // works fine
transfer(a, c, 10);      // syntax error
```

In the first case, a function `transfer(int*, int*, int)` is compiled. In the second case, a function `transfer(double*, double*, int)` is compiled. In this last case, a is an `int*` type, but c is a `double*`. The template mechanism cannot produce an actual function because these are two different types. This leads to the syntax error "failure to unify the two argument types."

- ```
  for (int i = 0; i < size; i++)
      to[i] = from[i];
  ```

This `for` loop performs the actual transfer. It does it array-element by array-element, which is generally more efficient than a byte transfer.

The template function requires that the type be properly instantiated. It does not allow two distinct types to be used in this form of array transfer. It continues to provide type safety, which is important to program correctness.

C++ uses the keyword `template` to provide parametric polymorphism, which allows the same code to be used with respect to various types, in which the type is a parameter of the code body. This is a form of generic programming. Many of the classes used in the text so far contained data of a particular type, although the data have been processed in the same way regardless of type. Using templates to define classes and functions allows us to reuse code in a simple, type-safe manner that lets the compiler automate the process of type instantiation—that is, when a type replaces a type parameter that appeared in the template code.

6.1 Template Class stack

Here, we modify the `ch_stack` type from Section 4.11, *A Container Class Example: ch_stack*, on page 187, to have a parameterized type. This is a prototypical container class. It is a class whose chief purpose is to hold values. Rather than write a version of this class for each type, we can write generic code using the `template` syntax.

In file templateStack.cpp

```
// Template stack implementation

template <class TYPE>
class stack {
public:
    explicit stack(int size = 100)
        : max_len(size), top(EMPTY), s(new TYPE[size])
        { assert(s != 0); }
    ~stack() { delete []s; }
    void   reset() { top = EMPTY; }
    void   push(TYPE c) { s[++top] = c; }
    TYPE   pop() { return s[top--]; }
    TYPE   top_of() const { return s[top]; }
    bool   empty() const { return top == EMPTY; }
    bool   full() const { return top == max_len - 1; }
private:
    enum   { EMPTY = -1 };
    TYPE*  s;
    int    max_len;
    int    top;
};
```

The syntax of the class declaration is prefaced by

```
template <class identifier>
```

This identifier is a template argument that essentially stands for an arbitrary type. Throughout the class definition, the template argument can be used as a type name. This argument is instantiated in the declarations. A template declaration usually has global or namespace scope, can be a member of a class, and can be declared within another template class. An example of a `stack` declaration using this is

```
stack<char>      stk_ch;         // 100 char stack
stack<char*>     stk_str(200);   // 200 char* stack
stack<complex>   stk_cmplx(500); // 500 complex stack
```

This mechanism saves us rewriting class declarations in which the only variation would be the type declarations, providing a type-safe, efficient, and convenient way to reuse code.

Polymorphic Genie: Capable of Assuming Any Type

When a template class is used, the code must always use the angle brackets as part of the declaration.

In file templateStack.cpp

```cpp
// Reversing an array of char* represented strings

void reverse(char* str[], int n)
{
    stack<char*>  stk(n);
    int  i;

    for (i = 0; i < n; ++i)
        stk.push(str[i]);
    for (i = 0; i < n; ++i)
        str[i] = stk.pop();
}
// Initialize stack of complex numbers from an array

void init(complex c[], stack<complex>& stk, int n)
{
    for (int i = 0; i < n; ++i)
        stk.push(c[i]);
}
```

Member functions, when declared and defined inside the class, are, as usual, inline. When defining them externally, you must use the full angle bracket declaration. So, when defined outside the template class,

```
TYPE  top_of() const { return s[top]; }
```

would be written as

```
template<class TYPE> TYPE stack<TYPE>::top_of() const
    { return s[top]; }
```

Yes, this is ugly and takes some getting used to, but the compiler otherwise would not know that TYPE was a template argument. As another example, we write the file scope definition of the destructor for `template<class TYPE> stack`:

```
template<class TYPE> stack<TYPE>::~stack()
    { delete []s; }
```

A C++ programmer would use the Standard Template Library (STL) class `std::stack`. The code presented in this section allows you to better appreciate the container classes provided by the standard library. See Chapter 7, *Standard Template Library*, for more on STL.

Now that's what I call a generic waiter—he can balance anything!

6.2   Function Templates

Many functions have the same code body, regardless of type; for example, initializing the contents of one array from another of the same type uses the same code body. The essential code is

```
for (i = 0; i < n; ++i)
   a[i] = b[i];
```

Many programmers automate this with a simple macro:

```
#define  COPY(A, B, N) \

    {int i; for (i=0; i < (N); ++i) (A)[i] = (B)[i]; }
```

Programming that works regardless of type is a form of generic programming. The use of `define` macros is a form of generic programming. Its advantages are several, including simplicity, familiarity, and efficiency. There is familiarity because of a long tradition in C programming of using such macros. It is very efficient. There is no function call overhead.

The disadvantages of using macros include type safety, unanticipated evaluations, and scoping problems. Using `define` macros can often work, but doing so is not type-safe. Macro substitution is a preprocessor textual substitution that is not syntactically checked until later. Another problem with `define` macros is that they can lead to repeated evaluation of a single parameter. Definitions of macros are tied to their position in a file and not to the C++ language rules for scope. The code

```
#define CUBE(X) ((X)*(X)*(X))
```

behaves differently from the code

```
template<class T> T cube (T x) { return x * x * x;}
```

When `cube(sqrt(7))` is invoked, the function `sqrt(7)` is called once, not three times as with the CUBE `define` macro.

Templates are safer when types can be mixed in an expression and conversions are inappropriate.

In file copy1.cpp

```
template<class TYPE>
void copy(TYPE a[], TYPE b[], int n)
{
    for (int i = 0; i < n; ++i)
        a[i] = b[i];
}
```

The invocation of copy() with specific arguments causes the compiler to generate the function based on those arguments. If it cannot, a compile-time error results. What are the effects of the following calls?

In file copy1.cpp

```
double  f1[50], f2[50];
char    c1[25], c2[50];
int     i1[75], i2[75];
char*   ptr1 = c1, *ptr2 = c2;

copy(f1, f2, 50);
copy(c1, c2, 10);
copy(i1, i2, 40);
copy(ptr1, ptr2, 15);
copy(i1, f2, 50);
copy(ptr1, f2, 50);
```

The last two invocations of copy() fail to compile because their types cannot be matched to the template type. This is called a unification error. The types of the arguments do not conform to the template. How the compiler generates this matching is discussed in the next section. If we were to cast f2 as

```
copy(i1, static_cast<int* >(f2), 50);
```

compilation would occur. However, the result would be an inappropriate form of copying. Instead, we need to have a generic copying procedure that accepts two distinct class type arguments.

In file copy2.cpp

```
template<class T1, class T2>
void copy(T1 a[], T2 b[], int n)
{
    for (int i = 0; i < n; ++i)
        a[i] = b[i];
}
```

This form has an element-by-element conversion. This is usually the appropriate and safer conversion.

See, any cookie shape is possible!

6.2.1   Signature Matching and Overloading

A generic routine often cannot work for special cases. The following form of swapping template works on basic types:

In file swap.cpp

```
// Generic swap

template <class T>
void swap(T& x, T& y)
{
    T  temp;

    temp = x;
    x = y;
    y = temp;
}
```

A function template is used to construct an appropriate function for any invocation that matches its arguments unambiguously:

```
int      i, j;
char     str1[100], str2[100], ch;
complex  c1, c2;
char *s1 = str1, *s2 = str2;

swap(i, j);              // i j int-okay
swap(c1, c2);           // c1, c2 complex-okay
swap(str1[50], str2[33]); // both char variables-okay
swap(i, ch);            // i int ch char-illegal
swap(str1, str2);       // illegal
swap(s1, s2);       // legal-but may not be intention
```

In the first three cases, the template compiles and runs as expected. The case of swap(i, ch) yields a syntax error, as the two arguments are not the same type. In the case of swap(str1, str2), str1 and str2 are array names. They are pointer values that cannot be modified. Therefore, for this type, the code x = y; cannot compile. In the last case, swap(s1, s2), the arguments are the same type and are modifiable. The swap(s1, s2) function compiles and executes, but the contents of the arrays that the pointers represent are not copied; only the pointers themselves are swapped.

To have swap() work for strings represented as character arrays, we write the following special case:

```
void swap(char* s1, char* s2)
{
    int  max_len;

    max_len = (strlen(s1) >= strlen(s2)) ?
                strlen(s1) : strlen(s2);
    char* temp = new char[max_len + 1];

    strcpy(temp, s1);
    strcpy(s1, s2);
    strcpy(s2, temp);
}
```

This specific version of swap() swaps the two strings represented by pointer values. With this specialized case added, an exact match of this nontemplate version to the signature of a swap() invocation takes precedence over the exact match found by a template substitution. This is a dangerous swap routine, as the longer string might overflow the memory that had been allocated for the shorter string. When multiple functions are available, the overloaded function-selection algorithm given below determines which to use.

Overloaded Function-Selection Algorithm

1. Exact match with some trivial conversions on nontemplate functions

2. Exact match using function templates

3. Ordinary argument resolution on nontemplate functions

6.2.2   How to Write a Simple Function: `square()`

Let us review what we know about writing a simple function. We choose the function `square()` as our test case.

```
// Hand-coding genericity by overloading the function

inline int square(int n)
{
    return n * n;
}
inline double square(double x)
{
    return x * x;
}
```

Here, we use a text editor to copy the basic code and change types as needed. The function `square()` is overloaded for as many signatures as needed. The downside in this is the effort to do this mundane coding task manually. It is also error-prone because, in copying and changing types by hand, mistakes are made.

```
// Macro square

#define SQUARE(X) ((X)*(X))
```

Here, we use a preprocessor to inline substitute code where necessary, independent of type. The macro is also error-prone, because textual substitution occurs without language rules being checked. It is only after the substitution that the compiler checks for syntax errors.

```
// Poor attempt at genericity using void*

inline double square(void* p)
{
    double* temp = reinterpret_cast<double*>(p);
    return (*temp) * (*temp);
}
```

Here, we use a `void*` as the argument type, which is error-prone because it uses a system-dependent cast. It works through conversion to `double`, which may be inappropriate.

And the winner is template coding:

```
// C++ template

template <class T>
inline T square(T n)
{
    return n * n;
}
```

The code is easily generated based on testing for a simple native type. It works universally when the multiplication `operator*` is defined. It is automatically generated as necessary for arbitrary signatures. You can test your understanding of this concept by doing exercise 4 on page 318.

6.3   Generic Code Development: Quicksort

Sorting is an important algorithm for many applications. Sorting needs to be accomplished on many different types. Sorting needs to be compactly coded and highly efficient. Thus, sorting functions are a prime candidate for generic coding. We develop the code for quicksort—a highly efficient, well-known sorting method. Quicksort was created by C. Anthony R. Hoare and described in his 1962 paper "Quicksort" (*Computer Journal,* vol. 5, no. 1). Of all the various sorting techniques, quicksort is perhaps the most widely used internal sort. An internal sort is one in which all the data to be sorted fit entirely within main memory.

First, we program the quicksort for a specific type. Then we show how easy it is to convert it to generic code. Our quicksort code is as follows:

In file quicksort.cpp

```
// Quicksort
inline void swap(int& x, int& y)
{
    int  t;
    t = x;
    x = y;
    y = t;
}

inline void order(int& x, int& y)
{
    if (x > y) swap(x, y);
}
```

```
bool find_pivot(int *left, int *right,
                int *pivot_ptr);

int* partition(int *left, int *right, int pivot);

void quicksort(int *left, int *right)
{
    int    *p, pivot;
    if (find_pivot(left, right, &pivot)) {
        p = partition(left, right, pivot);
        quicksort(left, p - 1);
        quicksort(p, right);
    }
}
```

Quicksort is usually implemented recursively. The underlying idea is to divide and conquer. Suppose that in main() we have declared a to be an array of size N. After the array has been filled, we can sort it with the call

```
quicksort(a, a + N - 1);
```

The first argument is a pointer to the first element of the array; the second argument is a pointer to the last element of the array. In the function definition for quicksort(), it is convenient to think of these pointers as being on the left and right side of the array, respectively. The function find_pivot() chooses, if possible, one of the elements of the array to be a pivot element. The function partition() is used to rearrange the array so that the first part consists of elements all of whose values are less than the pivot, and the remaining part consists of elements all of whose values are greater than or equal to the pivot. In addition, partition() returns a pointer to an element in the array. Elements to the left of the pointer all have value less than the pivot, and elements to the right of the pointer, as well as the element pointed to, all have value greater than or equal to the pivot. Once the array has been rearranged with respect to the pivot, quicksort() is invoked on each subarray.

```
bool find_pivot(int *left, int *right, int *pivot_ptr)
{
    int    a, b, c, *p;
    a = *left;                          // left value
    b = *(left + (right - left) / 2);   // middle value
    c = *right;                         // right value
    order(a, b);
    order(a, c);
    order(b, c);        // order these 3 values
    if (a < b) {        // pivot is higher of 2 values
        *pivot_ptr = b;
        return true;
    }

    if (b < c) {
        *pivot_ptr = c;
        return true;
    }
    for (p = left + 1; p <= right; ++p)
        if (*p != *left) {
            *pivot_ptr = (*p < *left) ? *left : *p;
            return true;
        }
    return false;       // all elements have same value
}
```

Ideally, the pivot should be chosen so that at each step the array is partitioned into two parts, each with an equal (or nearly equal) number of elements. This would minimize the total amount of work performed by `quicksort()`. Because we do not know a priori what this value should be, we try to select for the pivot the middle value from among the first, middle, and last elements of the array. In order for there to be a partition, there has to be at least one element that is less than the pivot. If all the elements have the same value, a pivot does not exist and `false` is returned by the function.

```
int *partition(int *left, int *right, int pivot)
{
   while (left <= right) {
      while (*left < pivot)
        ++left;
      while (*right >= pivot)
        --right;
      if (left < right) {
       swap(*left, *right);
       ++left;
       --right;
      }
   }
   return left;
}
```

The major work is done by `partition()`. We want to explain in detail how this function works. Suppose we have an array `a[]` of 12 elements:

7   4   3   5   2   5   8   2   1   9   -6   -3

When `find_pivot()` is invoked, the first, middle, and last elements of the array are compared. The middle value is 5, and because this is larger than the smallest of the three values, this value is chosen for the pivot value. The following simulation shows the values of the elements of the array after each pass of the outer `while` loop in the `partition()` function. The elements that were swapped in that pass are underlined.

```
Unordered data:  7  4  3  5  2  5  8  2  1  9 -6 -3
First pass:     -3  4  3  5  2  5  8  2  1  9 -6  7
Second pass:    -3  4  3 -6  2  5  8  2  1  9  5  7
Third  pass:    -3  4  3 -6  2  1  8  2  5  9  5  7
Fourth pass:    -3  4  3 -6  2  1  2  8  5  9  5  7
```

Notice that after the fourth pass, the elements with index 0 to 6 have value less than the pivot and that the remaining elements have value greater than or equal to the pivot. The address of `a[7]` is returned from `partition()` when it finishes the fourth pass and exits.

6.3.1 Converting to a Generic `quicksort()`

Now let us convert the quicksort to work with generic data. The key is to identify any types that need to be generalized. The original algorithm works with `int` data. Let us change this step by step to work with data of type T.

In file genericQuicksort.cpp

```
template <class T>
inline void swap(T& x, T& y)
{
    T t;
    t = x;
    x = y;
    y = t;
}

template <class T>
inline void order(T& x, T& y)
{
    if (x > y) swap(x, y);
}
```

Dissection of the `swap()` and `order()` Functions

■ ```
template <class T>
inline void order(T& x, T& y)
```

The key to writing templates is to preface the code with `template` and the appropriate number of type identifiers, usually identifiers T1, T2, and so on. Normally, only one type is parameterized, and for this case `class T` is usual. The function normally uses T as part of its signature. Later, when `order()` is called with a given type, as in `order(x, y)`, with these being `doubles`, the compiler generates code to specifically handle that type. One downside is that for each use of `order()` with different types, a code body is generated. Schemes for generic coding using `void*` can avoid these multiple code bodies, also referred to as code bloat.

■ ```
{
    if (x > y) swap(x, y);
}
```

The code is no different from for the `int` case. The compiler gives you a syntax error if the operator > is not defined for a particular type T.

```
■ template <class T>
  inline void swap(T& x, T& y)
  {
      T t;
```

Here, both the signature and a block variable are using type T.

```
■     t = x;
      x = y;
      y = t;
  }
```

This code should work universally because `operator=` is defined for any type. However, the user needs to check that semantics for `operator=` should be a deep copy, that is, a copy of the data itself, not just a copy of a pointer to the data.

Once the algorithm and its general coding scheme are understood, it is relatively easy to find the specific type, in this case `int`, that needs to be parameterized and change it to a parameterized type T. We show the remaining code parameterized without comment.

```
// Forward declarations of auxiliary functions

template <class T>
bool find_pivot(T *left, T *right, T *pivot_ptr);

template <class T>
T* partition(T *left, T *right, T pivot);

template <class T>
void quicksort(T *left, T *right)
{
    T   *p, pivot;
    if (find_pivot(left, right, &pivot)) {
        p = partition(left, right, pivot);
        quicksort(left, p - 1);
        quicksort(p, right);
    }
}
```

```
template <class T>
T *partition(T *left, T *right, T pivot)
{
    while (left <= right) {
        while (*left < pivot)
            ++left;
        while (*right >= pivot)
            --right;
        if (left < right) {
            swap(*left, *right);
            ++left;
            --right;
        }
    }
    return left;
}

template <class T>
bool find_pivot(T *left, T *right, T *pivot_ptr)
{
    T   a, b, c, *p;
    a = *left;                              // left value
    b = *(left + (right - left) / 2);   // middle value
    c = *right;                             // right value
    order(a, b);
    order(a, c);
    order(b, c);    // order these 3 values
    if (a < b) {    // pivot is higher of 2 values
        *pivot_ptr = b;
        return true;
    }
    if (b < c) {
        *pivot_ptr = c;
        return true;
    }
    for (p = left + 1; p <= right; ++p)
        if (*p != *left) {
            *pivot_ptr = (*p < *left) ? *left : *p;
            return true;
        }
    return false;  // all elements have same value
}
```

Let us test this code on two different array types.

In file genericQuicksort.cpp

```cpp
int main()
{
    cout << "quicksort\n";
    int a[12]={7, 4, 3, 5, 2, 5, 8, 2, 1, 9, -6, -3 };

    for (int i = 0; i < 12; i++)
        cout << a[i] << " , ";
    quicksort(a, a + 11);
    cout << "\n\nquicksorted\n";
    for (int i = 0; i < 12; i++)
        cout << a[i] << " , ";
    cout << endl;
    // Now use doubles
    double b[6] = { 7.8, 4.9, 3.8, 5.0, 2.8, 5.3 };
    for (int i = 0; i < 6; i++)
        cout << b[i] << " , ";
    quicksort(b, b + 5);
    cout << "\n\nquicksorted\n";
    for (int i = 0; i < 6; i++)
        cout << b[i] << " , ";
    cout << endl;
}
```

The standard C library provides qsort(), a generic quicksort routine using void*. An extended discussion of this technique can be found in *A Book on C: 4th Edition*, by Al Kelley and Ira Pohl (Addison-Wesley, 2000), pages 372 to 380.

6.4 Class Templates

In the stack<T> example given in Section 6.1, *Template Class stack*, on page 283, we have an ordinary case of class parameterization. In this section, we wish to discuss various special features of parameterizing classes.

6.4.1   Friends

Template classes can contain friends. A friend function that does not use a template specification is universally a friend of all instantiations of the template class. A friend function that incorporates template arguments is specifically a friend of its instantiated class.

```
template <class T>
class matrix {
public:
   friend void  foo_bar();          // universal
   friend vect<T>  prod(vect<T> v); // instantiated
   .....
};
```

6.4.2   Static Members

Static members are not universal but are specific to each instantiation.

```
template <class T>
class foo {
public:
   static int  count;
   .....
};

.....
foo<int>      a;
foo<double>   b;
```

The static variables foo<int>::count and foo<double>::count are distinct.

6.4.3   Class Template Arguments

Both classes and functions can have several class template arguments. Let us write a function that converts one type of value to a second type, provided the first type is at least as wide as the second type.

In file coerce.cpp

```
template <class T1, class T2>
bool coerce(T1& x, T2 y)
{
   if (sizeof(x) <= sizeof(y))
      return false;
   x = static_cast<T1>(y);
   return true;
}
```

This template function has two possibly distinct types as template arguments.

Other template arguments include constant expressions, function names, and character strings.

In file templateArray.cpp

```
template <class T, int n>
class assign_array {
public:
   T  a[n];
};
.....
assign_array<double,50>  x, y;
.....
x = y;        // should work efficiently
```

The benefits of this parameterization include allocation off the stack, as opposed to allocation from free store. On many systems, the former is more efficient. The type is bound to the particular integer constant; thus, operations involving compatible-length arrays are type-safe and checked at compile time. (See exercise 1 on page 318.)

6.4.4   Default Template Arguments

A template provider can decide that there is a common case that should be provided as a default.

```
template<class T = double>
class point{
   .....
private:
   T x, y, z;  // T is commonly double
}
```

This template can be used with an explicit parameter or with the parameter omitted as follows:

```
point <int> i_pt;     // the coordinates are int
point <double> d_pt;  // the coordinates are double
point < > d_pt2;      // the coordinates are double
```

6.4.5   Member Templates

Members may themselves be templates inside the template class. This feature of the ANSI standard has yet to be implemented on some compilers.

```
template <class T1>
class foo {
public:
    // class member template
    template <class T2>
    class fooprime {
        .....
        // can use T1 and T2 in fooprime
    };
    // can only use T1 in foo
    .....
};

foo<int>::fooprime<char>   a;
```

There can also be function member templates. Check your local compiler documentation to see whether these constructs are available.

6.5   Parameterizing the Class vector

Let us improve on the native C++ array by creating a container class. A defect of the array as found in C and C++ is that it is easy to have out-of-bounds errors resulting in difficult-to-find runtime bugs. We parameterize the class, naming it vector in anticipation of discussing and understanding the Standard Template Library (STL) class std::vector. The new class is used in conjunction with iterators and algorithms. An iterator is a pointer or a pointerlike variable used for traversing and accessing container elements.

In file vect_it.h

```
// Template-based vector type

template <class T>
class vector {
public:
   typedef T* iterator;
   explicit vector(int n = 100);// make size n array
   vector(const vector<T>& v);   // copy vector
   vector(const T a[], int n);   // copy an array
   ~vector() { delete []p; }
   iterator begin() { return p; }
   iterator end() { return p + size; }
   T& operator[](int i);      // range-checked element
   vector<T>& operator=(const vector<T>& v);
private:
   T*   p;                    // base pointer
   int  size;                 // number of elements
};
```

Basically, the `template` definition uses T everywhere the class acts on values stored in individual elements. Thus, the declaration of the private base pointer p is type T.

The definition of member functions in file scope includes the scope-resolved label *classname*<T>. The following constructors for vector<T> use T as the type specification to new:

```
template <class T>
vector<T>::vector(int n) : size(n)
{
   assert(n > 0);
   p = new T[size];
   assert(p != 0);
}
```

The preceding code is the default constructor because of the default argument of 100 given in its declaration within the class. We use the keyword `explicit` to disallow its use as a conversion from `int` to `vector`. Assertions are used to guarantee that the constructor performs its contractual obligations when given appropriate input.

```
template <class T>
vector<T>::vector(const T a[], int n)
{
    assert(n > 0);
    size = n;
    p = new T[size];
    assert(p != 0);
    for (int i = 0; i < size; ++i)
        p[i] = a[i];
}
```

This constructor converts an ordinary array to a vector. The copy constructor defines a deep copy of the vector v.

```
template <class T>
vector<T>::vector(const vector<T>& v)
{
    size = v.size;
    p = new T[size];
    assert(p != 0);
    for (int i = 0; i < size; ++i)
        p[i] = v.p[i];
}
```

The following code defines vector indexing by overloading the bracket operator. The return type for the bracket operator is "reference to T," as this is an alias for the item stored in the container. Using this return type allows the bracket operator to access the item in the container as an lvalue.

```
template <class T> T& vector<T>::operator[](int i)
{
    assert (i >= 0 && i < size);
    return p[i];
}
```

Notice that we can test to make sure that the array bounds are not exceeded. With operator[] overloaded, we can access vectors as if they were native C++ arrays. We also need to provide an overloaded assignment operator.

```
template <class T>
vector<T>& vector<T>::operator=(const vector<T>& v)
{
    assert(v.size == size);
    for (int i = 0; i < size; ++i)
        p[i] = v.p[i];
    return *this;
}
```

Client code is almost as simple as with nonparameterized declarations. To use these declarations, you simply add within angle brackets the specific type that instantiates the template. These types can be native types, such as `int` in the example, or user-defined types. The following code uses these templates:

In file vect_it.cpp

```
int main()
{
    vector<double> v(5);
    vector<double>::iterator p;
    int  i = 0;

    for (p = v.begin(); p != v.end(); ++p)
        *p = 1.5 + i++;

    do {
        --p;
        cout << *p << " , ";
    } while (p != v.begin());
    cout << endl;
}
```

The output from this program is

```
5.5, 4.5, 3.5, 2.5, 1.5,
```

The values are in reverse order to how they are stored. This is a consequence of iterating back from the iterator value `v.end()`. (See exercise 6 on page 319.)

6.6   Using STL: `string`, `vector`, and `complex`

The C++ standard library makes heavy use of templates. It is not necessary to be able to code templates, but it is vital to be able to use template code. This section discusses a range of useful template types provided by the standard library and by STL. The full use of STL is such an important and extensive topic that it is the subject of Chapter 7, *Standard Template Library*.

6.6.1   *string* **and basic_string<>**

The *string* library is a very extensive library that uses templates to create a family of string types. This library should be used in preference to *cstring*, the older C standard library for char* strings.

It is simple enough to use string as a type. This is in effect a basic container type, specialized to contain the type char. In reality, string is the template basic_string<charT> with the instantiation char and can be used typically as well to store the wider character type wchar_t. This is useful when the limited ASCII character set does not suffice to express the needed character set, as is the case for many foreign languages, such as Chinese, Japanese, Finnish, or Korean. The basic_string<> class represents a sequence of characters. It contains all the usual operations of a sequence container, as well as standard string operations such as concatenation.

There is no need to use the basic_string<> template directly because the types string and wstring are typedefs for, respectively, basic_string<char> and basic_string<wchar_t>.

The following example shows some of these features:

In file templateString.cpp

```cpp
// String class to rewrite a sentence.

#include <iostream>
#include <string>
using namespace std;

int main()
{
   string sentence, words[10];
   int  pos = 0, old_pos = 0, nwords, i = 0;

   sentence = "Eskimos have 23 ways to ";
   sentence += "describe snow";
   while (pos < sentence.size()) {
      pos = sentence.find(' ', old_pos);
      words[i].assign(sentence, old_pos,
                      pos - old_pos);
      cout << words[i++] << endl;       // print words
      old_pos = pos + 1;
   }
```

```
        nwords = i;
        sentence = "C++ programmers ";
        for (i = 1; i < nwords -1; ++i)
            sentence += words[i] + ' ';
        sentence += "windows";
        cout << sentence << endl;
    }
```

The `string` type is used to capture each word from an initial sentence in which the words are separated by the space character. The position of the space characters is computed by the `find()` member function. Then the `assign()` member function is used to select a substring from `sentence`. Finally, a new sentence is constructed using the overloaded `operator=()`, `operator+=()`, and `operator+()` functions to perform assignments and concatenations.

Note that it is important to check the local system documentation, as different vendors have employed their own specifications.

6.6.2   vector<> in STL

We developed a useful generalization of an arraylike container, the `vector<>`. A fully developed `std::vector<>` is found in the STL library *vector*. In most cases, it is preferable to use this type instead of the native array type. It is safer than native arrays, because it checks to see if you are out of range. It is more flexible than native arrays because it is resizable and has many associated standard methods. It is very easy to substitute for native arrays because it works as given with array notation. Here is an example:

```
#include <vector>
using namespace std;

template<class T>
T* find(vector<T> data, T v)
{
    int  i;

    for (i = 0; i < data.size(); i++)
        if (data[i] == v);
            return &data[i];
    return 0; // indicates failure to find v
}
```

Notice that the code looks typical of an array. The extra feature is that `size()` is a method that returns the length of the vector.

6.6.3   Using `complex<>`

The `complex<>` template found in the library *complex* provides a complex number type. It is compatible with the other numerical types. In earlier C++ libraries, this was not a template. It was a type based on the following data description:

```
class complex{
    // ·····methods
    private:

    double x, y;
};
```

This is replaced by

```
template <class SCALAR>
class complex{
    // ·····methods
    private:

    SCALAR x, y;
};
```

This allows users to decide on needed precision of the underlying type. Usually, this would be `float`, `double`, or `long double`. Here is some simple code testing this type:

In file complex.cpp

```
#include <iostream>
#include <complex>
using namespace std;

int main()
{
    complex<double> x(1,2.1), y;

    cout << "x = " << x << endl;
    y = x + 1.0;
    cout << "\ny = " << y << endl;
    // if (x < y) not allowed - no standard definition
    //     cout << "x less than y" << endl;
}
```

The `complex` type is important to scientists and engineers. It shows how easy it is to extend C++ to new domains. For example, many scientists programmed in FORTRAN90, which has a complex number type. Thus, C++ readily can be used to replace FORTRAN programs needing the complex type.

Notice how the commented out lines involve using the less-than operator. It is not defined in the standard library for this type, so the template compilation fails to instantiate it. If you have your own definition for this operator, you could specifically overload it and then this code would work.

6.6.4   *limits* and Other Useful Templates

The *limits* library describes the characteristics of the fundamental types on the local system. The template class `numeric_limits<>` provides this information for all numeric types. Instead of a different macro identifier for each data type characteristic, such as INT_MAX, the local system maximum `int` value, the class defines a single static function, named `max()`, which returns the appropriate values, such as `numeric_limits<int>::max()`. Using a template class greatly reduces the number of symbolic names that need to be defined to describe the local system.

The following is an example of using these functions:

In file limits.cpp

```
#include <iostream>
#include <limits>
using namespace std;

int main()
{
    cout << numeric_limits<char>::digits
         << " char\n ";
    cout << numeric_limits<unsigned char>::digits
         << " u  char\n";
    cout << numeric_limits<wchar_t>::digits
         << " wchar_t\n";
    cout << numeric_limits<int>::max()
         << " max int\n";
    cout << numeric_limits<double>::max()
         << " max double " << endl;
}
```

The `digits` field yields the number of bits representing the magnitude of the type.

Two other template libraries that are not discussed here but that are very important for certain specialized computations are *valarray* and *memory*. The *valarray* library provides templates for scientific vector computations that can be parallelized. Typically, this is useful on certain vector-parallel supercomputers. The *memory* library provides the `auto_ptr<>` template that aids management of data dynamically allocated by `new` expressions.

6.7 Software Engineering: Reuse and Generics

Reuse is a key to holding down software costs. Writing and testing new code is always expensive. Templates are a critical means of providing efficient reusable code. Unlike the `#define` macro, templates are type-safe and properly scoped.

As indicated in this chapter, templates are frequently no more expensive to develop than specialized code. Typically, the programmer writes the specialized case for a given type. This type should have characteristics representative of the different types the generic code would be instantiated with. The specialized code should be debugged and carefully tested until satisfactory. Then the programmer rewrites the specialized code in template form.

6.7.1 Debugging Template Code

As with ordinary code, you have syntax errors that the compiler finds and runtime errors that the programmer must hopefully find. In the case of template code, the syntax errors are of two varieties. One is just an error regardless of type instantiation; the second is an error because of a particular instantiation. Here is some code we wrote earlier in the chapter; however, it is modified to have an error, a missing semicolon:

```
template <class T1, class T2>
bool coerce(T1& x, T2 y)
{
    if (sizeof(x) <= sizeof(y))
        return false                 // missing semicolon
    x = static_cast<T1>(y);
    return true;
}
```

This type of error is readily detected upon compilation. Now consider using the code with the semicolon correction, as follows:

```
int main()
{
    int i = 6;
    struct s { int first, second; }x;

    coerce(i, x);
    cout << i;
}
```

Here is code that again has a syntax error, but this error is specific to the type instantiation. We are asking a `struct` variable to be cast to an `int` variable. Different compilers note this error with messages that can be difficult to decipher. You should try it on whatever C++ compilers you are using.

```
int main()
{
    int i = 6;
    double x = 5.5;

    coerce(i, x);
    cout << i;
}
```

Here is code that works, but the Borland compiler properly indicates that there is unreachable code. This is because the test

```
if (sizeof(x) <= sizeof(y))
```

is instantiated for the types `int` and `double` and the expression is always true. Needless to say, code that is generic and uses casting is highly suspect. As a general software engineering rule, you should stay away from code that is likely to have nonportable behavior.

6.7.2   Special Considerations

Many current C++ template implementations make a distinction between template parameters for functions and those for classes. Functions allow only class arguments, which must occur in the template function signature as part of the type description of at least one of the function parameters. The following is okay:

```
template <class TYPE>
void  maxelement(TYPE a[], TYPE& max, int size);

template <class TYPE>
int  find(TYPE* data);
```

The following was previously illegal but is now legal according to the ANSI standard:

```
template <class TYPE>
TYPE  convert(int i) { TYPE temp(i); return temp; }
```

In the ANSI standard, the function is invoked as follows:

```
// Newly allowed explicit function instantiation
```

```
convert<double>(i + j);
```

Since it was previously illegal, the function instantiation may not work on some systems. The restriction exists because these compilers must use the arguments at function invocation to deduce which functions are created. A workaround is possible by creating a class whose sole member is a parameterized static function, as follows:

```
template <class TYPE>      // other arguments possible
class convert_it {
public:
   static TYPE convert(int i)
            { TYPE temp(i); return temp; }
};

int main()
{
   convert_it<double> D;

   cout << D.convert(5) << endl;  // outputs a double
}
```

6.7.3   Using typename

The keyword typename can be used inside templates instead of the keyword class to declare template type parameters. The keyword is needed when class would not allow the template declaration to be correctly parsed.

```
template<class T1, class T2>
T1 foo(T1* w, T2 data)
{
   typename T1:: y * z; // a pointer declaration
   .....
};
```

Without the typename declaration, the compiler would not know whether foo() was declaring z of type T1::y* or multiplying y times z. Other subtle situations exist that require this form.

6.8   Dr. P's Prescriptions

- Use templates instead of `void*` genericity.

- First write an archetypal case and test, and then recode generically and test.

- Use templates for any standard code to enhance reuse.

- Avoid a commitment to a particular container type.

- Be general where possible.

- Use templates for containers, such as `stack` or `tree`.

- Use iterators in preference to indices for access to containers.

Before templates were used, generic code in C++ was written using `void*` arguments to functions. This generic pointer type can accept any specific pointer type as an argument. This code can largely be replaced with templates. The code is again compile-time type-checked. Also, template functions need not manipulate arguments indirectly with pointers.

It can be difficult to write and test generic code from scratch. Concreteness is a great aid to the program developer. Pick a type that represents the archetypal case. Develop the code for this case and test, making sure it's correct. Finally, convert this to template code and retest with selected types.

Templates are especially good for code that is repeatedly required with different types. Container class code is usefully generalized by coding with templates. A container is an object whose primary purpose is to store values. A classic example of a container is a stack. Templates allow such code to be reused over arbitrary types with type safety that is checked at compile time.

C++ is designed to be template friendly. Code, when designed as a template, benefits from greater abstraction than corresponding specialized code. What we mean by this is that programmers are normally overly clever. This leads to hard-to-maintain code with possibly subtle bugs. Generic code must be correct over a wide range of types and cannot indulge in cleverness.

Iterators avoid the commitment to a particular container type. In contrast, using indices to access arrays does not allow for pointer traversal as used in list and tree containers. Generalization benefits by avoiding commitments.

6.9 C++ Compared with Java

Unlike C++, Java does not have templates. Java does not have void* or macro code mechanisms. Instead, each class in Java can be viewed as an extension of the superclass Object. This is done implicitly. The Object superclass provides for a type of generic programming and achieves some of the ideas of polymorphism accomplished by the use of templates in C++. The use of Object in writing generic code is based on inheritance and is discussed in *Java by Dissection*, by Pohl and McDowell (Addison-Wesley, 1999), pages 244 to 249.

Java does have string types. They are built-in and come in two important classes: String and StringBuffer. We begin our discussion of the class String with an example that uses two operations defined for String: length() and charAt(). A string can be viewed as a sequence of characters. The method length() is used to find the number of characters in the string. The method charAt() is used to select individual characters from a string. The first character in the string is at position zero, and the last is at position *length* – 1, in which *length* is the number of characters in the string.

We use the String class to determine whether a string is a palindrome, a string that reads the same backward or forward. A simple example is the word *eye*. Here is the Java code from *Java by Dissection*, pages 190–192, and its output.

In file Palindrome.java

```java
// Check if a string is a palindrome
public class Palindrome {
    public static void main(String[] args) {
        String str1 = "eye", str2 = "bye";
        System.out.println("Palindrome detection");
        System.out.println(str1 + " " +
                            isPalindrome(str1));
        System.out.println(str2 + " " +
                            isPalindrome(str2));
    }
```

```
static boolean isPalindrome(String s) {
    int  left = 0;
    int  right = s.length() - 1;
    while (left < right) {
        if (s.charAt(left) != s.charAt(right))
            return false;
        left++;
        right--;
    }
    return true;
}
}
```

```
Palindrome detection
eye true
bye false
```

Dissection of the *Palindrome* Program

■ ```
public static void main(String[] args) {
    String str1 = "eye", str2 = "bye";
    System.out.println("Palindrome detection");
    System.out.println(str1 + " " +
                       isPalindrome(str1));
    System.out.println(str2 + " " +
                       isPalindrome(str2));
}
```

We use the method `main()` to test our `isPalindrome()` method. We declare two variables of type `String` and assign them initial values. Except for the objects of type `String` or created by literals, we create all other class objects by using the keyword `new`.

■ `static boolean isPalindrome(String s)`

For methods that perform a test and return a boolean, the method's name commonly begins with the prefix `is`.
```

■
```
int left = 0;
int right = s.length() - 1;
```

The operation `length()` is applied to the `String` variable s. For the same reason that arrays are indexed starting at 0, the position of the first character in a `String` is position, or index, 0; therefore, the position of the last character is *length* – 1.

■
```
while (left < right) {
    if (s.charAt(left) != s.charAt(right))
        return false;
    left++;
    right--;
}
return true;
```

The method `charAt()` implements the operation of extracting a single, selected character from a string, based on the position of the character in the string. Each pair of corresponding characters is tested for inequality. The first pair that disagrees causes the method to terminate with a value of `false`. If the iteration reaches the middle of the string without disagreement, the loop terminates. The method then returns with a value of true.

The methods `length()` and `charAt()` are called *instance methods* because they operate on a specified instance of the class `String`. This corresponds to C++'s nonstatic member functions. Note that in the palindrome example, we preceded the method calls `length()` and `charAt()` with a `String` variable separated by a dot. That's how we specify the object upon which the method is to operate.

We can modify a `String` variable to refer to different objects, but we can't change an actual `String` object to let it contain different characters. However, the standard Java class `StringBuffer` does provide string objects that are modifiable. Like a `String` object, a `StringBuffer` object represents a sequence of characters. In addition, the class `StringBuffer` provides *mutator methods* that can be used to change the sequence of characters represented by the `StringBuffer`. For example, the method `reverse()` can reverse the character sequence contained in `StringBuffer`.

```
StringBuffer str = new StringBuffer("ABCD");
str.reverse();
System.out.println(str);                    // prints  DCBA
```

Note that `str.reverse()` doesn't return a new `StringBuffer` that is the reverse of `str`. Instead, it actually modifies the `StringBuffer` referred to by `str`.

It should come as no surprise to readers familiar with arrays that the `StringBuffer` class internally stores the characters of the represented string in an array. Consequently, a `StringBuffer` object has two sizes: One is called the *length,* and the other is called the *capacity.* The object's length, like the length of a `String` object, is the number of characters in the represented string. The object's capacity is the number of characters that can be stored in the `StringBuffer` before the `StringBuffer` must do a relatively expensive operation of adding additional storage. This information is helpful to an understanding of some of the methods that are part of the `StringBuffer` class.

Summary

- C++ has a void pointer type that can be used to create generic code. Generic code is code that can work with different types.

- C++ uses templates to provide parametric polymorphism. The same code is used with different types, in which the type is a parameter of the code body.

- Both classes and functions can have several class template arguments. In addition to class template arguments, class template definitions can include constant expressions, function names, and character strings as template arguments. A common case is to have an `int` argument that parameterizes a size.

- A nontemplate, specialized version of a function may be needed when the generic routine does not work. When multiple functions are available, the overloaded function-selection algorithm determines which to use.

Overloaded Function-Selection Algorithm

1. Exact match with some trivial conversions on nontemplate functions

2. Exact match using function templates

3. Ordinary argument resolution on nontemplate functions

- A class such as `vector<>` or `stack<>` is a form of container class. It is used to hold and retrieve values of other types. An iterator is a pointer or a pointerlike variable used for traversing and accessing container elements. It is useful to traverse container classes using iterators.

- The *string* library is a very extensive library that uses templates to create a family of string types. This library should be used in preference to *cstring*, the older C standard library for `char*` strings.

- The `complex<>` template found in the library file *complex* provides a complex number type. It is compatible with the other numerical types.

- A fully developed `std::vector<>` is found in the STL library *vector*. It is preferable to use this type instead of the native array type. It is safer than native arrays because it checks to see if you are out of range. It is more flexible than native arrays because it is resizable and has many associated standard methods.

- The *limits* library describes the characteristics of the fundamental types on the local system. The template class `numeric_limits<>` provides this information for all numeric types.

Review Questions

1. In C, one can use `void*` to write generic code, such as `memcpy()`. In C++, writing generic code uses the keyword _____.

2. Rewrite as a template function the macro

   ```
   #define  SQ(A) ((A) * (A))
   ```

   Mention a reason why using the template is preferable to using the macro.

3. Using templates to define classes and functions allows us to reuse code in a simple, type-safe manner that lets the compiler automate the process of type _____—that is, when a type replaces a type parameter that appeared in the template code.

4. A _____ is an object whose primary purpose is to store values.

5. An iterator is a pointer or a pointerlike variable used for _____.

6. One downside is that for each use of a template function with different types, _____ is generated.

7. A friend function that does not use a template specification is a friend of _____.

8. Are static template members universal or specific to each instantiation? _____.

9. Unlike the #define macro, templates are _____ and _____.

10. The keyword _____ can be used inside templates instead of the keyword class to declare template type parameters.

Exercises

1. Rewrite stack<T> in Section 6.1, *Template Class stack*, on page 283, to accept an integer value for the default size of the stack. Now client code can use such declarations as

   ```
   stack<int, 100>  s1, s2;
   stack<char, 5000>  sc1, sc2, sc3;
   ```

   Discuss the pros and cons of this additional parameterization.

2. Define a template for fixed-length stacks that allocates a compile-time-determined size array to store the stacked values.

3. The code

   ```
   #define CUBE(X) ((X)*(X)*(X))
   ```

   behaves differently from the code

   ```
   template<class T> T cube (T x){ return x * x * x;}
   ```

   Explain the difference when cube(sqrt(7)) is invoked. When would the two coding schemes give different results?

4. Write a generic exchange() function with the following definition, and test it:

   ```
   template<class TYPE>
   void exchange(TYPE& a, TYPE& b, TYPE& c)
   {
   // replace a's value by b's and b's by c's
   // and c's by a's
   }
   ```

5. Write a generic function that, given an arbitrary array and its size, rotates its values with

   ```
   a[1] = a[0] , a[2] = a[1], ·····,
   a[size - 1] = a[size - 2], a[0] = a[size - 1]
   ```

6. For the *vect_it* program in Section 6.5, *Parameterizing the Class vector*, on page 302, write the member function template to print the entire `vector` range.

```
<class T> void vector<T>::print()
```

7. Rewrite the overloaded assignment operator to be more general:

```
template <class T>
vector<T>& vector<T>::operator=(const vector<T>& v)
// allow different size vectors to be assigned
// must delete and reallocate storage for left-hand
// argument and avoid in a = a
```

8. Write a generic function that requires swapping of two `vector<T>`s of different types. (See Section 6.5, *Parameterizing the Class vector*, on page 302.) Assume that both array types have elements that are assignment convertible.

9. Using `vector<T>` and its associated iterator class, code a generic vector internal sorting routine of your choice, but not quicksort (see Section 6.5, *Parameterizing the Class vector*, on page 302). Compare its running time with the STL sort routine for vectors of 100; 1,000; and 10,000 elements.

10. *(Project)* Create a parametric string type. The basic type is to act as a container class that contains a `class T` object. In the prototype case, the object is a `char`. The normal end-of-string sentinel is `0`. The standard behavior should model the functions found in the *string* library. The class definition could parameterize the sentinel as well. Such a type exists in the standard library *string*.

11. Sorting functions are natural candidates for parameterization. Rewrite the following generic bubble sort using templates:

```
void bubble(int d[], int how_many)
{
   int   temp;
   for (int i = 0; i < how_many - 1;   ++i)
      for (int j= 0; j < how_many - 1 - i; ++j)
         if (d[j] < d[j + 1]) {
            temp = d[j];
            d[j]= d[j + 1];
            d[j + 1] = temp;
         }
}
```

What happens if this is instantiated with a class in which `operator<()` is not defined? What would you need to do to get this to sort `char*` strings lexicographically?

Standard
Template Library

The standard template library (STL) is the C++ library providing generic programming for many standard data structures and algorithms. The STL provides three types of components—containers, iterators, and algorithms—that support a standard for generic programming.

The library is built using templates and is highly orthogonal in design. It is orthogonal in that components can be used in combination with one another on native and user-provided types through proper instantiation of the various elements of the STL. The following sections serve only as an overview and brief introduction to the STL, which is large and complicated. Many newer systems have important further extensions to the STL.

7.1 A Simple STL Example

We start with an example of using the container class `vector`. It was briefly discussed in Section 6.6.2, *vector<> in STL*, on page 306. This class is a generalization of the native array type in C++ and, as such, is easily understood and used. Indeed, one of the most effective uses of the STL is to replace the use of ordinary C++ arrays with STL vectors. The STL `vector` type has many important advantages over the array, such as dynamic expansion, thus avoiding overflow.

Further, it can be readily navigated with both iterators and indices and has a rich interface of built-in operations.

In file stl_vector1.cpp

```
// Simple STL vector program

#include <iostream>
#include <vector>
using namespace std;

int main ()
{
    vector<int> v(100);      // 100 is vector's size

    for (int i = 0; i < 100; ++i)
        v[i] = i;
    for (vector<int>::iterator p = v.begin();
        p != v.end(); ++p)
        cout << *p << '\t';
    cout << endl;
}
```

Dissection of the *stl_vector* Program

■ `// Simple STL vector program`

```
#include <iostream>
#include <vector>
using namespace std;
```

The library *vector* contains the STL's template for the component vector<>.

■ `vector<int> v(100);      // 100 is vector's size`

The STL container vector is used in place of an ordinary int array. As with any other template, it is instantiated with an existing type. Here, we use the native type int. The template class has a number of constructors. The one used here generates an int vector of size 100.

```
■ for (int i = 0; i < 100; ++i)
     v[i] = i;
```

The first `for` statement is written in exactly the same manner as a C++ loop on ordinary data. In most instances, vectors can be used in place of native arrays without changing working code besides the declarations.

```
■ for (vector<int>::iterator p = v.begin();
     p != v.end(); ++p)
     cout << *p << '\t';
```

The second `for` statement is written using the iterator p. An iterator behaves as a pointer. STL provides the member functions `begin()` and `end()` as initial and terminal position values for the container. Note that `end()` returns the iterator position (or address), one past the last element of the container. Thus, `end()` is a guard location, or a value signaling that you are finished traversing the container.

The next example uses the list container, an iterator, and the generic algorithm `accumulate()`. The *list* and *numeric* libraries are required.

In file stl_container.cpp

```
#include <iostream>
#include <list>                    // list container
#include <numeric>                 // for accumulate
using namespace std;

// Using the list container

void print(list<double> &lst)
{
    list<double>::iterator p;      // traverse iterator

    for (p = lst.begin(); p != lst.end(); ++p)
        cout << *p << '\t';
    cout << endl;
}
```

```
int main()
{
    double w[4] = { 0.9, 0.8, 88, -99.99 };
    list<double> z;

    for (int i = 0; i < 4; ++i)
        z.push_front(w[i]);
    print(z);
    z.sort();
    print(z);
    cout << "sum is "
         << accumulate(z.begin(), z.end(), 0.0)
         << endl;
}
```

In this example, a list container is instantiated to hold `doubles`. An array of `doubles` is pushed into the list. The `print()` function uses an iterator to print each element of the list in turn. Notice again that iterators work like pointers. Both the list and the vector have the standard `begin()` and `end()` member functions for starting and ending locations of the container. Also, the list interface includes a stable sorting algorithm, the `sort()` member function. In a stable sort, equal elements remain in the same relative position. The `accumulate()` function is a generic function in the *numeric* package that uses `0.0` as an initial value and computes the sum of the list container elements by going from the starting location `z.begin()` to the ending guard location `z.end()`.

Notice that `print()` itself could be parameterized by using an iterator range and a return value of the position where the printing leaves off, making it a more general algorithm. Let us do this:

```
// Using the iterator range
// b is the beginning location
// e is the guard location and ends the iteration

template <class Iterator>
Iterator print(Iterator b, Iterator e)
{
    for (Iterator p = b; p != e; ++p)
        cout << *p << '\t';
    cout << endl;
    return p; //guard value
}
```

This version of print is far more general. It works on any standard container, including native array types. It also illustrates some conventions that STL uses. Typically, the ending location is a guard value and is the location one past the last element processed. Thus, the loop termination test is p != e; so as not to process this location.

7.2 Containers

Containers come in two major families: sequence and associative. Sequence containers (vectors, lists, and deques) are ordered by having a sequence of elements. The vector is the most useful. The deque is a double-ended queue container, conveniently added to at both front and back. The list makes internal insertion and deletion efficient and convenient. Associative containers (sets, multisets, maps, and multimaps) have keys for looking up elements. The set is a container that stores a value according to an ordering relationship. A set contains only unique values. The multiset allows multiple copies of the same item to be stored. The map container is a basic associative array and requires that a comparison operation on the stored elements be defined. The multimap is a generalization of a map that allows nonunique keys. So, one key value may be linked to more than one value.

The two varieties of container share a similar interface.

STL Typical Container Interfaces

- Constructors, including default and copy constructors
- Element access
- Element insertion
- Element deletion
- Destructor
- Iterators

Containers are traversed using iterators that are available as templates and optimized for use with STL containers.

In file stl_deque.cpp

```
// A typical container algorithm

template <class Summable>
Summable sum(deque<Summable> &dq)
{
    deque<Summable>::iterator p;
    Summable s = 0;

    for (p = dq.begin(); p != dq.end(); ++p)
        s += *p;
    return s;
}
```

Dissection of the deque sum() Function

- `template <class Summable>`
  `Summable sum(deque<Summable> &dq)`

We sum the elements contained in this double-ended queue container dq. It is passed by reference to avoid copying costs for the potentially large data structure. The choice for identifier `Summable` is used to indicate that the instantiated type should have properties that allow for addition and should recognize a value of 0. It is a convention to capitalize the template class identifier because it is a meta-variable that is instantiated with an actual type when used by the compiler to produce machine code.

- `deque<Summable>::iterator p;`

The deque container is traversed using an `iterator`. The iterator `p` is dereferenced to obtain each stored value in turn. This algorithm works with sequence containers and all types having `operator+=()` defined. Containers allow equality and comparison operators, and have an extensive list of standard data and function members.

- `for (p = dq.begin(); p != dq.end(); ++p)`
     `s += *p;`

This is a standard traversal idiom for STL containers. Notice how it works for ordinary pointers as well. This algorithm would be more general if instead of a specific container type it used a parameterization based on an iterator range.

Container classes, as shown in Table 7.1, are designated as CAN in the following description of their interface. The identifier CAN was chosen because a can is something that holds items.

Table 7.1 STL Container Definitions	
`CAN::value_type`	Type of value held in the CAN
`CAN::reference`	Reference type to value
`CAN::const_reference`	const reference
`CAN::pointer`	Pointer to value type
`CAN::iterator`	Iterator type
`CAN::const_iterator`	const iterator accessing const values
`CAN::reverse_iterator`	Reverse iterator moving backward
`CAN::const_reverse_iterator`	const reverse iterator
`CAN::difference_type`	Represents the difference between two `CAN::iterator` values
`CAN::size_type`	Size is an integral type that can represent a `difference_type` value

All container classes have these definitions available. For example, in using the vector container class, `vector<char>::value_type` means a character value is stored in the vector container and could be traversed with a `vector<char>::iterator`. For example:

In file stl_vector_char.cpp

```
#include <iostream>
#include <typeinfo>
#include <vector>
using namespace std;

int main() {
   char c;
   vector<char>::value_type v;
   if (typeid(c) == typeid(v))
      cout << "vector<char>::value_type is just char"
           << endl;
   else
      cout << "vector<char>::value_type differs "
           << "from char" << endl;
}
```

Containers have an extensive list of standard member functions, as shown in Table 7.2.

Table 7.2 STL Container Members	
`CAN::CAN()`	Default constructor
`CAN::CAN(c)`	Copy constructor
`c.begin()`	Beginning location of CAN `c`
`c.end()`	Guard location of CAN `c`
`c.rbegin()`	Beginning used by a reverse iterator
`c.rend()`	Guard used by a reverse iterator
`c.size()`	Number of elements in CAN
`c.max_size()`	Largest possible `size`
`c.empty()`	`true` if the CAN is empty
`c.swap(d)`	Swap two CANs

Containers allow equality and comparison operators, as shown in Table 7.3.

Table 7.3 STL Container Operators	
`==  !=  <  >  <=  >=`	Equality and comparison operators using `CAN::value_type`

7.2.1   Sequence Containers

Sequence containers (`vector`, `list`, and `deque`) have a sequence of accessible elements. In many cases, the C++ array type can also be treated as a sequence container. In the *stl_vector2* program, we create a five-element `vector` v. The *deque* and *vector* libraries are used.

In file stl_vector2.cpp

```
// Sequence Containers - insert a vector into a deque
// Simple STL vector program

#include <iostream>
#include <vector>
#include <deque>
using namespace std;
```

```
int main()
{
    int  data[5] = { 6, 8, 7, 6, 5 };
    vector<int>  v(5, 6);              // 5 element vector
    deque<int>  d(data, data + 5);
    deque<int>::iterator p;
    cout << "\nDeque values" << endl;
    for (p = d.begin(); p != d.end(); ++p)
        cout << *p << '\t';           // print:6 8 7 6 5
    cout << endl;
    d.insert(d.begin(), v.begin(), v.end());
    for (p = d.begin(); p != d.end(); ++p)
        cout << *p << '\t';// print:6 6 6 6 6 8 7 6 5
    cout << endl;
}
```

Dissection of the *stl_vector* Program

■ ```
int data[5] = { 6, 8, 7, 6, 5 };
vector<int> v(5, 6);   // 5 element vector
deque<int> d(data, data + 5);
deque<int>::iterator p;
```

The vector v initializes a five-element int container to value 6. The deque d uses the iterator values data and data + 5 to initialize a five-element double-ended queue container. This is one of the standard container class constructors. Notice how it uses an iterator range to pass in arguments for the constructor. Many of the STL functions use iterator ranges as arguments. Here, array pointers are used as iterator values. The starting value is the pointer address d, and the ending guard value is the pointer address d + 5. The iterator p is declared but is not initialized. The deque<int> d is initialized sequentially to the five values 6, 8, 7, 6, and 5.

■ ```
for (p = d.begin(); p != d.end(); ++p)
    cout << *p << '\t';           // print:6 8 7 6 5
```

In this standard idiom, notice that d.end() is used to terminate the loop, because it is the end-of-container iterator guard value. Also notice that the ++ increment has pointer semantics advancing the iterator to the next container position. Dereferencing also works analogously to pointer semantics.

- `d.insert(d.begin(), v.begin(), v.end());`

The `insert()` member function places the range of iterator values `v.begin()` up to but not including `v.end()` at the position `d.begin()`. The `insert()` member function is very typical of member functions in STL, using the first iterator value as an insertion point and an iterator range for the values to be inserted.

- `for (p = d.begin(); p != d.end();++p)`
    `cout << *p << '\t';// print:6 6 6 6 6 6 8 7 6 5`

As a consequence of inserting five new elements of value 6 at the front of the deque d, the output of the traversal loop for d is now the 10 elements, as shown in the comment.

Some sequence container member functions are given in Table 7.4. Sequence classes are designated as SEQ in the following description of their interface; these are in addition to the already described CAN interface. End values designated in Table 7.4 below as `e_it` are understood as guard values.

Table 7.4 STL Sequence Members	
`SEQ::SEQ(n, v)`	n elements of value v
`SEQ::SEQ(b_it, e_it)`	Starts at b_it and goes to e_it
`c.insert(w_it, v)`	Inserts v before w_it
`c.insert(w_it, v, n)`	Inserts n copies of v before w_it
`c.insert(w_it, b_it, e_it)`	Inserts b_it to e_it before w_it
`c.erase(w_it)`	Erases the element at w_it
`c.erase(w_it, e_it)`	Erases w_it to e_it

7.2.2   Associative Containers

The associative containers (sets, multisets, maps, and multimaps) have key-based accessible elements and an ordering relation `Compare`, which is the comparison method for the associative container. In Section 7.6, *STL: Function Objects*, on page 361, we show you how to program such a method as a class that has the function call `operator()` overloaded.

Briefly, a set is a container that stores a unique value according to an ordering relationship. For example, it might store a series of strings according to lexicographic (alphabetic or dictionary order) comparison, or integers according to their value. The multiset is a generalization of a set that can store multiple copies of the same item. The map is a container that has a pair of values. Each element is a key-value pair. It allows you to look up the value based on the key in an efficient manner. This is also known as an associative array. The multimap generalizes map to allow nonunique keys. So, one key may be linked to more than one value.

We have an example of using the *map* and *string* libraries:

In file stl_age.cpp

```
// Associative Containers-looking up ages

#include <iostream>
#include <map>
#include <string>
using namespace std;

int main()
{
   map<string, int, less<string> > name_age;

   name_age["Pohl,Laura"] = 12;
   name_age["Dolsberry,Betty"] = 39;
   name_age["Pohl,Tanya"] = 14;
   cout << "Laura is " << name_age["Pohl,Laura"]
        << " years old." << endl;
}
```

Dissection of the *stl_age* Program

■ `#include <map>`
  `#include <string>`

These are two standard library header files needed for the `map` container where it is used for looking up information based on a `string`.

■ `map<string, int, less<string> > name_age;`

The `map` `name_age` is an associative array where the key is a `string` type and the `Compare` object is `less<string>`. The `map` is a template that requires three arguments. This means that an `int` value is stored in the `map` and found using a `string` value. The ordering relationship is `less<string>`.

- ■ ```
  name_age["Pohl,Laura"] = 12;
  name_age["Dolsberry,Betty"] = 39;
  name_age["Pohl,Tanya"] = 14;
  ```

  The ages of the three people are stored in the `map` `name_age`.

- ■ ```
  cout << "Laura is " << name_age["Pohl,Laura"]
       << " years old." << endl;
  ```

  Here, associative retrieval is used to get back the age of Laura Pohl. Unlike an ordinary array, which takes constant time to retrieve a stored value, the `map` requires logarithmic time per lookup.

The associative containers have several standard constructors for initialization. What distinguishes these constructors from sequence container constructors is the use of a comparison method. The insertions work when no element of the same key is already present.

Associative classes are shown as ASSOC in Table 7.5. Keep in mind that these are in addition to the already described CAN interface.

Table 7.5 STL Associative Definitions	
`ASSOC::key_type`	Retrieval key type
`ASSOC::key_compare`	Comparison method object for keys
`ASSOC::value_compare`	Comparison method object for values

The associative containers have several standard constructors for initialization, as shown in Table 7.6.

Table 7.6 STL Associative Constructors	
`ASSOC()`	Default constructor using `Compare`
`ASSOC(cmp)`	Constructor using `cmp` as the comparison method
`ASSOC(b_it, e_it)`	Uses element range `b_it` to `e_it` using `Compare`
`ASSOC(b_it, e_it, cmp)`	Uses element range `b_it` to `e_it` and `cmp` as the comparison method

What distinguishes associative constructors from sequence container constructors is the use of a comparison method, as in Table 7.7.

Table 7.7 STL Insert and Erase Member Functions	
`c.insert(t)`	Inserts t, if no existing element has the same key as t; returns `pair <iterator, bool>` with `bool` being `true` if t was not present
`c.insert(w_it, t)`	Inserts t with `w_it` as a starting position for the search; fails on sets and maps if key value is already present; returns position of insertion
`c.insert(b_it, e_it)`	Inserts the elements in this range
`c.erase(k)`	Erases elements whose key value is k, returning the number of erased elements
`c.erase(w_it)`	Erases the pointed-to element
`c.erase(b_it, e_it)`	Erases the range of elements

The insertion works when no element of the same key is already present, as seen in Table 7.8.

Table 7.8 STL Member Functions	
`c.find(k)`	Returns iterator to element having given key k; otherwise, ends
`c.count(k)`	Returns the number of elements with key k
`c.lower_bound(k)`	Returns iterator to first element having value greater or equal to key k
`c.upper_bound(k)`	Returns iterator to first element having value greater than key k
`c.equal_range(k)`	Returns an iterator pair for `lower_bound` and `upper_bound`

The associative containers are sets, multisets, maps, and multimaps. They have key-based accessible elements. These containers have an ordering relation, `Compare`, which is the comparison method for the associative container.

As a further associative container example, we use a multiset to count the number of times each vegetable enters our diet in the course of 100 meals. We use a random number generator to select which vegetable we will have in a given meal. Besides printing out the number of times each vegetable is in a meal, we will print out how the multiset stores this information.

In file stl_multiset.cpp

```
// Associative Containers-checking up on your diet

#include <iostream>
#include <set>       // used for both set and multiset
#include <vector>
using namespace std;

enum vegetables { broccoli, tomato, carrot, lettuce,
                  beet, radish, potato };

int main() {
   vector<vegetables> my_diet(100);
   vector<vegetables>::iterator pos;
   vegetables veg;
   multiset<vegetables, greater<vegetables> > v_food;
   multiset<vegetables, greater<vegetables>
                                    >::iterator vpos;

   for (pos = my_diet.begin(); pos != my_diet.end();
       ++pos) {
     *pos = static_cast<vegetables>(rand() % 7);
     v_food.insert(*pos);
   }

   cout << "How often a vegetable is eaten." << endl;
   cout << " broccoli, tomato, carrot, lettuce,"
        <<"beet, radish, potato " << endl;
   for (veg = broccoli; veg <= potato;
       veg = static_cast<vegetables>(veg + 1) )
     cout << v_food.count(veg) << endl;
   cout << "\nOffering of vegetables" << endl;
   for (vpos = v_food.begin(); vpos != v_food.end();
          ++vpos)
     cout << *vpos << '\t';
   cout << endl;
}
```

Dissection of *stl_multiset* Program

- ```
#include <set>   // used for both set and multiset
#include <vector>
using namespace std;
enum vegetables { broccoli, tomato, carrot,
                  lettuce, beet, radish, potato };
```

This program generates a random diet of vegetables. It then uses the special properties of multiset to perform a count on how often each vegetable is eaten in our diet. The set elements are taken from the type vegetable. The *set* library file contains both the set and multiset templates.

- ```
vector<vegetables> my_diet(100);
vector<vegetables>::iterator pos;
vegetables veg;
```

We store into the vector my_diet a selection of vegetables. The vector is declared to be size 100 and to have an associated iterator variable pos. The variable veg is of the enumerated type vegetables.

- ```
multiset<vegetables, greater<vegetables> > v_food;
multiset<vegetables, greater<vegetables>
                              >::iterator vpos;
```

The multiset requires a comparison relationship that is used to order and efficiently retrieve elements of the set. Notice how an iterator gets declared. All the template arguments must be reproduced when declaring the related iterator.

- ```
for (pos = my_diet.begin(); pos != my_diet.end();
     ++pos) {
   *pos = static_cast<vegetables>(rand() % 7);
   v_food.insert(*pos);
}
```

We randomly generate the seven possible vegetables. These values are inserted into both a vector my_diet and a multiset v_food.

- ```
for (veg = broccoli; veg <= potato;
     veg = static_cast<vegetables>(veg + 1))
   cout << v_food.count(veg) << endl;
```

The count() method of a multiset prints the count for each value the multiset stores. Thus, v_food.count(broccoli) tells us how many times we eat broccoli.
```

7.2.3   Container Adaptors

Container adaptor classes modify existing containers to produce various public behaviors based on an existing implementation. Three provided container adaptors are `stack`, `queue`, and `priority_queue`. The `stack` can be adapted from `vector`, `list`, and `deque` and needs an implementation that supports back, `push_back`, and `pop_back` operations. From these underlying operations and representations, the `stack` adaptor template produces the equivalent standard `stack` container with operations for `pop` and `push`. The `stack` is a last-in-first-out data structure.

The `queue` can be adapted from `list` or `deque` and needs an implementation that supports `empty`, `size`, `front`, `back`, `push_back` and `pop_front` operations. From these underlying operations and representations, the `queue` adaptor template produces the equivalent standard `queue` container with operations for `pop` and `push`. The `queue` is a first-in-first-out data structure.

The `priority_queue` is a queue that has values accessible in an order decided by a comparison operation. It can be adapted from `vector` or `deque` and needs an implementation that supports `empty`, `size`, `push_back`, `pop_back`, and `front` operations. It also needs a comparison function object, and its underlying container must support random-access iteration.

We adapt the `stack` from an underlying `vector` implementation. Notice that the STL ADTs replace our individually designed implementations of these types. The *stack*, *vector*, and *string* libraries are required.

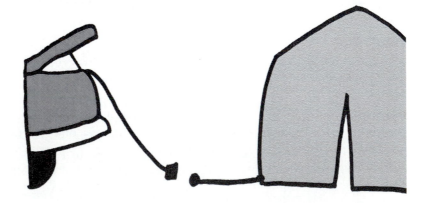

Well, I did bring the heater, but I forgot the plug adaptor!

In file stl_stack.cpp

```cpp
// Adapt a stack from a vector

#include <iostream>
#include <stack>
#include <vector>
#include <string>
using namespace std;

int main()
{
   stack<string, vector<string> > str_stack;
   string quote[3] =
         { "The wheel that squeaks the loudest\n",
           "Is the one that gets the grease\n",
           "Josh Billings\n" };

   for (int i = 0; i < 3; ++i)
      str_stack.push(quote[i]);
   while (!str_stack.empty()) {
      cout << str_stack.top();
      str_stack.pop();
   }
}
```

The output from this program is

```
Josh Billings
Is the one that gets the grease
The wheel that squeaks the loudest
```

Dissection of *stl_stack* Program

■ ```cpp
  int main()
  {
     stack<string, vector<string> > str_stack;
  ```

The stack uses an underlying representation. In this case, it uses a vector. In effect, it is a facade for the vector implementation that restricts the use of vector to a last-in-first-out data structure, namely, the stack. The template's first argument is the type stored in the stack, in this case, a string. The second argument is the stack's implementation.
  ```

```
■ for (int i = 0; i < 3; ++i)
      str_stack.push(quote[i]);
```

The basic operation is a push onto the stack. Notice how the three strings are lines from a common adage. After being pushed onto the stack, they have the last line on the top of the stack.

```
■ while (!str_stack.empty()) {
      cout << str_stack.top();
      str_stack.pop();
  }
```

The top of the stack is printed. Then the stack element is popped. This continues until the stack is empty. This results in the adage printed line by line in reverse order. Notice how `push()`, `pop()`, `empty()`, and `top()` are all standard methods for the stack container.

Special functions exist for adaptor classes, as is shown in Table 7.9 through Table 7.11.

Table 7.9 STL Adapted `stack` Functions	
`void push(const value_type& v)`	Places v on stack
`void pop()`	Removes top element of stack
`value_type& top() const`	Returns top element of stack
`bool empty() const`	Returns `true` if stack is empty
`size_type size() const`	Returns number of elements in stack
`operator==` *and* `operator<`	Equality and lexicographically less than

In the minimal description in the tables, the use of the equality operator or less-than operator causes the entire contents of two stacks to be compared for equality or less-than, respectively. The less-than is lexicographic, meaning the first elements are compared, and that continues in sequence, element pair by element pair, until a less-than is determined. Check your vendor's product for specific system-dependent implementations. In general, it is best to stay with the standard. This avoids locking you into particular products.

Table 7.10 STL Adapted queue Functions	
`void push(const value_type& v)`	Places v on end of queue
`void pop()`	Removes front element of queue
`value_type& front() const`	Returns front element of queue
`value_type& back() const`	Returns back element of queue
`bool empty() const`	Returns `true` if queue is empty
`size_type size() const`	Returns number of elements in queue
`operator==` *and* `operator<`	Equality and lexicographically less than

Table 7.11 STL Adapted priority_queue Functions	
`void push(const value_type& v)`	Places v in `priority_queue`
`void pop()`	Removes top element of `priority_queue`
`value_type& top() const`	Returns top element of `priority_queue`
`bool empty() const`	Checks for `priority_queue` empty
`size_type size() const`	Shows number of elements in `priority_queue`

7.3 Iterators

Navigation over containers is by iterator. As seen in our earlier examples, iterators should be thought of as an enhanced pointer type. Here is a simple example of iterator and pointer use:

In file stl_iterator.cpp

```
// Compare iterator and pointer traversal

#include <iostream>
#include <set>
using namespace std;
```

```
int main()
{
    int  primes[4] ={ 2, 3, 5, 7 }, *ptr = primes;
    set<int, greater<int> > s;
    set<int, greater<int> > :: const_iterator c_it;
    while (ptr != primes + 4)
        s.insert(*ptr++);

    cout << "The primes below 10 : " << endl;
    for (c_it = s.begin(); c_it != s.end(); ++c_it)
        cout << *c_it << '\t';
    cout << endl;
}
```

The preceding program uses an iterator for a set container to output one-digit primes. Such an iterator needs to have the ability to increment and to be dereferenced. Notice how the iteration travels over a range from s.begin() until s.end(). This idiom is repeated throughout the examples found here.

There are five iterator types: input, output, forward, bidirectional, and random-access. Not all iterator types may be available for a given container class. For example, random-access iterators are available for vectors but not for maps.

Input iterators support equality operations, dereferencing, and increment. An iterator that satisfies these conditions can be used for one-pass algorithms that read values of a data structure in one direction. A special case of the input iterator is the istream_iterator.

Output iterators support dereferencing restricted to the left-hand side of assignment and increment. An iterator that satisfies these conditions can be used for one-pass algorithms that write values to a data structure in one direction. A special case of the output iterator is the ostream_iterator.

Forward iterators support all input/output iterator operations, as well as unrestricted use of assignment. This allows position within a data structure to be retained from pass to pass. Therefore, general one-directional multipass algorithms can be written with forward iterators.

Bidirectional iterators support all forward iterator operations as well as both increment and decrement. Therefore, general bidirectional multipass algorithms can be written with bidirectional iterators.

Random-access iterators support all bidirectional iterator operations, as well as address arithmetic operations, such as indexing. Also, random-access iterators support comparison operations. Therefore, algorithms, such as `quicksort`, that require efficient random access in linear time can be written with these iterators.

Container classes and algorithms dictate the category of iterator available or needed; therefore, `vector` containers allow random-access iterators, but `list`s do not. Sorting generally requires a random-access iterator, but finding requires only an input iterator.

7.3.1   Iterators for *istream* and *ostream*

An `istream_iterator` is derived from an input iterator to work specifically with reading from streams. An `ostream_iterator` is derived from an output iterator to work specifically with writing to streams. We write a program that prompts for five numbers, reads them, and computes their sum, with I/O using these iterators. The template for `istream_iterator` is instantiated with a *<type>* and some older compilers require instead *<type, distance>*. This distance is usually specified by `ptrdiff_t`. More recent STL implementations do not require the `ptrdiff_t` argument, as it is defaulted. As defined in *cstddef* or *stddef*, it is an integer type representing the difference between two pointer values. Both *vector* and *iterator* libraries are needed.

In file stl_io.cpp

```
// Use of istream_iterator and ostream_iterator

#include <iterator>
#include <iostream>
#include <vector>
using namespace std;
```

```
int main()
{
    vector<int> d(5);
    int   i, sum;

    cout << "enter 5 numbers" << endl;
    istream_iterator<int> in(cin);
    ostream_iterator<int> out(cout, "\t");
    sum = d[0] = *in;      // input first value
    for (i = 1; i < 5; ++i) {
        d[i] = *++in;          // input consecutive values
        sum += d[i];
    }
    for (i = 0; i < 5; ++i)
        *out = d[i];           // output consecutive values
    cout << "sum = " << sum << endl;
}
```

Dissection of the *stl_io* Program

■ `vector<int> d(5);`

The vector container is the workhorse of STL. If you learn only this one part of the library, you gain 90 percent of the benefit from using it. Here, we have a simple vector constructor that gets us five elements.

■ `cout << "enter 5 numbers << endl;`
`  istream_iterator<int> in(cin);`

The `istream` iterator `in` is constructed with the argument `cin`. This is, of course, the standard input stream, normally the keyboard. The iterator must input `int` values as specified by its template parameter. Some older compilers require the use of `ptrdiff_t`, which is a distance type that the iterator uses to advance in getting a next element. It is the number of bytes each `int` requires for storage. If it is required, the `istream_iterator` statement is replaced by

```
    istream_iterator<int, ptrdiff_t> in(cin);
```

■ `ostream_iterator<int> out(cout, "\t")`

The `ostream_iterator` out is constructed with the output stream `cout` and the `char*` delimiter `\t`. Thus, the tab character is issued to the stream `cout` after each `int` value is written. Recent implementations of `istream_iterator` do not require the `ptrdiff_t` argument.

```
■ sum = d[0] = *in;    // input first value
  for (i = 1; i < 5; ++i) {
     d[i] = *++in;      // input consecutive values
     sum += d[i];
  }
```

The iterator `in` is a pointerlike object. When dereferenced, it forces a next value to be fetched from the standard input stream. Here, we obtain five values and place them in an array while summing them.

```
■ for (i = 0; i < 5; ++i)
     *out = d[i];       // output consecutive values
  cout << " sum = " << sum << endl;
```

Here, we use the output iterator `out` to take values from the array `d[]` and print them to the standard output stream. These five values are spaced using the tab character. We could as well have used `*out = sum,` but then we could have not commented the output with the string `" sum = "`.

The output stream iterator is isomorphic to the input stream iterator. When a value is assigned to the iterator, it is written to the instantiated output stream, using operator `<<`. As seen in the preceding example, the output stream iterator must specify the associated output stream as a parameter to the constructor. An optional second parameter to the constructor is a string that is used as a separator between values.

An `ostream_iterator` is derived from an `output_iterator` to work specifically with writing to streams. The `ostream_iterator` can be constructed with a `char*` delimiter, in this case `\t`. Thus, the tab character is issued to the stream `cout` after each `int` value is written. In this program, the iterator `out`, when it is dereferenced, writes the assigned `int` value to `cout`:

In file stl_o_iterator.cpp

```
// Use of ostream_iterator iterator

#include <iostream>
#include <iterator>
using namespace std;
```

```
int main()
{
    int  d[5] = { 2, 3, 5, 7, 11 };          // primes
    ostream_iterator<int> out(cout, "\t");

    for (int i = 0; i < 5; ++i)
        *out = d[i];
    cout << endl;
}
```

Simple file manipulations can be coded by using input and output stream iterators and various algorithms in the standard library. The following example reads a file of integers, removes all occurrences of the value 0, and copies the remaining values, separating each value with a comma:

In file stl_io_iterator.cpp

```
// Use istream_iterator & ostream_iterator iterator

#include <iostream>
#include <iterator>
#include <algorithm>
using namespace std;

void main()
{
    istream_iterator<int> input (cin), eof;
    ostream_iterator<int> output (cout, ",");

    // remove 0 from file redirected to cin
    // print file to cout
    remove_copy (input, eof, output, 0);
}
```

7.3.2   Iterator Adaptors

Iterators can be adapted to provide backward traversal and traversal with insertion. Reverse iterators reverse the order of iteration; with insert iterators, insertion takes place instead of the normal overwriting mode. All standard container classes define reverse iterators. The following example uses a reverse iterator to traverse a sequence. The *vector* library is required.

In file stl_adaptor.cpp

```cpp
// Use of the reverse iterator

#include <iostream>
#include <vector>
using namespace std;

template <class ForwIter>
void print(ForwIter first, ForwIter last,
           const char* title)
{
   cout << title << endl;
   while (first != last)
      cout << *first++ << '\t';
   cout << endl;
}
int main()
{
   int      data[3] = { 9, 10, 11 };
   vector<int> d(data, data + 3);

   print(d.begin(), d.end(), "Original");
   print(d.rbegin(), d.rend(), "Reverse");
}
```

This program uses a reverse iterator to change the direction in which the print() function prints the elements of vector d.

Ah, here's the problem. I keyed "reverse_iterator" instead of "reverse_rudder"!

STL Iterator Adaptors

- Reverse iterators—reverse the order of iteration
- Insert iterators—insertion takes place instead of the normal overwriting mode

In Table 7.12, we briefly list adaptors and their purpose, as found in this library.

Table 7.12 STL Iterator Adaptors	
`reverse_bidirectional_ iterator;`	Reverses normal direction of iteration using `rbegin()` and `rend()` for range
`reverse_iterator;`	Reverses normal direction of iteration using `rbegin()` and `rend()` for range
`inserter(c, p);`	Inserts into `c` at position `p`
`front_inserter(c);`	Inserts at front of container and requires `push_front()`
`back_inserter(c);`	Inserts at back of container and requires a `push_back()` member

7.4   Algorithms

The STL algorithms library contains the following four categories:

- Sorting algorithms
- Nonmutating sequence algorithms
- Mutating sequence algorithms
- Numerical algorithms

These algorithms generally use iterators to access containers instantiated on a given type. The resulting code can be competitive in efficiency with special-purpose codes.

7.4.1   Sorting Algorithms

Sorting algorithms include general sorting, merges, lexicographic comparison, permutation, binary search, and similar operations. These algorithms have versions that use either `operator<()` or a `Compare` object and often require random-access iterators.

The following program uses the quicksort function `sort()` from the STL *algorithm* library to sort over elements d to e.

In file stl_sort1.cpp

```cpp
// Using sort() from STL

#include <iostream>
#include <algorithm>
using namespace std;

const int N = 5;

int main()
{
    int    d[N], i, *e = d + N;

    for (i = 0; i < N; ++i)
        d[i] = rand();
    sort(d, e);
    for (i = 0; i < N; ++i)
        cout << d[i] << '\t';
    cout << endl;
}
```

This is a straightforward use of the library `sort` algorithm operating on the built-in array `d[]`. Ordinary pointer values can be used as iterators. We present some sorting algorithms in Table 7.13 through Table 7.17.

These algorithms have a form that uses a `Compare` object replacing `operator<()`, as in

```cpp
template<class RandAcc, class Compare>
void sort(RandAcc b, RandAcc e, Compare comp);
```

Here is another sorting example:

In file stl_sort2.cpp

```cpp
#include <iostream>
#include <algorithm>
using namespace std;

// Using sort() from STL
```

Table 7.13   STL Sort-Related Library Functions

`sort(b, e);`	Quicksort over elements in range b to e
`sort(b, e, comp);`	Quicksort algorithm over elements in range b to e using `comp` for ordering
`stable_sort(b, e);`	Stable sorting algorithm over elements in range b to e. In stable sort, equal elements remain in their relative same position
`partial_sort` `(b, m, e)`	Partial sorting algorithm over elements in range b to e. Range b to m filled with elements sorted up to position m
`partial_sort_copy` `(b, e,` `result_b,` `result_e)`	Partial sorting algorithm over elements in range b to e. Elements sorted taken from input iterator range and copied to random-access iterator range when smaller of two ranges is used
`nth_element` `(b, n, e)`	nth element placed in sorted order, with rest of elements partitioned by it. For example, if fifth position is chosen, four smallest elements are placed to left of it. Remaining elements placed to right of it and are greater than or equal to it
`merge (b1, e1, b2,` `e2, result_b)`	Elements in range b1 to e1 and b2 to e2 are merged to starting position `result_b`
`inplace_merge` `(b, m, e)`	Elements in range b to m and m to e are merged in place

Table 7.14   More STL Sort-Related Library Functions

`binary_search(b, e, t)`	true if t is found in b to e
`lower_bound(b, e, t)`	First position for placing t while maintaining sorted order
`upper_bound(b, e, t)`	Last position for placing t while maintaining sorted order
`equal_range(b, e, t)`	Returns iterator pair for range where t can be placed while maintaining sorted order
`next_permutation(b, e)`	Produces next permutation
`prev_permutation(b, e)`	Produces previous permutation
`lexicographical_compare` `(b1, e1, b2, e2)`	Returns true if sequence 1 is lexicographically less than sequence 2

Table 7.15 STL Sort-Related Heap Functions	
push_heap(b, e)	Places the location e's element into an already existing heap
pop_heap(b, e)	Swaps the location e's element with the b location's element and reheaps
sort_heap(b, e)	Performs a sort on the heap
make_heap(b, e)	Creates a heap

Table 7.16 STL Sort Related Min and Max Functions	
min(t1, t2)	Return the minimum of t1 and t2 that are call-by-reference arguments
max(t1, t2)	Return the maximum
min_element(b, e)	Return the position of the minimum
max_element(b, e)	Return the position of the maximum

Table 7.17 STL Sort Related Set Functions	
set_union (b1, e1, b2, e2, r)	Returns the union as output iterator r
set_intersection (b1, e1, b2, e2, r)	Returns the set intersection as output iterator r
set_difference (b1, e1, b2, e2, r)	Returns the set difference as output iterator r
set_symmetric_difference (b1, e1, b2, e2, r)	Returns the set symmetric difference as output iterator r

```
// Class MyLess works for any class T that has
// operator<() defined

template<class T>
class MyLess {
public:
   bool operator()(const T& obj1, const T& obj2)
      { return obj1 < obj2; }
};
```

```
// Function MyGreater works for any class T with
// operator>() defined

template<class T>
bool MyGreater (const T& obj1, const T& obj2)
    { return obj1 > obj2; }

const int N = 5;

int main()
{
    int  i, d[N], *e = d + N;
    MyLess<int> MyLessObj;

    for (i = 0; i < N; ++i)
        d[i] = rand()%100;
    sort(d, e, MyLess<int>()); // use comparison class
    for (i = 0; i < N; ++i)
        cout << d[i] << '\t';
    cout << endl;
    sort(d, e, MyGreater<int>); // use comparison func
    for (i = 0; i < N; ++i)
        cout << d[i] << '\t';
    cout << endl;
    sort(d, e, MyLessObj);       // use comparison method
    for (i = 0; i < N; ++i)
        cout << d[i] << '\t';
    cout << endl;
}
```

7.4.2 Nonmutating Sequence Algorithms

Nonmutating algorithms do not modify the contents of the containers they work on. A typical operation is searching a container for a particular element and returning its position.

In the following program, the nonmutating library function `find()` in the *algorithm* library is used to locate the element t:

In file stl_find.cpp

```
// Use of the find function
#include <iostream>
#include <algorithm>
#include <string>
using namespace std;
```

```
int main()
{
    string words[5] = { "my", "hop", "mop", "hope",
                        "cope"};
    string*   where;

    where = find(words, words + 5, "hop");
        cout << *++where << endl;                    // mop
    sort(words, words + 5);
    where = find(words, words + 5, "hop");
        cout << *++where << endl;                    // hope
}
```

Dissection of the *stl_find* Program

■ #include <algorithm>

The *algorithm* header is where many STL standard generic algorithms are declared.

■ string words[5] = { "my", "hop", "mop", "hope",
                      "cope"};
   string*   where;

As usual, native arrays can be used with STL algorithms and treated as random-access containers.

■ where = find(words, words + 5, "hop");

This program uses find() to look for the position of the word *hop*.

■ cout << *++where << endl;   // mop

The word after *hop* in the array is *mop*.

■ sort(words, words + 5);
  where = find(words, words + 5, "hop");
  cout << *++where << endl;   // hope

After sorting the array words[], the word after *hop* is now *hope*.

We present some of the library functions for algorithms in Table 7.18. We briefly list other algorithms and their purpose as found in this library in Table 7.19.

Table 7.18 STL Nonmutating Sequence Library Functions	
find(b, e, t)	Finds the position of t in the range b to e
find(b, e, p)	Finds the position of the first element that makes the predicate true in the range b to e; otherwise, the position e is returned

Table 7.19 STL Nonmutating Sequence Library Functions	
count(b, e, t, n)	Returns count n of elements equal to t
count_if(b, e, p, n)	Returns count n of elements that make predicate p true
adjacent_find(b, e)	Returns first position of adjacent elements that are equal; otherwise, returns e
adjacent_find (b, e, bp)	Returns first position of adjacent elements satisfying binary predicate bp; otherwise, returns e
mismatch(b1, e1, b2)	Returns iterator pair indicating positions where elements don't match from sequences starting with b1 and b2
mismatch (b1, e1, b2, bp)	As above, with binary predicate bp used instead of equality
equal(b1, e1, b2)	Returns true if indicated sequences match; otherwise, returns false
equal (b1, e1, b2, bp)	As above, with binary predicate bp used instead of equality
search(b1, e1, b2, e2)	Returns iterator where second sequence is contained in first; if not, returns e1
search (b1, e1, b2, e2, bp)	As above, with binary predicate bp used instead of equality

7.4.3 Mutating Sequence Algorithms

Mutating algorithms can modify the contents of the containers they work on. A typical operation is reversing the contents of a container.

In the following program, the mutating library functions reverse() and copy() are used. The *vector* and *algorithm* libraries are required.

In file stl_reverse.cpp

```
// Use of mutating copy and reverse
```

```
#include <iostream>
#include <string>
#include <algorithm>
#include <vector>
using namespace std;

int main()
{
   string first_names[5] = {"laura", "ira",
        "buzz", "debra", "twinkle"};
   string last_names[5] = {"pohl", "pohl",
        "dolsberry", "dolsberry", "star"};
   vector<string> names(first_names, first_names+5);
   vector<string> names2(10);
   vector<string>::iterator p;

   copy(last_names, last_names + 5, names2.begin());
   copy(names.begin(), names.end(),
        names2.begin()+5);
   reverse(names2.begin(), names2.end());
   for (p = names2.begin(); p != names2.end(); ++p)
      cout << *p <<'\t';
   cout << endl;
}
```

The first invocation of the mutating function `copy()` places `last_names` in the container `vector names2`. The second call to `copy()` copies in the `first_names` that had been used in the construction of the `vector names`. The function `reverse()` reverses all the elements, which are then printed out.

We present the library prototypes for mutating algorithms in Table 7.20.

Table 7.20	STL Mutating Sequence Library Functions
`copy(b1,e1,b2)`	Copying algorithm for elements b1 to e1. The copy is placed starting at b2. Position returned is guard value of end of copy.
`copy_backward(b1,e1,b2)`	Copying algorithm for elements b1 to e1. The copy is placed starting at b2 and runs backward from e1 into b2. Position returned is `b2-(e1 - b1)`.
`for_each(b, e, f)`	Applies the function f to each value found in the range b to e

Table 7.20 STL Mutating Sequence Library Functions	
`reverse(b, e)`	Reverses in place the elements b to e
`reverse_copy(b1, e1, b2)`	Reverse copying algorithm for elements b1 to e1. Copy in reverse is placed starting at b2 and runs backward from e1 into b2. Position returned is b2 + (e1 - b1).
`unique(b, e)`	Adjacent duplicate elements in the range b to e are erased, and position returned is end of resulting range

The remaining library functions are briefly described in Table 7.21.

Table 7.21 STL Mutating Sequence Library Functions	
`unique(b, e, bp);`	Adjacent duplicate elements in range b to e with binary predicate bp satisfied are erased. Returns end of resulting range.
`unique_copy(b1, e1, b2)`	Results are copied to b2 with original range unchanged
`unique_copy(b1, e1,` `        b2, bp)`	If binary predicate bp is satisfied, results are copied to b2 with original range
`next_permutation(b, e)`	Rearranges the elements in range b to e according to the next permutation
`prev_permutation(b, e)`	Produces previous permutation
`swap(t1, t2)`	Swaps t1 and t2
`iter_swap(b1, b2)`	Swaps pointed-to locations
`swap_range` `   (b1, e1, b2)`	Swaps elements from b1 to e1 with those starting at b2; returns b2 + (e1 - b1)
`transform` `   (b1, e1, b2, op)`	Using unary operator op, transforms the sequence b1 to e1, placing it at b2; returns end of output location

`transform`
`   (b1, e1, b2,`
`    b3, bop)`
	Uses binary operator bop on two sequences starting with b1 and b2 to produce sequence b3; returns end of output location

`replace(b, e, t1, t2)`	Replaces in range b to e value t1 by t2
`replace_if` `   (b, e, p, t2)`	Replaces in range b to e elements satisfying predicate p by t2

Table 7.21 STL Mutating Sequence Library Functions	
`replace_copy` `(b1, e1, b2, t1, t2)`	Copies and replaces into b2 range b1 to e1 with value t1 replacing t2
`replace_copy_if` `(b1, e1, b2, p, t2)`	Copies and replaces into b2 range b1 to e1 with elements satisfying predicate p replacing t2
`remove(b, e, t)`	Removes elements of value t
`remove_if()`, `remove_copy()`, `remove_copy_if()`	These correspond to `replace()` methods, except that values are removed
`fill(b, e, t)`	Assigns t to range b to e
`fill_n(b, n, t)`	Assigns n ts starting at b
`generate (b, e, gen)`	Assigns to range b to e by generator gen
`generate_n` `(b, n, gen)`	Assigns n values starting at b using gen
`rotate(b, m, e)`	Rotates leftward elements of range b to e; element in position *i* ends up in position *(i + n − m) % n,* where *n* is range size, m is midposition and b is first position
`rotate_copy` `(b1, m, e1, b2)`	As above, but copies to b2 with original unchanged
`random_shuffle(b, e)`	Shuffles the elements
`random_shuffle` `(b, e, rand)`	Shuffles the elements using the supplied random number generator rand
`partition` `(b, e, p)`	Range b to e is partitioned to have all elements satisfying predicate p placed before those that do not satisfy p
`stable_partition` `(b, e, p)`	As above, but preserving relative order

7.4.4 Numerical Algorithms

Numerical algorithms include sum, inner product, and adjacent difference. In the following program, the function `accumulate()` from the *numeric* library performs a vector summation, and `inner_product()` performs a vector inner product.

In file stl_numeric.cpp

```cpp
// Vector accumulation and inner product

#include <iostream>
#include <numeric>
using namespace std;

int main()
{
    double v1[3] = { 1.0, 2.5, 4.6 },
           v2[3] = { 1.0, 2.0, -3.5 };
    double sum, inner_p;

    sum = accumulate(v1, v1 + 3, 0.0);
    inner_p = inner_product(v1, v1 + 3, v2, 0.0);
    cout << "sum = " << sum << ", product = "
         << inner_p << endl;
}
```

The output from this program is

```
sum = 8.1, product = -10.1
```

Dissection of the *stl_numeric* Program

■ `#include <numeric>`

This is the header for STL generic numerical algorithms.

■ `sum = accumulate(v1, v1 + 3, 0.0);`

This function behaves as expected on numerical types, where + is defined. The `accumulate` algorithm takes the starting and ending positions and, as a third argument, the initial value, normally `0.0`, to start accumulating the sum with. In this case, we add the three elements initialized in the `double` array `v1[]`.

■ `inner_p = inner_product(v1, v1 + 3, v2, 0.0);`

This function behaves as expected on numerical types, where + and *
are defined. The `inner_product` algorithm takes the starting and ending positions of a first sequence and, as a third argument, the starting
position for a second sequence. The fourth argument is normally `0.0`
and is the starting value for accumulating the inner product value.
Each position is then multiplied and accumulated to produce the inner
product. In this case, we compute

`v1[0] * v2[0] + v1[1] * v2[1] + v1[2] * v2[2]`

The library prototypes for numerical algorithms are shown in Table
7.22.

Table 7.22 STL Numerical Library Functions	
`accumulate(b, e, t)`	Successive elements from range b to e are summed and added to sum t
`accumulate` `(b, e, t, bop)`	Successive elements from range b to e are summed with sum function `bop(sum, element)` and added to t
`inner_product` `(b1, e1, b2, t)`	Returns inner product from two ranges starting with b1 and b2; this product is initialized to t, usually 0
`inner_product (b1,` `e1, b2, t, bop1, bop2)`	Returns generalized inner product using bop1 to sum and bop2 to multiply
`partial_sum` `(b1, e1, b2)`	Produces a sequence of element sums starting at b2 that is the partial sum of the terms from range b1 to e1
`partial_sum` `(b1, e1, b2, bop)`	As above, using bop for summation
`adjacent_difference` `(b1, e1, b2)`	Produces sequence starting at b2 that is adjacent difference of terms from range b1 to e1
`adjacent_difference` `(b1, e1, b2, bop)`	As above, using bop for difference

Numerical Integration Made Easy

7.5

STL provides the basic computations for many more sophisticated algorithms. By using STL, programmers can easily implement those algorithms. We use numerical integration as an example. The idea is to generate a series of points, using a generator. A generator is a class that defines the function by overloading `operator()`, the function call operator. The STL algorithm

```
generate(iterator b, iterator e, generator g)
```

is used to produce a `vector` of values in the range (0, 1) for the function. The *algorithm*, *numeric*, and *vector* libraries are all required.

In file stl_integration1.cpp

```cpp
// Simple integration routine for x * x over (0, 1)

#include <iostream>
#include <numeric>
#include <algorithm>
#include <vector>
using namespace std;

// The function is represented in class gen

class gen {      // generator for integrated function
public:
   gen(double x_zero, double increment)
     : x(x_zero), incr(increment) { }
   double operator()() { x += incr; return x * x; }
private:
   double x, incr;
};

double integrate(gen g, int n)  // integrate on (0,1)
{
   vector<double> fx(n);

   generate(fx.begin(), fx.end(), g);
   return(accumulate(fx.begin(), fx.end(), 0.0) / n);
}
```

```
int main()
{
    const int n = 10000;

    gen g(0.0, 1.0/n);
    cout << "integration program x**2" << endl;
    cout << integrate(g, n) << endl;
}
```

Dissection of the *stl_integration* Program

- ```
  class gen { // generator for integrated function
  public:
      gen(double x_zero, double increment)
        : x(x_zero), incr(increment) { }
      double operator()() {x += incr; return x * x; }
  private:
      double x, incr;
  };
  ```

To write a generator, we must write a class that overloads the function call operator with no arguments. In this case, `gen::operator()()` is used to increment a value x. The class constructor is used to initialize the variable x and the increment for it, `incr`. The idea is to use this to generate a sequence of values where the function is numerically integrated.

- ```
  double integrate(gen g, int n)  // integrate (0,1)
  {
      vector<double> fx(n);
  ```

We use the generator to integrate between 0 and 1 in increments of 1/n. The values of the expression x * x at the points between 0 up to and including 1 are stored in vector `fx`.

- ```
  generate(fx.begin(), fx.end(), g);
  ```

The generator object g is used to generate the n x * x values at increments of 1/n.

- ```
  return(accumulate(fx.begin(), fx.end(), 0.0) / n);
  ```

This numerical sum is an approximation to integrating $f(x) = x^2$.

```
■ int main()
  {
      const int n = 10000;

      gen g(0.0, 1.0/n);
      cout << "integration program x**2" << endl;
      cout << integrate(g, n) << endl;
  }
```

The generator object is initialized with an increment of 1/10,000. That means 10,000 points are used for the evaluation. On our local system, the answer is 0.333383. The answer if worked out by calculus is 1/3. So the numerical solution is accurate to four significant digits.

We can write a more accurate numerical integrator. We approximate the area under the curve by a sequence of rectangles whose height is the value of the function and whose width is the increment. An increment gives us two choices for a height, and in the previous example, we have chosen the right end point to compute it. We could improve the numerical accuracy of integration by bounding the area between rectangles based on the smaller heights and one based on the larger heights.

In file stl_integration2.cpp

```
// Simple integration routine for x * x over (0, 1)

#include <iostream>
#include <numeric>
#include <algorithm>
#include <vector>
using namespace std;

// The function is represented in class gen

class gen {     // generator for integrated function
public:
    gen(double x_zero, double increment)
     : x(x_zero), incr(increment) { }
    double operator()() { x += incr; return x * x; }
private:
    double x, incr;
};
```

```
// Integrate on (0,1)

double integrate(gen g, int n, double& diff)
{
   vector<double> fx(n + 1), sm(n), lg(n);
   double s, l;

   generate(fx.begin(), fx.end(), g);
   for (int i = 0; i < n; ++i)
      if (fx[i] > fx[i + 1]) {
         sm[i] = fx[i + 1]; lg[i] = fx[i];
      }
      else {
         sm[i] = fx[i]; lg[i] = fx[i + 1];
      }
   s = accumulate(sm.begin(), sm.end(), 0.0) / n;
   l = accumulate(lg.begin(), lg.end(), 0.0) / n;
   diff = l - s;
   return(s + l) / 2;
}

int main()
{
   const int n = 10000;

   gen g(0.0, 1.0/n);
   cout << "integration program x**2" << endl;
   double d, i = integrate(g, n, d);
   cout << "integral = " << i << " +/- "
        << (d / 2) << endl;
}
```

The second version of `integrate()` produces a more reliable estimate, with an error estimate calculated in `diff`. In this method, we get a result of 0.333333 on our system, which is accurate to six digits.

7.6   STL: Function Objects

It is useful to have function objects to further leverage the STL library. For example, many of the previous numerical functions had a built-in meaning using + or *, but also had a form in which user-provided binary operators could be passed in as arguments. Defined function objects can be found in *function* or built. Function objects are classes that have `operator()` defined. These are inlined and are compiled to produce efficient object code.

In file stl_function.cpp

```
// Using a function object minus<int>

#include <iostream>
#include <numeric>
using namespace std;

int main()
{
  double v1[3] = { 1.0, 2.5, 4.6 }, sum;

  sum = accumulate(v1, v1 + 3, 0.0, minus<int>());
  cout << "sum = " << sum << endl;      // sum = -7
}
```

Accumulation is done using integer minus for the binary operation over the array v1[]. Therefore, the double values are truncated, with the result being –7.

There are three defined function object classes.

STL Defined Function Object Classes

■ Arithmetic function objects

■ Comparison function objects

■ Logical function objects

We use Table 7.23 to briefly list algorithms and their purpose as found in this library. Arithmetic function objects are often used in numerical algorithms, such as accumulate().

Table 7.23 STL Arithmetic Function Objects	
`<class T> struct plus`	Add for type T
`<class T> struct minus`	Subtract for type T
`<class T> struct times`	Multiply for type T, obsolete
`<class T> struct multiplies`	Multiply for type T
`<class T> struct divides`	Divide for type T
`<class T> struct modulus`	Modulus operator for type T
`<class T> struct negate`	Unary minus for type T

The comparison methods are frequently used with sorting algorithms, such as merge().

Table 7.24 STL Comparison Function Objects	
`equal_to`	Equality of 2 operands
`not_equal_to`	Inequality of 2 operands
`greater`	Comparison by greater (>) of 2 operands
`less`	Comparison by less (<) of 2 operands
`greater_equal`	Comparison by greater or equal (>=) of 2 operands
`less_equal`	Comparison by less or equal (<=) of 2 operands

Table 7.25 STL Logical Function Objects	
`logical_and`	Performs logical and (&&) on two operands
`logical_or`	Performs logical or (||) on two operands
`logical_not`	Performs logical negation (!) on single argument

7.6.1   Building a Function Object

To better understand the library-provided function objects, let us see how to provide our own. Let us write a binary operator that alternates between being plus and minus. This is frequently used in alternating series in mathematics.

```
int alternate(int x, int y)
{
    static int sign = -1;
    sign = -sign;
    return x + (y * sign);
}
```

It could be used as the binary operator for `accumulate()` as follows:

```
sum = accumulate(v1, v1 + 3, 0.0, alternate);
```

This function `alternate()` could be used in place of `minus<int>()`. It would then add and subtract alternate terms when used by `accumulate()`. This would work on arguments that are `int` or convertible to `int`.

More generally, we can write a template class with `operator()` overloaded.

```
template <class T>
class alternate {
public:
    T operator()(const T& x, const T& y) const
    {
        static int sign = -1;
        sign = -sign;
        return x + (y * sign);
    }
};
```

Now this will work on arbitrary types that support the various arithmetic operations found in the definition of `operator()`. It could be used as the binary operator for `accumulate()` as follows:

```
sum = accumulate(v1, v1 + 3, 0.0, alternate<int>());
```

7.6.2 Function Adaptors

A function adaptor is a function object. It allows function objects to be composed with each other or with other functions. STL provides some predefined function adaptors.

STL Function Adaptors

- Negators for negating predicate objects
- Binders for binding a function argument
- Adaptors for pointer to a function

In the following example, we use a binder function `bind2nd()` to transform an initial sequence of values to a sequence where these values doubled.

In file stl_fadaptor.cpp

```
// Use of the function adaptor bind2nd

#include <iostream>
#include <algorithm>
#include <functional>
#include <string>
using namespace std;
```

```
template <class ForwIter>
void print(ForwIter first, ForwIter last,
           const string& title)
{
  cout << title << endl;
  while (first != last)
    cout << *first++ << '\t';
  cout << endl;
}

int main()
{
  int  data[3] = { 9, 10, 11 };

  print(data, data + 3, "Original values");
  transform(data, data + 3, data,
            bind2nd(multiplies<int>(), 2));
  print(data, data + 3, "New values");
}
```

Dissection of the *stl_fadaptor* Program

- ```
  #include <algorithm>
  #include <functional>
  #include <string>
  ```

As with all STL programs we need to include the appropriate libraries. The function `transform()` comes from the *algorithm* library. The function adapter `bind2nd()` and the function object `multiplies<int>()` come from the *functional* library.

- ```
  transform(data, data + 3, data,
            bind2nd(multiplies<int>(), 2));
  ```

The `transform()` function has as its first two arguments the iterator range for the values that are transformed. Here, we transform the array elements `data[0]`, `data[1]`, and `data[2]`. The transformed values are placed starting at the destination iterator value, which is the third argument. Here, this starts at the beginning of the array `data`. The fourth argument is a unary function operator. Here, this is `bind2nd()`. Its purpose is to adapt the `multiplies<int>()` operator, which is binary, to a unary operator. It makes the second argument the integer constant 2. This has the effect of doubling each element value in the original iterator range.

Where the function object `multiplies<int>` is not available, use `times<int>`, as this is an earlier implementation of this object. We use Table 7.26 to briefly list algorithms and their purpose.

Table 7.26 STL Function Adaptors	
`not1(p)`	Returns `!p` where p is unary predicate
`not2(p)`	Returns `!p` where p is binary predicate
`binder1st<Op> bind1st (op, t)`	Binary op has first argument bound to `t`; a function object is returned
`binder2nd<Op> bind2nd (op, t)`	Binary op has second argument bound to `t`; a function object is returned
`ptr_fun(T (*f)(Arg))`	Constructs a `pointer_to_unary_function<Arg, T>`
`ptr_fun(T (*f) (Arg1, Arg2))`	Constructs a `pointer_to_binary_function <Arg1, Arg2, T>`

7.7   Allocators

Allocator objects manage memory for containers. They allow implementations to be tailored to local system conditions while maintaining a portable interface for the container class. Allocator definitions include `value_type`, `reference`, `size_type`, `pointer`, and `difference_type`. We briefly list allocator member functions as found in this library in Table 7.27.

Table 7.27 STL Allocator Members	
`allocator();` `~allocator();`	Constructor and destructor for allocators
`pointer address(r);`	Returns address of r
`pointer allocate(n);`	Allocates memory for n objects of `size_type` from free store
`void deallocate(p);`	Deallocates memory associated with p
`size_type max_size();`	Returns largest value for `difference_type`; in effect, largest number of elements allocatable to a container

7.8   Software Engineering: STL Use

The not-invented-here syndrome is especially costly when developing software. Programmers are uncomfortable using others' code. However, STL is to be greatly preferred to specially developed code. It is far easier to maintain and is highly portable and efficient. When possible, it is desirable to use library functions that are known to be efficient, debugged, and well documented.

When extending STL, you should write in an STL style. This means that algorithms should be coded to use the weakest iterator class that leaves the code efficient. This also means that code should work on parameters that are iterator ranges.

Let us write code that will count how many of a given character appear in a vector of `char`:

```
int count(vector<char> & v, char comp)
{
    int  count = 0;
    vector<char>::iterator p;

    for (p = v.begin(); p !=v.end(); ++p)
        count += (comp == *p);
    return count;
}
```

This is not properly general. There is no reason to limit the container to the vector. Better is the following:

```
template<class InIterator>
int count(InIterator b, InIterator e, char comp)
{
    int  count = 0;

    for(; b != e; ++b)
        count += (comp == *b);
    return count;
}
```

Iterator ranges and template code is in the style of STL. This version is far more reusable. One last generalization is to not tie the algorithm to finding a character `comp` but instead to allow it to be whatever the iterator value type is. This will be left as an exercise.

7.8.1   Syntax Bugs

There is a tricky lexical problem that leads to confusion when first using templates. It is found in the following template instantiation:

```
vector<vector<int>> b; // may give a syntax error
```

Here, we expect to declare a `vector` of `vectors` of `int`. Certainly a very useful container. The problem is that the `>>` is interpreted as the token for the bit-shift operator. This does not make sense here. Instead, you should use extra space, as in:

```
vector<vector<int> > b; // space makes it okay
```

Once you get used to STL, you will want to replace native array code with `vector` code. The advantages of `vector` use outweigh any minor loss of efficiency or storage utilization advantages for native arrays. The `vector` container is safer. It is typically used with iterators that safeguard the user from falling out of range. It is more flexible. For example, a `vector` can automatically expand.

In file stl_vec_is_best.cpp

```cpp
// Use of vector is better than array

#include <iostream>
#include <vector>
using namespace std;

int main()
{
   vector<int> d(5); //usually only 5 numbers
   int  i, sum = 0;

   cout << "\nEnter integers - 0 terminates" << endl;
   for (i = 0; cin >> d[i] && d[i] != 0; ++i)
     sum += d[i];
     cout << "sum = " << sum << endl;
}
```

7.9   Dr. P's Prescriptions

- For sequence containers, think vector first, deque second, and list last.

- Use the most efficient container for a computation.

- When adapting, remember that the underlying structure determines efficiency.

- Use iterator parameters rather than container variables.

- Use the weakest iterator category compatible with the function.

- Use the most efficient algorithm for a computation.

- Modify or adapt existing STL algorithms.

- Understand function composition.

- Make sure your vendor implements the standard.

The vector is generally the easiest container to use. It is a simple generalization of the array and as such is most familiar to programmers. It is also often the most efficient over a large class of operations. It should be your default container choice. The deque is the next most useful. Its ability to add to both ends of the data structure in linear time is its greatest strength. It also supports random access. The list in many ways is the most expensive container class. Its chief benefit is to give you insertion and deletion of internal elements in constant time without destroying existing iterator values. Again, be guided by the most frequent operations required by your problem in making these choices.

There is relative ease in switching among containers. One container can be constructed by passing an iterator range from another container. Do not be afraid of using multiple representations for some problems that dictate a combination of space-operation cost trade-offs. The point of STL is to use a more efficient algorithm. Usually, this involves selecting the appropriate container.

Container adaption results in a supported interface, such as a stack or priority queue, that hides the underlying container implementation. Nevertheless, the different implementations dictate the efficiency of the resulting data structure. Your choice should be sensitive to what operations and space constraints are important to your problem. When in doubt, profile your program.

Iterator sequences are not tied to a particular type of container. Container types are a narrower style of representation than iterator ranges. Ergo, using iterator sequences leaves algorithms more general and hence more reusable.

Our modus operandi in generic programming is to make the program as general as possible without degrading efficiency. This leads to rule 2; namely, use the weakest iterator type compatible with an efficient implementation of a computation.

The STL algorithms are expected to be efficient. The generalized sort is an efficient version of quicksort and compares favorably in most cases to running `qsort()` as found in the C standard library.

As in the preceding example of numerical integration, STL routines can be readily employed and adapted to perform significant computations without resorting to special codes. In many cases, a lack of understanding of the mathematical concept of function composition prevents a programmer from fully mastering the notion and techniques of adaptation. Many of these concepts are routinely used in functional languages or logic-based languages such as Lisp, ML, Scheme, and Prolog. It can be useful to look at examples written in those languages to better understand how these ideas can apply to STL.

Many vendors have variations on the STL standard. There can also be problems with the vendors' support of template compilation. These algorithms have been tested on the latest Sun Microsystem compiler and with Borland 5.1 and found to work. There were some problems with Microsoft C++ version 6.0. Generally, these can be easily remedied by looking at your vendor's documentation.

7.10   C++ Compared with Java

Unlike C++, Java does not have templates. Instead, each class in Java can be viewed as an extension of the superclass `Object`. This is done implicitly. The `Object` superclass provides for a type of generic programming and achieves some of the ideas of polymorphism accomplished by the use of templates in C++.

There is a Java Generic Library (JGL) that corresponds roughly to STL for C++. The use of `Object` in writing generic code is based on inheritance and is discussed in Chapter 8, *Inheritance and OOP*.

The package *java.util* has several useful containers, including `LinkedList` and `Stack`. The Java array type is safer than the C++ native array, so in some sense it more closely approximates the `vector`. A Java array is allocated off the heap. It also has a `length` member that dynamically tracks the array size. This is described in detail in *Java by Dissection*, by Ira Pohl and Charlie McDowell, (Addison-Wesley, 1999), page 147.

Summary

- The standard template library (STL) is the C++ library that provides generic programming for standard data structures and algorithms.

- Containers come in two major families: sequence and associative. Sequence containers (vectors, lists, and deques) are ordered by having a sequence of elements. Associative containers (sets, multisets, maps, and multimaps) have keys for looking up elements.

- Container adaptor classes modify existing containers to produce different public behaviors, based on an existing implementation. Three provided container adaptors are `stack`, `queue`, and `priority_queue`.

- Iterators can be thought of as an enhanced pointer type. The five iterator types are input, output, forward, bidirectional, and random-access. Not all iterator types may be available for a given container class. For example, random-access iterators are available for vectors but not for maps.

- The STL algorithm's library contains the following four categories: sorting algorithms, nonmutating sequence algorithms, mutating sequence algorithms, and numerical algorithms. These algorithms generally use iterators to access containers instantiated on a given type. The resulting code can be competitive in efficiency with special-purpose codes.

- It is useful to have function objects to further leverage the STL library. Defined function objects can be found in *function* or built. Function objects are classes that have `operator()` defined. These are inlined and are compiled to produce efficient object code.

- When extending STL you should write in an STL style. This means that algorithms should be coded to use the weakest iterator class that leaves the code efficient. This also means that code should work on parameters that are iterator ranges.

Review Questions

1. The three components of STL are _____, _____, and _____.

2. An iterator is like a _____ type in the kernel language.

3. The member _____ is used as a guard for determining the last position in a container.

4. Name two STL sequence container classes.

5. Name two STL associative container classes.

6. Can STL be used with ordinary array types? Explain.

7. True or false: A template argument can be only a type.

8. A nonmutating STL algorithm, such as `find()`, has the property _____.

Exercises

1. Using a random number generator, generate 10,000 integers between 0 and 9,999. Place them in a `list<int>` container. (See Section 7.1, *A Simple STL Example*, on page 323.) Compute and print the median value. What did you expect? Compute the frequencies of each value; in other words, how many 0s were generated, how many 1s were generated, and so forth. Print the value with the greatest frequency. Use a `vector<int>` to store the frequencies.

2. Recode `print(const list<double> &lst)` to be a template function that is as general as possible. (See Section 7.1, *A Simple STL Example*, on page 323.)

3. Write an algorithm for `vector<> v` that adds the values stored in the elements `v[2 * i]`, the even-valued indices of the vector. Test it on ints and doubles.

4. Write a program that inputs a string. It then separates the string into a list of words. Finally, it should sort the list of words and print out this list. You need to use `list<string>` and can use any of STL.

5. For `list<T>`, write the member function

    ```
    iterator list<T>::insert(iterator w_it, T v);
    ```

    which inserts v before `w_it` and returns an iterator pointing at the inserted element. (See Section 7.1, *A Simple STL Example*, on page 323.)

6. For `list<T>`, write the member function

    ```
    void list<T>::erase(iterator w_it);
    ```

    which erases the element pointed at by `w_it`. (See Section 7.1, *A Simple STL Example*, on page 323.)

7. Write an algorithm to find the second largest element stored in an arbitrary container class. Use STL containers `vector<T>`, `list<T>`, and `set<T>` to test that it works regardless of the container. Write the algorithm, assuming that a forward iterator is available and comparison is understood.

8. Write and test the template code for the STL library function `count_if(b, e, p, n)`, where p is a predicate and n is the summing variable.

9. Rewrite the flushing program of Section 4.7, *An Example: Flushing*, on page 174, to use STL container classes.

10. Rewrite exercise 9 to use `random_shuffle()` instead of the special purpose routine found in the original code. Why is this better methodology?

11. Improve the *stl_multiset.cpp* program by having the output appear as `vegetable was eaten k times` instead of a simple unlabeled integer. One way to do this is to create an array of vegetable names indexed by the vegetables enumeration value.

12. Change the ordering of vegetables in the previous exercise to be `lesser<vegetable>` and print the result.

13. Use a map to create a table of foods and calories per portion. For example carrots—45, ice cream—250, and so on. Place at least 10 foods in your map. Use a random number generator to pick 4 foods per meal. Print out the meal and its calorie total.

14. Write a comparison object that uses the square of an objects value for comparison. Therefore, a large negative number is

greater than a small positive number using this comparison object. Generate in a vector the integers –100 to +100 and use an STL sort with this comparison object. Print out the result.

15. Write an STL algorithm `product(b1, e1, b2, c1)` that multiplies the elements starting at `b1` by the elements starting at `b2` and places the results starting at `c1`. The parameter `e1` is the guard value for the first sequence.

16. *(Project)* Design a data type `class matrix` that uses vectors to hold rectangular arrays of elements. How should iterators be implemented for such a two-dimensional container? You need to think about basic accessing operations and algorithms such as matrix addition and multiplication.

Inheritance and OOP

I nheritance is the powerful code-reuse mechanism of deriving a new class from an old one. That is, the existing class can be added to or altered to create the derived class. Through inheritance, a hierarchy of related types that share code and interfaces can be created.

Many useful types are variants of one another, and it is frequently tedious to produce the same code for each. A derived class inherits the description of the base class, which can then be altered by adding members and modifying existing member functions and access privileges. The usefulness of inheritance can be seen by examining how taxonomic classification compactly summarizes large bodies of knowledge.

For example, knowing the concept *mammal* and knowing that an elephant and mouse are both mammals allows our descriptions of them to be considerably more succinct than they are otherwise. The root concept contains the information that mammals are warm-blooded higher vertebrates and that they nourish their young through mammary glands. This information is inherited by the concept of both mouse and elephant, but it is expressed only once: in the root concept. In C++ terms, both elephant and mouse are derived from the base class *mammal*.

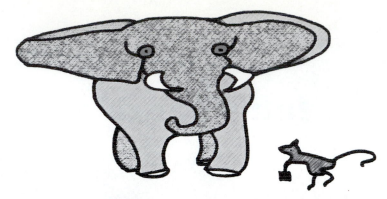

Hey! Don't flatten me, I'm your cousin from Chicago!

C++ supports virtual member functions: functions declared in the base class and redefined in a derived class. A class hierarchy that is defined by public inheritance creates a related set of user types, all of whose objects may be pointed at by a base-class pointer. By accessing the virtual function through this pointer, C++ selects the appropriate function definition at runtime. The object being pointed at must carry around type information so that this distinction can be made dynamically, a feature typical of object-oriented code. Each object knows how it is to be acted on. This is a form of polymorphism called pure polymorphism.

Inheritance should be designed into software to maximize reuse and to allow a natural modeling of the problem domain. With inheritance, the key elements of the OOP design methodology are as follows:

OOP Design Methodology

1. Decide on an appropriate set of types.

2. Design in relationships among types and use inheritance to share code.

3. Use virtual functions to process like objects polymorphically.

8.1   A Derived Class

A class can be derived from an existing class by using the form

> class *class-name* : (public|protected|private)$_{opt}$*base-name*
> {
>   *member declarations*
> };

As usual, the keyword `class` can be replaced by the keyword `struct`, with the implication that members are by default `public`. One aspect of the derived class is the visibility of its inherited members. The keywords `public`, `protected`, and `private` are used after the colon to specify how the base-class members are to be accessible to the derived class. The keyword `protected` is introduced to allow data hiding for members that must be available in derived classes but that otherwise act like private members. It is an intermediate form of access between public and private.

Consider developing software to track everyone at a college or university. First, everyone is a person. Then some people are employees and some people are students. Each of these two major categories has further subcategories: undergraduate and graduate students, staff and faculty employees. Understanding a university leads to a natural hierarchy of the groups that participate at the university.

The `person` class has members that describe a person, such as name and gender.

In file person.h

```
class person {
public:
   person(const string& nm, int a,
          char g) : name(nm), age(a), gender(g) { }
   void print() const { cout << *this << endl; }
   friend ostream& operator<<(ostream& out,
                               const person& p);
protected:
   string name;
   int   age;
   char gender;              // male == 'M', female == 'F'
};
```

```
ostream& operator<<(ostream& out, const person& p)
{
    return (out << p.name << ", age is " << p.age
                << ", gender is " << p.gender);
}
```

The class `person` has the access keyword `protected`, which makes its members inaccessible to nonclass methods. We could use `person` in a code fragment, as follows:

```
// Declare and initialize

person abe(string("Abe Pohl"), 92, 'M');
cout << abe << endl;         // Abe info printed out
```

The output from these statements is

```
Abe Pohl, age is 92, gender is M
```

We can now create a new class for representing students that is derived from class `person`. The idea is that a student is a type of person, and this idea is expressed by `student` inheriting `person`'s code.

In file student.h

```
enum year { fresh, soph, junior, senior };
const string year_label[]= { "freshman", "sophomore",
                             "junior", "senior" };

class student: public person {
public:
    student(const string& nm, int a, char g,
            double gp, year yr)
        : person(nm, a, g), gpa(gp), y(yr) { }
    void print() const { cout << *this << endl; }
    friend ostream& operator<<(ostream& out,
                               const student& s);
protected:
    double gpa;
    year y;
};
```

```
ostream& operator<<(ostream& out, const student& s) {
    return(out << static_cast<person>(s) << ", "
                << year_label[s.y] << ", gpa = "
                << s.gpa);
}
```

Dissection of the student Class

- ```
  enum year { fresh, soph, junior, senior };

  const string year_label[]={"freshman",
                  "sophomore", "junior", "senior" };
  ```

An enumerated type is used to describe a student's year at college. The corresponding string entries are used in the output.

- ```
  class student: public person {
  ```

The keyword `public` means two things in this context. One is that `student` inherits the members of `person` and keeps their access at the same visibility level. So if in `person`, the member `gender` is `protected`, it remains `protected` in `student`. But it also means that `student` is a subtype of `person`. This is important in that it allows code that is written to operate on `person` to also operate on `student`.

- ```
  student(const string& nm, int a, char g,
          double gp, year yr)
          : person(nm, a, g), gpa(gp), y(yr) { }
  ```

Here, we have the constructor for `student`. Inside the constructor's initializer list is the class identifier `person` called with three arguments. This calls the `person` constructor to initialize the part of `student` that consists of its `person`'s members.

- ```
  void  print() const; { cout << *this << endl; }
  friend ostream& operator<<(ostream& out,
                                  const student& s);
  protected:
      double  gpa;
      year  y;
  };
  ```

The method declared here is `student::print()`, but recall that `person::print()` is imported through inheritance, so there are two `print` methods in `student`. The overloaded operator `>>` must be made a friend and then defined outside the class.

```
■  ostream& operator<<(ostream& out,
                       const student& s) {
   return(out << static_cast<person>(s) << ", "
              << year_label[s.y] << ", gpa = "
              << s.gpa);
   }
```

This overloads the output operator for printing so that the standard output << can be used with **student** objects. The method first invokes the output of **person**, in this case **name**, **age**, and **gender**. The rest of the code prints out the string corresponding to member y and the **gpa**. Notice that **out** is returned so that multiple objects can be output with a single statement.

We could use **student** in a code fragment as follows:

```
student abe(string("Abe Pohl"), 92, 'M', 3.9, soph);
cout << abe << endl;      // abe info printed out
```

The output from this print statement is

```
Abe Pohl, age is 92, gender is M, soph, gpa = 3.9
```

In this example, **student** is the derived class and **person** is the base class. The use of the keyword **public** following the colon in the derived-class header means that the protected and public members of **person** are to be inherited as protected and public members of **student**. Private members are inaccessible. Public inheritance also means that the derived class **student** is a subtype of **person**. Thus, a student *is a* person, but a person does not have to be a student. This subtyping relationship is called the ISA relationship, or interface inheritance.

A derived class is a modification of the base class, inheriting the public and protected members of the base class. Only constructors, destructors, and member function **operator=()** cannot be inherited. Thus, in the example of **student**, the **person** members **name**, **age**, **gender**, and **print()** are inherited. Frequently, a derived class adds new members to the existing class members. This is the case with **student**, which has two new data members and a redefined member function **print()**, which is overridden. The function definitions of **person::print()** and **student::print()** are distinct. Implementation of the member function of the derived class is different from that of the base class. This is different from overloading, in which the same function name can have different meanings for each unique signature.

Benefits of Using a Derived Class

- Code is reused: `student` uses existing, tested code from `person`.

- The hierarchy reflects a relationship found in the problem domain. When speaking of persons, the special grouping student is an outgrowth of the real world and its treatment of this group.

- Various polymorphic mechanisms allow client code to treat `student` as a subtype of `person`, simplifying client code while granting it the benefits of maintaining these distinctions among subtypes.

8.1.1 More Unified Modeling Language (UML)

A standard relationship between two classes is the inheritance relation. It is usual to have the base class at the top of the diagram and the derived class underneath, with an arrow pointing up from the derived class to the base class.

A key inheritance relationship between classes is the ISA or subtype relationship. In the following basic UML diagram, we show the person-student class diagram.

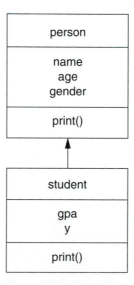

Basic inheritence in UML

8.2 A Student ISA Person

The first thing to understand about C++ inheritance logic is that public inheritance is used to generate subtypes, so in the first example, a `student` is a `person`. This implies that wherever `person` is allowed, so is `student`. We extend our previous example:

In file person.h

```
class person {
public:
    person(const string& nm, int a, char g):
            name(nm), age(a), gender(g) { }
    void print() const { cout << *this << endl; }
    friend ostream& operator<<(ostream& out,
                                const person& p);
    int get_age() const { return age; }
protected:
    string  name;
    int  age;
    char  gender;          // male == 'M', female == 'F'
};

// Overloaded and operator<<

ostream& operator<<(ostream& out, const person& p)
{
    return (out << p.name << ", age is " << p.age
            << ", gender is " << p.gender); }
}

// older can work with student as well

const person& older(const person& a, const person& b)
{
    if (a.get_age() >= b.get_age())
        return a;
    else
        return b;
}
```

In file student.cpp

```cpp
int main()
{
    // declare and initialize
    person abe(string("Abe Pohl"), 92,'M');
    person sam(string("Sam Pohl"), 66, 'M');
    student phil(string("Philip Pohl"), 68, 'M',
                 3.8, junior);
    student laura(string("Laura Pohl"), 12, 'F',
                  3.9, fresh);
    cout << abe << endl;     // info on abe is printed
    cout << phil << endl;

    person* ptr_person;
    ptr_person = &abe;
    ptr_person -> print();
    ptr_person = &phil;
    ptr_person -> print();

    cout << "older is " << older(abe, sam) << endl;
    cout << "older is " << older(abe, phil) << endl;
    cout << "older is " << older(laura, phil) << endl;
}
```

The output from this program is

```
Abe Pohl, age is 92, gender is M
Philip Pohl, age is 68, gender is M, junior, gpa = 3.8
Abe Pohl, age is 92, gender is M
Philip Pohl, age is 68, gender is M
older is Abe Pohl, age is 92, gender is M
older is Abe Pohl, age is 92, gender is M
older is Philip Pohl, age is 68, gender is M
```

Dissection of the *student* Program

■ `int get_age() const { return age;}`

It is standard methodology to provide accessor methods rather than
allow the variables accessed to be `public`.

```
ostream& operator<<(ostream& out,
                    const person& p)
{
   return (out << p.name << ", age is " << p.age
              << ", gender is " << p.gender); }
}
```

It is also customary to provide an overloaded `operator<<` for output.

```
■ const person& older(const person& a,
                      const person& b)
  {
     if (a.get_age() >= b.get_age())
        return a;
     else
        return b;
  }
```

We use pass-by-reference for aggregates because it is more efficient than pass-by-value, as this mechanism avoids unneeded argument copying. The key point here is that a publicly derived class from `person`, namely `student`, can be passed as well to this function's arguments.

```
■ person abe(string("Abe Pohl"), 92,'M');
  person sam(string("Sam Pohl"), 66, 'M');
  student phil(string("Philip Pohl"), 68, 'M',
               3.8, junior);
  student laura(string("Laura Pohl"), 12, 'F',
                3.9, fresh);
  cout << abe << endl;     // info on abe is printed
  cout << phil << endl;
```

We have two `persons` and two `students`. When we go to print `abe`, he prints as expected—namely, his name, age, and gender. When we print `phil`, he prints as a `student`. So, we get his college year and GPA printed. Note that `abe` uses `person::print()` and `phil` uses `student::print()`.

```
■ person* ptr_person;
  ptr_person = &abe;
  ptr_person -> print();
```

Here also, the function `person::print()` is called.

■ ```
ptr_person = &phil;
ptr_person -> print();
```

Here also, the function `person::print()` is called. But here we can get confused, because the object pointed at is `student::phil`. Nevertheless, the pointer type is `person`. In this situation, the pointer type determines which method to call.

■ ```
cout << "older is " << older(abe, sam) << endl;
cout << "older is " << older(abe, phil) << endl;
cout << "older is " << older(laura, phil) << endl;
```

In the first case, `abe` and `sam` are type `person`, so there is no problem. The second case is mixed, with `phil` being of type `student`. The third case has `laura` and `phil` both of type `student`. The function `older(person, person)` works regardless.

A student is a type of person, a person is a type of ape—they all derive from DNAS/GENOME.

8.3   Virtual Functions: Dynamic Determination

Overloaded member functions are invoked by a type-matching algorithm that includes having the implicit argument matched to an object of that class type. All this is known at compile time, and it allows the compiler to select the appropriate member directly. As becomes apparent, it is nice to dynamically select at runtime the appropriate member function from among base- and derived-class functions. The keyword `virtual`, a function specifier that provides such a mechanism, may be used only to modify member function declarations. The combination of virtual functions and public inheritance is our most general and flexible way to build a piece of software. This is a form of pure polymorphism.

An ordinary virtual function must be executable code. When invoked, its semantics are the same as those of other functions. In a derived class, it can be overridden, and the function prototype of the derived function must have a matching signature and return type. The selection of which function definition to invoke for a virtual function is dynamic. In the typical case, a base class has a virtual function, and derived classes have their versions of this function. A pointer to base class can point at either a base-class object or a derived-class object. The member function selected depends on the class of the object being pointed at, not on the pointer type. In the absence of a derived type member, the base-class virtual function is used by default.

Note the difference in selection of the appropriate overridden virtual function from an overloaded member function. The overloaded member function is selected at compile time based on its signature, and it can have distinct return types. A virtual function is selected at runtime based on the object's type, which is passed to it as its `this` pointer argument. Also, once it is declared `virtual`, this property is carried along to all redefinitions in derived classes. It is unnecessary in the derived class to use the function modifier `virtual`.

This note says to take my medicine at 8 o'clock, but which one?

Consider the following *virtual_sel* program example:

In file virtual_sel.cpp

```
// Virtual function selection

class Base {
public:
   virtual void  print() const
      { cout << " inside Base" << endl; }
};
class Derived : public Base {
public:
   // virtual as well
   void  print() const
      { cout << " inside Derived" << endl; }
};
int main()
{
   Base    b;
   Derived    f;
   Base*  pb = &b;          // points at a Base object

   pb -> print();          // call Base::print()
   pb = &f;                // points at Derived object
   pb -> print();          // call Derived::print()
}
```

The output of this program is

```
inside Base
inside Derived
```

Dissection of the *virtual_sel* Program

■ ```
class Base {
public:
   virtual void print() const
      { cout << " inside Base" << endl; }
};
```

The base class Base has the virtual method print(). We know when it executes by its output " inside Base".
```

```
■ class Derived : public Base {
  public:
        void  print() const        // virtual as well
        { cout << " inside Derived" << endl; }
  };
```

The derived class `Derived` has the overridden virtual method `print()`. We could have explicitly used the keyword `virtual` in its declaration, but this is unnecessary because this property is inherited from the base class method. We know when it executes by its output, `" inside Derived"`. Now an object of type `Derived` is also an object of type `Base` because it is derived by `public` inheritance.

```
■ int main()
  {
     Base    b;
     Derived    f;
     Base*  pb = &b;          // points at Base object
```

We test what gets called by having both class types used with a pointer pb. A base class pointer can be used to point at any object derived from its class.

```
■ pb -> print();          // call Base::print()
```

The pointer holds the address of `Base b`. It calls `Base::print()`.

```
■ pb = &f;               // points at Derived object
  pb -> print();          // call Derived::print()
```

The pointer is assigned the address of `Derived f`. It calls `Derived::print()`. In OOP terminology, the object is sent the message `print()`, and it selects its own version of the corresponding method. Thus, the pointer's base type is not the determining method (function) selection. Different class objects are processed by different functions, determined at runtime. Facilities that allow the implementation of ADTs, inheritance, and dynamic objects are the essentials of OOP.

It is important to notice that this did not happen with the last section example of `student` and `person`, because there the `print()` methods were not virtual. It is the normal case in inheritance that overridden methods be declared virtual. This allows them to select appropriate behavior at runtime. As a simple exercise, redo `person` with virtual functions. Should the `get_age()` method be virtual? Virtual functions require added work at runtime and are less efficient than nonvirtual methods. C++ programmers use them only where needed.

8.3.1 Overloading and Overriding Confusion

Virtual functions and member function overloading cause confusion.
Consider the following program:

In file virtual_err.cpp

```cpp
#include <iostream>
using namespace std;

class Base {
public:
   virtual void foo(int i)
      { cout << "Base::i = " << i << endl; }
   virtual void foo(double x)
      { cout << "Base::x = " << x << endl; }
};

class Derived : public Base {
public:
   void foo(int i)
      { cout << "Derived::i = " << i << endl; }
};
class Derived2 : public Derived {
public:
   void foo(int i)
      { cout << "Derived2::i = " << i << endl; }
   void foo(double d)
      { cout << "Derived2::d = " << d << endl; }
};
int main()
{
   Derived  d;
   Derived2  d2;
   Base  b, *pb = &d;

   b.foo(9);            // selects Base::foo(int);
   b.foo(9.5);          // selects Base::foo(double);
   d.foo(9);            // selects Derived::foo(int);
   d.foo(9.5);          // selects Derived::foo(int);
   pb -> foo(9);        // selects Derived::foo(int);
   pb -> foo(9.5);      // selects Base::foo(double);
   pb = &d2;
   pb -> foo(9);        // selects Derived2::foo(int);
   pb -> foo(9.5);      // selects Derived2::foo(double)
}
```

Dissection of the *virtual_error* Program

■
```
class Base {
public:
    virtual void foo(int i)
        { cout << "Base::i = " << i << endl; }
    virtual void foo(double x)
        { cout << "Base::x = " << x << endl; }
};
```

Here, we have a classic case of signature overloading. In overloading, the compiler at compile time statically selects which method to call.

■
```
class Derived : public Base {
public:
    void foo(int i)
        { cout << "Derived::i = " << i << endl; }
};
```

The base-class member function `Base::foo(int)` is overridden. So far, this is not confusing. However, the base-class member function `Base::foo(double)` is inherited in the derived class but is not overridden. Here is the cause of the confusion:

```
d.foo(9);              // selects Derived::foo(int);
d.foo(9.5);            // selects Derived::foo(int);
pb -> foo(9);          // selects Derived::foo(int);
pb -> foo(9.5);        // selects Base::foo(double);
```

In the statement `d.foo(9.5)`, the `double` value 9.5 is converted to the integer value 9. To call the hidden member function, we need to use scope resolution as in `d.Base::foo(double)`. On the other hand, when called with a pointer `pb -> foo(9.5)`, the `Base::foo(double)` is selected. Obviously, this a confusing situation that should be avoided. When overriding base class virtual functions that are overloaded, be sure to overload all of their definitions. This is what was done in `Derived2`, which does not suffer the same confusion.

Only nonstatic member functions can be virtual. The virtual characteristic is inherited. Thus, the derived-class function is automatically virtual, and the presence of the `virtual` keyword is usually a matter of taste. Constructors cannot be virtual, but destructors can be. As a rule of thumb, any class having virtual functions should have a virtual destructor. Some compilers, such as the latest version of *g++*, issues a warning if a class has virtual members and a nonvirtual destructor.

8.3.2   **A Canonical Example: Class shape**

Virtual functions allow runtime decisions. Consider a computer-aided design application in which the area of the shapes in a design has to be computed. The various shapes are derived from the shape base class.

In file shape.cpp

```
class shape {
public:
   virtual double  area() const { return 0; }
   // virtual double area is default behavior
protected:
   double  x, y;
};

class rectangle : public shape {
public:
   rectangle(double h = 0.0, double w = 0.0)
      : height(h), width(w) { }
   double  area() const { return (height * width); }
private:
   double  height, width;
};

class circle : public shape {
public:
   circle(double r = 0.0) : radius(r) { }
   double  area() const
      { return (PI * radius * radius); }
private:
   double   radius;
};
```

In such a class hierarchy, the derived classes correspond to important, well-understood types of shapes. The system is readily expanded by deriving further classes. The area calculation is a local responsibility of a derived class.

Client code that uses the polymorphic area calculation looks like this:

```
const int N = 3;

int main()
{
    shape*  p[N];
    p[0] = new rectangle(2, 3);
    p[1] = new rectangle(2.5, 2.001);
    p[2] = new circle(1.5);

    double tot_area = 0.0;

    for (int i = 0; i < N; ++i)
        tot_area += p[i] -> area();
    cout << tot_area << " is total area" << endl;
}
```

A major advantage here is that the client code does not need to change if new shapes are added to the system. Change is managed locally and propagated automatically by the polymorphic character of the client code.

8.4 Abstract Base Classes

A type hierarchy begins with a base class that contains a number of virtual functions. They provide for dynamic typing. In the base class, virtual functions are often dummy functions and have an empty body. In the derived classes, however, virtual functions are given specific meanings. In C++, the pure virtual function is introduced for this purpose. A pure virtual function is one whose body is normally undefined. Notationally, such a function is declared inside the class, as follows:

```
virtual function prototype = 0;
```

The pure virtual function is used to defer the implementation decision of the function. In OOP terminology, it is called a *deferred method*.

A class that has at least one pure virtual function is an *abstract class*. In a type hierarchy, it is useful for the base class to be an abstract class. This base class has the basic common properties of its derived classes but cannot itself be used to declare objects. Instead, it is used to declare pointers or references that can access subtype objects derived from the abstract class.

We explain this concept while developing a primitive form of ecological simulation. OOP was originally developed as a simulation methodology using Simula67. Hence, many of its ideas are easily understood as an attempt to model a particular reality.

The world in our example has various forms of life interacting; they inherit the interface of an abstract base class called `living`. Each position in a grid defined to be the world can either have a life-form or be empty. We shall have foxes as an archetypal predator, with rabbits as prey. The rabbits eat grass. Each of these life-forms lives, reproduces, and dies each iteration of the simulation.

In file predator.cpp

```cpp
// Predator-Prey simulation using class living

enum state { EMPTY, GRASS, RABBIT, FOX, STATES };

const int DRAB = 3, DFOX = 6, TMFOX = 5,
          CYCLES = 5, N = 40;

// DRAB rabbits die at 3, DFOX foxes at 6,
// TMFOX too many foxes, CYCLES of simulation,
// N size of square world

class living;                  // forward declaration
typedef living* world[N][N];

class living {                 // what lives in world
public:
    virtual state  who() = 0;  // state identification
    virtual living*  next(world w) = 0;
protected:
    int  row, column;          // location
    void sums(world w, int sm[]);
};

void living::sums(world w, int sm[])
{
    int  i, j;

    sm[EMPTY] = sm[GRASS] = 0;
    sm[RABBIT] = sm[FOX] = 0;
    for (i = -1; i <= 1; ++i)
        for (j = -1; j <= 1; ++j)
            sm[w[row + i][column + j] -> who()]++;
}
```

Dissection of the `living` Abstract Base Class

- ```
  class living;                    // forward declaration
  typedef living* world[N][N];
  ```

The class `living` represents different life-forms, such as rabbits and grass. The life-forms are placed on an N by N square world.

- ```
  class living {                   // what lives in world
  public:
      virtual state  who() = 0; // state identity
      virtual living*  next(world w) = 0;
  protected:
      int  row, column;            // location
      void sums(world w,int sm[]);
  };
  ```

This abstract base class is used as the base class for all derived individual life-forms needed by the simulation. There are two pure virtual functions and one ordinary member function, `sums()`. The pure virtual functions must be defined in any concrete class derived from `class living`. Virtual functions incur a small additional runtime cost over normal member functions. Therefore, we use virtual functions only when necessary to our implementations. Our simulation has rules for deciding who goes on living based on the populations in the neighborhood of a given square. These populations are computed by `sums()`. Note that the neighborhood includes the square itself.

- ```
  void living::sums(world w, int sm[])
  {
      int  i, j;

      sm[EMPTY] = sm[GRASS] = 0;
      sm[RABBIT] = sm[FOX] = 0;
      for (i = -1; i <= 1; ++i)
          for ( j = -1; j <= 1; ++j)
              sm[w[row + i][column + j] -> who()]++;
  }
  ```

This function collects the values of the different life-forms in the region immediately surrounding the life-form's position in the world, namely (`row`, `column`). Each life-form has rules that use this sum to see if they propagate, die off, or stay alive.

The inheritance hierarchy is one level deep.
  ```

```
// Currently only predator class

class fox : public living {
public:
    fox(int r, int c, int a = 0) : age(a)
        { row = r; column = c; }
    state  who() { return FOX; }// deferred fox method
    living*  next(world w);
protected:
    int  age;                    // used to decide on dying
};
```

```
// Currently only prey class

class rabbit : public living {
public:
    rabbit(int r, int c, int a = 0) : age(a)
        { row = r; column = c; }
    state  who() { return RABBIT; }
    living*  next(world w);
protected:
    int  age;
};
```

```
// Currently only plant life

class grass : public living {
public:
    grass(int r, int c) { row = r; column = c; }
    state who() { return GRASS; }
    living* next(world w);
};
```

```
// Nothing lives here

class empty : public living {
public:
    empty(int r, int c) { row = r; column = c; }
    state  who() { return EMPTY; }
    living*  next(world w);
};
```

Notice that the design allows other forms of predator, prey, and plant
life to be developed, using a further level of inheritance. The characteristics of how each life-form behaves are captured in its version of
next().

Grass can be eaten by rabbits. If there is more grass than the rabbits in the neighborhood can eat, the grass remains; otherwise, it is

eaten up. (Feel free to substitute your own rules, as these are highly limited and artificial.)

```
living* grass::next(world w)
{
   int  sum[STATES];

   sums(w, sum);
   if (sum[GRASS] > sum[RABBIT])          // eat grass
      return (new grass(row, column));
   else
      return (new empty(row, column));
}
```

Rabbits die of old age if they exceed a defined limit DRAB; they are eaten if there are an appropriate number of foxes nearby.

```
living* rabbit::next(world w)
{
   int  sum[STATES];

   sums(w, sum);
   if (sum[FOX] >= sum[RABBIT])  // eat rabbits
      return (new empty(row, column));
   else if (age > DRAB)          // rabbit is too old
      return (new empty(row, column));
   else
      return (new rabbit(row, column, age + 1));
}
```

Foxes die of overcrowding or old age.

```
living* fox::next(world w)
{
   int  sum[STATES];

   sums(w, sum);
   if (sum[FOX] > TMFOX)              // too many foxes
      return (new empty(row, column));
   else if (age > DFOX)              // fox is too old
      return (new empty(row, column));
   else
      return (new fox(row, column, age + 1));
}
```

Empty squares are competed for by the various life-forms.

```
living* empty::next(world w)      // fill empty square
{
   int  sum[STATES];

   sums(w, sum);
   if (sum[FOX] > 1)
      return (new fox(row, column));
   else if (sum[RABBIT] > 1)
      return (new rabbit(row, column));
   else if (sum[GRASS] > 0)
      return (new grass(row, column));
   else
      return (new empty(row, column));
}
```

The rules in the various versions of `next()` determine a possibly complex set of interactions. Of course, to make the simulation more interesting, other behaviors, such as sexual reproduction, whereby the animals have gender and can mate, could be simulated.

The array type `world` is a container for the life-forms. The container has the responsibility of creating its current pattern. The container needs to have ownership of the `living` objects so as to allocate new ones and delete old ones.

```
// World is all empty

void init(world w)
{
   int  i, j;

   for (i = 0; i < N; ++i)
      for (j = 0; j < N; ++j)
         w[i][j] = new empty(i,j);
}
```

This routine creates an empty world. Each square is initialized by the `empty::empty()` constructor.

```
// New world w_new is computed from old world w_old

void update(world w_new, world w_old)
{
   int  i, j;

   for (i = 1; i < N - 1; ++i)    // borders are taboo
      for (j = 1; j < N - 1; ++j)
         w_new[i][j] = w_old[i][j] -> next(w_old);
}
```

This routine updates the `world`. The old state of the world stored in `w_old[][]` is used to compute what lives in the new state `w_new[][]`. This is computed from rules that `next()` uses.

```
// Clean world up

void dele(world w)
{
   int  i, j;

   for (i = 1; i < N - 1; ++i)     //borders are taboo
      for (j = 1; j < N - 1; ++j)
         delete(w[i][j]);
}
```

This routine returns memory to the heap (free store). In a long-running large simulation, all these calls to `new` would burn up too much memory if not for this reclamation routine.

```
void eden(world w)
{
   int  i, j;

   for (i = 2; i < N - 2; ++i)
      for (j = 2; j < N - 2; ++j) {
         delete(w[i][j]);
         if ( (i + j) % 3 == 0)
            w[i][j] = new rabbit(i, j);
         else
            if ( (i + j) % 3 == 1)
               w[i][j] = new fox(i, j);
            else
               w[i][j] = new grass(i, j);
      }
}
```

We need a first state of the `world`. This version of an `eden()` routine should be replaced by a routine that allows the user to establish the Garden of Eden pattern.

```
void pr_state(world w)
{
   int  i, j;

   for (i = 0; i < N; ++i) {
      cout << endl;
      for (j = 0; j < N; ++j)
         cout << static_cast<int>(w[i][j] -> who());
   }
   cout << endl << endl;
}
```

**If the fox is eating the rabbit, which eats the grass,
can the fire be far behind?**

The simulation has odd and even worlds, which alternate as the basis
for the next cycle's calculations.

```
int main()
{
   world  odd, even;
   int    i;

   init(odd);  init(even);
   eden(even);            // generate initial world
   pr_state(even);        // print Garden of Eden state
   for (i = 0; i < CYCLES; ++i) {        // simulation
      if (i % 2) {
         update(even, odd);
         pr_state(even);
         dele(odd);
      }
      else {
         update(odd, even);
         pr_state(odd);
         dele(even);
      }
   }
}
```

The code runs the simulation for a number of iterations specified by the constant CYCLES. The reader should experiment with modifications of this code. The structure of the program lets you easily modify the rules and the initial configuration. More advanced modifications would improve the user interface and add other life-forms.

8.5   Templates and Inheritance

Templates and inheritance are jointly an extremely powerful reuse technique. Parameterized types can be reused through inheritance. Such use parallels that of inheritance in deriving ordinary classes. Templates and inheritance are both mechanisms for code reuse, and both can involve polymorphism. They are distinct features of C++ and, as such, combine in various forms. A template class can derive from an ordinary class, an ordinary class can derive from an instantiated template class, and a template class can derive from a template class. Each of these possibilities leads to different relationships.

In some situations, templates lead to unacceptable cost in the size of the object module. Each instantiated template class requires its own compiled object module. This can be remedied by using a template to inherit the base class.

The derivation of a class from an instantiated template class is basically no different from ordinary inheritance. In the following example, we assume that we already have a template class stack<class T>. For example, it can be obtained from STL. It is used as a base class for a safe character stack.

```
// Safe character stack

class safe_char_stack : public stack<char> {
public:
   // test push and pop
   void  push(char c)
    { assert (!full()); stack<char>::push(c); }
   char  pop()
    { assert (!empty()); return (stack<char>::pop()); }
};
```

The instantiated class stack<char> is generated and reused by safe_char_stack.

This example can be usefully generalized to a template class:

```
// Parameterized safe stack

template <class TYPE>
class safe_stack : public stack<TYPE> {
public:
    void  push(TYPE c)
      { assert (!full()); stack<TYPE>::push(c); }
    TYPE  pop()
      { assert (!empty()); return (stack<TYPE>::pop()); }
};
```

It is important to notice the linkage between the base class and the derived class. Both require the same instantiated type. Each pair of base and derived classes is independent of all other pairs.

8.6   Multiple Inheritance

The examples in the text thus far require only single inheritance; that is, they require that a class be derived from a single base class. This feature can lead to a chain of derivations wherein class B is derived from class A, class C is derived from class B, . . . , and class N is derived from class M. In effect, N ends up being based on A, B, . . . , M. This chain must not be circular, however; a class cannot have itself as an ancestor.

Multiple inheritance allows a derived class to be derived from more than one base class. The syntax of class headers is extended to allow a list of base classes and their privacy designations. For example:

```
class student {
    .....
};
class worker {
    .....
};
class student_worker: public student, public worker {
    .....
};
```

In this example, the derived class `student_worker` publicly inherits the members of both base classes. This parental relationship is described by the inheritance directed acyclic graph (DAG). The DAG is a graph structure whose nodes are classes and whose directed edges point from base to derived class. To be legal, a DAG cannot be circular; thus, no class may, through its inheritance chain, inherit from itself. Note, this is similar to the UML diagrams for these classes, but with the arrows reversed.

When identically named members are derived from different classes, ambiguities may arise. These derivations are allowed, provided the user does not make an ambiguous reference to such a member. For example:

```
class worker {
public:
   const int  soc_sec;
   const char* name;
   .....
};
class student {
public:
   const char* name;
   .....
};
class student_worker: public student, public worker {
public:
   void print() { cout << "ssn: " << soc_sec << "\n";
                  cout << name; ..... }        // error
   .....
};
```

In the body of `student_worker::print()`, the reference to `soc_sec` is fine, but the reference to `name` is inherently ambiguous. The problem can be resolved by properly qualifying `name` using the scope resolution operator.

With multiple inheritance, two classes can be derived from a common ancestor. If both classes are used as base classes in the ordinary way by their derived class, it has two subobjects of the common ancestor. If this duplication is not desirable, it can be eliminated, using virtual inheritance. An example is

```
class student: virtual public person {
   .....
};
class worker: virtual public person {
   .....
};
class student_worker: public student, public worker {
   .....
};
```

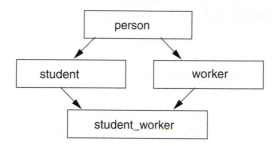

DAG of Multiple Inheritance

Without the use of `virtual` in this example, `class student_worker` would have objects of `class student::person` and `class worker::person`. The order of execution for initializing constructors in base and member constructors is given in the following list.

Constructor Execution Order

1. Base classes initialized in declaration order

2. Members initialized in declaration order

3. The body of the constructor

Virtual base classes are constructed before any of their derived classes and before any nonvirtual base classes. Construction order depends on their DAG. It is a depth-first, left-to-right order. Destructors are invoked in the reverse order of constructors. These rules, although complicated, are intuitive.

On many systems, a concrete example of multiple inheritance can be found in the *iostream* library. This library contains the class `iostream`, which can be derived from `istream` and `ostream`. However, it is an interesting comment on multiple inheritance that more recent implementations have gone back to single-inheritance designs.

8.7 RTTI and Other Fine Points

Runtime type identification (RTTI) provides a mechanism for safely determining the type pointed at by a base-class pointer at runtime and involves `dynamic_cast`, an operator on a base-class pointer; `typeid`, an operator for determining the type of an object; and `type_info`, a structure providing runtime information for the associated type. It is used with classes having virtual functions. The `dynamic_cast` operator has the form

```
dynamic_cast< type >( v )
```

where *type* must be a pointer or reference to a class type and *v* must be a corresponding pointer value or reference value. This cast is implemented as follows:

```
class Base { virtual void foo(); ····· };
class Derived : public Base { ····· };

void fcn(Base* ptr)
{
    Derived* dptr = dynamic_cast<Derived*>(ptr);
    ·····
}
```

In this example, the cast converts the pointer value `ptr` to a `Derived*`. If the conversion is inappropriate, a value of 0, the NULL pointer, is returned. This is called a downcast. Dynamic casts also work with reference types.

The operator `typeid()` can be applied to a *typename* or to an expression to determine the exact type of the argument. The operator returns a reference to the class `type_info`, which is supplied by the system and is defined in the header file *typeinfo* (some compilers use *type_info*). The class `type_info` provides both a `name()` member function that returns a string that is the type name and overloaded equality operators. Remember to check the local implementation for the complete interface of this class.

```
Base* bptr;
·····// print typename of what current bptr points at
cout << typeid(*bptr).name() << endl;
·····
if (typeid(*bptr) == typeid(Derived)) {
    ·····                     // appropriate for Derived
}
```

Bad dynamic casts and `typeid` operations can be made to throw the exceptions `bad_cast` and `bad_typeid`, so the user can choose between dealing with the NULL pointer or catching an exception. (See Section 10.9, *Standard Exceptions and Their Uses*, on page 471.)

8.7.1   Finer Points

A difficulty in learning C++ is the many distinctions and rules pertaining to the use of functions. We have described most of the extensions and now show some distinctions.

Function Use in C++

■　A virtual function and its derived instances having the same signature must have the same return type, with some minor exceptions. Notice that nonvirtual member functions with the same signature can have different return types in derived classes. For example, if the base class function returns its own type, then the derived class function can return its type.

■　All member functions except constructors and overloaded `new` and `delete` can be virtual.

■　Constructors, destructors, overloaded `operator=`, and friends are not inherited.

■　Conversion functions of `operator` *type*`()` and the operators `=`, `()`, `[]`, and `->` can be overloaded only with nonstatic member functions. Overloading operators `new` and `delete` can be done only with static member functions. Other overloadable operators can be done with friend, member, or ordinary functions.

■　A union may have constructors and destructors but not virtual functions. It can neither serve as a base class nor have a base class. Members of a union cannot require constructors or destructors.

■　Access modification is possible, but using it with public inheritance destroys the subtype relationship. Access modification cannot broaden visibility, but it can narrow it. For example:

In file access_mod.cpp

```
// Access modification

class Base {
public:
    int  k;
protected:
    int  j, n;
private:
    int  i;
};
```

```
class Derived : public Base {
public:
   int  m;
   Base::n; // illegal protected access can't broaden
private:
   Base::j; // otherwise default is protected
};
```

8.8   Software Engineering: Inheritance and Design

At one level, inheritance is a code-sharing technique. At another level, it reflects an understanding of the problem and relationships between parts of the problem space. Much of public inheritance is the expression of an ISA relationship between the base and derived classes. The rectangle is a shape. This is the conceptual underpinning for making shape a superclass and allowing the behavior described by its public member functions to be interpretable on objects within its type hierarchy. In other words, subclasses derived from the superclass share its interface.

A design cannot be specified in a completely optimal way. Design involves trade-offs between the various objectives one wishes to achieve. For example, generality is frequently at odds with efficiency. Using a class hierarchy that expresses ISA relationships increases our effort to understand how to compartmentalize coding relationships and potentially introduces coding inefficiencies by having various layers of access to the (hidden) state description of an object. However, a reasonable ISA decomposition can simplify the overall coding process. For example, a shape-drawing package need not anticipate shapes that might be added in the future. Through inheritance, the class developer imports the base-class shape interface and provides code that implements operations, such as draw. What is primitive or shared remains unchanged. Also unchanged is the client's use of the package.

An undue amount of decomposition imposes its own complexity and ends up being self-defeating. There is a granularity decision whereby highly specialized classes do not provide enough benefit and are better folded into a larger concept.

Single inheritance (SI) conforms to a hierarchical decomposition of the key objects in the domain of discourse. Multiple inheritance (MI) is more troubling as a modeling or problem-solving concept. In MI, the new object is composed of several preexisting objects and is usefully thought of as a form of each. The term mixin is used to mean a class composed using MI, with each base class orthogonal. Much of the time, there is an alternative HASA formulation. For example, is a vampire bat a mammal that happens to fly, a flying machine that happens to be a mammal, or both a flying machine and a mammal? Depending on what code is available, developing a proper class for vampire bat might involve an MI derivation or an SI with appropriate *HASA* members.

MI presents problems for the type theorist: `student` might be derived from `person`, and `employee` might be derived from `person`. But what about a student-employee? Generally, types are best understood as SI chains.

None of this diminishes the attraction of MI as a code-reuse technique. It is clearly a powerful generalization of SI. As such, it probably fits in with the style of some programmers. Just as some programmers prefer iteration to recursion, some prefer SI and aggregation to MI and composition. In aggregation, we create a big object by having class members for each subpart.

8.8.1　Subtyping Form

ADTs are successful insofar as they behave like native types. Native types, such as the integer types in C, act as a subtype hierarchy. This is a useful model for publicly derived type hierarchies, and it promotes ease of use through polymorphism. Here is a recipe for building such a type hierarchy. The base class is made abstract and is used for interface inheritance. The derived class implements this interface concretely.

```
class Abstract_Base {
public:
   // interface-largely virtual
   Abstract_Base();                    // default ctor
   Abstract_Base(const Abstract_Base&);  // copy ctor
   virtual ~Abstract_Base() = 0;       // pure virtual
   .....
protected: // used instead of private for inheritance
   .....
private:   // often empty-no future design constraint
   .....
};
```

```
class Derived: virtual public Abstract_Base {
public:
    // Concrete instance
    Derived();                        // default ctor
    Derived(const Derived&);          // copy ctor
    ~Derived();                       // dtor
    Derived& operator=(const Derived&);  // assignment
    .....
protected: // instead of private-inheritance expected
    .....
private:   // used for implementation details
    .....
};
```

It is usual to leave the base class of the hierarchy abstract, yielding the most flexible design. Generally, no concrete implementation is developed at this point. By using pure virtual functions, we are precluded from declaring objects of this type. Notice that the ~Abstract_Base() function is pure. This level of the design focuses on public interface. These are the operations expected of any subtype in the hierarchy. In general, basic constructors are expected and may not be virtual. Also, most useful aggregates require an explicit definition of assignment that differs from default assignment semantics. The destructor is virtual because response must be at runtime and is dependent on the object's size, which can vary across the hierarchy. Finally, virtual public inheritance ensures that in MI schemes we do not have multiple copies of the abstract base class.

8.8.2   Code Reuse

Private inheritance does not have a subtype, or ISA relationship. In private inheritance, we reuse a base class for its code. We call private derivation a LIKEA relationship, or implementation inheritance, as opposed to interface inheritance. The LIKEA relationship comes in handy when diagramming the class relationships in a complicated software system. Because private and protected inheritance do not create type hierarchies, they have more limited utility than does public inheritance. In a first pass in understanding these concepts, nonpublic inheritance can be skipped.

Code reuse is often all you want from inheritance. The template methodology is simpler and more runtime efficient; it is simpler because instantiation requires only a single type placed in the template declaration. In inheritance, we need to derive the whole interface, substituting appropriate types. It is more runtime efficient because it often avoids indirection. Inheritance allows special cases to be developed for each type, if necessary; it does not lead to large object-code modules. Remember, each template instantiation is compiled to object code.

8.9   Dr. P's Prescriptions

- Use interface inheritance, called ISA inheritance.

- Usually, a base class is abstract.

- Minimize interactions between classes.

- Base-class destructors are usually virtual.

- Avoid deep hierarchies.

- Avoid multiple inheritance.

Public inheritance creates a class hierarchy in which a derived class object is a form of base-class object. This is called ISA inheritance; it is also referred to as interface inheritance, as opposed to implementation inheritance. Class hierarchies should be about interface inheritance. In the classic example, an abstract base class `shape` describes the properties and behaviors of all `shape` types using virtual and pure virtual member functions. The derived classes LIKEA `circle` implement the specifics. The `circle` ISA `shape`. A base-class reference or pointer can be assigned a derived-class object or address. Manipulation by such a reference or pointer can be polymorphic— namely, by using virtual functions, the properly overridden function defined in the derived class is called dynamically. Usually, such a base class is abstract. This identifies the class as an important type to be used polymorphically. It guarantees that the compiler insists on overridden member function definitions where concrete behavior for derived types is needed.

Base-class destructors should be virtual. In most cases, derived classes have different resource requirements, implying that returning resources through destructor finalization needs to be dynamic.

Overdoing complexity by using deep hierarchies or multiple inheritance leads to code that can be inefficient and difficult to maintain and modify.

8.10 C++ Compared with Java

Like C++, Java has the inheritance mechanism, which extends a new class from an existing one. Java uses different terminology with respect to inheritance. The Java base class is called the superclass. The extended class adds to or alters the inherited superclass methods. This is used to share an interface and to create a hierarchy of related types. In Java, ordinary class inheritance is single inheritance. Java also has interface inheritance, which can be used as a restricted form of multiple inheritance.

Consider designing a database for a college. The registrar must track various types of students. We start with the superclass `Person1`. This class is identical to `Person` in Section 4.14, *C++ Compared with Java*, on page 197 except that the `private` instance variables are changed to have access `protected`. This access allows their use in the subclass but otherwise acts like `private`.

In file Person1.java

```
// An elementary Java implementation of type Person

class Person1 {
    public void setName(String nm) { name = nm; }
    public void setAge(int a) { age = a; }
    public void setGender(char b) { gender = b; }
    public String toString()  { return(name + " age is "
                     + age + " gender is " + gender);    }
    protected String name;
    protected int age;
    protected char gender; // male 'M', female 'F'
};
```

Now we derive `Student` from `Person1`:

```
class Student extends Person1 {
   private String college;
   private byte year;         // 1=fr, 2=so, 3=jr, 4=sr
   private double gpa;        // 0.0 to 4.0
   public void setCollege(String nm)
       { college = nm; }
   public void setYear(byte a) { year = a; }
   public void setGpa(double g) { gpa = g; }
   public String toString()
       { return (super.toString() + " college is "
               + college); }
   public Student()
       { super.setName("Unknown");
         college = "Unknown"; }
   public Student(String nm)
       { super.setName(nm); college = "Unknown"; }
   public Student(String nm, int a, char b)
       { name =nm; age =a; gender = b; }
};
```

In this example, Student is the subclass, and Person1 is the superclass. Notice the use of the keyword super, which provides a means
of accessing the instance variables or methods found in the superclass.

The inheritance structure provides a design for the overall system.
The superclass Person1 leads to a design whereby the subclass Stu-
dent is derived from it. Other subclasses, such as GradStudent or
Employee, could be added to this inheritance hierarchy.

In Java, polymorphism comes from both method overloading and
method overriding. Overriding occurs when a method is redefined in
the subclass. The toString() method is in Person1 and is redefined
in Student extended from Person1.

```
// Overriding the toString() method

class Person1 {
   protected String name;
   .....
   public String toString() { return (name
       + " age is " + age +    " gender is "
       + gender); }
   .....
};
```

```
class Student extends Person1 {
   private String college;
   .....
   public toString()
       { return(super.toString() + " college is "
       + college); }
   .....
};
```

The overridden method `toString()` has the same name and signature in both the superclass `Person1` and the subclass `Student`. Which one gets selected depends on what is being referenced at runtime. For example:

```
// StudentTest.java uses Student, which uses Person1

public class StudentTest {
   public static void main (String[] args)
   {
       Person1 q1;
       q1 = new Student();
       q1.setName("Charles Babbage");
       System.out.println(q1.toString());
       q1 = new Person1();
       q1.setName("Charles Babbage");
       System.out.println(q1.toString());
   }
}
```

The variable `q1` can refer to either the `Person1` object or the subtype `Student` object. At runtime, the correct `toString()` is selected. The `setName()` method is known at compile time, since it is the superclass `Person1` method.

Summary

■ Inheritance provides the ability to create new derived classes by adding to or altering existing classes. Through inheritance, a hierarchy of related, code-sharing ADTs can be created.

■ A class can be derived from an existing class using the form

class *class-name* : (public|protected|private)_{opt}*base-name*
{
    member declarations
};

As usual, the keyword `class` can be replaced by the keyword `struct`, with the implication that members are by default `public`.

■ The keywords `public`, `private`, and `protected` are available as visibility modifiers for class members. A public member is visible throughout its scope. A private member is visible to other member functions within its own class and to friend functions. A protected member is visible to other member functions within its class, within friend functions, and within any class immediately derived from it. These visibility modifiers can be used within a class declaration in any order and with any frequency.

■ The default visibility for a base class is private if the keyword `class` is used; it is public if the keyword `struct` is used.

■ The derived class has its own constructors, which invoke the base-class constructor. A special syntax is used to pass arguments from the derived-class constructor back to the base-class constructor:

function header : *base-classname* (*argument list*)

■ A publicly derived class is a subtype of its base class. A variable of the derived class can in many ways be treated as if it were the base-class type. A pointer whose type is pointer to base class can point to objects of the publicly derived class type.

■ A reference to the derived class may be implicitly converted to a reference to the public base class. It is possible to declare a reference to a base class and to initialize it to a reference to an object of the publicly derived class.

■ The keyword `virtual` is a function specifier that provides a mechanism to dynamically select at runtime the appropriate member function from among base- and derived-class functions. This specifier may be used only to modify member function declarations. This is called overriding. This ability to dynamically select a routine appropriate to an object's type is a form of polymorphism.

■ Inheritance provides for code reuse. The derived class inherits the base-class code and typically modifies and extends the base class. Public inheritance also creates a type hierarchy, allowing further generality by providing additional implicit type conversions. Also, at a runtime cost, it allows for runtime selection of overridden virtual functions. Facilities that allow the implementation of inheritance and the ability to process objects dynamically are the essentials of OOP.

■ A pure virtual function is a virtual member function whose body is normally undefined. Notationally, a pure virtual function is declared inside the class, as follows:

virtual *function prototype* = 0;

The pure virtual function is used to defer the implementation decision of the function. In OOP terminology, it is called a deferred method. A class that has at least one pure virtual function is an abstract class. It is useful for the base class in a type hierarchy to be an abstract class. As such, the base class would define the interface for its derived classes but cannot itself be used to declare objects.

Review Questions

1. In class X : Y { · · · · · }, X is a _____ class and Y is a class.

2. True or false: If D inherits from B privately, D is a subtype of B.

3. The term overriding refers to _____ functions.

4. An abstract base class contains a _____.

5. The subtyping relationship is called the _____.

6. True or false: Template classes cannot be base classes.

7. What is wrong with the following?

```
class A:B {·····};
class B:C {·····};
class C:A {·····};
```

8. In multiple inheritance, why is virtual inheritance used?

9. The class type_info provides a name() member function that _____.

10. True or false: Constructors, destructors, overloaded operator=, and friends are not inherited.

Exercises

1. For `student` and `grad_student` code, input member functions that read input for each data member in their classes. (See Section 8.1, *A Derived Class*, on page 378.) Use `student::read` to implement `grad_student::read`.

2. Pointer conversions, scope resolution, and explicit casting create a wide selection of possibilities. Using `main()`, discussed in Section 8.1.1, *A Student ISA Person*, on page 382, which of the following work, and what is printed?

   ```
   reinterpret_cast<grad_student *>(ps) -> print();
   dynamic_cast<student *>(pgs) -> print();
   pgs -> student::print();
   ps -> grad_student::print();
   ```

   Print out and explain the results.

3. Create an abstract class `Counter`. It should have only pure virtual functions. It should have a method `click()` that would advance the counter. It should have methods `get()` and `set()` for accessing and mutating the counter's value.

4. Create a concrete class `Timer` derived from the abstract class `Counter`. This class should simulate a timer that has seconds and minutes as readout. Write a program that tests this implementation.

5. Develop a class `Clock` based on `Timer`. It should have the same functionality as an ordinary house clock or watch. Write a program that tests this implementation.

6. Write a `class stack` that stores values that are `void*`. This is a form of generic stack. Implement operations that are available for the STL `stack`. Now derive privately a form of this stack that stores `ints`. Write some code testing this. One such standard test would be to use the stack for reversing a set of values. Compare this approach to one using STL. Why should STL be preferred? Are there any advantages to the use of `void*` and inheritance instead of templates?

7. Derive an integer vector class from the STL `class vector<int>` that has 1 as its first index value and n as its last index value.

   ```
   int_vector x(n);      // vector whose range is 1 to n
   ```

8. Generalize the previous exercise by deriving a template class that creates the index range 1 to n.

```
vec_1<double> x(n); // vector whose range is 1 to n
```

9. For the following program, explain when both overriding and overloading take place:

```
class B {
public:
   B(int j = 0) : i(j) {}
   virtual void  print() const
      { cout << " i = " << i << endl; }
   void  print(char *s) const
      { cout << s << i << endl; }
private:
   int  i;
};

class D : public B {
public:
   D(int j = 0) : B(5), i(j) {}
   void  print() const
         { cout << " i = " << i << endl; }
   int  print(char *s) const
         { cout << s << i << endl; return i; }
private:
   int  i;
};

int main()
{
   B   b1, b2(10), *pb;
   D   d1, d2(10), *pd = &d2;

   b1.print(); b2.print(); d1.print(); d2.print();
   b1.print("b1.i = "); b2.print("b2.i = ");
   d1.print("d1.i = "); d2.print("d2.i = ");
   pb = pd;
   pb -> print(); pb -> print("d2.i = ");
   pd -> print(); pd -> print("d2.i = ");
}
```

10. Modify class D in the previous exercise to be

```
class D2 : private B {
public:
    B::i;                   // access modification
    void  print_i()
    {
        cout << i << " inside D2 and B::i is "
             << B::i << endl;
    }
};
```

What is changed in the output from that program?

11. Define a base class person that contains universal information, including name, address, birth date, and gender. Derive from this class the following classes:

```
class student : virtual public person {
// ····· relevant additional state and behavior
};

class worker : virtual public person {
// ····· relevant additional state and behavior
};

class student_worker: public student, public worker
{
    ·····
};
```

Write a program that reads a file of information and creates a list of persons. Process the list to create, in sorted order by last name, a list of all people, a list of people who are students, a list of people who are employees, and a list of people who are student-employees. On your system, can you easily produce a list in sorted order of all students who are not employees?

12. Add a new life-form to the predator-prey simulation found in Section 8.4, *Abstract Base Classes*, on page 395.

13. *(Project)* Design and implement a graphical user interface (GUI) for the predator-prey simulation of Section 8.4, *Abstract Base Classes*, on page 395. It is beyond the scope of this book to describe various available GUI toolkits. The program should draw each iteration of the simulation on the screen. You should be able to directly input a Garden of Eden starting position. (See Section 8.4, *Abstract Base Classes*, on page 395, for the game-of-life simulation.) You should also be able to provide other settings for the simulation, such as the size of the simulation. Can you allow the

user to define other life-forms and their rules for existing, eating, and reproducing? Make the graphical interface as elegant as possible. The user should be able to position it on the screen, resize it, and select icons for the various available life-forms.

14. *(Java)* Add `GraduateStudent` to the Java class hierarchy in Section 8.10, *C++ Compared with Java*, on page 414. Note how Java uses capitalization instead of an underscore to separate words in an identifier. This is stylistic. C++ derives its heritage directly from C and adopted C style. Java has a SmallTalk influence and has styles adopted from that culture.

15. *(Java)* Develop the Java version of the shape hierarchy in Section 8.3.2, *A Canonical Example: Class* `shape`, on page 393.

16. *(Java)* Develop the predator-prey simulation in Java, using the *SWING* library to provide a graphical interface. (See Section 8.4, *Abstract Base Classes*, on page 395, for the predator-prey C++ simulation.) This is one area that Java excels in.

Input/Output

This chapter describes input/output in C++, using *iostream* and its associated libraries. The standard input/output library for C, described by the header *cstdio*, is still available in C++. However, C++ introduces *iostream*, which implements its own collection of input/output functions.

Stream I/O is described as a set of classes in *iostream*. These classes overload the put to and get from operators << and >>. Streams can be associated with files, and examples of file processing using streams are discussed in this chapter. A lot of file processing requires character-handling macros, which are found in *ctype*. These are also discussed here.

In OOP, objects should know how to print themselves, and in this text we have frequently made print() a member function of a class. Notationally, it is also useful to overload << for user-defined ADTs. In this section, we develop output functions for the types card and deck to illustrate these techniques.

9.1 The Output Class `ostream`

Output is inserted into an object of type `ostream`, declared in the header file *iostream*. An operator `<<` is overloaded in this class to perform output for the standard types. The overloaded left-shift operator is called the *insertion*, or *put to*, operator. The operator is left-associative and returns a value of type `ostream&`. The standard output `ostream` corresponding to `stdout` is `cout`, and the standard output `ostream` corresponding to `stderr` is `cerr`.

The effect of executing a simple output statement, such as

```
cout << "x = " << x << '\n';
```

is to print to the screen a string of four characters, followed by an appropriate representation for the output of x, followed by a new line. The representation depends on which overloaded version of `<<` is invoked.

The class `ostream` contains public members, such as

```
ostream& operator<<(int i);
ostream& operator<<(long i);
ostream& operator<<(double x);
ostream& operator<<(char c);
ostream& operator<<(const char* s);
ostream& put(char c);
ostream& write(const char* p, int n);
ostream& flush();
```

The member function `put()` outputs the character representation of c. The member function `write()` outputs the string of length n pointed at by p. The member function `flush()` forces the stream to be written. Since these are member functions, they can be used as follows:

```
cout.put('A');              // output A

char*  str = "ABCDEFGHI";
cout.write(str + 2, 3);     // output CDE
cout.flush();               // empty buffer to stream
```

9.2   Formatted Output and *iomanip*

The put to operator << produces by default the minimum number of characters needed to represent the output. As a consequence, output can be confusing, as seen in the following example:

```
int  i = 8, j = 9;

cout << i << j;               // confused: prints 89
cout << i << "   " << j;      // better: prints 8   9
cout << "i= " << i << " j= " << j; // best: i= 8 j= 9
```

Two schemes that we have used to properly space output are to have strings separating output values and to use \n and \t to create new lines and tabbing. We can also use manipulators in the stream output to control output formatting.

A manipulator is a value or a function that has a special effect on the stream on which it operates. A simple example of a manipulator is endl, defined in *iostream*, which outputs a newline and flushes the ostream.

```
x = 1;
cout << "x = " << x << endl;
```

This immediately prints the line

```
x = 1
```

Another manipulator, flush, flushes the ostream, as in

```
cout << "x = " << x << flush;
```

This has almost the same effect as the previous example but does not advance to a new line.

The manipulators dec, hex, and oct can be used to change integer bases. The default is base 10. The conversion base remains set until it is explicitly changed.

In file manip.cpp

```
// Using different bases in integer I/O

int main()
{
    int  i = 10, j = 16, k = 24;
    cout << i << '\t' << j << '\t' << k << endl;
    cout << oct << i << '\t' << j << '\t' << k << endl;
    cout << hex << i << '\t' << j << '\t' << k << endl;
    cout << "Enter 3 integers, e.g. 11 11 12a" << endl;

    cin >> i >> hex >> j >> k;
    cout << dec << i << '\t' << j << '\t' << k << endl;
}
```

The resulting output is

```
10        16        24
12        20        30
a         10        18
Enter 3 integers, e.g. 11 11 12a
11        17        298
```

Dissection of the *manip* Program

■ int   i = 10, j = 16, k = 24;

In this program, we show how to use manipulators to help format output.

■ cout << i << '\t' << j << '\t' << k << endl;

The default is decimal output with no separation. In this case, the tab character is used to separate the values. Better would be

```
    cout << "i = " << i << "\tj = " << j
         << "\tk = "<< k << endl;
```

■ cout << oct << i << '\t' << j << '\t' << k << endl;

The manipulator oct changes to an octal representation, so the value of i, which is decimal 10, is printed as the octal 12.

■ `cout << hex << i << '\t' << j << '\t' << k << endl;`

The manipulator `hex` changes to a hexadecimal representation, so the value of `i`, which is decimal 10, is printed as the hexadecimal a.

■ `cout << "Enter 3 integers, e.g. 11 11 12a" << endl;`

`cin >> i >> hex >> j >> k;`
`cout << dec << i << '\t' << j << '\t' << k << endl;`

Input streams can also set the base using manipulators. Thus, for `cin` the variable of `i` is read in as decimal, but the manipulator `hex` changes the base for the next values. The base manipulator is persistent. If we had not reset `cout` to `dec`, the values would have printed as hexadecimal because the last setting for `cout` was hexadecimal. Thus, the value of `j` input as hexadecimal 11 prints as decimal 17. The value of `k` input as hexadecimal 12a prints as decimal `298`.

The preceding manipulators are found in *iostream*. Other manipulators are found in *iomanip*. For example, `setw(int width)` is a manipulator that changes the default field width for the next formatted I/O operation to the value of its argument. This value reverts to the default. Table 9.1 briefly lists the standard manipulators, the function of each, and the location where each is defined.

Table 9.1 I/O Manipulators		
Manipulator	Function	File
`endl`	Outputs newline and flush	*iostream*
`ends`	Outputs null in string	*iostream*
`flush`	Flushes the output	*iostream*
`dec`	Uses decimal	*iostream*
`hex`	Uses hexadecimal	*iostream*
`oct`	Uses octal	*iostream*
`ws`	Skips white space on input	*iostream*
`skipws`	Skips white space	*iostream*
`noskipws`	Does not skip white space	*iostream*
`boolalpha`	Prints `true` and `false`	*iostream*
`noboolalpha`	Prints 1 and 0	*iostream*
`fixed`	Prints using format 123.45	*iostream*

Table 9.1 I/O Manipulators		
Manipulator	Function	File
`scientific`	Prints using format 1.2345e+02	*iostream*
`left`	Fills characters to right of value	*iostream*
`right`	Fills characters to left of value	*iostream*
`internal`	Fills characters between sign and value	*iostream*
`setw(int)`	Sets field width	*iomanip*
`setfill(int)`	Sets fill character	*iomanip*
`setbase(int)`	Sets base format	*iomanip*
`setprecision(int)`	Sets floating-point precision	*iomanip*
`setiosflags(long)`	Sets format bits	*iomanip*
`resetiosflags(long)`	Resets format bits	*iomanip*

A further example demonstrates the use of `setw`, `setfill`, and `setprecision` manipulators.

In file format.cpp

```
// Display use of formatting manipulators

#include <iostream>
#include <iomanip>
using namespace std;

// pi to 21 places
const long double pi = 3.14159265358979323846L;

inline long double area(long double rad)
    { return (pi * rad * rad); }
```

```
int main()
{
    long double  r;

    cout << "\nEnter radius: ";
    cin >> r;
    cout << "\nArea is " << setw(20) << area(r);
    cout << "\nArea is " << setw(20)
         << setprecision(10) << area(r);
    cout << "\nArea is " << area(r);
    cout << "\nArea is " << setprecision(20)
         << area(r) << endl;
    cout << setfill('*');
    cout << setprecision(4) << setw(20) << r << endl;
}
```

The output from this program when 1.0 is entered for r is

```
Enter radius:
Area is             3.14159
Area is          3.141592654
Area is 3.141592654
Area is 3.141592653589793238
********************1
```

Dissection of the *format* Program

■ #include <iomanip>

This file contains many of the standard manipulators, such as setw() and setprecision().

■ const long double pi = 3.14159265358979323846L;

We want to display a large number of digits in this test program.

```
■  cout << "\nArea is " << setw(20) << area(r);
```

The width for printing the `area(r)` is 20 characters. It prints as

```
Area is             3.14159
```

This is right-adjusted and prints by default six significant digits.

```
■  cout << "\nArea is " << setw(20)
       << setprecision(10) << area(r);
   cout << "\nArea is "  << area(r);
   cout << "\nArea is " << setprecision(20)
       << area(r) << endl;
```

Notice how these change the number of significant digits printed.

```
■  cout << setfill('*');
   cout << setprecision(4) << setw(20) << r << endl;
```

This prints 19 fill characters `*` and `r`, which is exactly `1`.

```
*******************1
```

In C++, being good at manipulation and willing to use it isn't a character flaw!

As expected, the `setprecision()` yields a different number of decimal digits of floating-point precision. Be careful not to exceed the meaningful precision of the result. The fill character by default is blank, and here in the last line of output, it was changed to the star. The output widths are adjusted per each output value. Otherwise, the default width is the exact number of characters needed to display a result.

9.3   User-Defined Types: Output

User-defined types have typically been printed by creating a member function print(). Let us use the types card and deck as an example of a simple user-defined type. We write out a set of output routines for displaying cards:

In file print_deck.cpp

```
// Card output

const char pips_symbol[14] = { '?', 'A', '2', '3', '4',
        '5', '6', '7', '8', '9', 'T', 'J', 'Q', 'K' };
const char suit_symbol[4] = { 'c', 'd', 'h', 's' };

enum suit { clubs, diamonds, hearts, spades };

class pips {
public:
   void  assign(int n) { p = n % 13 + 1; }
   void  print() { cout << pips_symbol[p]; }
private:
   int  p;
};

class card {
public:
   suit  s;
   pips  p;
   void  assign(int n)
      { cd = n; s = suit(n / 13); p.assign(n); }
   void  pr_card()
      { p.print(); cout << suit_symbol[s] << "  "; }
   suit  get_suit() { return s; }
   pips  get_pips() { return p; }
private:
   int  cd;                        // a cd is from 0 to 51
};
```

```
class deck {
public:
    void  init_deck();
    void  shuffle();
    void  deal(int, int, card*);
    void  pr_deck();
private:
    card d[52];
};

void deck::pr_deck()
{
    for (int i = 0; i < 52; ++i) {
        if (i % 13 == 0)        // 13 cards to a line
            cout << endl;
        d[i].pr_card();
    }
    cout << endl;
}
```

Each card is printed out in two characters. If d is a variable of type deck, then d.pr_deck() prints out the entire deck, 13 cards to a line.

In keeping with the spirit of OOP, it would also be nice to overload << to accomplish the same aim. The operator << has two arguments—an ostream& and the ADT—and it must produce an ostream&. You want to use a reference to a stream and to return a reference to a stream, whenever overloading << or >>, because you do not want to copy a stream object. Let us write these functions for the types card and deck:

In file print_deck.cpp

```
ostream& operator<<(ostream& out, pips& x)
{
    return (out << pips_symbol[x.p]);
}

ostream& operator<<(ostream& out, card& cd)
{
    return (out << cd.p << suit_symbol[cd.s]);
}
```

```
ostream& operator<<(ostream& out, deck& x)
{
    for (int i = 0; i < 52; ++i) {
        out << x.d[i];
        if ((i + 1) % 13 == 0)          // 13 cards to a line
            out << endl;
        else
            out << "  ";
    }
    return out;
}
```

The functions that operate on `pips` and `deck` need to be friends of the corresponding class, because they access private members.

See Section 5.17, *Overloading << and >>,* on page 253 for more examples of overloading the `<<` operator.

9.4   The Input Class `istream`

An operator `>>` is overloaded in `istream` to perform input for the standard types. The overloaded right-shift operator is called the *extraction*, or *get from*, operator. The standard input `istream` corresponding to `stdin` is `cin`.

The effect of executing a simple input statement, such as

```
cin >> x >> i;
```

is to read from standard input, normally the keyboard, a value for `x` and then a value for `i`. White space is ignored and is only used to separate tokens in the input stream.

The class `istream` contains public members, such as

```
istream& operator>>(int& i);
istream& operator>>(long& i);
istream& operator>>(double& x);
istream& operator>>(char& c);
istream& operator>>(char* s);
istream& get(char& c);
istream& get(char* s, int n, char c = '\n');
istream& getline(char* s, int n, char c = '\n');
istream& read(char* s, int n);
```

The member function `get(char& c)` inputs the character representation to `c`, including white space characters. The member function `get(char* s, int n, int c = '\n')` inputs into the string pointed at by `s` at most `n` – 1 characters, up to the specified delimiter character `c` or an end-of-file (EOF). A terminating 0 is placed in the output string. The optionally specified default character acts as a terminator but is not placed in the output string. If not specified, the input is read up to the next newline. The member function get-line() works like get(char*, int, char = '\n'), except that it discards rather than keeps the delimiter character in the designated istream. The member function read(char* s, int n) inputs into the string pointed at by s at most n characters. It sets the failbit if an end-of-file is encountered before n characters are read. (See Section 9.8, *Using Stream States*, on page 437.) In systems that have implemented ANSI standard exceptions, the ios_base::failure exception may be thrown.

```
cin.get(c);          // one character
cin.get(s, 40);      // length 40 or terminated by \n
cin.get(s, 10, '*'); // length 10 or terminated by *
cin.getline(s, 40);  // same as get but \n discarded
```

Other useful member functions are

```
int gcount();     // number of recently extracted chars
istream& ignore(int n=1, int delimiter=EOF); // skips
int peek();       // get next char without extraction
istream& putback(char c);   // puts back character
```

When overloading the >> operator to produce input to a user-defined type, the typical form is

```
istream& operator>>(istream& p, user-defined-type& x)
```

If the function needs access to private members of x, it must be made a friend of class x. A major point is to make x a reference parameter so that its value can be modified.

9.5   Files

C systems have stdin, stdout, and stderr as standard files. In addition, systems may define other standard files, such as stdprn and stdaux. Abstractly, a file may be thought of as a stream of characters that are processed sequentially. The standard C++ files are shown in Table 9.2.

The C++ stream input/output ties the first three of these standard files to cin, cout, and cerr, respectively. Typically, C++ ties cprn and caux to their corresponding standard files, stdprn and stdaux. There is also clog, which is a buffered version of cerr. Other files can be opened or created by the programmer. We show how to do this in the context of writing a program that double-spaces an existing file into an existing or new file. The file names are specified on the command line and passed into argv.

Table 9.2	Standard Files		
C	C++	Name	Connected To
stdin	cin	Standard input file	Keyboard
stdout	cout	Standard output file	Screen
stderr	cerr	Standard error file	Screen
stdprn	cprn	Standard printer file	Printer
stdaux	caux	Standard auxiliary file	Auxiliary port

File I/O is handled by including *fstream*, which contains the classes ofstream and ifstream for output and input file-stream creation and manipulation. To properly open and manage an ifstream or ofstream related to a system file, you must first declare it with an appropriate constructor.

```
ifstream();
ifstream(const char*, int = ios::in,
         int prot = filebuf::openprot);
ofstream();
ofstream(const char*, int = ios::out,
         int prot = filebuf::openprot);
```

The constructor of no arguments creates a variable that is later associated with an input file. The constructor of three arguments takes as its first argument the named file. The second argument specifies the file mode. The third argument is for file protection.

The arguments for file mode are defined as enumerators in class ios, as shown Table 9.3.

Table 9.3	File Modes
Argument	Mode
ios::in	Input mode
ios::app	Append mode
ios::out	Output mode
ios::ate	Open and seek to end-of-file
ios::nocreate	Open but do not create mode
ios::trunc	Discard contents and open
ios::noreplace	If file exists, open fails

Thus, the default for an `ifstream` is input mode, and the default for an `ofstream` is output mode. If file opening fails, the stream is put into a bad state. The mode can be tested with the `!` operator. In libraries built with exceptions, the `failure` exception can be thrown.

Other important member functions found in *fstream* include

```
// Opens ifstream file

void open(const char*, int = ios::in,
        int prot = filebuf::openprot);
// Opens ofstream file

void open(const char*, int = ios::out,
        int prot = filebuf::openprot);
void close();
```

These functions can be used to open and close appropriate files. If you create a file stream with the default constructor, you would normally use `open()` to associate it with a file. You could then use `close()` to close the file and to open another file, using the same stream. Typically a file stream will be closed automatically when it goes out of scope. Additional member functions in other I/O classes allow for a full range of file manipulation. The following program uses both the *fstream* and the *cstdlib* libraries:

In file double_space.cpp

```
// A program to double space a file.
// Usage: executable f1 f2
// f1 must be present and readable
// f2 must be writable if it exists

#include <fstream>
#include <cstdlib>
using namespace std;

void double_space(ifstream& f, ofstream& t)
{
    char   c;

    while (f.get(c)) {
        t.put(c);
        if (c == '\n')
            t.put(c);
    }
}
```

```
int main(int argc, char** argv)
{
   if (argc != 3) {
      cout << "\nUsage: " << argv[0]
           << " infile  outfile" << endl;
      exit(1);
   }
   ifstream  f_in(argv[1]);
   ofstream  f_out(argv[2]);

   if (!f_in) {
      cerr << "cannot open " << argv[1] << endl;
      exit(1);
   }
   if (!f_out) {
      cerr << "cannot open " << argv[2] << endl;
      exit(1);
   }
   double_space(f_in, f_out);
}
```

Dissection of the *double_space* Program

■ `void double_space(ifstream& f, ofstream& t)`

This function is a typical file-manipulation function. It is idiomatic of much of C++ file processing. In this case, there is an input file that is processed with the results going to an output file.

■ `char  c;`

  `while (f.get(c)) {`

Much of file processing is handled one character at a time. The expression `f.get(c)` returns as 0 when the stream can no longer be read. Otherwise, it returns with a nonzero value and reads into `c` the character value, including white space characters.

■ `t.put(c);`
  `if (c == '\n')`
     `t.put(c);`

The loop places each character into the output file. It tests each character for being a newline. Where a newline is found, it outputs a second newline, thus double-spacing the file.

```
■ int main(int argc, char** argv)
  {
      if (argc != 3) {
          cout << "\nUsage: " << argv[0]
                  << "  infile  outfile" << endl;
          exit(1);
      }
```

This is idiomatic for generating an executable that utilizes command line arguments. The resulting code would be something like

double_space my_input my_output

Here, the expectation is that there are three strings on the command line. The name of the executable is followed by the input and output file names. This correct usage is tested by main().

```
■ ifstream  f_in(argv[1]);
  ofstream  f_out(argv[2]);
```

The declarations of the two streams cause constructor invocation to properly open these files.

```
■ if (!f_in) {
      cerr << "cannot open " << argv[1] << endl;
      exit(1);
  }
  if (!f_out) {
      cerr << "cannot open " << argv[2] << endl;
      exit(1);
  }
  double_space(f_in, f_out);
```

We test that the constructors properly opened the two files. If there is no error exit, the double_space() function is invoked.

9.6 Using Strings as Streams

The class stringstream allows strings to be treated as iostreams. When using stringstreams, the *sstream* library must be included. An older library *strstring* does the same for char* strings. Check your system to determine which of these libraries is available.

The istringstream is used when input is from a string rather than from a stream. The overloaded >> get from operator may be used with istringstream variables. The forms for declaring an istringstream variable are

```
istringstream name (char* s);
istringstream name (char* s, int n);
```

where s is a string to use as input, n is the optional length of the input buffer, and *name* is used instead of cin. If n is not specified, the string must be terminated with a 0. The end-of-string sentinel is treated as an EOF. An example follows:

In file str_stream.cpp

```
#include <iostream>
#include <sstream>                        // replaces strstream
#include <cstdlib>
using namespace std;

int main()
{
    string  name;
    int  total;
string scores[5] = { "Vicki 2", "Nicole 5", "Boston 8",
                     "Chris 7", "Don 3" };
istringstream ist(scores[4]);// ist uses scores[4]
ist >> name >> total;        // name: Don, total: 3
cout << "\nname: " << name << "  total: "
     << total << endl;  }
```

Here, we have a series of five strings stored in an array. We take scores[4] as the initializer for ist. Then the overloaded extraction operator >> can be used to assign "Don" to name and 3 to total.

The ostringstream declarations have the following forms:

```
ostringstream name();
ostringstream name(char* s, int n,
                   int mode = ios::out);
```

where s is pointer to buf to receive string, n is the optional size of buffer, and mode specifies whether the data are to be put into an empty buffer (ios::out) or appended to the existing null-terminated string in the buffer (ios::app or ios::ate). If no size is specified, the buffer is dynamically allocated. The ostringstream variable may use the overloaded put to operator << to build the string. The use of ostringstream is particularly useful when you want to construct a single string from information kept in a variety of variables. In the following example, note that ost2 must contain an existing null-terminated string in order for the append to work correctly.

```
ostringstream ost1;
ostringstream ost2 (charbuf, 1000, ios::app);

ost1 << name << "  " << score << endl;
ost2 << address << city << endl << ends;
```

9.7   The Functions and Macros in *ctype*

The system provides a standard header file, *ctype.h*, or *ctype*, which contains a set of functions used to test characters and a set of functions used to convert characters, as shown in Table 9.4. These functions may be implemented as macros or as inline functions. This is mentioned here because of its usefulness in C++ input/output. Those functions that only test a character return an int value. The argument is type int.

Table 9.4 ctype Functions	
Function	Nonzero (true) Is Returned if c Is
isalpha(c)	A letter
isupper(c)	An uppercase letter
islower(c)	A lowercase letter
isdigit(c)	A digit
isxdigit(c)	A hexadecimal digit
isspace(c)	A white space character
isalnum(c)	A letter or digit
ispunct(c)	A punctuation character
isgraph(c)	A printing character, except space
isprint(c)	A printable character
iscntrl(c)	A control character
isascii(c)	An ASCII code

Other functions, as shown in Table 9.5, provide for the appropriate conversion of a character value. Note that these functions do not change the value of c stored in memory.

The ASCII code functions are usual on ASCII systems.

Table 9.5 ctype Conversion Functions	
`toupper(c)`	Changes `c` from lowercase to uppercase
`tolower(c)`	Changes `c` from uppercase to lowercase
`toascii(c)`	Changes `c` to ASCII code

9.8   Using Stream States

Each stream has an associated state that can be tested. The states on existing systems are

```
enum io_state { goodbit, eofbit, failbit, badbit };
```

ANSI systems propose the type `ios_base::iostate` to be a bitmask type defining these values. When the values other than `goodbit` are set by an I/O operation, ANSI systems can throw the I/O standard exception `ios_base::failure`. Associated with this exception is a member function `what()` returning a `char*` message that gives a reason for the failure.

The values for a particular stream can be tested by using the public member functions in Table 9.6.

Table 9.6 Stream State Functions	
`int good();`	Nonzero if not EOF or other error bit set
`int eof();`	Nonzero if istream `eofbit` set
`int fail();`	Nonzero if `failbit`, `badbit` set
`int bad();`	Nonzero if `badbit` set
`int rdstate();`	Returns error state
`void clear(int i=0);`	Resets error state
`int operator!();`	Returns `true` if `failbit` or `badbit` set
`operator void*() const;`	Returns `false` if `failbit` or `badbit` set

Testing for a stream's being in a nongood state can protect a program from hanging up. A stream state of `good` means that the previous input/output operation worked and that the next operation should also. A stream state of EOF means that the previous input operation returned an end-of-file condition. A stream state of `fail` means that the previous input/output operation failed but that the stream is usable once the error bit is cleared. A stream state of bad means that the previous input/output operation is invalid but that the stream may be usable once the error condition is corrected.

It is also possible to directly test a stream. It is nonzero if it is in either a good or an EOF state.

```
if (cout << x)          // output succeeded
   .....
else
   .....                // output failed
```

The following program counts the number of words coming from the standard input. Normally, this would be redirected to use an existing file. The program illustrates ideas discussed in this and the previous two sections.

In file word_count.cpp

```
// The word_count program for counting words
// Usage: executable < file

int  found_next_word();

int main()
{
   int  word_cnt = 0;

   while (found_next_word())
      ++word_cnt;
   cout << "word count is " << word_cnt << endl;
}
int found_next_word()
{
   char  c;
   int   word_sz = 0;

   cin >> c;
   while (!cin.eof() && !isspace(c)) {
      ++word_sz;
      cin.get(c);
   }
   return word_sz;
}
```

A non–white space character is received from the input stream and is assigned to c. The while loop calls the isspace() function in the *ctype* library to test that adjacent characters are not white space. The loop terminates when either an end-of-file character or a white space character is found. The word *size* is returned as 0 when the only non–white space character found is the end-of-file. One last point: The loop cannot be rewritten as

```
while (!cin.eof() && !isspace(c)) {
    ++word_sz;
    cin >> c;
}
```

because this would skip white space.

9.9   Mixing I/O Libraries

Throughout this text, *iostream* has been used. It is perfectly reasonable to want to continue using *stdio*. This is the standard in the C community, and it is well understood. Its disadvantage is that it is not type-safe.

We are switching from C to C++, and want to start using the newer *iostream* library, but I've got 240,000 lines of C code to integrate that use stdio!

Functions such as `printf()` use unchecked variable-length argument lists. Stream I/O requires, as arguments to its functions and over-loaded operators, assignment-compatible types. You might also want to mix both forms of I/O. Synchronization problems can occur because the two libraries use different buffering strategies. This can be avoided by calling

```
ios::sync_with_stdio();
```

The following program coordinates the two libraries:

In file mix_io.cpp

```
// The mix_io program with synchronized I/O

unsigned long fact(int n)
{
    unsigned long  f = 1;

    for (int i = 2; i <= n; ++i)
        f *= i;
    return f;
}
int main()
{
    int n;

    ios::sync_with_stdio();

    do {
        cout << "\nEnter n positive or 0 to halt: ";
        scanf("%d", &n);
        printf("\n fact(%d) = %ld", n, fact(n));
    } while (n > 0);
    cout << "\nend of session" << endl;
}
```

Note that for integer values greater than 12, the results overflow. It is safe to mix `stdio` and `iostream`, provided they are not mixed on the same file.

9.10   Software Engineering: I/O

STL containers and iterators are a natural pattern to use when writing code for input/output streams. Both model the sequence abstraction. STL provides special input and output iterators for handling I/O. These again demonstrate how sequences are a very powerful software design tool. Let us write a routine that reads a file into a `vector`, outputs its contents, and sums the `vector`.

In file io_iterators.cpp

```cpp
// Use of istream_iterator and ostream_iterator

#include <iterator>
#include <iostream>
#include <fstream>
#include <vector>
#include <numeric>
using namespace std;

int main()
{
    int  sum;
    istream_iterator<int>  in(*new ifstream("data"));
    istream_iterator<int> eos;
    ostream_iterator<int> out(cout, "\t");
    vector<int> v(in, eos);

    copy(v.begin(), v.end(), out);
    sum = accumulate(v.begin(), v.end(), 0);
    cout << "sum = " << sum << endl;
}
```

Dissection of the *io_iterators* Program

- `istream_iterator<int> in(*new ifstream("data"));`

This opens a file for input. The file's name is *data*. This is used to initialize the `istream_iterator` in. Note that some older compilers require the use of `ptrdiff_t` parameter as follows:

```cpp
istream_iterator<int, ptrdiff_t>
                    in(*new ifstream("data"));
```

- `istream_iterator<int> eos;`

This establishes the end-of-stream iterator. This allows us to use `in` as the beginning of the stream and `eos` as the end-of-stream guard. Note that some older compilers require the use of `ptrdiff_t` parameter as follows:

```cpp
istream_iterator<int, ptrdiff_t> eos;
```

- `ostream_iterator<int> out(cout, "\t");`

This constructs the correspondence between `cout` and the iterator out. Using this iterator injects a tab character after each `int` value output.

> ■ `vector<int> v(in, eos);`
>
> This creates a vector initialized from the file *data*. It reads all integer values until it hits the end-of-file.
>
> ■ `copy(v.begin(), v.end(), out);`
>
> The `copy()` algorithm writes the `vector` `v` to `cout`. This is a simple, powerful idiom for stream output from any sequence.

9.11   Dr. P's Prescriptions

- ■ Remember GIGO—garbage in, garbage out.

- ■ Input should be prompted for and checked by echoing.

- ■ Output should be easily readable by a user of the program who does not have source code available.

- ■ Use *iostream* instead of *cstdio*.

- ■ Provide overloaded functions << and >> in classes.

Garbage in, garbage out is one of the prime axioms of computation. This implies that the program must check input as rigorously as possible. I/O is critical to the user of your program. Without meaningful I/O the program is useless. In this text, we have kept many of the examples simple, and the text programs assume that a user will enter meaningful data. In real-world programs, the user interface has to be robust. This implies that the user will be prompted for appropriate data. The program will test that the input is what the user intended by asking the user to confirm that the data is correct. In the case of incorrect data, the user will be allowed to reenter new data.

Output needs to be formatted in a readable manner. Think in terms of the naive user being able to read the output without having to understand any detail of the program or algorithm.

One important improvement on *iostream* over *cstdio* is its type safety. There are reasons to use *cstdio*, such as maintenance of legacy code or a need for special formatting, but in most cases the *iostream* functionality is preferred.

There is an expectation in the C++ community that any user-defined type will have overloaded the << and >> for output and input, respectively. This design consistency is a trait of a good object-oriented programmer.

9.12   C++ Compared with Java

Java has type-safe I/O but does not have operator overloading. In Java, most output to the terminal is done using `println()`, as we discussed in Section 2.11, *C++ Compared with Java*, on page 76. Java also has the GUI library *Swing,* which is discussed extensively in *Java by Dissection*, by Ira Pohl and Charlie McDowell (Addison-Wesley 1999), Chapters 7 and 8. In this section, we present an example of Java writing to a file. This is taken from *Java by Dissection,* Section 10.2, pages 347–348.

The simplest way to write text to a file requires the use of two different classes—PrintWriter and FileWriter—both from the standard package `java.io`. The class `PrintWriter` has the familiar methods `print()` and `println()` that we've been using to write to the console. To create a `PrintWriter` object that is associated with a particular file, we must first create a `FileWriter` object for that file. This object is then passed to the constructor for the `PrintWriter`, as shown in the following example:

In file HelloFile.java

```
//Writing to a Java file

import java.io.*;

class HelloFile {
    public static void main(String[] args)
       throws java.io.IOException
    {
       PrintWriter out =
         new PrintWriter(new FileWriter("hello.txt"));
       out.println("Hello, file system!");
       out.close();
    }
}
```

If you run this program, it creates a file, *hello.txt*, which you can view with any text editor. The contents of the file are the one line:

Hello, file system!

Dissection of the `HelloFile` Program

■ `import java.io.*;`

We must import the package `java.io`. That is where the `PrintWriter` and `FileWriter` classes are defined.

■ `public static void main(String[] args)`
　　`throws java.io.IOException`

Many of the methods for I/O can generate an I/O exception. As discussed in Chapter 10, *Exceptions and Program Correctness*, an exception is something unexpected that occurs. Often, an exception is really an error. In this example, if the output file couldn't be opened for some reason, an `IOException` would be generated. A statement or method that generates an exception is said to "throw an exception." The class `IOException` is defined in the package `java.io`. We can either give the full name of the exception, `java.io.IOException`, as in this example, or, because we are importing `java.io.*`, we can use the shorter name, `IOException`.

■ `PrintWriter out =`
　　`new PrintWriter(new FileWriter("hello.txt"));`

The class `FileWriter` needs the name of the file as a string. This name can include directory information, which is platform-dependent. When no directory information is specified, the file is created in the operating system's notion of the current directory. The resulting `FileWriter` object is used to construct a `PrintWriter` object.

■ `out.println("Hello file system!");`
`out.close();`

Anything that we can do with `System.out.print()` or `System.out.println()`, we can do with the corresponding method from `PrintWriter`. Closing the file when the program terminates is essential. Failure to close the `PrintWriter` stream may cause some or all of the output not to appear in the file because of unflushed buffers.

Why do we need the two classes `PrintWriter` and `FileWriter`? The reason is that the Java I/O package is designed to support many different types of input/output processing. Think of the classes in the package as building blocks. By assembling the correct set of building blocks, you can meet many different I/O processing needs. You can use the class `FileWriter` to write a stream of text characters into a file, but the methods in `FileWriter` are fairly primitive and support only the writing of text from `String`, `char`, and `char[]` values. The class `PrintWriter` from the same package can generate a stream of text characters from any value. The primary methods in class `Print-Writer` are the familiar `print()` and `println()` used for writing to the console. By passing a `FileWriter` object to the constructor of a `PrintWriter`, you are logically creating a sequence or pipeline of processing steps.

You can use the class `PrintWriter` to create text streams that go somewhere other than to a file. For example, you can also use a `PrintWriter` to write over a network or to write to a character array. The output of the `PrintWriter` is sent to the stream specified in the constructor. In this case, it is a `FileWriter`.

Summary

- Output is inserted into an object of type `ostream`, declared in the header file *iostream*. An operator `<<` is overloaded in this class to perform output for the standard types. The overloaded left_shift operator is called the insertion, or put to, operator. The standard output `ostream` is `cout`.

- The operator `>>` is overloaded in `istream` to perform input for standard types. The overloaded right-shift operator is called the extraction, or get from, operator. The standard input `istream` is `cin`.

- A manipulator is a value or a function that has a special effect on the stream on which it operates. Common ones include `endl` and `setw()`.

- Code for overloading `operator<<` often looks like

```
ostream& operator<<(ostream& out, type& x)
{
    out << x.part << ·····// output members
    return out;
}
```

- File I/O is handled by including *fstream*, which contains the classes `ofstream` and `ifstream` for output and input file-stream creation and manipulation. To properly open and manage an `ifstream` or `ofstream` related to a system file, you must first declare it with an appropriate constructor.

- The `istringstream` is used when input is from a string rather than from a stream. The overloaded >> get from operator may be used with `istringstream` variables.

- Each stream has an associated state that can be tested. The states on existing systems are tested with *streamname*`.good()` and are

  ```
  enum io_state { goodbit, eofbit, failbit, badbit };
  ```

- Synchronization problems can occur because the two I/O libraries, *iostream* and *cstdio*, use different buffering strategies. This can be avoided by calling

  ```
  ios::sync_with_stdio();
  ```

Review Questions

1. What two standard output streams are provided by *iostream*?

2. What *ctype* method capitalizes alphabetic characters?

3. How is EOF tested for when using `cin`?

4. Name two manipulators and describe their purpose.

5. What method can be used to read strings from a file?

6. The class _____ allows strings to be treated as `iostreams`, and the _____ library must be included.

7. In OOP, objects should know how to print themselves, and it is best to do this by _____ for user-defined ADTs.

8. Synchronization problems can occur when using `stdio` and `iostream` in the same program because the two libraries use different buffering strategies, which can be avoided by calling _____.

9. Fill in the C++ stream names and their default physical connection devices in Table 9.7.

10. File I/O is handled by including _____, which contains the classes _____ and _____ for output and input file-stream creation and manipulation.

Table 9.7	Standard Files		
C	C++	Name	Connected to
stdin		Standard input file	
stdout		Standard output file	
stderr		Standard error file	
stdprn		Standard printer file	
stdaux		Standard auxiliary file	

Exercises

1. Write an array of strings to a file named *strings.txt*. Initialize the array with the four strings "I am", "a text", "file written", and "to strings.txt".

2. Create an array of strings that receive their input from the file *save.txt*. Specify the number of strings by asking the user to enter the number of lines to be read. Echo the strings read to cout.

3. Redo the preceding exercise to end when the input is a special sentinel string. For example, you may use an empty string as the sentinel.

4. Write a program that prints 1,000 random numbers to a file.

5. Write a program to read 1,000 random numbers in the range 0 to 1 from a file (see exercise 4) and plot their distribution. That is, divide the interval 0–1 into tenths and count the numbers that fall into each tenth. This gives you some confidence in their randomness.

6. Modify the preceding two exercises to allow the user to specify the number of random numbers and the name of the file on the command line. Store the number of generated numbers as the first entry in the file.

7. Read a text file and write it to a target text file, changing all lowercase to uppercase and double-spacing the output text.

8. Modify the program in the previous exercise to number each nonblank line.

9. Write a class `dollar`. Have its overloaded I/O operators print a number such as 12345.67 as $12,345.67. You should decide whether this class should internally store a dollar amount as two `int`s or a simple `double`.

10. Write a program that reads a text file and computes the relative frequency of each of the letters of the alphabet. You can use an array of length 26 to store the number of occurrences of each letter. You can use `tolower()` to convert uppercase letters. Subtracting `'a'` then gives you a value in the range 0 to 25, inclusive, which you can use to index into the array of counts.

11. Run the program from the previous exercise on several large text files and compare the results. How can you use this information to break a simple substitution code?

12. Compile the following program and put the executable code into the file *try_me*:

```
#include <iostream>

int main( )
{
    cout << "A is for apple" << endl;
    cerr << "and alphabet pie!" << endl;
}
```

Execute the program so you understand its effects. What happens when you redirect the output? Try the command

try_me > temp

Make sure you read the file *temp* after you do this. If UNIX is available to you, try the command

try_me >& temp

This causes the output that is written to `cerr` to be redirected, too. Make sure that you look at what is in *temp*. You may be surprised!

13. Write a program to number the lines in a file. The input file name should be passed to the program as a command line argument. The program should write to `cout`. Each line in the input file should be written to the output file with the line number and a space prepended.

14. Modify the program you wrote in the previous exercise so that the line numbers are right-adjusted. The following output is *not* acceptable:

    ```
    .....
    9 This is line nine.
    10 This is line ten.
    ```

15. Our program that double-spaces a file can be invoked with the command

    dbl_space infile outfile

    But if *outfile* exists, it is overwritten; this is potentially dangerous. Rewrite the program so that it writes to `stdout` instead. Then the program can be invoked with the command

    dbl_space infile > outfile

    This program design is safer. Of all the system commands, only a few are designed to overwrite a file. After all, nobody likes to lose a file by accident.

16. Write the function `getwords(in, k, words)` so that it reads k words from a file using the input stream `in` and places them in the string `words`, separated by newlines. The function should return the number of words successfully read and stored in `words`. Write a program to test your function.

17. Write a program that displays a file on the screen 20 lines at a time. The input file should be given as a command line argument. The program should display the next 20 lines after a carriage return has been typed. (This is an elementary version of the *more* utility in UNIX.)

18. Modify the program you wrote in the previous exercise. Your program should display one or more files given as command line arguments. Also, allow for a command line option of the form -*n*, where *n* is a positive integer specifying the number of lines that are to be displayed at one time.

19. Write a program called *search* that searches for patterns. If the command

    search hello my_file

    is given, then the string pattern *hello* is searched for in the file *my_file*. Any line that contains the pattern is printed. (This program is an elementary version of *grep*.) *Hint:* Use STL functions.

20. (*Java*) In the following Java example, we demonstrate how to detect an EOF with the standard Java class `BufferedReader`. The program opens the file specified on the command line and echoes its contents to the console. Rewrite this code as C++.

```java
// Echo.java - echo file contents to the screen
// Java by Dissection page 365.

import java.io.*;
class Echo {
    public static void main(String[] args)
                            throws IOException {
        if (args.length < 1) {
            System.out.println("Usage: " +
                                "java Echo filename");
            System.exit(0);
        }

        BufferedReader input =
         new BufferedReader(new FileReader(args[0]));
        String line = input.readLine();
        while (line != null) {
            System.out.println(line);
            line = input.readLine();
        }
    }
}
```

Exceptions and Program Correctness

This chapter describes exception handling in C++. Exceptions are generally unexpected error conditions. Normally, these conditions terminate the user program with a system-provided error message. An example is floating-point divide-by-zero. Usually, the system aborts the running program. C++ allows the programmer to attempt to recover from these conditions and continue program execution.

Assertions are program checks that force error exits when correctness is violated. One point of view is that an exception is based on a breakdown of a contractual guarantee among the provider of a code, the code's manufacturer, and the code's client. (See Section 11.1.1, *ADTs: Encapsulation and Data Hiding*, on page 484.) In this model, the client needs to guarantee that the conditions for applying the code exist, and the manufacturer needs to guarantee that the code works correctly under these conditions. In this methodology, assertions enforce the various guarantees.

10.1 Using the *assert* Library

Program correctness can be viewed in part as a proof that the computation terminated with correct output, dependent on correct input. The user of the computation had the responsibility of providing correct input. This was a precondition. The computation, if successful, satisfied a postcondition. Providing a fully formal proof of correctness is an ideal but is not usually done. Nevertheless, such assertions can be monitored at runtime to provide very useful diagnostics. Indeed, the discipline of thinking out appropriate assertions frequently causes the programmer to avoid bugs and pitfalls.

The C and C++ communities are increasingly emphasizing the use of assertions. The standard library *assert* provides a macro, `assert`, which is invoked as

    assert(*expression*);

If the *expression* evaluates as `false`, execution is aborted with diagnostic output. The assertions are discarded if the macro `NDEBUG` is defined.

Let us use assertions in template code for a stack container.

In file templateStack.cpp

```
// Template stack implementation

template <class TYPE>
class stack {
public:
   explicit stack(int size = 100)
      : max_len(size), top(EMPTY)
      { assert(size > 0); s = new TYPE[size];
        assert(s != 0); }
   ~stack() { delete []s; }
   void   reset() { top = EMPTY; }
   void   push(TYPE c) { assert(top < max_len - 1);
                         s[++top] = c; }
   TYPE   pop() { assert(top >= 0); return s[top--]; }
   TYPE   top_of() const { return s[top]; }
   bool   empty() const { return top == EMPTY; }
   bool   full() const { return top == max_len - 1; }
```

```
private:
   enum    { EMPTY = -1 };
   TYPE*   s;
   int     max_len;
   int     top;
};
```

The use of assertions replaces the ad hoc use of conditional tests with a more uniform methodology. This is better practice. The downside is that the assertion methodology does not allow a retry or other repair strategy to continue program execution. Also, assertions do not allow a customized error message, although it would be easy to add this capability.

Dissection of the stack Class

■ `explicit stack(int size = 100)`
```
        : max_len(size), top(EMPTY)
        { assert(size > 0);
          s = new TYPE[size]; assert(s != 0); }
```

The constructor is `explicit` to prevent its use as a conversion from `int` to `stack`. The `assert(size > 0)` tests the precondition that a legitimate value for this parameter was passed in to the constructor. The `assert(s != 0)` checks that the pointer s is not 0. On many C++ systems, this is the indicator that allocation with `new` failed. We discuss what happens when exception logic is used to signal this memory allocation error in Section 10.9, *Standard Exceptions and Their Uses*, on page 469.

■ `void  push(TYPE c) { assert(top < max_len - 1);`
```
                            s[++top] = c; }
```

Here, the assertion tests that the stack does not overflow. This is a precondition for the `push()` working correctly.

■ `TYPE  top_of()const { return s[top]; }`

Here, assertions that `top` has a valid value are unnecessary because the other methods guarantee that `top` is within the bounds `EMPTY` and `max_len`.

It is possible to make this scheme slightly more sophisticated by providing various testing levels, as are found in the Borland C++ *checks* library. Under this package, the flag _DEBUG can be set to

```
_DEBUG 0    no testing
_DEBUG 1    PRECONDITION tests only
_DEBUG 2    CHECK tests also
```

The idea is that once the library functions are thought to be correct, the level of checking is reduced to testing preconditions only. Once the client code is debugged, all testing can be suspended.

The following bubble sort does not work correctly:

In file bad_bubble1.cpp

```cpp
// Incorrect bubble sort

void swap(int a, int b)
{
    int  temp = a;

    a = b;
    b = temp;
}
void bubble(int a[], int size)
{
    int  i, j;

    for (i = 0; i != size - 1; ++i)
        for (j = i ; j != size - 1; ++j)
            if (a[j] < a [j + 1])
                swap (a[j], a[j + 1]);
}
int main()
{
    int  t[10] = { 9, 4, 6, 4, 5, 9, -3, 1, 0, 12};

    bubble(t, 10);
    for (int i = 0; i < 10; ++i)
        cout << t[i] << '\t';
    cout << "\nsorted? " << endl;
}
```

As an exercise, place assertions in this code to test that it is working properly. (See exercise 1 on page 479.)

10.2   C++ Exceptions

C++ introduces a context-sensitive exception-handling mechanism. It is not intended to handle the asynchronous exceptions defined in *signal*, such as SIGFPE, which indicates a floating-point exception. The context for handling an exception is a `try` block. The handlers are declared at the end of a `try` block, using the keyword `catch`.

C++ code can raise an exception in a `try` block by using the `throw` expression. The exception is handled by invoking an appropriate handler selected from a list found at the end of the handler's `try` block. An example of this follows:

In file simple_throw.cpp

```
int main()
{
cout << "\nEnter positive integer " <<
    "(negative will cause exception)" << endl;
    try {
        double x;
        cin >> x;
        if (x < 0)
            throw(x);
        else sqrt(x);
        .....
    }
    catch(double x)
        { cerr << "x = " << x << endl; abort(); }
}
```

The `throw(x)` has a double argument and matches the `catch(double x)` signature. The `catch(double x)` is called an exception handler. It is expected to perform an appropriate action where an incorrect value has been passed as an argument to `sqrt()`. For example, an error message and abort are normal.

10.3   Throwing Exceptions

Syntactically, throw expressions come in two forms:

```
throw expression
throw
```

The `throw` *expression* raises an exception. The innermost `try` block in which an exception is raised is used to select the `catch` statement that processes the exception. The `throw` with no argument can be used inside a `catch` to rethrow the current exception. This `throw` is typically used when you want a second handler called from the first handler to further process the exception.

The expression thrown is a temporary object that persists until exception handling is completed. The expression is caught by a handler that may use this value, as follows:

In file throw1.cpp

```
int foo()
{
   int  i = 0;         // illustrates an exception thrown
   // ····· code that affects i
      if (i < 0)
         throw i;
   return i;
}
int main()
{
   try {
      foo();
   }
   catch(int n)
      { cerr << "exception caught\n" << n << endl; }
}
```

The integer value thrown by `throw i` persists until the handler with the integer signature `catch(int n)` exits and is available for use within the handler as its argument.

Dissection of the *throw* Program

■
```
int foo()
{
    int  i = 0;      // illustrates exception thrown
    // ····· code that affects i
    if (i < 0)
        throw i;
    return i;
}
```

The `throw` expression has a simple syntax. It throws some value. In this case, the value is a negative integer. The idea is that `foo()`, to be correct, must return an integer value greater than or equal to zero. The `if` test, like an assertion, detects an incorrect computation and throws an exception that interrupts the normal flow of control for `foo()`. Normal execution would have been to return a value i to the point in `main()` where `foo()` is called.

■
```
int main()
{
    try {
        foo();
```

The `try` block is a scope within which an exception is caught. An exception, such as the `throw` i inside `foo()`, is caught at the end of the `try` block.

■
```
    }
    catch(int n)
        { cerr << "exception caught\n" << n << endl; }
```

A list of handlers, namely `catch(`*signature*`) {` *catch executable* `}`, comes at the end of the `try` block. The `throw` expression has a type, in this case `int`, which must match the `catch` signature.

When a nested function throws an exception, the process stack is unwound until an exception handler is found. This means that block exit from each terminated local process causes automatic objects to be destroyed.

In file throw2.cpp

```
void foo()
{
   int  i, j;
   .....
   throw i;    // foo() terminates with i persisting
               // as the exception object
               // i and j are destroyed
   .....       // this code won't be reached
}
void call_foo()
{
   int  k;
   .....
   foo();      // when foo() throws i call_foo() exits
               // exception object from foo() persists
               // k is destroyed
   .....
}
int main()
{
   try {
      call_foo();          // exception object persists
   }
   catch(int n) { ..... }  // catch(i) is executed
}
```

10.3.1   Rethrown Exceptions

Using throw without an expression rethrows a caught exception. The catch that rethrows the exception cannot complete the handling of the existing exception. This catch passes control to the nearest surrounding try block, where a handler capable of catching the still existing exception is invoked. The exception expression exists until all handling is completed. Control resumes after the outermost try block that last handled the rethrown expression.

An example of rethrowing of an exception follows:

```
void foo()
{
   try {
      .....
      throw i;
   }
   catch(int n)
   {
   if (n > 0)        // handle for positive values here
      .....
      return;
   }
   else {            // handle n <= 0 partially
      .....
      throw;         // rethrown
   }
}
```

Assuming that the thrown expression was of integer type, the rethrown exception is the same persistent integer object that is handled by the nearest handler suitable for that type.

I don't understand why I have to put in this error detection code: My code is always perfect, the machine has infinite resources, and I'm quite sure the interface code is every bit as perfect as my own!

10.3.2   Exception Expressions

Conceptually, the thrown expression passes information to the handlers. Frequently, the handlers do not need this information. For example, a handler that prints a message and aborts needs no information from its environment. However, the user might want additional information printed so that it can be used to select or help decide the handler's action. In this case, it can be appropriate to package the information as an object.

```
class stack_error {
public:
    stack_error(stack& s, string message);
};
```

Now, throwing an expression using an object of type `stack_error` can be more informative to a handler than just throwing expressions of simple types.

```
.....
throw stack_error(stk, "out of bounds");
.....
```

Let us use these ideas to write a complete example:

In file stack_error1.cpp

```
// Example of using an stack_error object
// Version 1. Uwe F. Mayer

#include <iostream>
#include <string>
using namespace std;

class stack{    // extremely simple stack
public:
    char s[100];
};

class stack_error {
public:
    stack_error(stack& s, const string message) :
                st(s), msg(message) { }
    void* get_stack() const { return &st; }
    const string& get_msg() const { return msg; }
private:
    stack& st;
    string msg;
};
```

```
int main()
{
    stack stk;
    try {
        throw stack_error(stk,"out of bounds");
    }
    catch(stack_error& se)
    {
        cerr << se.get_msg()
             << " for stack stored at "
             << se.get_stack() << endl;
        abort();
    }
}
```

Dissection of the *stack_error* Program

- ```
  class stack_error {
  public:
      stack_error(stack& s, const string message) :
                  st(s), msg(message) { }
      void* get_stack() const { return &st; }
      const string& get_msg() const { return msg; }
  ```

We create a specialized object that is used in conjunction with stack errors. It allows us to bundle information within a single object. It also allows us to have member functions that can provide different pieces of information. It can be used as the base class for a hierarchy of exception objects. The const string& return type for get_msg() is for efficiency reasons.

- ```
  private:
      stack& st;
      string msg;
  };
  ```

The hidden-away data members are used for diagnostic purposes.

- ```
  throw stack_error(stk,"out of bounds");
  ```

In main(), we throw our exception.
  ```

```
■ catch(stack_error& se)
  {
     cerr << se.get_msg()
           << " for stack stored at "
           << se.get_stack() << endl;
     abort();
  }
```

The `catch` uses the different `stack_error` methods to provide diagnostic information before aborting. In this case, the address of the `stack stk` prints as a hexadecimal number on most systems.

10.4   try Blocks

Syntactically, a `try` block has the form

> try
> *compound statement*
> *handler list*

The `try` block is the context for deciding which handlers are invoked on a raised exception. The order in which handlers are defined determines the order in which a handler for a raised exception of matching type is tried.

```
try {
   .....
   throw ("SOS");
   .....
   io_condition eof(argv[i]);
   throw (eof);
   .....
}
catch(const char* s) {·····}
catch(io_condition& x) {·····}
```

Conditions Under Which Throw Expression Matches the Catch Handler Type

- ■ An exact match

- ■ A derived type of the public base-class handler type

- ■ A thrown object type that is convertible to a pointer type that is the `catch` argument

It is an error to list handlers in an order that prevents them from being called. For example:

```
catch(void* s)          // any char* would match
catch(char* s)          // this needs to come first
catch(BaseTypeError& e) // always on DerivedTypeError
catch(DerivedTypeError& e)  // before BaseTypeError
```

There are further subtleties in ordering when `const` is used in the type. As an exercise, determine the preference between `catch(const char* s)` and `catch (char* s)`.

A `try` block can be nested. If no matching handler is available in the immediate `try` block, a handler is selected from its immediately surrounding `try` block. If no handler that matches can be found, a default behavior is used. This is by default `terminate()` (see Section 10.8, *terminate() and unexpected()*, on page 468).

10.5   Handlers

Syntactically, a handler has the form

```
catch  (formal argument)
compound statement
```

The `catch` looks like a function declaration of one argument without a return type.

In file catch.cpp

```
catch(string& message)
{
    cerr << message << endl;
    exit(1);
}

catch( ... )        // default action to be taken
{
    cerr << "THAT'S ALL FOLKS." << endl;
    abort();
}
```

An ellipsis signature matching any argument type is allowed. Also, the formal argument can be an abstract declaration: It can have type information without a variable name, such as `catch(int)`. Such a handler cannot use the value of the thrown expression.

The handler is invoked by an appropriate `throw` expression. At that point, the `try` block is exited. The system calls clean up functions that include destructors for any objects that were local to the `try` block. A partially constructed object has destructors invoked on any parts of it that are constructed subobjects. The program resumes at the statement after the `try` block.

10.6 Converting Assertions to Exceptions

We revisit our `template class stack` and use exceptions instead of assertions. Here, we can see that the exception logic is more dynamic because the handlers can be more informed than with asserts. The asserts print an assertion failure message and abort the program. Exception handlers can print arbitrary information and either abort the program or attempt to continue the program.

In file stack_error2.cpp

```
// Template stack with preconditions instead
// of assertions

#include <iostream>
using namespace std;

template <class T> void precondition (bool cond,
                    const string message, T throw_exp)
{
   if (!cond) {
      cerr << message << endl;
      throw throw_exp;
   }
}
```

This function template provides a generic precondition test. If the boolean expression passed in for the parameter `cond` is `false`, a message is printed, and an exception of type T is thrown. Similar generic `postcondition()` and `invariant()` tests can be coded.

```
// Replace asserts with precondition tests.
// We assume std::bad_alloc is thrown if new fails

template <class TYPE>
class stack {
public:
    explicit stack(int size = 100) :
        max_len(size), top(EMPTY)
        { precondition((size > 0),
          "Incorrect Allocation", 0);
          s = new TYPE[size]; }
    ~stack() { delete []s; }
    void  reset() { top = EMPTY; }
    void  push(TYPE c)
    {precondition(!full(), "Stack OverFlow", max_len);
       s[++top] = c; }
    TYPE  pop()
      { precondition(!empty(), "Stack UnderFlow ", 0);
        return s[top--]; }
    TYPE  top_of()const { return s[top]; }
    bool  empty()const { return top == EMPTY; }
    bool  full()const { return top == max_len - 1; }
private:
    enum   { EMPTY = -1 };
    TYPE*  s;
    int    max_len;
    int    top;
};
```

Let us write a `main()` that tests these assertions:

```
int main() {

    try{
        cout << "allocates for -1 " << endl;
        stack<char> d(-1);
    } catch(int n) { cerr << "stack error n="
                                 << n << endl; }
    try{
        stack<int> f(2);
        f.push(1);
        f.push(2);
        f.push(3);
    } catch(int n) { cerr << "stack error n= "
                                 << n << endl;}

}
```

The output from this program is

```
allocates for -1
Incorrect allocation
stack error n = 0
Stack OverFlow
stack error n = 2
```

Dissection of the `precondition()` Function

■ `precondition((size > 0),`
  `"Incorrect Allocation", 0);`

This prints Incorrect allocation and throws a value of 0.

■ `void push(TYPE c)`
  `{ precondition(!full(), "Stack OverFlow", max_len);`
  `    s[++top] = c; }`

The `push()` method has as a precondition the test for `stack` full. If it fails, then it prints the message Stack Overflow and throws a value of `max_len`.

■ `stack<char> d(-1);`

This is an incorrect size leading to a precondition exception thrown by the constructor.

■ `} catch(int n)`
  `        { cerr << "stack error n= " << n << endl; }`

Upon failure, the `catch()` prints out that a stack error has occurred with n = `max_len`.

■ `stack<int> f(2);`
  `f.push(1);`
  `f.push(2);`
  `f.push(3);`

In this try block, the stack overflows. There are three pushes onto a size 2 stack.

This is what happens when you build tiny little stacks, then go pushing all that data on! It's just a good thing you told me to throw a "strangle the programmer" exception, or I would have had to shut down this entire installation.

10.7   Exception Specification

Syntactically, an exception specification is part of a function declaration or a function definition and has the form

> *function header* throw (*type list*)

The *type list* is the list of types that a throw expression within the function can have. The function definition and the function declaration must specify the exception specification identically. If the list is empty, the compiler may assume that no throw is executed by the function, either directly or indirectly.

```
void foo() throw(int, stack_error);
void noex(int i) throw();
```

If an exception specification is left off, the assumption is that an arbitrary exception can be thrown by such a function. Violations of these specifications are runtime errors and are caught by the function unexpected().

As an example, let us write a template function postcondition() with an exception specification:

```
template <class T> void postcondition
        (bool cond, const string message,
         T throw_exp) throw(T)
{
   if (!cond) {
      cerr << message << endl;
      throw throw_exp;
   }
}
```

**For all our listeners out there who may be unfamiliar with the
new expansion team, the Silicon Valley Exceptions, we have to
say that they don't have a running game at all. But they sure can
catch and throw exceptionally well!**

10.8   terminate() **and** unexpected()

The system-provided function `terminate()` is called when no handler has been provided to deal with an exception. The `abort()` function, called by default, immediately terminates the program, returning control to the operating system. Another action can be specified by using `set_terminate()` to provide a handler. These declarations are found in the *except* library.

The system-provided handler `unexpected()` is called when a function throws an exception that was not in its exception-specification list. By default, the `terminate()` function is called; otherwise, a `set_unexpected()` can be used to provide a handler.

10.9   Standard Exceptions and Their Uses

C++ compilers and library vendors provide standard exceptions. For example, the exception type `bad_alloc` is thrown by the ANSI compiler if the `new` operator fails to return with storage from free store. The `bad_alloc` exception is in the *exception* library.

Here is a program that lets you test this behavior:

In file except.cpp

```
#include <iostream>
#include <exception>     // standard exceptions here
using namespace std;

int main()
{
   int  *p, n;

   try {
      while (true) {
         cout << "enter allocation request:" << endl;
         cin >> n;
         p = new int[n];
      }
   }
   catch(bad_alloc) { cerr << "bad_alloc" << endl; }
   catch(...) { cerr << "default catch" << endl; }
}
```

This program loops until it is interrupted by an exception. On our system, a request for 1 billion integers invokes the `bad_alloc` handler.

A frequent use of standard exceptions is in testing casts. The standard exception `bad_cast` is declared in file *exception*.

In file bad_cast.cpp

```
#include <iostream>
#include <exception>
using namespace std;

class A {
public:
   virtual void foo() { cout << "in A" << endl; }
};
```

```
class B: public A {
public:
    void foo() { cout << "in B" << endl; }
};
// Example by Ira Pohl and corrected by Uwe F. Mayer

int main()
{
    try {
        A a, *pa; B b;
        A& ar1= b;                              // legal
        // B& br1 = a;                          // illegal

        ar1.foo();
        pa = &b;
        A& ar2 = dynamic_cast<A&>(*pa); // succeeds
        ar2.foo();

        pa = &a;
        B& br2 = dynamic_cast<B&>(*pa);
                                    // fails, throws bad_cast
        br2.foo();
    }
    catch(bad_cast) { cerr << "dynamic_cast failed"
                            << endl; }
}
```

The standard library exceptions are derived from the base-class
`exception`. Two derived classes are `logic_error` and
`runtime_error`. Logic-error types include `bad_cast`, `out_of_range`,
and `bad_typeid`, which are intended to be thrown, as indicated by
their names. The runtime error types include `range_error`,
`overflow_error`, and `bad_alloc`.

The base class defines a virtual function.

```
virtual const char* exception::what() const throw();
```

This member function should be defined in each derived class to give
more helpful messages. The empty throw-specification list indicates
that the function should not itself throw an exception.

10.10 Software Engineering: Exception Objects

Paradoxically, error recovery is concerned chiefly with writing correct programs. Exception handling is about error recovery. Exception handling is also a transfer-of-control mechanism. The client/manufacturer model gives the manufacturer the responsibility of making software that produces correct output, given acceptable input. The question for the manufacturer is how much error detection and, conceivably, correction should be built in. The client is often better served by fault-detecting libraries, which can be used in deciding whether to attempt to continue the computation.

But if we throw an uncaught exception, it might blow up part of Moscow.

Error recovery is based on the transfer of control. Undisciplined transfer of control leads to chaos. In error recovery, one assumes that an exceptional condition has corrupted the computation, making it dangerous to continue. It is analogous to driving a car after realizing that the steering mechanism is damaged. Useful exception handling is the disciplined recovery when damage occurs.

In most cases, programming that raises exceptions should print a diagnostic message and gracefully terminate. Special forms of processing, such as real-time processing and fault-tolerant computing, require that the system not go down. In these cases, heroic attempts at repair are legitimate.

What can be agreed on is that classes can usefully be provided with error conditions. In many of these conditions, the object has member values in illegal states—values it is not allowed to have. The system raises an exception for these cases, with the default action being program termination.

But what kind of intervention is reasonable to keep the program running? And where should the flow of control be returned? C++ uses a termination model that forces the current `try` block to terminate. Under this regime, one either retries the code or ignores or substitutes a default result and continues. Retrying the code seems most likely to give a correct result.

Code is usually too thinly commented. It is difficult to imagine the program that would be too rich in assertions. Assertions and simple throws and catches that terminate the computation are parallel techniques. A well-thought-out set of error conditions detectable by the user of an ADT is an important part of a good design. An overreliance on exception handling in normal programming, beyond error detection and termination, is a sign that a program was ill-conceived, with too many holes, in its original form.

When designing classes, one could have an object's constructor look like the following:

```
Object::Object(arguments)
{
    if (illegal argument1)
        throw expression1;
    if (illegal argument2)
        throw expression2;
    .....                            // attempt to construct
}
```

The `Object` constructor now provides a set of thrown expressions for an illegal state. The `try` block can now use the information to repair or abort the incorrect operation.

```
try {

    // ····· fault-tolerant code

}
catch(declaration1) { /* fixup this case */ }
catch(declaration2) { /* fixup this case */ }
    .....
catch(declarationK) { /* fixup this case */ }
// correct or repaired-state values are now legal
```

When many distinct error conditions are useful for the state of a given object, a class hierarchy can be used to create a selection of related types to be used as throw expressions.

```
Object_Error {
public:
   Object_Error(arguments);      // capture useful info
```
members that contain thrown expression state
```
   virtual void repair()
      { cerr << "Repair failed in Object" << endl;
        abort(); }
};

Object_Error_S1 : public Object_Error {
public:
   Object_Error_S1(arguments);
```
added members that contain thrown expression state
```
   void repair(); // override to provide repair
};

.....           // other derived error classes as needed
```

These hierarchies allow an ordered set of catches to handle exceptions in a logical sequence. Remember: a base-class type should come after a derived-class type in the list of catch declarations.

10.11   Dr. P's Prescriptions

- Avoid the use of exceptions as a sophisticated transfer of control.

- Avoid using exceptions for continuing computations that have undiagnosed errors.

- Use exceptions and assertions to check preconditions and postconditions.

- Program by contract, where exceptions guarantee the terms.

- Use exceptions to test whether system resources are exhausted, unavailable, or corrupted.

- Use exceptions to provide soft, informative termination.

- Use exceptions to restart corrected computations.

- Exception handling is expensive; use only for error conditions.

- Exception specifications can cause unexpected program termination, even if the calling code is prepared to handle the exception.

- Beware of throwing pointers to local objects—otherwise, dangling references may be passed to the exception handler.

■ In general, it is safest and most efficient to catch complex exceptions by reference; this avoids extra copying as well as dangling references (as in catch-by-pointer).

Exceptions are often misused when they are used as a patch to fix code, much in the way the `goto` was used to hack changes to poorly designed programs. Exceptions are meant to detect errors; therefore, they should mostly be used to provide informed termination and soft failure.

Programming by contract is the ability of one part of the code to rely on guarantees from another part of the code. For example, to properly merge two lists, the merge code must rely on the input lists already being ordered. This is often done with assertions. The assertion methodology can be mimicked by exceptions that abort when guarantees are not met. An example of this is a `dynamic_cast` throwing a `bad_cast` exception when it is not able to provide the indicated conversion.

Exceptions should be thrown when requested resources are unavailable. The `std::bad_alloc` exception thrown by `new` when it fails is an example of this approach. In such cases, there may be ways to add to the system resources, allowing the program to continue.

Unless program termination is unacceptable, as in mission-critical real-time systems, ad hoc error correction and program resumption should be avoided. Such unexpected conditions should be diagnosed and the code redone. Special techniques exist for mission-critical code.

The last four tips were suggested by George Belotsky as further professional advice. Exception handling adds significant runtime expense. An assert methodology tied to a debug flag does not. In production code, you may want to eliminate exception handling. Exception specifications may cause the system-provided handler `unexpected()` to be called unnecessarily and is undesirable in production code. Pointers use can lead to dangling references and memory leaks. Be careful about these problems when using them as `catch` signatures. Finally, copying complex objects has significant expense. As with ordinary function call signatures, `catch` signatures can use call-by-reference to suppress this copying.

10.12   C++ Compared with Java

Java's exception-handling mechanism is integral to the language and heavily used for error detection at runtime. The mechanism is similar to the one found in C++. A Java exception is itself an object, which must be derived from the superclass `Throwable`. An exception is thrown by a method when it detects an error condition. The exception is handled by invoking an appropriate handler picked from a list of handlers, or catches. These explicit catches occur at the end of an enclosing `try` block. An uncaught exception is handled by a default Java handler that issues a message and terminates the program.

The following code robustly reads one integer from the console. If the user doesn't type an integer, he or she is prompted to try again. It is taken from *Java by Dissection*, by Ira Pohl and Charlie McDowell (Addison-Wesley 1999), pages 374–376, and uses the specially developed `tio` package. The source code is presented in Appendix D, *The tio Library*, and is available on the Web at ftp:// ftp.awl.com/cseng/authors/pohl-mcdowell/.

In file ExceptionExample.java

```java
import tio.*;

public class ExceptionExample {
    public static void main(String[] args) {
        int    aNumber = 0;
        boolean  success = false;
        String   inputString = "";
        System.out.println("Type an integer.");

        while (!success) {
            try {
                aNumber = Console.in.readInt();
                success = true;
            }
            catch (NumberFormatException e) {
                inputString = Console.in.readWord();
                System.out.println(inputString +
                    " is not an integer. Try again!");
            }
        }
        System.out.println("You typed " + aNumber);
        // continue with code to process aNumber
    }
}
```

Dissection of the ExceptionExample Program

■ `while (!success) {`

This loop continues until the assignment `success = true` is executed.

```
■ try {
      aNumber = Console.in.readInt();
      success = true;
  }
```

If a `NumberFormatException` occurs while any statement in the `try` block is being executed, control is immediately transferred to the first statement in the `catch` block. In this case, the call to `readInt()` may throw a `NumberFormatException`, in which case `aNumber` remains unchanged and the subsequent assignment `success = true` won't execute; hence the `while` loop repeats.

```
■ catch (NumberFormatException e) {
      inputString = Console.in.readWord();
      System.out.println(inputString +
                  " is not an integer. Try again!");
  }
```

Here, we ignore the parameter. Arriving at this `catch()` tells us all we need to know—a `NumberFormatException` occurred in the `try` block. Because `readInt()` is defined not to consume any nonwhite input characters if it fails, we use `readWord()` to read the offending white space delimited string of characters. We print an appropriate message and then continue with the statement following the `try-catch` statement. The exception has been handled, and normal execution resumes.

```
■ while (!success) {
      .....
      success = true;
      .....
  }
  System.out.println("You typed " + aNumber);
  // continue with code to process a Number
```

Eventually, the user types a legal integer, the assignment to success is reached, the end of the `try` block is reached, the `catch` block is skipped, and the loop exits.

Incorrectly entered input is a common programming error. In robust programs, input should be tested to determine whether it is both syntactically and semantically correct. Frequently, good practice is to ask the user to confirm the value entered. The following loop does just that:

```
while (confirm != 'Y') {
//    ..... ask for data in dollars
    System.out.println("Did you mean " + dollars);
    System.out.println("Please Enter Y or N:");
    confirm = Console.in.readChar();
}
```

This technique can be combined with the exception handling methodology of the preceding example.

Summary

- Exceptions are generally unexpected error conditions. Normally, these conditions terminate the user program with a system-provided error message. An example is floating-point divide-by-zero.

- The standard library *assert* provides the macro

  `assert(`*expression*`);`

  If the *expression* evaluates as `false`, then execution is aborted with diagnostic output. The assertions are discarded if the macro `NDEBUG` is defined.

- C++ code can raise an exception by using the `throw` expression. The exception is handled by invoking an appropriate handler selected from a list of handlers found at the end of the handler's `try` block.

- The `throw` expression raises an exception in a `try` block. The `throw` with no argument may be used in a `catch` to rethrow the current exception. Syntactically, `throw` comes in two forms:

  ```
  throw expression
  throw
  ```

- The `try` block is the context for deciding which handlers are invoked on a raised exception. The order in which handlers are defined determines the order in which a handler for a raised exception of matching type is tried. Syntactically, a `try` block has the form

  ```
  try
  compound statement
  handler list
  ```

- The `catch` looks like a function declaration of one argument without a return type. Syntactically, a handler has the form

  `catch` (*formal argument*)
  compound statement

- The type list is the list of types that a throw expression within the function can have. If the list is empty, the compiler may assume that no throw is executed by the function, either directly or indirectly. Syntactically, an exception specification is part of a function declaration and has the form

  function header `throw` (*type list*)

- The system-provided handler `terminate()` is called when no other handler has been provided to deal with an exception. The system-provided handler `unexpected()` is called when a function throws an exception that was not in its exception-specification list. By default, `terminate()` calls the `abort()` function. The default `unexpected()` behavior is to call `terminate()`.

Review Questions

1. True or false: In C++, `new` cannot throw an exception.

2. System exceptions, such as `SIGFPE`, are defined in _____.

3. The context for handling an exception is a _____ block.

4. The system-provided _____ is called when a function throws an exception that was not in its exception-specification list.

5. A standard exception class is _____ and is used for _____.

6. The system-provided handler _____ is called when no other handler has been provided to deal with an exception.

7. Handlers are declared at the end of a `try` block, using the keyword _____.

8. The _____ is the list of types a throw expression can have.

9. Name three standard exceptions provided by C++ compilers and libraries.

10. What two actions should most handlers perform?

Exercises

1. The following bubble sort does not work correctly. Place assertions in this code to test that it is working properly. Besides detecting errors, the placing of assertions in code as a discipline aids you in writing a correct program. Correct the program.

```
// Incorrect bubble sort

void swapIt(int a, int b)
{
   int  temp = a;

   a = b;
   b = temp;
}
void bubble(int a[], int size)
{
   int  i, j;

   for (i = 0; i != size - 1; ++i)
      for (j = i ; j != size - 1; ++j)
         if (a[j] < a [j + 1])
            swapIt (a[j], a[j + 1]);
}
int main()
{
   int  t[10] = { 9, 4, 6, 4, 5, 9, -3, 1, 0, 12};

   bubble(t, 10);
   for (int i = 0; i < 10; ++i)
      cout << t[i] << '\t';
   cout << "\nsorted?" << endl;
}
```

2. Use templates to write a generic version of the correct bubble sort, complete with assertions. Use a random number generator to generate test data. On what types can this be made to work generically?

3. Replace assertions with an equivalent version using exceptions.

4. Write a program that asks the user to enter a positive integer. Have it throw an exception when the user fails to enter a correct value. Have the handler write out the incorrect value and abort.

5. Rewrite the previous program to require the handler to ask the user for a correct value. The program should terminate printing

the correct value. Many programs try to ensure that input is failure proof. This is an aspect of good software engineering.

6. Recode the `ch_stack` class to throw exceptions for as many conditions as you think are reasonable. (See Section 5.1.5, *Constructing a Stack*, on page 218.) Use an enumerated type to list the conditions.

```
enum stack_error { overflow, underflow, ····· };
```

Write a `catch` that uses a `switch` statement to select an appropriate message and to terminate the computation.

7. Write a `stack_error` class that replaces the enumerated type in the previous exercise. Make this a base class for a series of derived classes that encapsulates each specific exception condition. The catches should be able to use overridden virtual functions to process the various thrown exceptions.

8. *(Java)* Recode in Java the `ch_stack` class, complete with exceptions. Java already throws exceptions if `new` fails to allocate storage, and Java automatically throws a range-error exception when an index is out of range.

CHAPTER 11

OOP Using C++

C++ is a hybrid language. The kernel language developed from C is classically used as a system-implementation language. As such, C++ is suitable for writing very efficient code. The class-based additions to the language support the full range of OOP requirements. Therefore, C++ is suitable for writing reusable libraries, and it supports both a generic and an object-oriented coding style.

In the 60s and 70s, the dominant programming methodology was structured programming that relied on breaking large programs into a series of function or procedure calls. Until the mid 1980s, procedural encapsulation was the dominant academic and professional programming paradigm. In the 1970s, SmallTalk, developed at Xerox Parc, pioneered a new paradigm, object-oriented programming (OOP). It ran on special hardware developed at Parc and was relatively expensive and inefficient in comparison with contemporary procedural languages, such as C and Pascal. C++ added objects to C. It allowed efficient compilation and execution of OOP on most platforms. Starting in 1985, it was embraced by industry very quickly. C++, as a hybrid OOP language, allows a multiparadigmatic approach to coding. The traditional advantages of C as an efficient, powerful procedural language are not lost. The key new ingredients in C++ are inheritance and polymorphism—that is, its capability to assume many forms.

Which form did you want, master?

11.1 OOP Language Requirements

We present four major OOP language characteristics below. These features cannot substitute for programmer discipline and community-observed convention, but they can be used to promote such behavior.

OOP Language Characteristics

- Encapsulation with data hiding: the ability to distinguish an object's internal state and behavior from its external state and behavior

- Type extensibility: the ability to add user-defined types to augment the native types

- Inheritance: the ability to create new types by importing or reusing the description of existing types

- Polymorphism with dynamic binding: the ability of objects to be responsible for interpreting function invocation

These features cannot substitute for programmer discipline and community-observed convention, but they can be used to promote such behavior.

Typical procedural languages, such as FORTRAN, Pascal, and C, have limited forms of type extensibility and encapsulation. These languages have pointer and record types that provide these features. C also has a scheme of file-oriented privacy, in its `static` file-scope declarations. Such languages as Modula-2 and Ada have more complete forms of encapsulation—namely, `module` and `package`, respectively. These languages readily allow users to build abstract data types (ADTs) and provide significant library support for many application areas. A language such as pure LISP supports dynamic binding. The elements in OOP have been available in various languages for at least 25 years.

LISP, Simula, and SmallTalk have long been in widespread use in both the academic and research communities. These languages are in many ways more elegant than C and C++. However, not until OOP elements were added to C was there any significant movement to use OOP in industry. Indeed, the late 1980s saw a bandwagon effect in adopting C++ that cut across companies, product lines, and application areas; industry needed to couple OOP with the ability to program effectively at a low level.

Also crucial was the ease of migration from C to C++. PL/1, by contrast, is rooted in FORTRAN and COBOL; Ada is rooted in Pascal. But C++ had C as a nearly proper subset. As such, the installed base of C code need not be abandoned. These other languages required a nontrivial conversion process to modify existing code from their ancestor languages.

The conventional academic wisdom is that excessive concern with efficiency is detrimental to good coding practices. This concern misses the obvious—namely, that product competition is based on performance. Consequently, industry values low-level technology. In this environment, C++ is a very effective tool.

11.1.1 ADTs: Encapsulation and Data Hiding

To fully appreciate the OOP paradigm, we must view the overall coding process as an exercise in shared and distributed responsibilities. These chapters have used the terms client to mean a user of a class and manufacturer to mean the provider of the class.

A client of a class expects an approximation to an abstraction. A stack, to be useful, has to be of reasonable size. A complex number must be of reasonable precision. A deck of cards must be shufflable, with random outcome in dealing hands. The internals of how these behaviors are computed is not a direct concern of the client. The client is concerned with cost, effectiveness, and ease of operation, not with implementation. This is the black box principle, and it has two components.

Black Box for the Client

- Simple to use, easy to understand, and familiar

- In a component relationship within the system

- Cheap, efficient, and powerful

Black Box for the Manufacturer

- Easy to reuse and modify; difficult to misuse and reproduce

- Profitable to produce with a large client base

- Cheap, efficient, and powerful

The manufacturer competes for clients by implementing an ADT product that is reasonably priced and efficient. It is in the manufacturer's interest to hide details of an implementation. This simplifies what the manufacturer needs to explain to the client, and it frees the manufacturer to allow internal repairs or improvements that do not affect the client's use. It restrains the client from dangerous or inadvertent tampering with the product.

A data-hiding scheme that restricts access of implementation detail to manufacturers guarantees client conformance to the ADT abstraction. The private parts are hidden from client code, and the public parts are available. It is possible to change the hidden representation without changing the public access or functionality. If done properly, client code need not change when the hidden representation is modified. The two keys to fulfilling these conditions are inheritance and polymorphism.

11.1.2   Reuse and Inheritance

Library creation and reuse are crucial indicators of successful language strategies. Inheritance, or deriving a new class from an old one, is used for code sharing and reuse, as well as for developing type hierarchies. Inheritance can be used to create a hierarchy of related ADTs that share both code and a common interface, a feature critical to the ability to reuse code.

Inheritance influences overall software design by providing a framework that captures conceptual elements that become the focus for system building and reuse. For example, InterViews is a C++ package that supports building graphical user interfaces for interactive, text, and graphics objects. These categories are readily composed to produce various applications, such as a CAD system, a browser, or a WYSIWYG editor.

OOP Design Methodology

1. Decide on an appropriate set of ADTs.

2. Design in their relatedness and use inheritance to share code and interface.

3. Use virtual functions to process related objects dynamically.

Inheritance also facilitates the black box principle and is an important mechanism for suppressing detail. It is hierarchical, and each level provides functionality to the next level that is built on it. In retrospect, structured programming methodology, with its process-centered view, relied on stepwise refinement to nest routines but did not adequately appreciate the need for a corresponding view of data.

11.1.3   Polymorphism

Polymorphism is the genie in OOP, taking instruction from a client and properly interpreting its wishes. A polymorphic function has many forms. Following the categorization developed by the programming theorists L. Cardelli and P. Wegner of Brown University, we make the following distinctions.

Types of Polymorphism

1. Coercion (ad hoc polymorphism): A function or operator works on several types by converting their values to the expected type. An example is conversion of arithmetic types in expressions.

   ```
   // x and d double, i int
   x = d + i; // int i is coerced to double
   ```

2. Overloading (ad hoc polymorphism): A function is called based on its signature, defined as the list of argument types in its parameter list. The integer-divide operator and float-divide operator are distinguished, based on their argument list.

   ```
   // type of division depends on type of a and b
   x = a / b ;
   ```

3. Inclusion (pure polymorphism): A type is a subtype of another type. Functions available for the base type work on the subtype. Such a function can have various implementations that are invoked by a runtime determination of subtype.

```
p -> draw()      // virtual function call
```

4. Parametric polymorphism (pure polymorphism): The type is
   left unspecified and is later instantiated. Templates provide
   this in C++.

```
template <class T> bool greater(T a, T b)
{
        return (a > b);
}
```

Polymorphism localizes responsibility for behavior. The client code
frequently requires no revision when additional functionality is
added to the system through manufacturer-provided code additions.

Polymorphism directly contributes to the black box principle. The
virtual functions specified for the base class are the interface used by
the client throughout. The client knows that an overridden member
function takes responsibility for a specific implementation of a given
action relevant to the object. The client need not know different routines for each calculation or different forms of specification. These
details are suppressed.

11.2 OOP: The Dominant Programming Methodology

OOP using C++ gained dazzling acceptance in industry from 1986 on,
despite acknowledged flaws and unfamiliarity with OOP strategies.
The reason for this is that C++ brought OOP technology to industry
in an acceptable way. C++ is based on an existing, widely used, successful language. C++ allows tight, efficient, portable code to be written. Type safety is retained, and type extensibility is general. C++
coexists with standard languages and does not require special system resources.

C was designed as a system-implementation language and as such
allows coding that is readily translated to efficiently use machine
resources. Software products gain competitive advantage from such
efficiency. Hence, despite complaints that traditional C was not a safe
or robust language to code in, C grew in its range of application. The
C community, by convention and discipline, used structured programming and ADT extensions. OOP made inroads into this professional community only when it was wed to C within a conceptual
framework that maintained its traditional point of view and advantages. Key to the bandwagon move to C++ has been the understanding that inheritance and polymorphism gain additional important
advantages over traditional coding practice.

Polymorphism in C++ allows a client to use an ADT as a black box. Success in OOP is characterized by the extent to which a user-defined type can be made indistinguishable from a native type. Polymorphism allows coercions to be specified that integrate the ADT with the native types. Objects from subtype hierarchies respond dynamically to function invocation, the messaging principle in OOP. Polymorphism also simplifies client protocols, and name proliferation is controlled by function and operator overloading. The availability of all four forms of polymorphism encourages the programmer to design with encapsulation and data hiding in mind. OOP is many things to many people. Attempts to define it are like blind men's attempts to describe an elephant. Recall the equation describing object orientation: OOP = type-extensibility + polymorphism.

In many languages and systems, the cost of detail suppression was runtime inefficiency or undue rigidity in the interface. C++ has a range of choices that allow both efficiency and flexibility. Also, the success of C++ was a precondition for the introduction of Java in 1995. Together, C++ and Java have established OOP as the dominant contemporary programming methodology.

The following example is amended from code developed by Andrew Koenig, the most important figure in the C++ community besides the inventor of C++, Bjarne Stroustrup. It is a demonstration of the power of type hierarchies and polymorphism. It is used to do expression evaluation.

An expression such as 2 * x + y can be represented as a tree, with each subexpression being a node. The following code uses an expression tree to evaluate an expression and print out its fully parenthesized form:

In file tree.cpp

```
// OOP = type-extensibility + polymorphism
// See also Andrew Koenig JOOP  August 1988

#include <iostream>
using namespace std;
```

```
class Node {
   friend class Tree;
   friend ostream& operator<<(ostream&, const Tree&);
protected:
   Node() { use = 1; }
   virtual ~Node() { }
   virtual void print(ostream&) const = 0;
   virtual int eval() const = 0;
private:
   int  use;         // reference count
};
```

Dissection of the Node Class

■ `friend class Tree;`

Because Tree contains Node as a subpart, we need to expose the pro-tected and private members of Node to Tree member functions. Our design leads to the unusual decision to hide Node constructors. This keeps Node from otherwise being used. This is in keeping with it, being used only for implementation of Tree and not as a separate data type.

■ `Node() { use = 1; }`
`virtual ~Node() { }`

Node is an abstract base class for a hierarchy of Node subtypes. You should always use a virtual destructor for these classes. This is to make sure that the proper cleanup is done within this polymorphic structure. Here, we build this as a reference counted structure. If you are unfamiliar with reference count ideas, see Section 5.5, *Strings Using Reference Semantics*, on page 229.

■ `virtual void print(ostream&) const = 0;`
`virtual int eval() const = 0;`

Here are two pure virtual functions. They must be overridden and defined for every concrete subclass.

In file tree.cpp

```cpp
class IntNode : public Node {
public:
   friend class Tree;
   int eval() const { return n; }
private:
   const int n;
   void print(ostream& o) const { o << n; }
   IntNode(int k): n(k) { }
};

class IdNode : public Node {
public:
   friend class Tree;
   int eval() const { return val; }
private:
   const char  name;
   int  val;
   void print(ostream& o) const { o << name; }
   IdNode(char id): name(id)
       { cout << "Enter value of " << name << ": ";
         cin >> val; }
};

class BinaryNode : public Node {
public:
   friend class Tree;
   int eval() const;
private:
   const char op;
   Tree left;
   Tree right;
   BinaryNode(char a, Tree b, Tree c):
              op(a), left(b), right(c) { }
   void print (ostream& o) const
       { o << "(" << left << op << right << ")"; }
};
```

```
int BinaryNode::eval() const
{
    int ans = 0;
    switch (op) {
    case '-': ans = (left.eval() - right.eval()); break;
    case '+': ans = (left.eval() + right.eval()); break;
    case '*': ans = (left.eval() * right.eval()); break;
    default:
      cerr << op << " not implemented" << endl; break;
    }
    return ans;
}
```

The various node types store different types of subexpressions. These are used to build the full expression tree.

Oh, yeah, next to my orange tree is an exotic C++ expression tree. It takes a lot of maintenance because it is prone to bug infestations.

Dissection of the BinaryNode, IdNode, and IntNode Classes

■ class IntNode : public Node {
    .....
    int eval() const { return n; }
    .....
    IntNode(int k): n(k) { }

The IntNode is a literal. It stores its value and returns it from eval(). The constructor just initializes an IntNode to its constant value.

```
■ class IdNode : public Node {
      .....
      int eval() const { return val; }
   private:
      const char name;
      int val;
      .....
      IdNode(char id): name (id)
         { cout << "Enter value of " << name << ": ";
           cin >> val; }
   };
```

The IdNode represents a variable. Its name can only be a single character. Its value is read in.

```
■ class BinaryNode : public Node {
      .....
      const char op;
      Tree left;
      Tree right;
      BinaryNode(char a, Tree b, Tree c):
                  op(a), left(b), right(c) { }
      void print (ostream& o) const
         { o << "(" << left << op << right << ")"; }
   };
```

Here, we see the power of this representation. The tree is a self-referential data structure. So a tree is made up of a left and right subtree. The print() method is polymorphic. It parenthesizes the expression and calls the output operator << to properly print the subexpressions. The constructor just performs initialization.

```
 int BinaryNode::eval() const
 {
    int ans = 0;
    switch (op) {
    case '-': ans= (left.eval()-right.eval());break;
    case '+': ans= (left.eval()+right.eval());break;
    case '*': ans= (left.eval()*right.eval());break;
    default:
      cerr << op <<" not implemented" <<endl; break;
    }
    return ans;
 }
```

The eval() function is both recursive and polymorphic. It calls itself on the two subtrees and then determines from the node type which overridden eval() method to call. Notice how convenient it is to extend the design by adding further operators as cases.

The next major piece is the expression tree. By adding further node types, such as a unary Node type and tree constructors, we can readily extend this code to more expression types.

In file tree.cpp

```cpp
class Tree {
public:
    Tree(int);                    // constant
    Tree(char);                   // variable
    Tree(char, Tree, Tree);       // binary operator
    Tree(const Tree& t) { p = t.p; ++p -> use; }
    ~Tree() { if (--p -> use == 0) delete p; }
    void operator=(const Tree& t);
    int eval() const { return p -> eval(); }
private:
    friend ostream& operator<<(ostream&, const Tree&);
    Node* p;                      // polymorphic hierarchy
};

void Tree::operator=(const Tree& t)
{
    if (this != &t) {
        ++t.p -> use;
        if (--p -> use == 0)
            delete p;
        p = t.p;
    }
}

ostream& operator<<(ostream& o, const Tree& t)
{
    t.p -> print(o);
    return (o);
}

Tree::Tree(int n) { p = new IntNode(n); }
Tree::Tree(char id) { p = new IdNode(id); }
Tree::Tree(char op, Tree left, Tree right)
    { p = new BinaryNode(op, left, right);
        left.p -> use++; right.p -> use++; }
```

Dissection of the Tree Class

```
Tree::Tree(int n) { p = new IntNode(n); }
Tree::Tree(char id) { p = new IdNode(id); }
Tree::Tree(char op, Tree left, Tree right)
    { p = new BinaryNode(op, left, right);
      left.p -> use++; right.p -> use++; }
```

Each of these constructors works with a different node type calling new to construct them.

■ `Tree(const Tree& t) { p = t.p; ++p -> use; }`
`~Tree() { if (--p -> use == 0) delete p; }`

The copy constructor and destructor use reference count semantics. This is a very important idiom that is used for many class types that need to construct objects by calling new.

■ `int eval() const { return p -> eval(); }`

The code for evaluation uses the base class Node pointer p to polymorphically call the correct overridden definition of eval().

■
```
ostream& operator<<(ostream& o, const Tree& t)
{
    t.p -> print(o);
    return (o);
}
```

The overloaded output operator<< also uses p polymorphically to produce a properly parenthesized expression.

■
```
void Tree:: operator=(const Tree& t)
{
    if (this != &t) {
        ++t.p -> use;
        if (--p -> use == 0)
            delete p;
        p = t.p;
    }
}
```

Although it is not used in this test example, we nevertheless provide an overloaded assignment operator. Anytime we provide a copy constructor, we also want to write code for assignment. Recall, this is a reference counted structure. So our copying is not expensive but requires pointer assignment semantics.

Finally, here is code to test our Tree expression class:

In file tree.cpp

```
int main()
{

    Tree t1 = Tree('*', Tree(5), Tree('+', 'A', 4));
    Tree t2 = Tree('+', Tree('-', 'A', 1),
            Tree('+', t1, 'B'));
    cout << "t1 = " << t1 << " ;   t2 = " << t2
        << endl;
    cout << "t1:" << t1.eval() << "   t2:" << t2.eval()
        << endl;
}
```

Presume that when prompted for variable A in the first `Tree t1,` we enter 3. Then the first tree evaluates to 35. It prints, fully parenthesized, as t1 = (5   * (A + 4)). Test this code and enter your own values for the variables in these expressions.

11.3   Designing with OOP in Mind

Most programming should involve the use of existing designs. For example, the mathematical and scientific communities have standard definitions of complex numbers, rationals, matrices, and polynomials. Each of these can be readily coded as an ADT. The expected public behavior of these types is widely agreed on.

The programming community has widespread experience with standard container classes. Reasonable agreement exists as to the behavior of stack, associative array, binary tree, and queue. Also, the programming community has many examples of specialized programming language oriented to a particular domain. For example, SNOBOL and its successor language, ICON, have powerful string-processing features that can be captured as ADTs in C++.

OOP attempts to emphasize reuse, which is possible on several scales. The grandest scale is the development of libraries that are effective for an entire problem domain. The upside is that reuse contributes in the long run to more easily maintained code. The downside is that a particular application does not need costly library development.

OOP requires programmer sophistication. More sophisticated programmers are better programmers. The downside is high training cost and the potential misuse of sophisticated tools.

OOP makes client code simpler and more readily extensible. Polymorphism can be used to incorporate local changes into a large-scale system without global modification. The downside can be runtime overhead.

C++ provides programming encapsulations through classes, inheritance, and templates. Encapsulations hide and localize. As systems get bigger and more complex, there is an increasing need for such encapsulations. Simple block structure and functional encapsulation of such languages as Pascal are not enough. The 1970s taught us the need for the module as a programming unit. The 1980s taught us that modules need to have a logical coherence supported in the language and that they must be derivable from one another. When supported by a programming language, encapsulations and relationships lead to increased programmer discipline. The art of programming is to blend rigor and discipline with creativity.

Occam's Razor is a useful design principle: Entities should not be multiplied beyond necessity—or beyond completeness, invertibility, orthogonality, consistency, simplicity, efficiency, or expressiveness. Such ideals can be in conflict and frequently involve trade-offs in arriving at a design.

This is possibly a little more complex than it needs to be just to hit a key.

Invertibility means that the program should have member functions that are inverses. In the mathematical types, addition and subtraction are inverses. In a text editor, add and delete are inverses. Some commands, such as negation, are their own inverses. The importance of invertibility in a nonmathematical context can be seen by the brilliant success of the *undo* command in text editing and the *recover* commands in file maintenance.

Completeness is best seen in Boolean algebra, in which the nand operation suffices to generate all possible Boolean expressions. But Boolean algebra is usually taught with negation, conjunction, and disjunction as the basic operations. Completeness by itself is not enough to judge a design by. A large set of operators is frequently more expressive.

Orthogonality means that each element of a design should integrate and work with all other elements without overlapping or being redundant. For example, on a system that manipulates shapes, one should have a horizontal move, a vertical move, and a rotate operation. In effect, these operations would be adequate to position the shape at any point on the screen.

Hierarchy is captured through inheritance. Designs should be hierarchical. It is a reflection of two principles—decomposition and localization. Both principles are methods of suppressing detail, a key idea in coping with complexity. However, there is a scale problem in such a design. How much detail is enough to make a concept useful as its own class? It is important to avoid a proliferation of specialized concepts. Too much detail renders the class design difficult to master.

11.4   Class-Responsibility-Collaborator

Designs can be aided by a diagramming process. Several object-oriented design (OOD) notations exist, and a number have been incorporated in CASE (computer-assisted software engineering) tools. The most comprehensive of these are based on Universal Modeling Language (UML), pioneered by Rational Software. Another useful, related low-tech scheme: the Class-Responsibility-Collaborator (CRC) note-card scheme.

A responsibility is an obligation the class must keep. For example, complex number objects must provide an implementation of complex arithmetic. A collaborator is another object that cooperates with this object to provide an overall set of behaviors. For example, integers and reals collaborate with complex numbers to provide a comprehensive set of mathematical behaviors.

11.4.1   CRC Cards

A CRC notecard is used to design a given class. The responsibilities of the class and the collaborators for that class are initially described. The back of the card is used to describe implementation detail. The front of the card corresponds to public behavior.

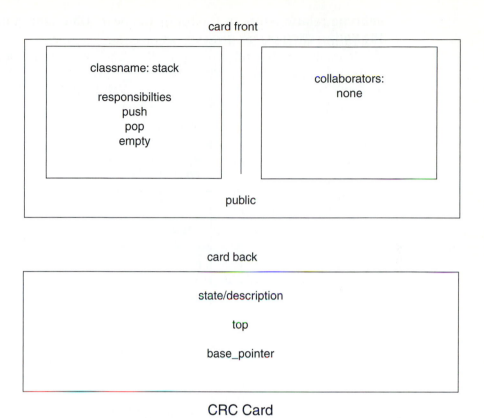

CRC Card

As the design process proceeds, the cards are rewritten and refined. They become more detailed and closer to a set of member function headers. The back of the card can be used to show implementation details, including ISA, LIKEA, and HASA relationships.

The attractiveness of this scheme is its flexibility. In effect, it represents a pseudocode refinement process that can reflect local tastes. The number of revisions and the level of detail and rigor are a matter of taste. (See the site at http://c2.com/doc/oopsla89/paper.html for a good description.)

A more formal system for documenting class architectures is Unified Modeling Language (UML), which we already discussed in Section 4.12.2, *Unified Modeling Language (UML) and Design*, on page 192. (See the UML site at http://www.rational.com/uml/ for a full description.) A class diagram describes the types and relationships in the system. It is very useful documentation, and a number of systems, such as Rational Rose, now provide automated tools to develop such documentation along with coding. A key relationship is the ISA or subtype relationship. In the following basic UML diagram, we show the Node-IdNode class diagram.

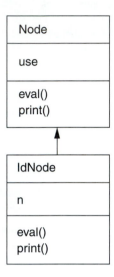

Basic ISA Inheritence in UML

Other relationships that can be depicted by UML include the part-whole or aggregation relationship (*HASA*), and the uses or collaborates relationship. For example, a Tree type uses a Node type as part of its representation. This is also called delegation.

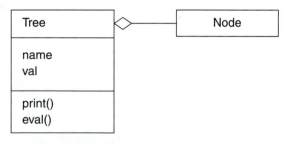

Basic HASA Relationship in UML

11.5 Design Patterns

Reuse is a primary theme in modern programming. In early times, reuse was limited to simple libraries of functions, such as the math functions found in *math.h* or the `char*` functions in *cstring*. In OOP, the class or template becomes a key construct for reuse. Classes and templates encapsulate code that conforms to certain designs. Thus, the iterator classes of STL are a design pattern. Recently, the concept of design pattern has proved very popular in defining medium-scale reuse. A design pattern has four elements.

Elements of a Design Pattern

1. The pattern terminology: for example, iterator

2. The problem and conditions: for example, visitation over a container

3. The solution: for example, pointerlike objects with a common interface

4. The evaluation: for example, the trade-off between defining an iterator on a vector and using a native array

A design pattern is an abstraction that suggests a useful solution to a particular programming problem. Often reuse is inexpensive, as with STL container and iterator design patterns that require only instantiation. Sometimes reuse is expensive, such as inventing a balanced-tree class with an interface conforming to STL sequence containers.

Design Patterns

1. *Iterator*, such as `vector::iterator`; organizes visitation on a container

2. *Composite*, such as `class grad_student`; composes complex objects out of simpler ones

OOP has stimulated reuse through design patterns. A design pattern is a software solution in search of a problem. Consider how the iterator logic of STL decouples visitation of container elements from specific details of the container. This idea is independent of computer language and is useful in C++, Java, and SmallTalk coding projects. This idea can be summarized as the iterator pattern.

The name is of great importance, as it increases the programmer's technical vocabulary. A name should be memorable and illuminate a key characteristic of the method. The problem identifies circumstances under which the pattern provides a solution. The solution shows how the pattern solves the problem. The consequences are a discussion of the cost-benefit trade-off in using the pattern.

When the pattern is discussed in a specific language context, it is often called a programming idiom. This is also sometimes used for smaller coding ideas. For example, in C++ or C, EOF is frequently used as a guard value to terminate file processing.

When the pattern is used in a wider context to provide a library of routines and components, it is called a framework. The STL can be considered a framework that makes heavy use of the iterator and template patterns, among others. In Java, the Java Foundation Classes, also known as *Swing*, support window development. They are implemented with the model-view-controller pattern.

11.6   A Further Assessment of C++

C++ is better than C in several ways. First, it can be used in place of C without change for most applications. Second, it extends C by including additional critical features that support object-oriented and generic programming. Third, it remedies some of C's defects.

C++ is largely a superset of C. There are some minor differences, such as the difference in semantics between void* in both languages and the fact that C++ treats control expressions as bool. Nevertheless, most running C code compiles and runs as C++ code.

C++ was designed, at first, to allow for classes and inheritance, the core functionality needed for object-oriented programming. This was done without sacrificing C's object code efficiency. The key idea was to extend struct's functionality to include access restrictions and member function declarations. The result is that the C++ language is philosophically consistent with C at its core. C++ also embraced generic programming using templates.

C++ remedies some of C's defects. C was a language of the 1970s. It relied on the preprocessor to provide macros and to define constants. C++ uses inline, template, and const to provide these facilities directly in the language. C is heavily criticized for its lack of type safety. Here, C++ provided *iostream,* a type safe I/O library, as a replacement for *stdio.h* in C. Also, C++ replaced unrestricted casting with four named casts. C++ added the bool type, which means that code that needs logical values, such as control expressions in conditional statements, no longer uses the traditional C interpretation of 0 as false and nonzero as true. C++ also provides more scoping constructs. In general, having scope enables you to manage complexity better. C++ allows `namespace` scope and nested `class` scope, both unavailable in C.

11.6.1   Why C++ Is Better Than Java

C++ compiles into efficient object code, while Java is interpreted. C++ is an almost proper superset of C. These two critical observations have important implications and advantages for C++ over Java.

Invariably, C++ runs faster than Java. This is true even for compiled Java code, in most cases. Java is designed to be independent of any local architecture. Therefore, it is easy to have a mismatch between a Java construct and the local machine. This is the price of Java, being largely machine-independent. C++ is allowed to define types that are convenient to the local architecture. There is a looser specification for C++, which allows a compiler writer to custom-tailor the compiler to the local system. C++ has low-level features, such as access to the bit representation of the word and inlining that allows great efficiency. C++ class methods can be nonvirtual and therefore do not require runtime dispatch overhead.

The C programmer is instantly a C++ programmer. The C programmer at first can be confused by the annoying changes to C code that allow it to run as Java. For example, in Java there cannot be external functions. All functions must be contained in a class. The syntax for `main()` is slightly different. Philosophically, Java is closer to Small-Talk than it is to C. Moving from C to C++ is relatively simple and does not require a break with existing C practice.

C++ has several critical features not found in Java, such as templates and operator overloading. Operator overloading is very important to C++'s use as a numerical algorithms language. Scientists and engineers like the ability to add numerical types, such as complex number, rational, matrix, and polynomial, while still using ordinary operators such as + and / for expressions over these types. C++ templates permit efficient generic programming that is type-safe. The implementation and use of STL, including important extensions to it, demonstrate the power of these techniques.

11.6.2   A Short Rebuttal

C++ is too large and complex. C++ is system-dependent. C++ is not Web-ready. C++ does not manage memory. Java is purely object-oriented and very type-safe. When teaching students programming, it is desirable to minimize complexity. This is possible by teaching a very restricted set of C++, but invariably issues such as signature matching, conversions, and memory management require sophisticated explanations. The mere fact that Java does not have the pointer type greatly simplifies the teaching of Java. We expand on this theme in Section 11.9, *C++ Compared with Java*, on page 503.

11.7 Software Engineering: Last Thoughts

Let us revisit our *tree.cpp* and examine software engineering lessons learned from this example. Imagine writing this code in a procedural programming style such as needed by C or Pascal. Invariably, it would be designed around a big `switch` statement, such as

```
switch (nodetype) {
case 1: ..... break; // unary operator
case 2: ..... break; // binary operator
.....
default: cerr << " Case not Found. " << endl;
        abort(); break;
}
```

What is required when we write a new version, possibly incorporating the evaluation of additional operators? We have to search out each such `switch` and update with the new case. In the case of our object-oriented code using a related hierarchy of **Node** types, we only need to add a new subclass. We do not have to do any global searches.

Notice that we did use a `switch` for evaluating a `BinaryNode`. This can be avoided by having further subclasses. In exercise 6 on page 514, you are asked to provide this switchless alternative and discuss its design trade-offs.

```
int BinaryNode::eval() const
{
   int ans = 0;
   switch (op) {
   case '-': ans = (left.eval() - right.eval()); break;
   case '+': ans = (left.eval() + right.eval()); break;
   case '*': ans = (left.eval() * right.eval()); break;
   default:
     cerr << op << " not implemented" << endl; break;
   }
   return ans;
}
```

Part of the trade-off comes from value returned by having subclasses of finer granularity. When you have software based on many little classes, you have fine granularity; with software based on very few large classes, you have coarse granularity. Fine granularity has the overhead of writing and maintaining many small classes of limited usefulness. Coarse granularity has the overhead of a relatively rigid design and the need for more revision and testing within these large classes.

11.8   Dr. P's Prescriptions

- KISS—keep it simple, stupid.
- Use standard libraries.
- Check that your compiler supports full, modern C++.

C++ has many obscure and complex features. For example, inheritance hierarchies tend to be overused. Remember, code needs to be understood, maintained, and extended by others not as clever as yourself. Low-level tricks based on heavy use of casting may provide a shortsighted benefit, but they can backfire when one is porting to another system. The most universal criticism of C++ is its great complexity. Sticking to essentials and idiomatic use promotes understanding of your code.

Do not reinvent the wheel—trite but true. STL is a great achievement and should be used extensively. It has excellent performance characteristics. Historically, starting with the FORTRAN scientific library package and continuing with the various UNIX libraries, libraries have been the most successful software reuse tool.

C++ compilers for ANSI C++ as described here may still be incomplete. Make sure you know what the vendors support, especially when it comes to recent changes in the use of namespaces, exception handling, templates, and libraries, particularly the Standard Template Library (STL). Vendors, such as Microsoft with its popular Visual C++, provide libraries and features that can be at variance with the standard.

11.9   C++ Compared with Java

Java shares with C++ the use of classes and inheritance to build software in an object-oriented manner. Also, both languages use data hiding and have methods that are bundled within the class.

Unlike C++, Java does not allow for conventional programming. Everything is encapsulated in a class. This forces the programmer to think and to design everything as an object. The downside is that conventional C code is not as readily adapted to Java as it is to C++. Java avoids most of the memory-pointer errors that are common to C and C++. Address arithmetic and manipulation are done by the compiler and the system, not the programmer. Therefore, the Java programmer writes safer code. Also, memory reclamation is automatically done by the Java garbage collector.

Another important concept in OOP is the promotion of code reuse through the inheritance mechanism. In Java, this is the mechanism of extending a new class, called a subclass, from an existing one, called the superclass. Methods in the extended class override the superclass methods. The method selection occurs at runtime and is a highly flexible polymorphic style of coding.

Java, in a strict sense, is completely portable across all platforms that support it. Java is compiled to byte code that is run on the Java virtual machine. This is typically an interpreter—code that understands the Java byte code instructions. Such code is much slower than native code on most systems. The trade-off here is universally consistent behavior versus loss of efficiency.

Java has extensively developed libraries for performing Web-based programming. Java also has the ability to write graphical user interfaces that are used interactively. Its thread package has secure Web communication features that let the coder write distributed applications.

Java is far simpler than C++ in the core language and its features. In some ways, this is deceptive in that much of the complexity is in its libraries. Java is far safer because of very strict typing, avoidance of pointer arithmetic, and well-integrated exception handling. It is system-independent in its behavior, so one size fits all. This combination of object orientation, simplicity, universality, and Web-sensitive libraries makes it the language of the moment.

Java programs are classes. A `class` has syntactic form that is derived from the C `struct`, which does not exist in Java. Data and functions are placed within classes. When a class is executed as a program, it starts by calling the member function `main()`.

Java is known for providing applets on Web pages. A browser is used to display and execute the applet. Typically, the applet provides a graphical user interface (GUI) to the code. The following discussion of an applet is taken from Chapter 8 of *Java by Dissection*, by Ira Pohl and Charlie McDowell (Addison-Wesley 1999). It uses the standard Java library *swing* for drawing components and the Java applet library *awt*.

Most GUIs have more than a single button to click or a single text field. As a result, we face two new questions: How do we arrange the GUI components when we have more than one? How do we respond to events from several different components?

To control the arrangement of GUI components, Java uses layout managers. A *layout manager* is an object that determines the location of components. One type of layout manager is implemented by the class `java.awt.GridLayout`. As the name implies, `GridLayout` arranges the components in a two-dimensional grid. We specify the number of rows and columns in the grid and then add the components, one at a time. Each new component is added into the next available cell in the grid.

In the following program, we use a `GridLayout` to arrange the components of a minicalculator, which is capable of adding and subtracting two numbers. The program includes two buttons: one for adding and one for subtracting. The `ActionListener` determines which button is clicked.

In file MiniCalc.java

```java
// Demo GridLayout

import java.awt.*;
import javax.swing.*;
class MiniCalc {
    public static void main(String[] args) {
        JFrame frame = new JFrame("MiniCalc");
        Container pane = frame.getContentPane();

        // create the major components
        JTextField firstNumber = new JTextField(20);
        JTextField secondNumber = new JTextField(20);
        JTextField result = new JTextField(20);
        JButton addButton = new JButton("Add");
        JButton subButton = new JButton("Subtract");

        // there are 4 rows of 2 components each
        pane.setLayout(new GridLayout(4, 2));

        // add all of the components to content pane
        pane.add(new JLabel("Enter a number"));
        pane.add(firstNumber);
        pane.add(new JLabel("Enter a number"));
        pane.add(secondNumber);
        pane.add(new JLabel("Result"));
```

```
            pane.add(result);
            pane.add(addButton);
            pane.add(subButton);

            // setup the listener, listening to the buttons
            // DoMath class is defnied separately
            DoMath listener =
              new DoMath(firstNumber, secondNumber,
                         result);
            subButton.addActionListener(listener);
            addButton.addActionListener(listener);
            frame.pack();
            frame.show();
        }
    }
```

The initial display looks like this:

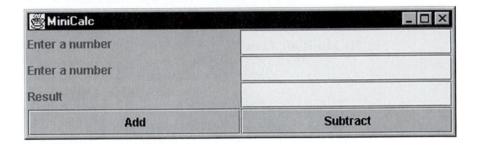

```
■ JTextField firstNumber = new JTextField(20);
  JTextField secondNumber = new JTextField(20);
  JTextField result = new JTextField(20);
  JButton addButton = new JButton("Add");
  JButton subButton = new JButton("Subtract");
```

Here, we create the `JButton` and `JTextField` components that are to be part of the GUI. The `JTextField` components are wide enough to display 20 characters.

```
■ pane.setLayout(new GridLayout(4, 2));
```

To have the content pane use a `GridLayout` manager, we must set the layout manager as shown. Other layout managers are, for example, `BorderLayout` and `FlowLayout`.

```
■ pane.add(new JLabel("Enter a number"));
  pane.add(firstNumber);
  pane.add(new JLabel("Enter a number"));
  pane.add(secondNumber);
  pane.add(new JLabel("Result"));
  pane.add(result);
  pane.add(addButton);
  pane.add(subButton)
```

We can now add the components to the grid. Instead of specifying a row and column number for each component, we simply add them one at a time. The components are added to the grid beginning in the upper left corner, filling the rows from left to right and moving to the next row when a row is full. Each of the `JTextField` components is placed in a row with a `JLabel` component, which is text that serves as a label. We haven't bothered to save a reference to the `JLabel` components in local variables because we don't need to refer to the labels after we've added them to the GUI.

```
■ DoMath listener =
      new DoMath(firstNumber, secondNumber, result);
  subButton.addActionListener(listener);
  addButton.addActionListener(listener);
```

Here, we create an instance of the class `DoMath`. The constructor for `DoMath` is passed the three text fields, which it needs in order to perform its task. The `DoMath` listener object is added as an `ActionListener` for both buttons.

■ `frame.pack();`
`frame.show();`

Now that we've added all the components to our GUI, we call `pack()`, which tells the JFrame to arrange the components according to the layout manager that we specified—in this case, a grid of four rows and two columns. Finally, the JFrame is ready to be shown.

We have now shown one way to control the arrangement of multiple components—with a `GridLayout`. We use the class `DoMath` to show how an object can listen to multiple buttons and determine which button was clicked.

In file DoMath.java

```java
// Respond to two different buttons

import javax.swing.*;
import java.awt.event.*;
class DoMath implements ActionListener {
   DoMath(JTextField first, JTextField second,
         JTextField result)
   {
      inputOne = first;
      inputTwo = second;
      output = result;
   }
   public void actionPerformed(ActionEvent e) {
     double first, second;
     first =
        Double.parseDouble(inputOne.getText().trim());
     second =
        Double.parseDouble(inputTwo.getText().trim());
     if (e.getActionCommand().equals("Add"))
        output.setText(String.valueOf(first + second));
     else            // must be the "Subtract" button
        output.setText(String.valueOf(first - second));
   }
   private JTextField inputOne, inputTwo, output;
}
```

Dissection of the *DoMath.java* Program

- ```
  import javax.swing.*;
  import java.awt.event.*;

  class DoMath implements ActionListener {
  ```

  This class uses `JTextField` from `javax.swing` and `ActionListener` and `ActionEvent` from `java.awt.event`. As with other listener classes, the class `DoMath` must implement the interface `ActionListener`.

- ```
  DoMath(JTextField first, JTextField second,
         JTextField result)
  ```

  The `DoMath` listener class has an explicit constructor; it cannot rely on the default constructor. An instance of `DoMath` needs references to the three text fields in the GUI—two for input and one for output. Each is saved in a private instance variable.

- ```
  public void actionPerformed(ActionEvent e) {
      double first, second;
      first =
        Double.parseDouble(inputOne.getText().trim());
      second =
        Double.parseDouble(inputTwo.getText().trim());
  ```

  Regardless of which button is clicked, we need to get the text strings from each of the input text fields and convert those strings to numbers. Here, we chose to convert them to primitive `double` values. The call `inputOne.getText()` returns the `String` object corresponding to the text typed into the `JTextField` component. We use the method `trim()` from the class `String` to eliminate any extraneous spaces a user may type before or after the number. This call isn't required, provided the user doesn't accidentally type any spaces in the text field. However, including it makes our program more robust—that is, less likely to generate an error when we could have given a normal response. The call `Double.parseDouble()` converts a `String` to a primitive `double` value.
  ```

```
■ if (e.getActionCommand().equals("Add"))
     output.setText(String.valueOf(first + second));
  else                // must be the "Subtract" button
     output.setText(String.valueOf(first - second));
```

The class `ActionEvent` defines the method `getActionCommand()`. When the event is generated by a button, this call returns the *action command string* associated with the button. By default, the action command string is the same as the label on the button. The action command string can be different from the label if the method `setCommandString()`, which is defined for the class `JButton`, is called. By testing the command string, we can determine which button was clicked. Once we know which button was clicked, we perform the appropriate operation and call `output.setText()` to set the text string displayed in the output text field. The call `String.valueOf()` is used to convert the `double` value to a `String`, as required by `setText()`.

■ `private JTextField inputOne, inputTwo, output;`

Here, we declare the private data members of the class that are initialized in the constructor.

Summary

- Object-oriented programming (OOP) and C++ were embraced by industry very quickly. As a hybrid OOP language, C++ allows a multiparadigmatic approach to coding. The traditional advantages of C as an efficient, powerful programmer's language are not lost. The key new ingredient is polymorphism, or the ability to assume many forms.

- Existing languages and methodology supported much of the OOP methodology by combining language features with programmer discipline. It is possible to create and use ADTs in a nonOOP language. Three examples in the C community are string, boolean, and file, which are pseudotypes in that they do not enjoy the same privileges as true types. What is gained by looking at these examples is a better understanding of the limits of extensibility in nonOOP.

- A black box for the client should be simple to use, easy to understand, and familiar; cheap, efficient, and powerful; and in a component relationship within the system. A black box for the manufacturer should be easy to reuse and modify and difficult to misuse and reproduce; cheap, efficient, and powerful; and profitable to produce for a large client base. In brief, the OOP design methodology involves deciding on an appropriate set of ADTs, designing in their relatedness, and using inheritance to share code and interface, using virtual functions to process related objects dynamically.

- Polymorphism directly contributes to the black box principle. The virtual functions specified for the base class are the interface used by the client throughout. The client knows that an overridden member function takes responsibility for a specific implementation of a given action relevant to the object.

- As a hybrid OOP language, C++ can cause the programmer a dialectical tension headache. The penchant of C programmers to focus on efficiency and implementation conflicts with the penchant of objectivists to focus on elegance, abstraction, and generality. The two demands on the coding process are reconcilable but require a measure of coordination and respect for the process.

- OOP is many things to many people. In many languages and systems, the cost of detail suppression was runtime inefficiency or undue rigidity in the interface. C++ has a range of choices that allow both efficiency and flexibility.

- Occam's Razor, a useful design principle, states that entities should not be multiplied beyond necessity—or beyond completeness, invertibility, orthogonality, consistency, simplicity, efficiency, or expressiveness. These principles can be in conflict and frequently involve trade-offs in arriving at a design.

- The Class Responsibility Collaborator (CRC) notecard scheme is used in OOD. A responsibility is an obligation the class must keep. A collaborator is another object that cooperates with this object to provide an overall set of behaviors. The responsibilities of the class and the collaborators for that class are initially described. The back of the card is used to describe implementation detail. The front of the card corresponds to public behavior.

- OOP has stimulated reuse of design patterns. A design pattern is a software solution in search of a problem. Consider how the iterator logic of STL decouples visitation of container elements from specific details of the container. This idea can be summarized as the iterator pattern. The name is of great importance, as it increases the programmer's technical vocabulary. The name should be clever and should illuminate a key characteristic of the method. The problem identifies circumstances under which the pattern provides a solution. The solution shows how the pattern solves the problem. The consequences are a discussion of the cost-benefit trade-off in using the pattern.

Review Questions

1. Name three typical characteristics of an object-oriented programming language.

2. True or false: Conventional academic wisdom is that excessive concern with efficiency is detrimental to good coding practice.

3. Through _____, a hierarchy of related ADTs can be created that share code and a common interface.

4. Name three properties of a black box for the client.

5. Name three properties of a black box for the manufacturer.

6. _____ methodology has a process-centered view and relies on stepwise refinement to nest routines but does not adequately appreciate the need for a corresponding view of data.

7. _____ is the genie in OOP, taking instruction from a client and properly interpreting its wishes.

8. Give an example of ad hoc polymorphism.

9. Describe at least two separate concepts for the keyword `virtual` as used in C++. Does this cause conceptual confusion?

Exercises

1. Consider the following three ways to provide a Boolean type:

```
// Traditional C using the preprocessor

#define   TRUE  1
#define   FALSE 0
#define   Boolean int

// ANSI C and C++ using enumerated types
// Prior to adoption of the native bool type

enum Boolean { false, true };
```

```
// C++ as a class

class Boolean {
   . . . . .
public:
   // various member functions
   // including overloading  !  &&  ||  ==  !=
};
```

What would be the advantages and disadvantages of each style? Keep in mind scope, naming and conversion problems. In what ways is it desirable for C++ to now have a native type `bool`?

2. C++ originally allowed the `this` pointer to be modifiable. One use was to have user-controlled storage management by assigning directly to the `this` pointer. The assignment of 0 meant that the associated memory could be returned to free store. Discuss why this is a bad idea. Write a program with an assignment of `this` = 0. What error message does your compiler give you? Can you get around this with a cast? Would this be a good idea?

3. The rules for deciding which definition of an overloaded function to invoke have changed since the first version of C++. One reason for this is to reduce the number of ambiguities. A criticism is that the rules allow matching through conversions that may be unintended by the programmer causing difficult-to-detect runtime bugs. One strategy is to have the compiler issue a diagnostic warning in such cases; another is to use casting defensively to inform the compiler of the intended choice. Discuss these alternatives after investigating how the rules have changed.

4. Add a `UnaryNode` class to our *tree.cpp* code from Section 11.2, *OOP: The Dominant Programming Methodology*, on page 487. It should deal with unary minus and unary plus. Unary plus is a no-op, meaning nothing is done. Test using the expressions +a – 3 * b and –a + b * –3.

5. Redo the previous exercise by including the increment and decrement operators. Write and run appropriate test cases.

6. (Uwe F. Mayer) Redo the *tree.cpp* from Section 11.2, *OOP: The Dominant Programming Methodology*, on page 489, to avoid the `switch` statements. Do this by writing further subclasses for the different binary operators. Discuss the benefits and drawbacks of this approach.

7. *(Java)* Java and C++ have different casting rules. Investigate the differences. C++ allows a wider range of casting opportunities. Is this desirable?

8. List three things that you would drop from the C++ language. Argue why each would not be missed. For example, it is possible to have protected inheritance, although it was never discussed in this text? Should it be in the language for completeness' sake? Can you write code that uses protected inheritance that demonstrates that it is a critical feature of language, as opposed to an extravagance?

9. *(Java)* Using *awt*, write a Java program that is a basic desktop calculator. Have buttons that indicate a series of operations, such as addition, multiplication, square root, and reciprocal; data fields to enter arguments; and a result field. If you have access to JFC *(Swing)*, use it. Document your design with CRC cards.

ASCII Character Codes

Table A.1		American Standard Code for Information Interchange							
	0	**1**	**2**	**3**	**4**	**5**	**6**	**7**	**8**	**9**
0	nul	soh	stx	etx	eot	enq	ack	bel	bs	ht
1	nl	vt	np	cr	so	si	dle	dc1	dc2	dc3
2	dc4	nak	syn	etb	can	em	sub	esc	fs	gs
3	rs	us	sp	!	"	#	$	%	&	'
4	(	)	*	+	,	-	.	/	0	1
5	2	3	4	5	6	7	8	9	:	;
6	<	=	>	?	@	A	B	C	D	E
7	F	G	H	I	J	K	L	M	N	O
8	P	Q	R	S	T	U	V	W	X	Y
9	Z	[	\	]	^	_	'	a	b	c
10	d	e	f	g	h	i	j	k	l	m
11	n	o	p	q	r	s	t	u	v	w
12	x	y	z	{	|	}	~	del		

Some Observations

- Character codes 0 through 31 and 127 are nonprinting.

- Character code 32 prints a single space.

- Character codes for digits 0 through 9 are contiguous.

- Character codes for letters A through Z are contiguous.

- Character codes for letters a through z are contiguous.

- The difference between a capital letter and the corresponding lowercase letter is 32.

Table A.2 The Meaning of Some of the Abbreviations			
bel	audible bell	ht	horizontal tab
bs	backspace	nl	newline
cr	carriage return	nul	null
esc	escape	vt	vertical tab

Operator Precedence and Associativity

Operators	Associativity
:: (*global scope*) :: (*class scope*)	Left to right
func() [] -> . (*postfix*) ++ (*postfix*) -- typeid(*e*) *type*(*e*) dynamic_cast<*type*>(*e*) static_cast<type>(*e*) reinterpret_cast<*type*>(*e*) const_cast<*type*>(*e*)	Left to right
++ (*prefix*) --(*prefix*) ! ~ & (*address*) sizeof(*e*) + (*unary*) - (*unary*) *(*indirection*) delete new (*type*)*e*	Right to left
.* ->*	Left to right
* / %	Left to right
+ -	Left to right
<< >>	Left to right
< <= > >=	Left to right
== !=	Left to right
&	Left to right
^	Left to right
|	Left to right
&&	Left to right
||	Left to right
?:	Right to left
= += -= *= /= %= >>= <<= &= ^= |=	Right to left
throw(*e*)	Left to right
, (*comma operator*)	Left to right

All operators in a given table entry, such as ++, new, and &, have equal precedence with respect to one another but have higher precedence than all the operators in the entries below them.

The associativity rule for all the operators in a given entry appears on the right side of the table.

String Library

A string type library is supplied by the C++ system including the standard header file *string*. It is the instantiation of a template class `basic_string<T>` with `char`. The string type provides member functions and operators that perform string manipulations, such as concatenation, assignment, or replacement. An example of a program using the string type for simple string manipulation follows:

In file poem.cpp

```cpp
// String class to write a poem
#include <string>
#include <iostream>
#include <cstdlib>
#include <vector>
using namespace std;

//pick a word at random
string& choose_word(vector<string> &word) {
    int i = rand() % 6;
    return word[i];
}
```

```
int main()
{
    int i, seed;
    string poem;
    vector<string> nouns(6), verbs(6), rhymes(6);

    cout << "enter seed: ";
    cin >> seed;
    cout << "enter dictionary: " << endl;

    for (i = 0; i < 6; ++i) {
        cin >> nouns[i];      // input words
        cin >> verbs[i];
        cin >> rhymes[i];
    }
    cout << "My random poem" << endl;
    for (int lines = 0; lines <4; ++lines)
        poem += choose_word(nouns) + ' '
              + choose_word(verbs)  + ' '
              + choose_word(rhymes) + '\n';
    cout << poem << endl;
}
```

The `string` type is used to store and manipulate each word conveniently. Notice how easy concatenation and assignment work with this type. These operations are overloaded in the library as well as the input/output operations.

The representation for a string of characters is presented in Table C.1. It is usual to have the instantiation `basic_string<wchar_t>` for a wide string type `wstring`. Other instantiations are possible as well.

Table C.1 String Private Data Members	
`char* ptr`	Contains the pointer to the initial character
`size_t len`	Contains the length of the string
`size_t res`	Contains the currently allocated size or, for an unallocated string, its maximum size

This implementation provides an explicit variable to track the string length; thus, string length can be looked up in constant time, which is efficient for many string computations.

C.1 Constructors

Table C.2 presents the six public `string` constructors. These constructors make it easy to declare and initialize strings from a wide range of parameters.

Table C.2 String Constructor Members	
`string()`	Creates an empty string
`string(const char* p)`	Constructs the implied string from the `char*` array p
`string(InputIterator b,` `        InputIterator e)`	Constructs the implied string from the `InputIterator` range from b to e
`string(const string& str,` `size_t pos=0, size_t n=npos)`	Copy constructor; npos is usually −1 and indicates that no memory was allocated
`string(const char* p, size_t n)`	Copies n characters, where p is the base address
`string(size_t n, char c)`	Constructs a string of n cs

These constructors make it quite easy to use the string type initialized from `char*` pointers, which is the traditional C method for working with strings. Many computations are readily handled as a vector of characters. This is also facilitated by the `string` interface.

C.2 Member Functions

Strings have some members that overload operators, as described in Table C.3.

The extensive set of public member functions lets you manipulate strings. In many cases, these functions are overloaded to work with `string`, `char*`, and `char`.

For the `append()` and `assign()` functions in Table C.4, all functions throw a `length_error` exception if the resulting lengths exceed `max_size()` and all return a reference to the implicit string argument.

Table C.3 String Overloaded Operator Members	
`string& operator=(s)`	Assigns from `string s`
`string& operator=(p)`	Assigns from `char* p` array
`string& operator=(c)`	Assigns from a single `char c`
`string& operator+=(s)`	Appends `string s`
`string& operator+=(p)`	Appends a `char*`
`string& operator+=(c)`	Appends a `char c`
`char operator[](pos)t`	Returns the character at `pos`
`char& operator[](pos)`	Returns the reference to the character at `pos`

Table C.4 `append()` and `assign()` Functions	
`string& append(s, pos, n)`	Appends n characters, starting at `pos` from `string s`
`string& append(p, n)`	Appends n characters from the `char* p` array
`string& append(p)`	Appends the characters from `char* p` array
`string& append(n, c)`	Appends n repetitions of `char c`
`string& assign(s, pos, n)`	Assigns n characters, starting at `pos` from `string s`
`string& assign(p, n)`	Assigns the first n characters of the `char* p` array
`string& assign(p)`	Assigns the `char* p` array
`string& assign(n, c)`	Assigns n repetitions of `char c`
`string& assign(b, e)`	Assigns members specified by the range `InputIterator b` to `InputIterator e`

In the following code examples, it is assumed that each statement starts with `s1` containing `"I am "` and `s2` containing `"7 years old"`.

```
s1.append(s2);          // s1 " I am 7 years old"
s2.append(s1,0,4);      // s2 "7 years old I am"
s1.assign(s2);          // s1 "7 years old"
s1.assign(s2);          // s1 "7 years old"
```

Table C.5 shows the use of some `insert()` functions. All `insert()` functions insert additional elements at the position specified by `pos`.

All variations also throw a `length_error` if the resulting string exceeds `max_size()`. Elements of the implicit string are moved apart as necessary to accommodate the inserted elements, and all return a reference to this string.

Table C.5 String `insert()` Functions	
`string& insert(pos, p, n)`	Inserts n characters of `char*` p array at `pos`
`string& insert(pos, p)`	Inserts `char*` p array at `pos`
`string& insert(pos, n, c)`	Inserts n repetitions of `char` c at `pos`
`string& insert(pos1, s1, pos2=0, n=0)`	Inserts at `pos1` in implied string, the lesser of n and `s1.size() - pos2` `characters` beginning at `pos2` of `string s1`

The `insert()` functions presented in Table C.6 work with iterators. These versions of `insert()` put additional elements in this string immediately before the character referred to by p. All of these versions require that p is a valid iterator on this string. The first two functions return the `iterator` p; the third returns `void`.

Table C.6 String `insert()` Iterator Functions	
`iterator insert(p, c)`	Inserts single `char` c at `iterator` p
`iterator insert(p, n, c)`	Inserts n repetitions of `char` c at `iterator` p
`iterator insert(p, b, e)`	Inserts at `iterator` p elements from range `iterator` b to `iterator` e

The following code illustrates the use of `insert()` and again assumes that `s1` contains `"I am "` and `s2` contains `"7 years old"`:

```
s1.insert(2, s2);          // s1 "I 7 years old am"
```

The inverse function is `remove()`.

Table C.7 briefly describes further public `string` member functions. The return types are shown explicitly.

You can lexicographically compare two strings by using `compare()`, a family of overloaded member function shown in Table C.8. The return `int` value is 0 if the strings have the same value, a negative number if the implied string is lexicographically before the string argument, and a positive number otherwise.

Table C.7   More String Members

`string& remove(pos, n s)`	Removes n number of characters at position pos
`string& replace(pos1, n1, str, pos2=0, n2=npos)`	Replaces at pos1 for n1 characters, the substring in `str` at pos2 of n2 characters
`string& replace(pos,n,p,n2)` `string& replace(pos,n,p)` `string& replace(pos,n,c)`	Replaces n characters at pos, using a `char*` p of n2 characters, or a `char*` p until null, or a character `c`
`size_t length()`	Returns the string length
`const char* c_str()`	Converts `string` to traditional `char*` representation
`const char* data()`	Returns the base address of the string representation
`void resize(n, c)` `void resize(n)`	Resizes the string to length n; the padding character c is used in the first function, and the `eos()` character is used in the second
`void reserve(res_arg)` `size_t reserve()`	Allocates memory for string; returns the size of the allocation
`size_t copy(p, n, pos=0)`	Copies the implicit string starting at pos into the `char*` p for n characters
`string substr(pos=0, n=npos)`	Returns substring of n characters of the implicit string

Table C.8   string compare() Functions

`int compare(s, pos=0, n=npos)`	Compares implicit string starting at pos for n characters with `string s`
`int compare(p, pos, n)`	Compares implicit string starting at pos for n characters with `char*` array p
`int compare(p, pos=0)`	Compares implicit string starting at pos with `char*` array p

The `find()` functions we present in Table C.9 perform a find operation. One group is discussed here; Table C.10 summarizes more variations of this group of member functions. In all cases, if the substring is found, its position is returned. If it is not found, `npos` is returned.

Table C.9 string `find()` Functions	
`size_t find(s, pos=0)`	Searches for `string` s starting at `pos`
`size_t find(p, pos, n)`	Searches for `char*` array p and starting at `pos` and going for n characters.
`size_t find(p, pos=0);`	Searches for `char*` array p starting at `pos`
`size_t find(c, pos=0)`	Searches for `char` c starting at `pos`

`size_t rfind(s, pos=npos)`
`size_t rfind(p, pos, n)`
`size_t rfind(p, pos=npos)`
`size_t rfind(c, pos=npos)`
	Like `find()` but scans the `string` s backward for a first match in the specified pattern: `string` s, `char*` array p, or `char` c

Further functions for finding strings and characters are briefly described in Table C.10.

Table C.10 String More Find Members	

`size_t find_first_of(s, pos=0)`
`size_t find_first_of(p, pos, n)`
`size_t find_first_of(p, pos=0)`
`size_t find_first_of (c,pos=0)`
	Searches for first character of any character in specified pattern: `string` s, `char*` array p, or `char` c

`size_t find_last_of(s, pos=npos)`
`size_t find_last_of(p, pos, n)`
`size_t find_last_of(p, pos=npos)`
`size_t find_last_of(c,pos=npos)`
	Searches backward for first character of any character in specified pattern: `string` s, `char*` array p, or `char` c

`size_t find_first_not_of(s, pos=0)`
`size_t find_first_not_of(p, pos, n)`
`size_t find_first_not_of(p, pos=0)`
`size_t find_first_not_of(c,pos=0)`
	Searches for first character that does not match any character in specified pattern: `string` s, `char*` array p, or `char` c

`size_t find_last_not_of(s, pos=npos)`
`size_t find_last_not_of(p, pos, n)`
`size_t find_last_not_of(p, pos=npos)`
`size_t find_last_not_of(c,pos=npos)`
	Searches backward for first character that does not match any character in specified pattern: `string` s, `char*` array p, or `char` c

C.3   Global Operators

The string package contains operator overloadings that provide input/output, concatenation, and comparison operators. These are intuitively understandable and are briefly described in Table C.11.

Table C.11 String Overloaded Global Operators	
`ostream& operator<<(o, s)`	Output `string` s to `ostream` o
`istream& operator>>(in, s)`	Input into `istream` in from `string` s
`string operator+(s1, s2)`	Concatenates `strings` **s1** and **s2**
`bool operator==(s1, s2)`	**true** if `strings` **s1** and **s2** are lexicographically equal
`<   <=   >   >=   !=`	As expected

The comparison operators and the concatenation `operator+()` are also overloaded with the four signatures as shown in Table C.12.

Table C.12 String Comparison Operators	
`bool operator==(p, s)`	Compares `char*` array p and `string` s
`bool operator==(c, s)`	Compares `char` c and `string` s
`bool operator==(s, p)`	Compares `strings` and `char*` array p
`bool operator==(s, c)`	Compares `string` s and `char` c

In effect, a comparison or concatenation of any kind can occur between string and a second argument that is a string, a character, or a character pointer.

The tio Library

The Java tio package was developed by Charlie McDowell as an aid in writing simple I/O in Java programs. Originally developed for the book *Java by Dissection*, by Ira Pohl and Charlie McDowell (Addison-Wesley, 1999), the downloadable source code may be found at www.cse.ucsc.edu/~charlie/java/tio/.

D.1 Console

```
package tio;
import java.io.*;

/**
 * The class Console is a convenience class.
 * It contains a static variable in that is
 * initialized to refer to a ReadInput object,
 * reading from the standard input stream
 * System.in.
 * It also contains a static variable out
 * that is initialized to refer to a
 * FormattedWriter, writing to the output
 * stream System.out.
 */
```

```
public class Console {
    public final static ReadInput in =
            new ReadInput(new
                            InputStreamReader(System.in));
    public final static FormattedWriter out =
            new FormattedWriter(System.out);
}
```

D.2   FormattedWriter

```
package tio;

import java.io.*;
import java.text.*;

/**
 * The class FormattedWriter contains
 * methods that allow for formatted printing.
 * It includes support for setting the width of the
 * output field, using left or right justification in
 * the output field, using an arbitrary fill
 * character, and setting the number of digits to the
 * right of the decimal point in floating-point
 * values.
 *
 * @author C. E. McDowell
 */

public class FormattedWriter extends PrintWriter {
    // constants for specifying justification
    public static final int LEFT = 1;
    public static final int RIGHT = 2;

    /**
     * Constructs a FormattedWriter object for an
     * OutputStream.
     *
     * @param os the OutputStream to write to
     */

    public FormattedWriter(OutputStream os) {
        super(os, true); // make default auto-flushing
    }
```

```java
/**
 * Constructs a FormattedWriter object for a
 * FileWriter.
 *
 * @param writer the FileWriter to write to
 */
public FormattedWriter(FileWriter writer) {
    super(writer, true);
}
/**
 * Constructs a FormattedWriter object for writing
 * to a file.
 *
 * @param filename the name of the file to write to
 */
public FormattedWriter(String filename)
    throws java.io.IOException
{
    this(new FileWriter(filename));
}
/**
 * Set the output field width. If the value being
 * printed is less than the width of the field,
 * then the field is padded with the pad character
 * (see setPadChar()). The field can be either left
 * or right justified (see setJustify()).
 *
 * @param width the width of the output field
 */
public void setWidth(int width) {
    if (width < 0)
        this.width = 0;
    else if (width > MAX_WIDTH)
        this.width = MAX_WIDTH;
    else
        this.width = width;
}
```

```java
/**
 * Set the number of digits to be printed to the
 * right of the decimal point in floating-point
 * values.
 *
 * @param places the number of places to the right
 *      of the decimal point
 */
public void setDigits(int places) {
    decimalPlaces = places;
    form.setMaximumFractionDigits(decimalPlaces);
}
/**
 * Set the justification to be LEFT or RIGHT.
 *
 * @param leftOrRight use FormattedWriter.LEFT
 *      or FormattedWriter.RIGHT
 * @exception IllegalArgumentException if not LEFT
 *      or RIGHT
 */
public void setJustify(int leftOrRight) {
    if (leftOrRight != LEFT && leftOrRight != RIGHT)
        throw new IllegalArgumentException(
            "use FormattedWriter.LEFT or" +
            " FormattedWriter.RIGHT");
    justify = leftOrRight;
}
/**
 * Set the character to be used in padding.
 * The default padding character is a blank.
 *
 * @param pad the character to use in padding
 */
public void setPadChar(char pad) {
    if (pad == ' ')
        padding = spaces;
    else if (pad == '0')
        padding = zeros;
    else
        padding = buildPadding(MAX_WIDTH, pad);
}
```

```java
/**
 * Print a String in a field of the current
 * width using the current padding character
 * and justification.
 *
 * @param s the String to print
 */
public void printf(String s) {
  if (s.length() >= width)
    super.print(s);
  else if (justify == LEFT)
    super.print(s +
      padding.substring(0, width - s.length()));
  else
    super.print(
      padding.substring(0, width-s.length())+s);
}


/**
 * Print a boolean in a field of the current
 * width, using the current padding character and
 * justification.
 *
 * @param value the value to print
 */
public void printf(boolean value) {
    printf(String.valueOf(value));
}
/**
 * Print a char in a field of the current
 * width, using the current padding character and
 * justification.
 *
 * @param value the value to print
 */
public void printf(char value) {
  printf(String.valueOf(value));
}
```

```
/**
 * Print an array of characters in a field of the
 * current width, using the current padding
 * character and justification.
 *
 * @param value the value to print
 */
public void printf(char[] value) {
  printf(String.valueOf(value));
}
/**
 * Print an int in a field of the current
 * width, using the current padding character and
 * justification.
 *
 * @param value the value to print
 */
public void printf(int value) {
  printf(String.valueOf(value));
}
/**
 * Print a long in a field of the current
 * width, using the current padding character and
 * justification.
 *
 * @param value the value to print
 */
public void printf(long value) {
  printf(String.valueOf(value));
}
/**
 * Print any Object in a field of the current
 * width, using the current padding character and
 * justification.
 *
 * @param value the value to print
 */
public void printf(Object value) {
  printf(value.toString());
}
```

```
/**
 * Print a double in a field of the current
 * width, with the current number of digits to the
 * right of the decimal point and using the current
 * padding character and justification.
 *
 * @param value the value to print
 */
public void printf(double value) {
   printf(trimDigits(String.valueOf(value)));
}
/**
 * Print a float in a field of the current
 * width, with the current number of digits to the
 * right of the decimal point and using the current
 * padding character and justification.
 *
 * @param value the value to print
 */
public void printf(float value) {
   printf(trimDigits(String.valueOf(value)));
}
/**
 * Same as printf() with a newline added at the
 * end.
 */
public void printfln(String s) {
   printf(s);
   println();
}
/**
 * Same as printf() with a newline added at the
 * end.
 */
public void printfln(boolean value) {
   printf(value);
   println();
}
/**
 * Same as printf() with a newline added at the
 * end.
 */
```

```
public void println(char value) {
  printf(value);
  println();
}
/**
 * Same as printf() with a newline added at the
 * end.
 */
public void println(char[] value) {
  printf(value);
  println();
}
/**
 * Same as printf() with a newline added at the
 * end.
 */
public void println(int value) {
  printf(value);
  println();
}
/**
 * Same as printf() with a newline added at the
 * end.
 */
public void println(long value) {
  printf(value);
  println();
}
/**
 * Same as printf() with a newline added at the
 * end.
 */
public void println(Object value) {
  printf(value);
  println();
}
/**
 * Same as printf() with a newline added at the
 * end.
 */
```

```java
public void printfln(double value) {
  printf(value);
  println();
}
/**
* Same as printf() with a newline added at the
* end.
*/
public void printfln(float value) {
  printf(value);
  println();
}

/*
* Trim the number of digits to the right of the
* decimal point if there is one.
*/
private String trimDigits(String value) {
  int places;

  if (decimalPlaces == -1)
     return value;
  int pos = value.indexOf(".");
  int exp = value.indexOf("E");

  if (exp == -1)
     places = value.length() - pos - 1;
  else
     places = exp - pos - 1;
  if (places <= decimalPlaces)
      return value;
  if (exp == -1)
     return round(value);
  else {
     String needsRounding=value.substring(0, exp);
     return round(needsRounding) +
        value.substring(exp);
  }
}
```

```
/*
 * Round the last digit of s. E.g., 1.2345 would be
 * returned as 1.235 and 1.234 would be returned as
 * 1.23.
 * This is done using a java.text.NumberFormat
 * object that had its decimal places set in
 * setDigits() above.
 */
private String round(String s) {
  // form is a java.text.NumberFormat object
  return form.format(Double.parseDouble(s));
}

/*
 * Create an array of pad characters used for
 * quickly building strings of pad characters
 * by a call to substring (see printfln(String s))
 */
private static String buildPadding(int width,
                                   char pad)
{
  StringBuffer sbuf = new StringBuffer(width);
  for (int i = 0; i < width; ++i)
     sbuf.append(pad);
  return sbuf.toString();
}

private static int MAX_WIDTH = 40;
private static final String spaces =
   buildPadding(MAX_WIDTH, ' ');
private static final String zeros =
   buildPadding(MAX_WIDTH, '0');
private String padding = spaces;
private int width = 0;
private int justify = LEFT;

// -1 means use max precision
private int decimalPlaces = -1;
// used in trimming decimal digits
private NumberFormat form =
     NumberFormat.getInstance();
```

D.3   PrintFileWriter

```java
package tio;

import java.io.*;

/**
 * The class PrintFileWriter is a
 * convenience class. It adds one constructor to its
 * parent class, PrintWriter. This new constructor
 * takes the name of a file.
 *
 * new PrintFileWriter(fileName) is the
 * same as
 * new PrintWriter(new FileWriter(fileName))
 *
 */
public class PrintFileWriter extends PrintWriter {
    public PrintFileWriter(String filename)
        throws IOException
    {
        super(new FileWriter(filename));
    }
}
```

D.4   ReadException

```java
package tio;

import java.io.*;

/**
 * The class ReadException is used to convert
 * java.io.IOExceptions into a subtype of
 * RuntimeException. By doing this, users of
 * ReadInput methods do not need to use throws
 * declarations, simplifying beginning programs.
 * Subtypes of RuntimeException do not need
 * to be declared using a throws clause.
 *
 * @author C. E. McDowell
 * @version 1.1, Released for Java by Dissection
 *
 */
```

```
public class ReadException extends RuntimeException {
   /**
    * Constructs a ReadException object with no
    * specific message.
    */
   public ReadException() {
      super();
   }
   /**
    * Constructs a ReadException object with the
    * specified message.
    *
    * @param message the error message
    */
   public ReadException(String message) {
      super(message);
   }
}
```

D.5   ReadInput

```
package tio;

import java.io.*;

/**
 * The class ReadInput contains methods that
 * allow for simple input of numbers, strings, and
 * characters from a text stream.
 *
 * @author C. E. McDowell
 * @version 1.1, release for Java by Dissection
 */
public class ReadInput {
   /**
    * Constructs a ReadInput object for reading from
    * any * Reader object.
    * @param input the Reader text stream to read
    * from.
    */
```

```java
public ReadInput(Reader input) {
    // look ahead over 1024 white space characters
    // when checking for the end of file mark
    this.input = new PushbackReader(input, 1024);
}
/**
* Constructs a ReadInput object for reading from a
* file.
*
* @param filename the name of the file from which
*       to read.
* @exception FileNotFoundException if the file
*       can't be opened.
*/

public ReadInput(String filename) {
    try {
        FileReader fin = new FileReader(filename);
        this.input = new PushbackReader(fin, 1024);
    }
    catch (java.io.IOException e) {
        throw new ReadException(e.toString());
    }
}
/**
* Constructs a ReadInput object for reading from
* any InputStream.
*
* @param input the InputStream to read from.
*/

public ReadInput(InputStream input) {
    this(new InputStreamReader(input));
}
/**
* Check to see if there are any non-white space
* characters left in the input. If used to
* terminate reading with readLine(), any trailing
* blank lines will be ignored. To read trailing
* blank lines, do not use hasMoreElements() and
* instead read with readLine() until an
* EOFException is thrown.
*
* @return true if the input contains more
* non-white space characters and false otherwise.
*/
```

```java
public boolean hasMoreElements() {
  try {
    if (atEof)
      return false;
    else if (whiteSpaceBuffered)
      //something followed the white space
      return true;
// look ahead to see if any non-white remain
    int nextChar = input.read();
    if (Character.isWhitespace((char)nextChar)) {
      // save white space incase readLine() next
      whiteSpaceBuffered = true;
      buffer[0] = (char)nextChar;
      for (bufferCount = 1; bufferCount < 1024;
           ++bufferCount)
      {
        nextChar = input.read();
        if (nextChar == -1) {
          atEof = true;
          break;
        }
        else if
        (!Character.isWhitespace((char)nextChar))
        {
          input.unread(nextChar);
          break;
        }
        buffer[bufferCount] = (char)nextChar;
      }  //end for
    }
    else if (nextChar == -1) {
      atEof = true;
      input.unread(nextChar);
    }
    else
      input.unread(nextChar);
    return !atEof;
  }
  catch(java.io.IOException e) {
    throw new ReadException(e.toString());
  }
}
```

```
/**
 * Read next character. White space is not skipped.
 * readChar() cannot be used to reread input
 * characters that resulted in a
 * NumberFormatException trying
 * to read a number. readLine() will return the
 * characters of a failed number read.
 *
 * @return the int value of the next character.
 */
public int readChar() {
  try {
    int result;
    // tokenRead will be true if a token was read
    // but couldn't be parsed. readChar() cannot
    // be used to reread such a token; discard it
    tokenRead = false;
    if (whiteSpaceBuffered) {
      input.unread(buffer, 0, bufferCount);
      whiteSpaceBuffered = false;
    }
    result = input.read();
    if (result == -1)
      atEof = true;
    return result;
  }
  catch (java.io.IOException e) {
    throw new ReadException(e.toString());
  }
}
/**
 * Attempt to interpret next white space delimited
 * input characters as a double.
 *
 * @return double value of the next, white space
 *      delimited input string.
 * @exception NumberFormatException if A3next input
 *      string does not contain a parsable double.
 */
```

```java
public double readDouble() {
  try {
     readToken();
     double result = Double.parseDouble(token);
     tokenRead = false; // token has been used up
     return result;
  }
  catch (java.io.IOException e) {
     throw new ReadException(e.toString());
  }
}
/**
 * Attempt to interpret next white space delimited
 * input characters as a float.
 *
 * @return the float value of the next, white space
 *      delimited input string.
 * @exception NumberFormatException if next input
 *      string does not contain a parsable float.
 */
public float readFloat() {
  try {
     readToken();
     float result = Float.parseFloat(token);
     tokenRead = false; // token has been used up
     return result;
  }
  catch (java.io.IOException e) {
     throw new ReadException(e.toString());
  }
}
/**
 * Attempt to interpret next white space delimited
 * input characters as an int.
 *
 * @return the int value of the next, white space
 *      delimited input string.
 * @exception NumberFormatException if next input
 *      string does not contain a parsable int.
 */
```

```java
public int readInt() {
    try {
      readToken();
      int result = Integer.parseInt(token);
      tokenRead = false; // token has been used up
      return result;
    }
  catch (java.io.IOException e) {
      throw new ReadException(e.toString());
  }
}
/**
* Read the next complete input line up to newline
* character. The terminating newline character is
* read and discarded. It is not part of the return
* string. If the previous read was an attempt to
* read a number that generated
* a NumberFormatException, readLine()
* will return the input line including the input
* characters that caused the exception. This can
* be used to try and recover from failure to read
* numeric input.
*
* @return the next input line as a String.
*/
public String readLine() {
  try {
      if (tokenRead) {
          tokenRead = false;
          return token + readLine(input);
    }
      else {
          return readLine(input);
      }
    }
  catch (java.io.IOException e) {
      throw new ReadException(e.toString());
  }
}
```

```
/**
 * Attempt to interpret next white space delimited
 * input characters as a long.
 *
 * @return the long value of the next, white space
 *      delimited input string.
 * @exception NumberFormatException if next input
 *      string does not contain a parsable long.
 */
public long readLong() {
  try {
    readToken();
    long result = Long.parseLong(token);
    tokenRead = false; // token has been used up
    return result;
  }
  catch (java.io.IOException e) {
    throw new ReadException(e.toString());
  }
}

/**
 * Read the next white space delimited string.
 *
 * @return the next, white space delimited input
 * string.
 */
public String readWord() {
  try {
    readToken();
    tokenRead = false; // token has been used up
    return token;
  }
  catch (java.io.IOException e) {
    throw new ReadException(e.toString());
  }
}

/**
 * Do the work of reading a line of text.
 * White space may have been buffered up from a
 * call to hasMoreElements(). If so, unread the
 * buffered white space then read one line.
 */
```

```java
private String readLine(PushbackReader in)
        throws IOException
{
  StringBuffer result = new StringBuffer(80);
  if (whiteSpaceBuffered) {
    in.unread(buffer, 0, bufferCount);
    whiteSpaceBuffered = false;
  }
  int nextChar = in.read();
  while (nextChar != -1 && nextChar != '\n' &&
        nextChar != '\r') {
    result.append((char)nextChar);
    nextChar = in.read();
  }
  if (nextChar == -1) {
    atEof = true;
    in.unread(nextChar);
  }
  else if (nextChar == '\r') {
    nextChar = in.read(); // check for cr/newline
    if (nextChar != '\n')
        in.unread(nextChar);
  }
  if (atEof && result.length() == 0)
    return null;
  else
    return result.toString();
}
/**
 * Read the next white space delimited string.
 * This will then be parsed by the appropriate
 * routine to return one of the desired types.
 */
```

```java
        private void readToken() throws IOException {
          if (atEof)
            throw new EOFException(
             "Attempt to read beyond the end of "
             "the stream.");
          if (!tokenRead) {
            //discard any buffered white space
            whiteSpaceBuffered = false;
            StringBuffer result = new StringBuffer(80);
            int nextChar = input.read();
            while
              (Character.isWhitespace((char)nextChar))
               nextChar = input.read();
            while (nextChar != -1 && nextChar != '\n' &&
                nextChar != '\r' &&
                !Character.isWhitespace((char)nextChar))
            {
               result.append((char)nextChar);
               nextChar = input.read();
            }
            token = result.toString();
            if (nextChar == -1)
              if(token.length() == 0)
                throw new EOFException(
                    "Attempt to read beyond the end "
                    "of the stream.");
              else
                atEof = true;
            input.unread(nextChar);
            tokenRead = true;
          }
        }

        private String token;
        private boolean tokenRead = false;
        private PushbackReader input;
        private boolean atEof = false;
        private boolean whiteSpaceBuffered = false;
        private char[] buffer = new char[1024];
        private int bufferCount;
    }
```

Index

M